Terrorist Movements and the Recruitment of Arab Foreign Fighters

Terrorist Movements and the Recruitment of Arab Foreign Fighters

A History from 1980s Afghanistan to ISIS

Roger Warren

I.B. TAURIS

LONDON • NEW YORK • OXFORD • NEW DELHI • SYDNEY

I.B. TAURIS
Bloomsbury Publishing Plc
50 Bedford Square, London, WC1B 3DP, UK
1385 Broadway, New York, NY 10018, USA
29 Earlsfort Terrace, Dublin 2, Ireland

BLOOMSBURY, I.B. TAURIS and the I.B. Tauris logo are
trademarks of Bloomsbury Publishing Plc

First published in Great Britain 2019

Cover design by Adriana Brioso
Cover image © GIUSEPPE CACACE/AFP/Getty Images

A catalogue record for this book is available from the British Library.

A catalog record for this book is available from the Library of Congress.

ISBN: HB: 978-1-7883-1498-5
PB: 978-0-7556-3650-1
ePDF: 978-1-7867-3621-5
eBook: 978-1-7867-2615-5

Series: Terrorism and Extremism Studies

Typeset by RefineCatch Limited, Bungay, Suffolk

To find out more about our authors and books visit
www.bloomsbury.com and sign up for our newsletters.

Contents

List of Figures

Acknowledgements

This book was born thirty years ago in 1989 while I navigated the markets of Peshawar and the weapons bazaars in Darra on the Afghan-Pakistani border, just after the Soviets had withdrawn from Afghanistan. By then the markets and bazaars were crowded with Arab foreign fighters and by absorbing their tales through their many different Arabic dialects, it stimulated an initial interest in Arab foreign fighters. Later in Iraq in 2003, I met other Arab foreign fighters which piqued my interest again, eventually leading to the crafting of this book. I must therefore acknowledge their personal influence on me as the subjects of this book.

I would like to thank my wife, Jacquie, who has been a mainstay throughout the rather lonely process of academic study. Her love, support and encouragement were crucial to the success of this book. Second, behind the scenes, my father and mother, Fred and Ann Warren, have always promoted academic thought, and this book is testimony to that encouragement.

Academically, I am indebted to the many scholars who offered guidance and influenced me on my journey. Specifically, I would like to thank the many lecturers at the Centre for the Study of Terrorism and Political Violence (CSTPV) at the University of St Andrews (UK), specifically Tim Wilson, Peter Lehr, Sarah Marsden and Kieran McConaghy. In addition, my PhD Viva Committee (Bernhard Blumenau and Jonathan Githens-Mazer) offered superb feedback and professional input, and this book reflects many of their most incisive comments. Finally, I am indebted to Julie Middleton of CSTPV who was always willing to help out a wayward student.

I must also acknowledge the support of friends, comrades and colleagues who patiently stood shoulder to shoulder with me, throughout this academic journey. In particular, I greatly appreciate the encouragement from Matt Minshall, Paul Leister and Robin Loewen. In addition, I also acknowledge the contributions from my many Omani, Kuwaiti and Emirati friends, who often contextualised my analysis; but due to the subject of the book, they prefer to remain anonymous. Lastly, a special thanks to Jasper Van Maaden for his understanding and help under rather tricky circumstances.

Finally, I would like to thank Joanna Godfrey and Olivia Dellow from Bloomsbury for their guidance, responsiveness and understanding. They ensured I remained clear of the many publishing pitfalls, including the need for professional copy-editing which was conducted superbly by Babette de Wet and Andrew Devine.

Roger Warren

Canada, 2019

1

Is One Man's Foreign Fighter Another Man's Terrorist?

Afghan war veterans, scattered throughout the world, could surprise the US with violence in unexpected locales.

US Department of State, 'The wandering mujahidin: Armed and dangerous', 1993.[1]

The majority of the leaders and planners behind the 9/11 attacks in America were veteran Arab foreign fighters from the 1980s Afghan jihad against the Soviet invaders. These Arab foreign fighters had arrived in Afghanistan with no known prior terrorist links, yet as a result of their participation in the Afghan jihad, they subsequently became involved in Islamist terrorist-related activities, that included the 9/11 attacks. In effect, their trajectory to involvement in terrorism was via participation in defensive jihad, as opposed to the direct 'fast track' route taken by the majority of 9/11 hijackers. The veteran Arab foreign fighters who became the leaders and planners behind the 9/11 attacks included Osama bin Laden, Khalid Shaykh Muhammad, Abu Faraj al-Libi, Abdul Rahman al-Nashiri and a rather less well-known Syrian called Muhammad Haydar Zammar, who was considered a key recruiter for three of the 9/11 pilots.[2] Zammar was born in 1961 in Aleppo, Syria and moved to Germany as a child before becoming a German citizen in 1982. In 1991, he travelled to Afghanistan to train and subsequently fight in a defensive jihad against Afghan communists after the Soviets had departed. Later in 1995, he then travelled to Bosnia to fight in another defensive jihad, this time against Serbian forces who were attacking Bosnian Muslims. He later returned to Afghanistan and became involved with, and was influenced by Al Qaeda, before returning to Hamburg, Germany where the 9/11 pilots were university students. His story is that of an ordinary young Syrian man who was raised in Germany, who fought to defend fellow Muslims from persecution, yet subsequently became a key terrorist operative. Muhammad

Haydar Zammar's story is not unique; indeed it appears to follow a well-worn trajectory that is punctuated by involvement in defensive jihad.

Ahmad Abdullah al-Shaya was an ordinary twenty-year-old single man from the religiously conservative town of Buraidah in Saudi Arabia. He had no Islamist (violent or non-violent) links, but was motivated to travel to Iraq in 2004 to protect fellow Muslims and 'to fight the Americans on Noble Jihad'.[3] His self-confessed objective was 'to kill the Americans, policemen, national guards and the American collaborators'.[4] However, two months after his arrival, having undergone training and indoctrination in Iraq, he executed a self-sacrificial 'martyrdom/suicide' attack killing twelve civilians and non-combatants. His story is also not unique, whereby an individual initially becomes a foreign fighter, but subsequently becomes involved in Islamist terrorism. His complete biography is covered in Chapter 3. Finally, to reinforce this phenomenon, Ahmad al-Darawi was a thirty-eight-year-old Egyptian man who was married with two children. A former police officer until 2007, he then became a sports marketer for a telecommunications firm. By all accounts from family and friends he was a mature, normal and ordinary man. During the Egyptian 2011 revolution as part of the Arab Spring, he became a prominent rights activist who decided to run (unsuccessfully) for parliament. Two years later (in June 2013) he travelled to Syria's Latakia province, and subsequently became the commander of foreign fighters in the Lions of the Caliphate Brigade. Al-Darawi's brigade pledged allegiance to the Islamic State in Iraq and the Sham (ISIS) in November 2013. In a (24 February 2014) Twitter post, he posted 'how sweet life is between the Quran and my Kalashnikov [rifle]'.[5] A few months later, in May 2014, he reportedly conducted a self-sacrificial ('martyrdom/suicide') attack against a Syrian military outpost.

The accounts of Muhammed Zammar, Abdullah al-Shaya and Ahmad al-Darawi are emblematic of many of the trajectories of Arab foreign fighters in 1980s Afghanistan, Iraq (post-2003) and Syria (post-2011), and raise a series of broad conundrums that require investigation. Specifically, to what extent did their geographic origin affect their initial involvement in defensive jihad? Did being an expatriate Arab living in Germany affect Zammar? Did living in a conservatively religious town affect al-Shaya? Prior to their respective involvements in defensive jihad, they all appeared ordinary men, yet what motivated their departures to a foreign battlefield? Were they radicalised prior to their involvement in defensive jihad or did that happen as a result of participation on the battlefield? Indeed, were they ever actually radicalised? Why were Arabs motivated to defend their co-religionists in other countries as foreign fighters? Although al-Shaya targeted civilians and non-combatants, and al-Darawi a Syrian military outpost, can one disaggregate self-sacrificial ('martyrdom/suicide') attacks based on targeting? Is there a difference between targeting civilians and targeting soldiers (foreign occupation and/or oppressive regime forces)? Are self-sacrificial ('martyrdom/ suicide') attacks conducted by non-state combatants comparable with those conducted by more conventional combatants (Vietnamese Viet Cong, German Hitler Youth, Japanese Kamikazes and Russian *Shtraf* companies)? To what extent did the situational context of defensive jihad (including indoctrination, the brutalisation of combat and obedience to authority) affect Zammar's, al-Shaya's and al-Darawi's subsequent behaviour? Was al-Shaya an Arab foreign fighter involved in a defensive jihad, or an Islamist terrorist involved in a terrorism against civilians? Are these two categories (Arab foreign fighters and Islamist terrorists) one and the same, or can boundaries be identified and drawn between them? Is it a case of one man's foreign fighter being another man's terrorist? Are there metrics that can be employed to distinguish between the two cohorts?

Then again, why does attempting to disaggregate the two cohorts really matter? The answer lies in the fact that by drawing distinctions between Arab foreign fighters and Islamist terrorists, it allows academics and policy makers to better understand the phenomena. There are clear policy implications of branding an individual a foreign fighter or an Islamist terrorist. This conundrum and matter of distinctions are not about mere semantics or intended to be some theoretical debate about various transnational cohorts and mobilisations. The need to distinguish between Arab foreign fighters and Islamist terrorists will facilitate, overlaps notwithstanding, a greater understanding of their respective initial mobilisations, and the situational factors (amongst others) that subsequently influenced and informed their respective decisions, behaviour and actions. It does not appear correct to simply assume that at the individual level, an Arab national who mobilises to fight abroad in a defensive jihad against a foreign army of occupation (or a despotic Arab regime), has the same motivation as an Arab national who conducts a self-sacrificial ('martyrdom/suicide') attack in a Baghdad market targeting civilians and non-combatants. In addition, by acknowledging important subtleties and nuances, individualised rehabilitation and reintegration programmes can be established to better reflect these subtleties.

However, the current conflation of these two cohorts is perhaps understandable given that some Arab foreign fighters do subsequently become involved in Islamist terrorist-related activities.[6] Indeed, a widely misunderstood reality is that whilst not all Arab foreign fighters embrace Islamist terrorism, many individuals in Al Qaeda and ISIS started their 'careers' as Arab foreign fighters. As Chapter 2 will demonstrate, there were veteran Arab foreign fighters involved in the 1993 World Trade Centre (WTC) attack, the 1995 Riyadh attacks, the 1998 East Africa bombings, the 2000 USS *Cole* attack, and finally the 9/11 attacks where four of the hijackers had previously participated in a defensive jihad in either Bosnia or Chechnya.[7] Moreover, this apparent conflation (between Arab foreign fighters and Islamist terrorists) is not just an issue in academia, inasmuch as the United Nations Security Council passed Resolution 2178 (in September 2014) that introduced another term – 'foreign terrorist fighters'.[8] In July 2015 at a meeting in Madrid, a United Nations Security Council Counter-Terrorism Committee (UNSC CTC) discussed the threat from 'foreign terrorist fighters' including, *inter alia*, those 'who travelled to Afghanistan during the 1980s ... and to Iraq ... during the 2000s'.[9] Yet those Arabs who travelled to Afghanistan during the 1980s were helping those labelled by former President Ronald Reagan (in 1982) as 'freedom fighters of Afghanistan'.[10] In effect, President Reagan was implicitly encouraging 'freedom fighters' to go to Afghanistan, only to be rebranded subsequently as 'foreign terrorist fighters', 'foreign fighters', or 'Islamist terrorists'. The irony of such rebranding was also recognised by the Arab foreign fighters themselves, as Anne Speckhard and Mubin Shaikh noted:

> those who opposed the Soviets were supported and called 'freedom fighters' and many were encouraged to go and fight to throw the Soviets out. So for many, it was hypocritical to now call those who resisted the United States invasion of Iraq, terrorists – rather than freedom fighters.[11]

Finally, it is instructive that the passing of the United Nations Security Council Resolution 2178 (pertaining to 'foreign terrorist fighters' mentioned earlier), did not escape academic scrutiny. Professor Alex Schmid suggested that 'a distinction ought to be made between a "Foreign Fighter" and a "Foreign *Terrorist* Fighter" but the Security Council chose not to do so';[12] while Professor David Malet argued correctly that 'the Security Council blurred all analytic distinctions'.[13] This book seeks to address directly the 'Western tendency to conflate foreign fighters and international terrorists',[14] and the inclination 'to lump all jihadis together in one category and to overlook important subtleties, nuances, and differences between them'.[15]

Although discussed in greater detail later in this chapter, Arab foreign fighters are defined in this book as ethnically Arab, religiously Sunni Muslim combatants, who participate in defensive jihad, with no apparent link to the conflict other than religious affinity with the Sunni Muslim side.[16] Yet some readers may ask why study Arab foreign fighters over Western foreign fighters? There are two main reasons. First, ethnically, Arabs are the most prolific group involved in contemporary defensive jihad and their impact on the battlefield involving self-sacrificial ('martyrdom/suicide') attacks is immeasurable. The sheer quantity of Arabs involved in defensive jihad offers the opportunity to examine large quantities of data, and this book draws on a personal dataset of 3,367 Arab foreign fighters. Second, Western Muslims tend to take the lead from their Arab comrades who possess the language and cultural skills having been raised in the Arab world. Aware that most defensive jihads are conducted in Muslim-majority countries, Western foreign fighters appear (in most instances) to subordinate themselves to Arab fighters.

Arab foreign fighters, also known as foreign Arab *mujahhideen*, have been involved in various defensive jihads fighting against the external aggression of foreign occupation forces and/or the internal aggression of unpopular autocratic regimes. Examples of defensive jihads against occupation forces would include those fighting the Soviets in 1980s Afghanistan, the Russians in 1990s Chechnya, and US-led coalition forces in Iraq (post-2003). Defensive jihads against unpopular autocratic regimes would include those against the Indian government in Kashmir, the Gaddafi regime in Libya, and the Assad regime in Syria (post-2011). Arab foreign fighters fight in defence of their Sunni Muslim co-religionists, and hence their battles are more generally labelled *jihad al-difaa* (defensive jihad). Their targeting is predominantly focused on occupation forces and/or forces representing unpopular autocratic regimes, to the almost total exclusion of civilians and non-combatants, although this often changes as the defensive jihad develops into a wider insurgency. It is this later change in targeting that is the focus of examination of this book, particularly in explaining why and how some Arab foreign fighters subsequently become involved in Islamist terrorist-related activities.

The Central Argument of this Book

The central argument developed in the main body of this book is that, overlaps notwithstanding,[17] Arab foreign fighters involved in jihad defending co-religionists against a foreign invader or an unpopular autocratic Arab regime, should not necessarily be deemed synonymous with Islamist terrorists. These two different cohorts or groups often have quite distinct motivations, ideologies and levels of radicalisation, although these differences do appear to diminish over time. The linkage therefore between Arab foreign fighters and Islamist terrorists appears to involve situational factors experienced over time whilst participating in the initial defensive jihad. The situational factors that increase levels of radicalisation include, but are not limited to, exposure to the brutalising effects of close combat in a war zone; being subjected to ideological (religious) indoctrination (as part of group training and socialisation); and the notion of obedience to authority. The term 'situational factors' was coined by Philip Zimbardo who deemed them 'factors outside the actor ... environmental processes unique to a given setting',[18] rather than dispositional qualities of 'genetic makeup, personality traits, character, free will and other dispositions'.[19]

Naturally implicit in this argument is that the Arab foreign fighters who are the focus of this book, had no known previous terrorist links prior to their involvement in defensive jihad. For instance, Ayman al-Zawahiri the current head of Al Qaeda, was a terrorist member of the Egyptian Islamic Jihad (EIJ) group prior to his involvement in the 1980s Afghan jihad. Therefore, whilst he is cited in this book, he lies outside the cohort of Arab foreign fighters who are examined due to his prior involvement in terrorist-related activities. Conversely, Osama bin Laden (the now deceased former head of Al Qaeda) is probably the best-known example of an Arab foreign fighter who had no known previous terrorist links prior to his involvement in the 1980s Afghan jihad, but who subsequently became involved in Islamist terrorism.

Lastly, this book argues somewhat counter-intuitively, that many Arab foreign fighters who travelled to participate in a defensive jihad, appeared to be ordinary men – in the sense of being 'regular, normal, customary, usual'[20] individuals. In the context of the Arab world, Asef Bayat in his seminal book, *Life as Politics: How Ordinary People Change the Middle East*, defined 'ordinary people' as 'the globalizing youth and other urban grass roots'.[21] Despite the term 'ordinary' being a normative rather than a social-scientific judgement, referring to 'ordinary people' and 'ordinary men' retains academic ballast, being effectively used by scholars such as Professors Fred Katz and Christopher Browning, respectively.[22] The notion of ordinariness of some Arab foreign fighters also perhaps confirms the suggestion that 'plain folk ... ordinary people ... have contributed to extraordinary evil'.[23] This argument could be extrapolated further to suggest that whilst some Arab foreign fighters may have been radicalised prior to arriving in a conflict zone, this did not appear to apply to all of them. This book challenges the commonly held notion that all (as opposed to some) Arab foreign fighters are somehow necessarily radicalised (prior to travelling). This becomes particularly relevant when comparing them to Western foreign fighters who also travelled to

Syria, but who fought *against* ISIS, alongside the Kurdish People's Protection Units (YPG). It begs the question whether the notion of radicalisation relies on a state-centric perspective that depends on which group individuals joined, and/or on which side they fought. Naturally measuring and assessing radicalisation is extremely difficult, and many of the findings on the non-radicalisation of many Arab foreign fighters in this book are more suggestive than definitive. In addition, such an assessment relies on a definition of radicalisation, and this is offered later in the chapter.

The Approach

The approach taken to address how and why some Arab foreign fighters cross a threshold to subsequently become involved in Islamist terrorist-related activities is to try to understand them as individuals and avoid the frequent demonisation of both Arab foreign fighters and Islamist terrorists. In essence it is an account, through the eyes of Arab foreign fighters themselves, of their motivations, their environment and their beliefs – however misconceived they may appear to those not involved in Islamist activism or not living in the Arab world. Broadly it is an empathetic account of Arab foreign fighters, in an attempt to try to understand them; however, empathy should not be confused with sympathy. Trying to understand Arab foreign fighter behaviour is not equivalent to condoning it, and trying to explain their rationales for violence does not imply any support or approval for it. This book is an attempt to address both Edward Hall's argument that 'a way to experience another group is to understand . . . the way their minds work',[24] and John Horgan's more recent observation 'that too little [attention] is paid to terrorists' own account of their activities as a means of constructing a sense of their involvement in terrorism'.[25] In the post-9/11 landscape, if one perceives all resistance to unprovoked state aggression as terrorism, it will allow states a monopoly on the use of violence.

This book relies on analysis of the personal data collected from open sources on 3,367 Arab foreign fighters, who were involved in one or more of three case study defensive jihads: 1980s Afghanistan, Iraq (post-2003) and Syria (post-2011). This unique dataset is understood to be the largest currently constructed on Arab foreign fighters. These defensive jihads were selected as they attracted the greatest number of Arab (and other) foreign fighters (compared to other defensive jihads),[26] thereby offering the largest amount of data for analysis. The dataset was created over six years between 2012 and 2018, drawing mainly on Arab language Islamist websites (most of which have now be taken down by authorities). It was constructed using data extracted from sources including '*idaara al-ʿaama lil-hudood biyaanaat mujahhid*' (ISIS General Border Administration *Mujahhid* Data); *shuhada'fi zaman al-ghurba* (Martyrs in a Time of Alienation);[27] *maloomaat shakhseeya khaasa bil-muhajjireen* (Special Personal Information of the Immigrants – sometimes known as the 'Sinjar Records');[28] the Violations Documentation Centre (for Syria); the Chicago Project on Security and Threats (CPOST) Suicide Attack Database; Guantanamo Bay Detainee Assessments; Dabiq (IS magazine pre-August 2016); Rumiyah (IS magazine post-August 2016); Inspire (AQ magazine); and the 'Abu Zubaydah diaries'.[29] In particular, the data offer a 'through-life' picture of many Arab foreign fighters, starting with their 'in-processing' into a group (for example, the ISIS General Border Administration *Mujahhid* Data forms) and finishing with their 'out-processing' (for example, their martyrdom eulogies). The data extracted from these sources include, but are not limited to, personal biographical data (name, nationality and age), roles and activities of the individuals, the environment in which they operated, motivations, ideological influences, previous experience of jihad, and finally kinship and social ties.

Whilst the research explores the initial motivational circumstances of Arab foreign fighters leading them to participate in a defensive jihad, the main focus of this book is on those who subsequently became involved in Islamist terrorist-related activities, as a result of the situational circumstances they experienced during defensive jihad. To support the analysis, this book uses several tools: it examines the initial and subsequent motives of Arab foreign fighters; it discerns at what stage in the radicalisation process they moved from targeting foreign forces to civilians and non-combatants; it draws on the psychological theories of Philip Zimbardo (situational perspectives) and Stanley Milgram (obedience to authority);[30] it leverages the ideology and proponents of political Islam;[31] and lastly it draws upon War Studies in order to better understand the behaviour of men in battle. By using these tools, this book explores and examines those Arab foreign fighters who subsequently became involved in Islamist terrorist-related activities, but also attempts to illuminate the other broad outcomes resulting from their involvement in defensive jihad. Often considered as *post-jihad trajectories*, they include reintegration back into Arab society and/ or remaining involved in defensive jihad (in another country, for example Afghanistan or Libya).

Key Terms and Concepts

The accounts of Muhammed Zammar, Abdullah al-Shaya and Ahmad al-Darawi (introduced earlier in the chapter) highlight a lot of the concepts that are key to helping answer the central question of this book. The eight key terms and concepts that are consistently referred to in this book are defensive jihad and foreign fighters; terrorism and Islamist terrorists; civilians and non-combatants; self-sacrificial ('martyrdom/suicide') attacks, and the notion of radicalisation. It is acknowledged that the terms are not static categories, but evolve over time and continue to be contested. Their interpretation varies depending on who is using the term(s) and for what purpose. Whilst definitions of key terms and concepts will be offered below, the overarching Islamist philosophy of the Arab foreign fighters' and Islamist terrorists' own interpretation of these terms, will be discussed and developed throughout the case study chapters.

The first pair of key terms is jihad and Arab foreign fighters. The notion of jihad is contested and dynamic in nature, changing in order to remain 'relevant to new circumstances'.[32] It is important to recognise that there are non-violent as well as violent manifestations of jihad. Non-violent jihad is often considered the greater jihad, while violent jihad is considered the lesser jihad.[33] The non-violent jihad is internal and spiritual in nature, possessing great theological depth within Islam. Violent jihad, however – sometimes labelled 'jihad by the sword'[34] – may be offensive or defensive. According to Quintan Wiktorowicz 'offensive jihad functions to promote the spread of Islam', whereas:

> defensive jihad . . . is a widely-accepted concept that is analogous to international norms of self-defense and Judeo-Christian just war theory.[35] According to most Islamic scholars, when an outside force invades Muslim territory it is incumbent on all Muslims to wage jihad to protect the faith and the faithful . . . At the root of defensive jihad is a theological emphasis on justness . . . defending the faith-based community against external aggression is considered a just cause *par excellence*.[36]

Such a view has Quranic support, for example Surah al-Buqarah 2: 190 advises Muslims to 'Fight in the way of Allah those who fight you but do not transgress'. It is clear that the Soviet invasion of Afghanistan and the US-led coalition invasion of Iraq represented a classic example of the need for defensive jihad against external aggression, requiring the involvement of all able-bodied Sunni Muslims. It is of note, however, that the notion of defensive jihad in Iraq was exploited by Abu Musab al-Zarqawi (the deceased former leader of Al Qaeda in Iraq) who declared in June 2005, that 'our jihad in Iraq is the same as in Afghanistan, Kashmir, Chechnya, and Bosnia – an honourable jihad'.[37] This confirms the view that Islamist terrorists often hijack the concept of defensive jihad,[38] thus contributing to the conflation of the two activities. It is worthy of inclusion that some scholars (such as Thomas Hegghammer) adopt the label 'classical jihad' to denote defensive jihad. As the Arab and wider Muslim world use the term 'defensive jihad' (*jihad al-difaa*), that term is used throughout this book.

The key to understanding defensive jihad is that it may be conceptualised as a religiously sanctioned defensive response to foreign (or regime) aggression, and that it can only be 'authorized by a legitimate representative of the Muslim community'.[39] Although the notion of a legitimate representative may be contested,[40] Abdullah Azzam, Abu Musab al-Zarqawi and Abu Bakr al-Baghdadi became the perceived legitimate representatives (of most Arab foreign fighters) for the defensive jihads in 1980s Afghanistan, Iraq (post-2003) and Syria (post-2011), respectively.[41] The necessity for involvement in a defensive jihad is enshrined within the notion of *fard*, which is:

> a Divinely instituted obligation ... there is *fard al-ayn*, or essential obligation which is incumbent upon all Muslims,[42] and *fard al-kifayah*, an obligation which is acquitted in the name of all, as long as it is performed by some.[43]

For example, many Islamic scholars believed that the jihad in 1980s Afghanistan was an individual duty for the Afghan people, and not for other Muslims (living outside Afghanistan). Therefore, with the local Afghan *mujahhideen* fully engaged in defensive jihad against the Soviets, any outside help, for example from the Arab world, would be considered the lesser *fard kifayya* (a collective religious obligation).

All Muslims who participate in defensive jihad are considered to be *mujahhideen* (in Arabic), and hence Arab foreign fighters could also be considered foreign Arab *mujahhideen*.[44] Generic foreign fighters are normally defined as 'non-indigenous, non-territorialized combatants who, motivated by religion, kinship, and/or ideology enter a conflict zone to participate in hostilities'.[45] As noted earlier, Arab foreign fighters are defined in this book as 'ethnically Arab, religiously Sunni Muslim combatants, who participate in a defensive jihad, with no apparent link to the conflict other than religious affinity with the Sunni Muslim side'. They are essentially Sunni Muslim combatants who are ethnically Arab, who originate from (in the sense of being born in) one of the seventeen countries in the Arab world,[46] and who participate in defensive jihad in a foreign space. The sense that they are 'foreign' is based on the 'Western concept of the state and of citizenship',[47] rather than Islamic concepts of the *umma*, which encompasses 'a people, a community; or a nation, in particular the "nation" of Islam which transcends ethnic or political definition'.[48]

The second pair of key terms in need of definition is terrorism and Islamist terrorist. This book is anchored by the 'revised academic consensus definition of terrorism' promoted by Professor Alex Schmid, and refers to:

> a conspiratorial practice of calculated, demonstrative direct violent action without legal or moral restraints, targeting mainly civilians and non-combatants, performed for its propagandistic and psychological effects on various audiences and conflict parties.[49]

The key conceptual point, which Schmid reinforces, is that the 'main direct victims of terrorist attacks are in general not any armed forces but are *usually civilians, non-combatants or other innocent and defenceless persons*'.[50] Aware that Islamist terrorists more generally target civilians and non-combatants, it appears that by identifying the targeting rationales of Arab foreign fighters and Islamist terrorists, it will assist with distinguishing between the two cohorts. This definition of terrorism is a cornerstone of the book, and is further reinforced and validated by Section 2656f(d) of Title 22 of the United States Code definition[51] and by Professor Boaz Ganor.[52] It is, however, recognised that this reliance on drawing distinctions between targeting patterns of the two transnational cohorts is potentially problematic, in that defining civilians and non-combatants is challenging. For example, are Iraqi men waiting outside Iraqi Army recruiting centres considered combatants, non-combatants, or civilians, and in whose eyes?

The term 'terrorist' could therefore simply be defined as a perpetrator of terrorism, however it is important to recognise 'that involvement and engagement in terrorism is best thought of as a *process*'.[53] The term terrorist therefore used in this book refers to an individual who is moving through a process from 'initially becoming engaged' to 'the point of engaging in terrorist events'.[54] This could also include involvement in terrorist-related activities, that involves providing material support.[55] Although a terrorist may subscribe to any religion (or be an atheist), this book examines Sunni Muslim Arab foreign fighters some of whom subsequently became involved in Islamist terrorist-related activities.[56] The term 'Islamist terrorist' deserves further explanation. 'Islamist' is used in this book in the sense of 'advocating Islam as a political as well as a religious system'.[57] Although Islamists may come in different shades,[58] they broadly promote the need for *Sharia* law, and a greater adherence to Islamic principles. The label 'Islamist' is adopted throughout this book, fully mindful that 'Islamist terrorist movements are a small minority compared to the overwhelming majority of Islamist movements which are non-violent'.[59]

The typology of Islamist terrorist-related activities also needs explaining and includes at least three variants. First, there is 'transnational' Islamist terrorism conducted by global terrorists (for example, Al Qaeda) who promote 'military confrontation with the United States and her allies, to avenge and deter non-Muslim oppression of Muslims'[60] – first referred to as the 'far enemy' by Egyptian ideologue Muhammad Abdul Salam Faraj.[61] Second, there is 'religious nationalist' terrorism[62] conducted by 'socio-revolutionaries' (for example, the Egyptian Islamic Group) against 'a Muslim regime perceived as illegitimate'[63] – often referred to as the 'near enemy' by Muhammad Abdul Salam Faraj. Lastly, the Islamist terrorism perpetrated by the Islamic State and Al Qaeda affiliated groups in both Iraq and Syria is arguably an ideologically hybrid version that incorporates 'religious nationalist' terrorism (against the state), but with a wider transnational targeting agenda (against civilians in Western, Asian or African countries).

The third pair of key terms is 'civilians and non-combatants'. By leveraging the different targeting patterns of Arab foreign fighters and Islamist terrorists, and by defining civilians and non-combatants, it is suggested that distinctions may be drawn between the two transnational cohorts. Unfortunately even under International Law, defining civilians is fraught with difficulty particularly in non-international conflicts.[64] According to the International Committee of the Red Cross in international armed conflicts, civilians are defined 'as persons who are not members of the armed forces', however, in 'non-international armed conflicts . . . the terms civilians and civilian population are used without defining them'.[65] There is broad agreement, however, that 'civilians who do not take a direct part in hostilities are included in the category of non-combatants'.[66] What is striking is that the US Department of State also uses the label non-combatant to mean, 'in addition to civilians, military personnel (whether or not armed or on duty) who are not deployed in a war zone or a war-like setting'.[67] Thus, whilst these definitions are the preserve of national and international bodies, they do suggest correctly that aspiring Iraqi volunteers outside military recruitment centres are civilians (as they are not yet members of the armed forces); and that the Al Qaeda attack on the USS *Cole* in Aden (in 2000) was terrorism, as the sailors were non-combatants in a non-war zone. Whilst contentious, making a targeting distinction explicit is not contrived, for Professor Alex Schmid also identified many other distinguished scholars (including Boaz Ganor, Joshua

Sinai, Mohammed Hafez and Ekaterina Stepanova) who also highlighted the need to distinguish between 'civilians/non-combatants' and combatants from a nation's armed forces.[68]

The fourth key term(s) are self-sacrificial ('martyrdom/suicide') attacks. These are highly contested terms, and are more generally labelled by states as 'suicide attacks'. This, however, ignores the context within which the attacks are made, the targeting rationale and history. These are all developed throughout the case study chapters, however a brief overview is warranted. Academically there is little consensus on a definition of 'suicide attack' except, rather bizarrely, that 'the perpetrator's death is a precondition of a successful attack'. One would therefore conclude based on this conventional wisdom that when a 'suicide bomber' survives (as does happen), despite killing civilians or military personnel, such an attack is not deemed to be a 'successful attack'. Few scholars are willing to challenge this disparity apart from Professors David Cook and Karin Fierke. Cook places 'martyrdom operations' inside inverted commas, being unwilling 'to take a stand on the question of whether people who die during the course of these actions are actually martyrs or not'.[69] Fierke places 'suicide/martyrdom' inside inverted commas, in order 'to highlight the tension in the relationship between the two concepts'.[70] This book occupies the middle ground, choosing the term 'self-sacrificial ("martyrdom/suicide") attack' in order to be apolitical, impartial and offer a more contextualised and realistic term.

The last key term in need of a definition is radicalisation. Much has been written about radicalisation, yet it remains an imprecise, contested and largely a politically expedient term, rather than an analytically useful term. There are no metrics to measure radicalisation despite many efforts including the Terrorism Radicalization Assessment Protocol (TRAP-18),[71] which is more focussed on the radicalisation of lone actor terrorists. Governments in the Arab world and the West use the term radicalisation as a 'catch-all' to explain why Islamists may become involved in non-violent and violent activism. Although radicalisation is often a pejorative label, it suggests the possible existence of a progression whereby an individual may move from point *a* (involvement in defensive jihad) and subsequently arrive at point *b* (involvement in Islamist terrorism). The most current and comprehensive definition of radicalisation was proposed by Professor Alex Schmid, and includes:

> an individual or collective (group) process whereby, usually in a situation of political polarisation, normal practices of dialogue, compromise and tolerance between political actors and groups with diverging interests are abandoned by

one or both sides in a conflict dyad in favour of a growing commitment to engage in confrontational tactics of conflict-waging. These can include either (i) the use of (non-violent) pressure and coercion, (ii) various forms of political violence other than terrorism or (iii) acts of violent extremism in the form of terrorism and war crimes.[72]

However, this definition may be too broad. First, including 'the use of (non-violent) pressure and coercion' under 'confrontational tactics of conflict-waging' is potentially problematic. For example, an eager and committed politician who is canvassing hard for (re)election on a front doorstep, adopting the 'use of (non-violent) pressure and coercion', could be considered radicalised! At the other end of Schmid's definitional spectrum, 'acts of violent extremism in the form of terrorism and war crimes' are also nestled under 'confrontational tactics of conflict-waging'. Therefore, by way of example, the US Army unit involved in the 1968 massacre of 504 unarmed Vietnamese women, children and old men in My Lai village, would also be considered radicalised – yet the unit was not considered to be so (and this dichotomy is discussed in detail in Chapter 6). It is worth noting that as far back as 2010, Professor Jonathan Githens-Mazer and Robert Lambert offered a persuasive argument on how the 'conventional wisdom on radicalisation' is a 'failed discourse'.[73]

Bearing in mind this lack of clarity and agreement amongst scholars and politicians, this book uses a broad and arguably more nuanced definition of radicalisation, namely an ideological process whereby groups or individuals begin to embrace views and beliefs of a more extremist nature, that may subsequently cross a threshold that leads to acts of illegal violence of varying degrees of brutality and morality. This personal definition of radicalisation would allow scholars and the general public to recognise the psychological and social influences acting on an individual or a group, but also to conceptualise the term as a gradual but not necessarily a linear process – perhaps like the board game 'Snakes and Ladders', whereby one may reach 100 (participation in terrorism), hover around 50 (non-violent activism) or simply descend down some snakes and return to zero (a normal civilian life).

Book Layout

This book is based on rigorous evidence-based research drawing on a dataset of 3,367 Arab foreign fighters, developed from primarily Arabic sources over a six-year period. It seeks to explain, through the eyes of Arab foreign fighters, why and how they became initially involved in defensive jihad, and how some subsequently became involved in Islamist terrorist-related activities. It is an empathetic account of Arab foreign fighters; however, it must be stressed that trying to understand and explain their motivations is not equivalent to condoning them, and in no part does this book excuse, exonerate or condone their behaviour.

The book is broken down into six chapters, with Chapter 1 having set the scene and covered the central question, the argument, and key terms/concepts. Chapters 2 to 4 constitute the three case study chapters of 1980s Afghanistan, Iraq (post-2003), and Syria (post-2011), that examine the circumstances of Arab foreign fighter initial participation in defensive jihad. Additionally, the case studies also explore their subsequent post-jihad trajectories, that include reintegration back into Arab society and/or remaining involved in defensive jihad. Chapter 5 provides analysis of, and reflections on, the findings from the three case study chapters and explores whether the analysis may apply more widely (including for Western foreign fighters). Finally, Chapter 6 provides a conclusion and recommendations.

Afghan Arabs in the Afghan Jihad: The Incubation of Modern Terrorism

The Afghan Arabs were 'not bloodthirsty people, the jihad was focused, and the philosophy of hatred and bloodshed did not exist'.

Abdullah Anas.[1]

Introduction

This chapter, the first of three case studies, examines the initial motivational factors behind Afghan Arab involvement in the Afghan jihad and their subsequent post-conflict trajectories that included becoming involved in Islamist terrorist-related activities. Such activities included involvement in the 1993 World Trade Centre (WTC) attack, the 1995 Riyadh attack, the 1998 East Africa attacks, the 2000 USS *Cole* attack and the 9/11 attacks. It examines empirically those Arabs who participated in the defensive jihad in 1980s Afghanistan by leveraging a dataset comprising of 394 Afghan Arabs (representing as a minimum, nearly 20 per cent of the total Afghan Arab cohort).[2] The label 'Afghan Arab' (also known as 'Arab-Afghan')[3] is defined in this book in time and space as an Arab male, predominantly from the Arab world,[4] who became involved in the defensive jihad in Afghanistan starting from December 1979 (the Soviet invasion) until April 1992 (the collapse of the Afghan communist regime under President Najibullah). In effect, they were Arab *mujahhideen*, assisting the Afghan *mujahhideen*. Whilst the nexus between veteran Afghan Arabs and their subsequent involvement in Islamist terrorism (both global and religious nationalist) constitutes the hub of this chapter, other trajectories of veteran Afghan Arabs are also explored, including their further involvement in defensive jihad (for example, Bosnia) or returning to their home countries.

The background to the Afghan jihad deserves illuminating. The Arab world at the time of the Soviet invasion of Afghanistan (in December 1979) was already reeling from two earlier momentous events that same year: the siege of the Grand Mosque in Mecca (17 November 1979) and the Iranian (Shi'a) revolution with the coming to power of the Grand Ayatollah Khomeini (December 1979). Additionally, the Cold War between the West and the communist Soviet Union was dividing the world. The siege of the Grand Mosque, led by Juhayman Saif al-Utaybi, was underpinned by his belief that 'Saudi Arabia's monarchy ... [was] illicit' and that the clergy 'had betrayed the faith, siding for reasons of political expediency with a regime they clearly knew to be violating Islamic rules'[5] – in effect a 'religious nationalist' agenda. As a result of the Mecca siege, the Saudi regime felt their legitimacy being challenged, thus by overtly supporting the Afghan *mujahhideen* resistance to the Soviet military invasion and occupation, it implicitly permitted and indeed supported, the involvement of Saudi youth in the Afghan jihad.

The second momentous event in 1979 was the Iranian (Shi'a) revolution, which had adopted a violent religious narrative that subsequently proved to be an inspiration to many Sunni Islamists who became emboldened to adopt this revolutionary (religious nationalist) model in their own home countries, particularly in Egypt, Algeria and Syria. Two notable religious nationalist examples would be the assassination of Egyptian President Muhammad Anwar Sadat in 1981, and the Muslim Brotherhood uprising in 1982 in Syria against the late President Hafez al-Assad. This resulted in many Arab regimes feeling their legitimacy being threatened by the emboldened and more politically aware Islamists, and hence they introduced policies of both appeasement and increased brutality. Appeasement came in the form of supporting external Islamist causes such as the Afghan jihad, in effect exporting militancy, whilst the brutality came in the form of mass arrests and prison torture. For example, in the 1982 uprising in Syria, the Syrian army 'killed up to 20,000 people'.[6]

The Soviet invasion of Afghanistan was predicated on propping up a deeply unpopular and beleaguered communist regime (within Afghanistan), that was resisted by the majority of the Afghan people. Having lost control over the majority of the country, apart from the cities, the Soviets viewed their intervention as coming to the aid of an ally in difficulty. With the backdrop of the Cold War, the West in general and the United States in particular were determined to challenge the Soviet occupation through proxies, by supporting the Afghan *mujahideen* and the Pakistan Inter-Services Intelligence (ISI) in financial aid and weaponry. US aid by 1982 amounted to an annual budget of $600 million, a figure matched by Gulf states, particularly Saudi Arabia.[7] Thus, the United States and the Gulf States were also indirectly (whether knowingly or not) supporting

Arab foreign fighters, including Shaykh Abdullah Azzam (a Jordanian who became the principal ideologue in Afghanistan having arrived in 1981), Shaykh Tameem al-Adnani (a Jordanian Islamist ideologue) and Osama bin Laden (the Saudi who later became the leader of Al Qaeda).

This chapter is broken down into two broad sections. The first analyses the broad backgrounds of the Arab foreign fighters, including their geographic origin, education and age, as well as the influence of religion (as perceived by those involved); the influence of kinship and social ties; and the possible impact of living as an Arab expatriate abroad. These were all identified as factors that appeared to contribute to the initial involvement of Arab foreign fighters in the Afghan jihad. This research was conducted by using a personal dataset comprised of 394 Afghan Arabs, allowing the analysis to be both evidence-based and empirically driven. The second part of this chapter examines the situational circumstances experienced by the Afghan Arabs during the Afghan jihad, which influenced their post-conflict trajectories (including subsequent involvement in Islamist terrorism, full or partial reintegration back into Arab society, or remaining involved in defensive jihad). This allows for some form of comparative analysis, particularly in trying to explain why some chose *not* to subsequently engage in Islamist terrorism, despite being exposed to the same situational circumstances in the Afghan jihad.

Afghan Arab Involvement in the 1980s Afghan Jihad

Overview

The 1980s defensive jihad in Afghanistan involved Afghan *mujahhideen* and Afghan Arabs fighting the Soviet military occupation – a conflict that has been covered by many scholars.[8] The Afghan Arabs travelled to Peshawar (on the Pakistan side of the Afghan border) and became involved in the defensive jihad as combatants (by crossing the border into Afghanistan), as instructors in military training camps, or as humanitarians within non-governmental organisations (NGOs) in Pakistan or Afghanistan.

The breakdown of the geographic origin by birth of the 394 Afghan Arabs from the dataset is presented in Figure 2.1. The actual total figures are used in preference to *per capita* (per one million) in order not to distort the analysis. For example, only six Afghan Arabs came from Qatar, but coming from such a small population (371,000 in 1985) gave the country the highest *per capita* rate of

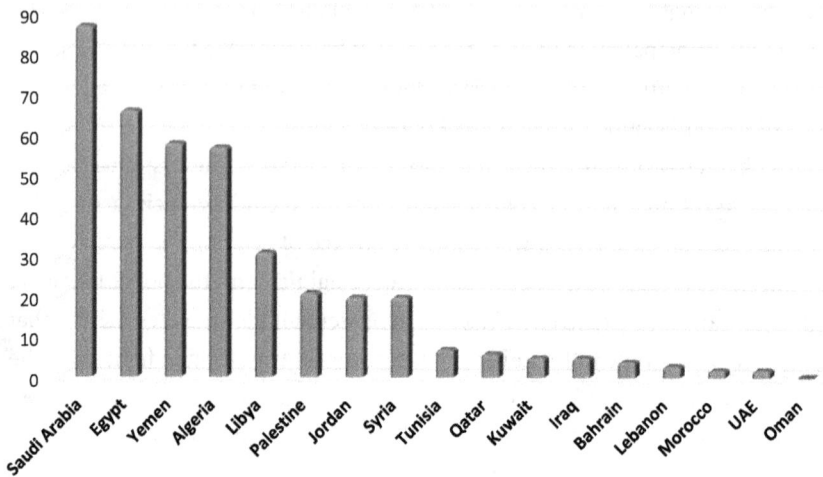

Figure 2.1 Afghan Arab geographic origin (n=394).

16.7 per one million of the population. Trying to provide meaningful analysis using such a low number of individuals (only six) was statistically insignificant.

The dataset shows the major cohorts of Afghan Arabs coming from countries like Saudi Arabia, Egypt and Yemen. A brief analysis of these geographic origins offers an insight into the contextual societal level (or structural) circumstances that may, or may not, have promoted involvement in the 1980s Afghan jihad. First, in the case of Saudi Arabia, the 'religious scholars, the Saudi ruling elite, and society at large fully supported the migration of young men to pursue jihad overseas'.[9] Former Yemeni foreign fighter and later Osama bin Laden's bodyguard, Nassir al-Bahri, recalled that 'Saudi authorities at the time were officially encouraging young men to join the holy war against the Soviet troops which had invaded Afghanistan'.[10] He also admitted to having been 'influenced by the sermons delivered by some speakers in the mosques in Jeddah [Saudi Arabia] about jihad in Afghanistan' adding that 'the instigation and call to jihad in the Friday sermons, the tape cassettes, the magazines, and other media . . . influenced him greatly'.[11]

Undoubtedly the most significant and influential individual behind the transnational mobilisation of Arab (and some Western) foreign fighters was a displaced Palestinian national, Shaykh Abdullah Yusuf Azzam (known thereafter as Abdullah Azzam). He was the principal ideologue who issued *fatwas* (religious proclamations) and whose speeches and cassettes were distributed throughout mosques all over the Arab and Western world. His influence as an ideologue espousing the need for involvement in defensive jihad in 1980s Afghanistan is covered later in this chapter. Arguably the second most significant Afghan Arab ideologue was also a displaced Palestinian national, Shaykh Tameem al-Adnani (known thereafter as Tameem al-Adnani) who, for example, influenced Saudi Afghan Arab, Wa'il Hamza Julaidan: 'Before I came to the Afghan jihad, I visited Shaykh Tameem to speak with him about the jihad . . . in the mosque, and due to that, his lectures on cassettes were passed between the young Muslims and spread like a light in the darkness, like fire in the woods'.[12]

The second most prolific cohort of Afghan Arabs came from Egypt. Their substantial involvement can be broadly explained by two push factors (i.e. considered grievances, broadly defined, that push an individual to act) orchestrated by the Egyptian regime. First, after the 1981 assassination of President Muhammad Anwar as-Sadat, the Egyptian regime targeted (violent and non-violent) Islamist groups. This resulted in mass arrests and prison sentences, leading many individuals to escape to Afghanistan once released from jail for fear of re-arrest.[13] Examples include Ayman al-Zawahiri (current leader of Al Qaeda), Ahmad Salama Mabrook (who twenty-five years later joined Jabhat al-Nusrah in Syria), and Abu Hani al-Misri (who later joined Ahrar al-Sham in Syria). Second, many Egyptian Islamists were also encouraged by the Egyptian regime to travel to Afghanistan in order to export jihad beyond their own nation-states.[14] As will be discussed later, the Egyptian Afghan Arabs with known pre-existing terrorist links, particularly to Egyptian Islamic Jihad (EIJ) or the Egyptian Islamic Group (EIG), greatly influenced those Afghan Arabs who had no known pre-existing terrorist links.

Finally, the involvement of so many Yemenis is less obvious. During the 1980s they were split as a country, one half being the communist People's Democratic Republic of Yemen (PDRY) and the other half being the Yemen Arab Republic (aka North Yemen). From the limited data available, it appears the majority of Yemeni Afghan Arabs came from the Yemen Arab Republic (Ibb, Marib, Sanaa, Khirash and Hudaydah), sometimes referred to as North Yemen. However North Yemen was divided into two halves, based on sectarian lines – with Sunni *Shafi's* in the southern half, and with Shi'a *Zaidis* in the north. The Sunni *Shafi's* resented the Shi'a *Zaidis* who controlled North Yemen.[15] The dataset suggests that the majority of Yemeni Afghan Arabs comprised of Sunni *Shafi's*. Finally, 21 per cent (twelve) of the Yemeni Afghan Arab cohort (fifty-eight) were actually (economic) expatriates, working in Saudi Arabia. Being away from family roots and living in a country that was promoting the narrative of the defensive jihad in Afghanistan may have contributed to their vulnerability and subsequent mobilisation. The issue of expatriate status and its connections with involvement in Islamist activities (violent and non-violent) is covered later in this chapter.

From the dataset, the Afghan Arabs were well represented educationally and career wise: fifty-two (13 per cent) of the 394 Afghan Arabs had a university education, with ten of them having gained their degrees in the United States: there were nine medical doctors, six engineers and thirty-eight bachelor's degree holders – a finding that is corroborated in previous studies.[16] This somewhat challenges the myth that such volunteers are uneducated, unemployed and from socially deprived backgrounds. Age wise, based on the available data of 105 Afghan Arabs, they varied between eleven and sixty-five years old,[17] with 51 per cent of them being under twenty-two-years-old. The average age was twenty-three and the median was twenty-four-years-old. In addition, only thirty-two were identified as married when they arrived in Afghanistan, a fact that when placed alongside their average age, may indicate the existence of 'biographical availability' – a situation denoting the 'absence of personal constraints that may increase the costs and risks of movement participation, such as full-time employment, marriage and family responsibilities'.[18] This finding chimes well with the scholarly literature, particularly as it 'is already well established in other spheres that young males are associated with a multitude of dangerous and high-risk activities'.[19] This perhaps suggests that those Afghan Arabs (with no known prior terrorist links) were just ordinary Arab men, in the sense of being 'regular, normal, customary, usual'[20] individuals, who were broadly representative of their societies with varying social–economic and educational levels, and having a broad spectrum of ages. If this was the case, what were the factors that persuaded some ordinary Arab men to become involved in the Afghan jihad? The first (and arguably the most influential) factor that emerged from the data was the centrality of religion and the ideological narrative.

The Centrality of Religion and the Ideological Narrative

The situational circumstances of the 1980s Afghan jihad need illuminating in order to understand the Afghan Arabs' initial motivations. For example, were the Afghan Arabs already radicalised prior to arriving in Afghanistan? Was the Afghan jihad actually Islamist terrorism, where civilians and non-combatants were targeted? Was the notion of martyrdom in the Afghan jihad actually a synonym for suicide attacks? To answer these questions and more, it is useful to examine the defensive jihad in 1980s Afghanistan through the eyes of those who were actually there, in order to answer the above questions. To do this, this chapter draws on the narratives of Abdullah Azzam and six other prominent Afghan Arabs.

Abdullah Azzam (1941–1989) was a Palestinian ideologue who has been labelled 'the father of the Afghan Arabs ... and a preeminent theoretician'.[21] In addition, as important as his ideological credentials were, he was also acknowledged as a 'charismatic authority' amongst the Afghan Arabs.[22] Abdullah Azzam was a pious child who joined the Muslim Brotherhood in his teenage years, and later (1966) gained a BA in *Shariah* Law from the University of Damascus. After the Israelis captured the West Bank in 1967, Shaykh Abdullah Azzam decided to resettle in Jordan (as an Arab expatriate), because he could not live under the Israeli occupation. He would later join the jihad against it. He later received an MA in *Shariah* Law and a PhD in *Usool al-Fiqh*[23] from the University of Al Azhar (in Egypt). The circumstances that inspired Shaykh Abdullah Azzam's involvement in the Afghan jihad are instructive. First, he had experienced the invasion and occupation of the West Bank by Israeli forces, and thus had genuine empathy for the Afghans who were under Soviet military occupation. Second, he had 'a chance meeting in Mecca' with Shaykh Kamal Sananiri[24] in October 1980 and 'was so influenced by what Sananiri had to say that he decided to go to Afghanistan'.[25] He went there in 1981, where he subsequently became the main pillar of the defensive jihad and published many treatises including, but not limited to, *Signs of the Merciful* in May 1982; *In Defence of Muslim Lands* in 1983; and *Join the Caravan* in 1987.

The six other prominent Afghan Arabs used in this chapter are Abdullah Anas – an Algerian who was one of the first and most prominent Afghan Arabs in Afghanistan; Mustafa Hamid (aka Abu Walid al-Misri) – an Egyptian, who was also one of the early arrivals in Afghanistan prepared to wage jihad against the Soviet invaders; Musa al-Qarni – a Saudi intellectual and former Afghan Arab 'who once led the incitement to jihad in Saudi Arabia and travelled to Afghanistan in the early days of jihad against the Russians';[26] Tameem al-Adnani – a Palestinian and the Director of the Afghan *Mujahhideen* Services Office;[27] and Noman Benotman[28] – a Libyan veteran of the Afghan jihad and former member of the *Shura* Committee of the Libyan Islamic Fighting Group (LIFG). Finally, Abu Zubaydah (aka Zayn Al Abidin Muhammad Husayn) was a Palestinian expatriate living in Saudi Arabia who maintained a personal diary of his experience as an Afghan Arab while in Afghanistan,[29] and who is used as an example, in that he epitomises many of the Afghan Arab fighters. These six prominent Afghan Arabs were selected due to open source availability, the senior positions many held during the Afghan jihad, and the content of their narrative that appears broadly devoid of rhetoric. Whilst not necessarily always being representative of the rank and file of the Afghan Arab cohort, their narratives are illuminating.

The Religious Ideology of Defensive Jihad in 1980s Afghanistan

The 'most pronounced reason' for participating in defensive jihad in Afghanistan was that it 'was a formally and religiously sanctioned war to defend the country and the land'.[30] This defensive narrative was based on perhaps the most influential publication of Abdullah Azzam, in his 1983 book *In Defence of Muslim Lands*, where he argued that 'one of the most important lost obligations is the forgotten obligation of fighting . . . [it] is the most important of the compulsory duties and arises [when] the *kuffar*[31] enter a land of the Muslims'.[32] Azzam's central argument was that 'if a piece of Muslim land the size of a hand span is infringed upon, then jihad becomes *fard ayn* [an individual religious obligation] on every Muslim',[33] and not just the Afghan people.

Azzam's interpretation of defensive jihad being *fard ayn* (an individual religious obligation)[34] for all Muslims appeared to challenge the accepted Islamic mores, in that 'the mainstream position of religious scholars at the time was that jihad was only an individual duty for the Afghans, not for all Muslims'.[35] Therefore, with the local Afghan *mujahhideen* fully engaged in the defensive jihad against the Soviets, any outside help (for example, from the Arab world) was considered *fard kifayya* (a collective religious obligation).[36] However, Abdullah Azzam had, by his own admission, changed the mainstream position among Muslim clerics, and had actually gained the support of Shaykh Abdul Aziz bin Bazz,[37] Shaykh Muhammad bin Uthaymin[38] and 'more than one hundred scholars from the entire Islamic world'.[39] Thus, with the defensive jihad in Afghanistan now being considered *fard ayn* (an individual religious obligation for all Muslims), it effectively unravelled nearly 1,400 years of Islamic consensus on defensive jihad. From once being considered *fard kifayya* (a collective religious obligation) for Muslims, this change in tack appeared to become accepted doctrine among many contemporary Islamists. This is the same broad doctrinal message that has resonated since the Afghan jihad in the Arab and wider Muslim world, particularly for the defence of Muslims in Bosnia, Chechnya, Afghanistan (post-2001), Iraq (post-2003), Libya (2011) and Syria, although the last three conflicts became more nuanced and sectarian in nature.

Additionally, Abdullah Azzam highlighted the injustices being inflicted upon Afghan co-religionists, in particular that 'Afghan children are being slaughtered, women are being raped, the innocent are killed and their corpses scattered'.[40] It sought to achieve an emotional resonance – the same that has been used to recruit Arab foreign fighters to the Syrian conflict.[41] Abdullah Azzam's narrative, of identifying with co-religionists in Afghanistan, and the glory gained by participation in jihad, was a powerful motivating factor for involvement in the Afghan jihad. Certainly, Nassir al-Bahri, a veteran Arab foreign fighter and later a bodyguard of Osama bin Laden wrote:

> I carried Abdullah Azzam's books and cassettes around with me. In them he talked about Paradise, the glory of jihad and what lies beyond death. His talks described the mysterious powers of the mujahid, who feels no pain as he dies a martyr from his injuries.[42]

The dataset shows further anecdotal evidence of the influence of Abdullah Azzam, including Moroccan Afghan Arab Hassan Walafee (aka Abu Tayyib al-Maghrabi),[43] who in response to meeting Abdullah Azzam in the United States in December 1988, promptly gave up his studies in Texas for jihad in Afghanistan; Abu Walid al-Gazi (aka Abu Walid al-Filistini) was inspired by Abdullah Azzam and subsequently travelled to Afghanistan in 1986; and Yemeni Afghan Arab Muhammad Ali al-Shuwaibi (aka Abu Jihad al-Sanaani) travelled to Afghanistan in 1989, also having been inspired by the rhetoric of Abdullah Azzam.[44]

The other six prominent Afghan Arabs used in this chapter also recall life in the 1980s Afghan jihad. According to Mustafa Hamid, the majority 'of those who fought in Afghanistan were youths who went thinking they were fighting for a fair and just cause',[45] reinforcing the notion that they were not necessarily radicalised. This may help explain why the Afghan Arabs (with no known pre-existing terrorist links) eschewed terrorist-related activities. Certainly, Tameem al-Adnani stressed that 'hijacking planes . . . killing innocent people, women, and civilians . . . is not jihad'. He argued that in 1980s Afghanistan, 'jihad was fighting for the sake of Allah . . . fighting those who fight you . . . the men . . . the Russians'.[46] This was echoed by two further Afghan Arabs: Abdullah Anas argued that the Afghan Arabs were 'not bloodthirsty people, the jihad was focused, and the philosophy of hatred and bloodshed did not exist';[47] while veteran Saudi Afghan Arab, Musa al-Qarni noted that 'many Arab young men who had joined the Afghan jihad . . . had only come to fight' the Soviet invaders.[48]

This suggestion that the majority (though not all) of Afghan Arabs were not necessarily radicalised prior to their involvement in defensive jihad is broadly (but not entirely) supported in the scholarly literature. According to Professor Olivier Roy, the Afghan Arabs 'did not come from the more radical milieu',[49] with other scholars explaining that that they 'came to Afghanistan just to fight jihad in support of their Afghan brethren'.[50] Despite this finding, academics such as Katerina Dalacoura still paint the Afghan Arabs as 'Islamic radicals fighting the Soviet Union in Afghanistan'.[51] Whilst perhaps misleading and unrepresentative, such labelling is consistent with, and emblematic of, the wider political and academic trend of 'associating the noble religious concept of jihad with illegitimate violence'.[52]

There is, however, some possibly anecdotal evidence that atrocities (akin to terrorism by non-state actors)[53] did take place during the 1980s Afghan jihad. Maybe these atrocities were conducted by more extreme Afghan Arabs with pre-existing terrorist links, however in 1989 a group of Afghan Arabs did massacre some Afghan communist troop prisoners near Jalalabad.[54] Perhaps, therefore, it was no coincidence that 'it was after Jalalabad that the western media started to call [the Afghan Arabs] terrorists' in Afghanistan.[55] Finally, veteran Afghan Arab Abdullah Anas, while comparing the 1980s Afghan jihad with the atrocities perpetrated in the Syrian conflict (post-2011), also argued that 'the word jihad has been stolen, hijacked … jihad will continue until the hereafter, but the challenge is, in what context, what circumstances, who declared the jihad, with who, when'?[56]

The Religious Nature of Martyrdom in the 1980s Afghan Jihad

Whilst the twentieth-century Islamic concept of martyrdom (*al-istishhaad*) is often viewed in the West as suicide (*al-intihaar*),[57] perhaps counter-intuitively there is no evidence of Afghan Arabs conducting self-sacrificial ('martyrdom/ suicide') attacks during the Afghan jihad. In the biographies of the 394 Afghan Arabs, whilst the *shaheed* (martyr) is revered, it is in accordance with the view of Abdullah Azzam in his book, *Defence of Muslim Lands*: a martyr *fee sabeel Allah* (in the cause of God). As one veteran Saudi Afghan Arab, Musa al-Qarni explained, 'there were no suicide operations at the time. The young men used to attack tanks and fighter aircraft with their personal weapons'.[58] Academically, this is corroborated by two scholars – Olivier Roy recognised that most Afghan Arabs 'were generally courageous, even fanatical fighters'[59] however as Mohammed Hafez noted, the 'Afghan Arabs did not engage in suicide attacks per se'.[60] This zeal and fanaticism displayed by the Afghan Arabs should not be confused (or conflated) with that of contemporary 'suicide bombers'. Whilst it is recognised that the

Afghan Arabs did develop a culture for martyrdom (in line with the writings of Abdullah Azzam), based on the evidence from the dataset, they only sought martyrdom *fee sabeel Allah*, fighting the Soviets in a conventional military sense. Importantly, Abdullah Azzam authored several books on martyrdom including *Martyrs: The Building Blocks of Nation*.[61] In it, he argued that:

> History does not write its lines except with blood. Glory does not build its loft[y] edifice except with skulls; honour and respect cannot be established except on a foundation of cripples and corpses. Empires, distinguished peoples, states and societies cannot be established except with examples. Indeed, those who think that they can change reality, or change societies, without blood, sacrifices and invalids, without pure, innocent souls, then they do not understand the essence of this *deen* [religion].[62]

The essence of Azzam's message is that a *mujahhid* must be willing to sacrifice his (or her) life for a meaningful cause, which in the case of 1980s Afghanistan was defending a fellow Muslim country from the Soviet invaders. Assaf Moghadam argued succinctly that 'Azzam understood martyrdom not as involving suicide missions *per se*, but as the death of any "true" Muslim waging jihad. Such martyrdom would wash away the jihadi's sins and bestow glory upon him.'[63]

In the obituary of Saudi Afghan Arab Yahya Sanyor al-Jaddawi,[64] considered to be the first 'martyr' from the Arabian Gulf to have been killed in Afghanistan in 1985, it refers to the Qur'anic view of martyrdom: 'Think not of those who are killed in the Way of Allah as dead. Nay, they are alive, with their Lord, and they have provision'.[65] Many Afghan Arabs sought martyrdom, such as Saudi Afghan Arab Abu Zubair al-Madani,[66] who 'always used to speak and think about one thing, which was martyrdom'. He survived Afghanistan fighting at Jaji, Jalalabad and Kabul, but had his wish fulfilled in Bosnia in 1992. Another case was Yemeni Afghan Arab Abu Uthman, who was motivated to become an Afghan Arab because he 'wanted to be a Muslim martyr',[67] which he did in 1989 on the battlefield at Shakardara, Afghanistan. Finally, and interestingly, Yemeni Afghan Arab Ali Hamza al-Bahlul, was initially recruited for jihad at a mosque in Sanna aptly named *masjid al-shuhada* (the Martyrs' Mosque).

The view is therefore taken that whilst the Afghan Arabs did embrace the religious underpinnings of jihad and martyrdom, based on the evidence from the 394 Afghan Arabs, they were only inclined to sacrifice their lives for God fighting the Soviets (or Afghan communists) in a conventional military sense. There is no evidence to support the view of BBC reporter Sarah Shah, who visited Afghanistan in 1986 and reported that 'the Arab volunteers in

Afghanistan … don't mind strapping explosives to themselves to become martyrs'.[68] In effect, it confuses the Islamic notion of 'martyrdom' with that of 'suicide'. Despite the nuance, it is a very fundamental point to take on board in order to truly understand the behavioural choices of the Afghan Arabs in the 1980s jihad. As noted in Chapter 1, in order to offer an impartial and nuanced account, the preferred terms used throughout this book are 'self-sacrificial attacks' and/or 'martyrdom/suicide' operations, in order to the ease the tension between the terms.

Research undertaken for this book has determined that there is no evidence of a single self-sacrificial ('martyrdom/suicide') attack targeting civilians or non-combatants, or an expression to commit one, during the Afghan jihad. This suggests that the Afghan Arabs (with no known prior terrorist links) were not necessarily radicalised, let alone terrorists. This appears to be counter-intuitive in the post-9/11 political landscape, but in the 1980s Afghan jihad, the Arab participants could be better thought of as noble idealists, albeit perhaps misguided; however their mobilisation was to subsequently spawn a transnational Islamist terrorist movement under the label Al Qaeda. This organisation, with its widespread use of self-sacrificial ('martyrdom/suicide') attacks targeting civilians and non-combatants, has in effect hijacked the original notion of 'martyrdom' extolled by Abdullah Azzam, and has paid little attention 'to constructing a theological argument justifying such attacks'.[69]

Kinship and Friendship Ties

Extracted from the dataset, just over 10 per cent (thirty-nine) of Afghan Arabs had some form of identifiable social affiliation connected to their involvement in the Afghan jihad, in the form of kinship or friendship ties. This finding is not new, for other scholars have recognised that 'the process of joining the jihad was fundamentally a social experience and the main vehicles of mobilisation were networks of kinship and friendship'.[70] However, the scale of the phenomenon is rarely presented empirically. Based on the dataset, it appears that kinship ties were more influential than friendship ties, although chance encounters that developed into friendship ties and subsequent involvement in the Afghan jihad were also numerous, and are covered later. In addition, during the Afghan jihad friendships were developed between Afghan Arabs that resulted in enduring relationships which may be better understood as 'comradeship ties', that were subsequently important in generating trust, loyalty and social cohesion.

Kinship Ties

Extracted from the dataset, the most usual kinship tie was that of brothers involved in Islamist militancy, be that the Afghan jihad or terrorism. Particular examples include Egyptian Afghan Arab Abu Ubaidah al-Banshiri (future AQ chief of operations), whose brother was involved in the assassination of President Sadat; Egyptian Afghan Arab Muhammad Shawqi al-Islambouli, whose brother (Khalid Shawqi al-Islambouli) was also involved in the assassination of President Sadat; Kuwaiti Afghan Arab Khalid Shaykh Muhammad (the mastermind of the 9/11 attacks) had three of his brothers involved in Afghan jihad; and Al Qaeda's current leader (2018) Ayman al-Zawahiri, had a brother (Muhammad al-Zawahiri) also involved in the Afghan jihad. Finally, anecdotally, there was the case of indirect sister involvement. For example, the thirteen-year-old sister of Yemeni Afghan Arab Abu Muslim al-Khalan, encouraged him to become an Afghan Arab by saying, 'had I been a boy, I would definitely have gone to Afghanistan'.[71]

The involvement of fathers is also enlightening. Saudi Afghan Arab Musab Saud al-Awseen at the age of nineteen was sent by his father to the Afghan jihad and was killed near Jalalabad on 24 October 1990;[72] Yemeni Afghan Arab Salim Umar al-Haddad,[73] was also sent by his father (an Islamic preacher) along with his three brothers; and finally Yemeni Afghan Arab Muhannad bin Attash was sent by his father along with four other brothers.[74] However, there were unsupportive fathers, who did not sanction or support the involvement of an offspring in the Afghan jihad. Take the case of Yemeni Afghan Arab Abu Hasan al-Jadawi; his family retrieved him from Afghanistan and burned his passport. However, he returned to Afghanistan after obtaining another passport and was later killed near Nangarhar.[75] It is interesting that this phenomenon has continued into the Syrian conflict, where leaked ISIS documents revealed cases in which fathers also came to retrieve their sons in 2014.[76]

However, the involvement of fathers also creates an interesting situation where realistically a child may have no option but to travel with his father. Abdullah Tufankashi (aka Abdullah al-Misri) moved to Afghanistan with his father (an Egyptian expatriate living in Saudi Arabia), and later, following in his father's footsteps, trained in Kandahar during Taliban rule. He was subsequently killed by US forces in Afghanistan in 2001. Huthaifa Azzam, son of Abdullah Azzam, also arrived in Afghanistan in 1982 aged twelve-years-old (a year after his father first visited) and later fought as an Afghan Arab. This story also chimes with that of Omar Khadr, the son of an Egyptian family living in Canada. He was born in 1986 and spent his early childhood life in Afghanistan during and after the Afghan jihad, although he made short visits back to Canada with his parents. However, on 22 July 2002 (aged fifteen) Khadr was involved in a battle with US forces that resulted in the death of a US soldier. Khadr was badly wounded and later captured, becoming the youngest detainee in Guantanamo Bay prison. These three examples of parental influence (beyond the control of the children themselves), raises interesting questions concerning their (un)willing involvement in Islamist-related activities, violent or non-violent. Although beyond the scope of this book, the case of Omar Khadr was a polarising issue in Canada, vis-à-vis his young age and his susceptibility to the prevailing narrative in Afghanistan after the 9/11 attacks. Many believed he was more akin to a vulnerable misguided child soldier, rather than an individual who was deemed by US authorities to be 'committed to extremist Islamic values ... and likely to pose a threat to the US, its interests or its allies'.[77]

Other family relationships also appeared to influence personal involvement in the Afghan jihad. Notable kinship ties include Osama bin Laden's cousin, Muhammad al-Habbashi (aka Abu Zubair al-Madani), who fought with Bin Laden at the Battle of Jaji in 1987, and as noted earlier, was subsequently killed in Bosnia alongside his brother, defending Bosnian Muslims. Beyond blood relatives as introduced earlier, kinship ties were established in Afghanistan based on marriages between relatives of Afghan Arabs that led to many new kinship ties between Arab foreign fighters. For example, Algerian Afghan Arab Abdullah Anas married the daughter of Abdullah Azzam; Egyptian Afghan Arab (and later one of Al Qaeda's top lieutenants) Saif al-Adil married the daughter of fellow Egyptian Afghan Arab Mustafa Hamid; and the daughter of Egyptian Afghan Arab (and former Al Qaeda military chief) Muhammad Atif (aka Abu Hafs al-Misri), later married Muhammad bin Laden (son of Osama bin Laden). The influence of kinship affiliations in the initial mobilisation and future stability of the Afghan jihad (and beyond) is important when trying to understand the trust and loyalty needed within groups involved in jihad (and Islamist terrorism). Although the available open source data may not have captured its real significance, other studies have revealed similar findings, particularly in the post-9/11 landscape.[78]

Friendship Ties

Although not as numerous as kinship ties, the dataset does reveal the influence of friendship ties involved in the Afghan jihad. This characteristic of friends deciding to join the Afghan jihad more as a group than as individuals often came from the same school, town or tribe. For example, Egyptian nationals Suhaib

Yusuf Arabi and Tariq Jarool Rabb, both fellow students from the University of Asyut, decided to travel together to Afghanistan,[79] as did Saudi national Suhaib al-Ghamidi and his friends Abu Walid and Ibn Masood.[80] Even chance encounters that very quickly developed into friendships were not uncommon, often leading to individual involvement in the Afghan jihad. For example, as mentioned earlier, it was a chance encounter in Mecca (Saudi Arabia) between Abdullah Azzam and Egyptian Shaykh Kamal Sananiri that subsequently led Abdullah Azzam to travel Afghanistan in 1981. It was also a chance encounter that subsequently led to the friendship between Abdullah Azzam and one of his students, Osama bin Laden, that subsequently led Bin Laden to travel to Afghanistan.

Expatriate Status

The final factor that emanated from the Afghan Arab dataset was the incidence of expatriate Arabs involved in the Afghan jihad. Being an Arab expatriate living, studying or working in a country away from their home, family, friends and possibly culture, appears in some cases to have influenced their decision to become Afghan Arabs. Out of the 394 biographies of Afghan Arabs, nearly 17 per cent (sixty-six) had been expatriates. Although the total number of expatriate Arabs in the 1980s is unclear, the 17 per cent still appears significant. Accepting that the total Afghan Arab cohort was about 2,000,[81] it represents less than 0.001 per cent of the Arab world population (168,154,961 in 1985 according to UN figures).[82] Had 17 per cent of all non-expatriate Arabs (those residing in their countries) joined the Afghan jihad, there would have been nearly 29 million Afghan Arabs, thus it appears that a substantially larger cohort of Arabs living outside their countries, were attracted to the idea of involvement in the Afghan jihad. Their biographies demonstrate the context of the 1980s in that many Palestinians had immigrated to Jordan (due to the Palestinian-Israeli conflict); many Algerians and Egyptians had resettled in the West (claiming political asylum); many Yemenis had resettled in Saudi Arabia (to seek employment as noted earlier); and finally, many Arabs had been studying in Western academic institutions (including fourteen in the United States), prior to travelling to Afghanistan.

Examples of these circumstances include Egyptian Afghan Arab Abu Hamza al-Misri, who had come to the United Kingdom on a student visa, and felt subsequently inclined to become an Afghan Arab (and later jailed for life in 2015 on terrorism charges in the United States); Egyptian Afghan Arab Ahmad Said Khadr, who lived in Canada and went to Afghanistan with his family to work in an NGO; and Egyptian Afghan Arab Muhsin bin Mitwalli Atwah, who was an expatriate in Iraq who later travelled to Afghanistan, and was subsequently the bomb maker in both of the 1998 attacks on the US embassies in Kenya and Tanzania. Whilst their reasons and motivations for becoming Afghan Arabs are unclear, a few anecdotal accounts do permeate the dataset. Algerian Afghan Arab Khalid Mustafa became involved in the Afghan jihad because he 'got fed up with his life' in the United States and United Kingdom;[83] Saudi Afghan Arab Abdullah al-Hudhayf was actually 'radicalised as a student' in the United States in the early 1980s';[84] and finally, Palestinian Afghan Arab Abu Anas became 'fed up of American society' whilst studying for an engineering degree in the United States, and decided to join the Afghan jihad instead.[85]

Whilst the common denominator of this cohort is that they were all expatriates, it is suggested that they appeared to be 'deracinated Arab youth, cut off from their families, feeling the sting of discrimination, and looking for some colourful purpose to orient their drifting lives'.[86] This is corroborated by Professor Andrew Silke, who noted that '[r]esearch has shown that most members ... joined the jihad while they were living in a foreign country or when they were otherwise isolated from older friends and family. Often these individuals were expatriates – students, workers, refugees – living away from home and family'.[87] Finally, although pertaining to Islamist terrorists (and not Afghan Arabs), Marc Sageman also identified in his study that '70 per cent joined in a country where they had not grown up. They were expatriates ... away from home and family'.[88] This suggests that as the kinship and friendship ties were broken due to living abroad, many may have experienced feelings including social isolation, lack of integration, racism, discrimination and marginalisation, particularly at a time of no mobile phones or Internet. Such feelings may have contributed to many expatriate Arabs taking up a cause (the Afghan jihad) and also escaping their current 'foreign' environment. By going to Afghanistan, although still a foreign environment, the social environment amongst like-minded Afghan Arabs was a complete change compared with the social isolation that many had experienced as expatriates. This change of environment is amply demonstrated in the diaries of an Afghan Arab called Abu Zubaydah.

The Epitome of an Afghan Arab – The Case of Abu Zubaydah

Zayn al-Abidin Muhammad Husayn, better known as Abu Zubaydah, was an Afghan Arab who was later deemed by the CIA to have been the 'third or fourth man in al-Qa'ida,'[89] a label that was quietly withdrawn in 2009. The circumstances that inspired his initial involvement in the Afghan jihad in 1991 are based on his personal diary released in 2013 through *Al Jazeera America* that was written in 1991 and 1992. The account does not suffer from *post hoc* rationalisation as it was written during his time in Afghanistan and was clearly never intended for public scrutiny. Arguably, the case of Abu Zubaydah epitomises many of the young Arab men of the 1980s and early 1990s, who wished to train to become a *mujahhid* and wage jihad against Soviet military occupation of Afghanistan. The four predominant circumstances that shaped his initial involvement in jihad were his expatriate status, his religiosity, a triggering event and social ties.

Abu Zubaydah had been a Palestinian expatriate living in Saudi Arabia, who exhibited feelings of social isolation. In his diary, he talks openly about being 'a Palestinian, with no homeland, no passport and no identity'. He expresses feelings of 'living among people who viewed him primarily as a refugee, [where] sometimes their looks utter words and show feelings of "burden on my country" ... while Jews are running loose in my country'. He confesses that those looks 'were to bother me ever since I was little. I used to ignore it but it is a fact that cannot be escaped'.[90] Interestingly, this feeling of social isolation continued when he was a student in India: 'I could not adjust properly to this country or its people'.[91] Through his personal writings, Abu Zubaydah felt like an outsider, who was never embraced by the societies in which he dwelled, despite his own acknowledged efforts at integration. These feelings translated into a sense of despair: 'I am lost, erratic, completely distracted and unsettled. I do not know for sure what I want or what I'm missing'.[92] Three months later, on the 6 January 1991, Abu Zubaydah decided to travel to Afghanistan.

It is worth examining his religiosity[93] prior to his departure, as it is a strength that he continually relied upon during his perceived adversity (loneliness, abusive father and marginalisation). He assesses his personal 'religiosity [as] up to 30 per cent okay; however up until now, I have not sensed that I have achieved God's approval [although] I never miss a prayer, or a fasting season'.[94] Although he rates his personal religiosity at 30 per cent, he measures his belief in God at 100 per cent and his narrative deserves to be quoted in full:

> I don't believe in anything except in God, of course, my trust in God cannot be doubted at all. The percentage in which I believe in anything does not exceed 50 per cent, but my belief in God, his angels, his books, his messengers, doomsday, and its destiny in all its good and evil, exceeds 100 per cent.[95]

It is clear that Abu Zubaydah was a pious man who tried to lead his life in accordance with the *Sunnah* (the Qur'an and the *Hadiths*) and he appears to have sought refuge in this belief. He makes every attempt to be a good Muslim and abide by the word of God. He even confesses to have rejected the advances of a flirtatious Indian girl called Flumina, 'for fear of God'.[96] It is therefore surprising that his reasons for going to Afghanistan appear deceptively simple.

On 6 January 1991, Abu Zubaydah writes that 'I have decided to visit Afghanistan, receive training and come back to finish my education. The intent is *bona fide*, God willing ... I trust in God and we seek refuge in him.' He also confesses that 'it is my friend Amin's idea and he will accompany me on the trip, God willing'.[97] This diary entry encompasses a lot of factors that contributed to Abu Zubaydah's decision to go to Afghanistan. First, it appears that he has been strongly influenced by a 'social tie' – Amin al-Jamil;[98] second, Afghanistan appeared to offer an escape or a solution to his feelings of isolation and marginalisation;[99] and third, Abu Zubaydah also had a 'triggering event' in that he was accused of anti-social behaviour in India and felt 'humiliated and disgraced'.[100] The concept and potential influence of a triggering event, often defined as an 'extremely provocative event'[101] should not be underestimated, in that it may tip an individual to act in ways that would normally appear out of character.

To fully exploit the personal writings of Abu Zubaydah, it is worth following his trajectory that moves beyond simply receiving training and returning to finish his education, to actually engaging in jihad against Afghan communists. He reveals the importance of two particular concepts: jihad and martyrdom. Having arrived in Afghanistan, Abu Zubaydah appears to have gone through a gradual, incremental, conceptual development in his notion of jihad and this is revealed in his diary. A week after his arrival in Afghanistan (19 January 1991) while staying at the *Bayt al-Shuhadaa* (House of Martyrs), he remarked that the 'spiritual atmosphere here is good; youth and elderly have given their souls to Almighty God, they traded off life and everything in it for jihad ... the idea of settling here is enticing me'.[102] Less than three months later, on 2 April 1991, his diary entry revealed: 'I feel settled down due to being mentally determined to be engaged in jihad. Jihad is the future and my future is jihad ... and we seek refuge in Allah'.[103] Finally in the week of 18–25 April 1991, Abu Zubaydah noted the conceptual development of jihad within himself: 'the idea of jihad for Allah's cause in its meaning and perception is revealing itself to me and becoming more refined', concluding that 'jihad now is an individual duty'.[104] As mentioned in Chapter 1, the notion of *fard ayn* (an individual duty) is considered a divinely instituted essential obligation which is incumbent upon all Muslims.

Almost sixteen years to the day, Abu Zubaydah again articulated most lucidly the notion of jihad, this time not in a diary but at his 2007 Guantanamo Bay Prison (JTF-GTMO) Combatant Status Review Tribunal Hearing. In his oral statement, he explained that:

> Defensive jihad means that if an aggressor or invader invades Muslim lands, no matter where, then it is every Muslim's duty to defend the land against the invader. For example, Russia against Afghanistan and Serbia against Bosnia. Our doctrine has always been to go after ... military targets, which includes military members or civilians who work for or directly support the military. Our doctrine was not the same as what Osama bin Laden and al-Qaida were promoting, which was and is a doctrine of offensive jihad.[105]

It is clear from Abu Zubaydah's diary entries that the longer he socialised and trained with fellow *mujahhideen*, the more he began to adopt the prevailing ideology at that time. The camp environment consisted of a mix of directed indoctrination, as well as socialisation of like-minded people, linked by their religious beliefs and ideology. However, care needs to be taken when interpreting Abu Zubaydah's diary entries, in order not to conflate the notion of jihad with terrorism, as nowhere does he indicate support for terrorism (including the killing of civilians and non-combatants). Although *mujahhid* and Islamist terrorist trajectories may have similarities and crossovers, during the Afghan Arab period they appeared largely distinct, with the Islamist terrorist trajectories being discussed in detail later in this chapter.

The second concept embraced by Abu Zubaydah was that of martyrdom. After just a week in Afghanistan (on 20 January 1991) while staying at the *Bayt al-Shuhadaa*, Abu Zubaydah first discusses, in parallel with the notion of jihad, the idea of martyrdom. In his diary, he writes: 'I desire becoming a martyr and God knows that I love that, because of all of its rewards and forgiveness of all sins ... Here, I mean martyrdom for Allah's cause; that is, to be a martyr'.[106] Again, most likely as a result of increased interaction with other *mujahhideen* and cut off from the outside world, less than three months after his arrival (8 April 1991) his desire for martyrdom became noticeably more intense with an increased sense of urgency. It is quoted necessarily in full:

> Martyrdom for Allah's cause. I become dreaming of it [*sic*] because of all I hear about its virtue and standing by Almighty God ... sometimes I wish for a bullet or a swift shell to take me to meet my Lord as a martyr ... I cannot wait: I want to be a martyr for Allah's cause quickly. I, and God is my witness, am longing to see the face of Almighty God, his gardens, and what he had promised.[107]

There are two key points concerning the desire for martyrdom emanating from Abu Zubaydah's diary entries. First, is the religious (Islamic) basis for such a desire, and second is the lack of suicidal intent. Drawing on the definition of suicide adopted by French sociologist Emile Durkheim (d. 1917), Abu Zubaydah was not necessarily seeking a 'case of death which results directly or indirectly from a positive or negative act, carried out by the victim himself, knowing that it will produce this result'.[108] It is clear from the writings of Abu Zubaydah that he and many of his cohort of Arab compatriots were seeking martyrdom through jihad, unequivocally in the cause of God. Their desire arguably has a degree of nobility and honour, in addition to a strong belief in the rewards after death. Perhaps most critically, Abu Zubaydah presents a persuasive narrative which lacks any real semblance of radicalisation, just a degree of imagined theological urgency. According to Marc Sageman, a medical doctor and forensic psychiatrist, Abu Zubaydah's 'diary shows him to be frighteningly normal'.[109] Finally, the absence of any suicidal intent is juxtaposed beside a desire to be killed in jihad as a result of enemy action ('a bullet or a swift shell'). Thus, while Abu Zubaydah expresses no desire to commit suicide, in the sense of being a 'suicide bomber', his desire to be killed in battle conforms to the interpretation of martyrdom championed by Abdullah Azzam. The actual desire amongst some Afghan Arabs to conduct self-sacrificial ('martyrdom/suicide') attacks only really came about after the end of the Afghan jihad (April 1992) and is discussed in detail in the forthcoming pages.

The Post-Jihad Trajectories of Veteran Afghan Arabs

The post-jihad landscape in Afghanistan cultivated a continued feeling of armed militancy among many veteran Afghan Arabs, and a need to remain involved in some form of Islamist violence. This violence was aimed at three main perceived enemy groups. First, there was the West in general, and the United States in particular, often labelled the 'far enemy' in Islamist circles. Second, there were the Arab regimes from where the majority of Afghan Arabs had originated (the near enemy). Lastly, there were countries and regimes that were deemed to be persecuting fellow Sunni Muslims, such as Serbian troops in the Bosnian war and Russian troops in the Chechen conflict. The attacks perpetrated against Western interests were, and continue to be, commonly understood as global or transnational terrorism, whereas attacks against Arab regimes are commonly understood as religious nationalist terrorism. In both cases, the targets of such attacks are primarily civilians and non-combatants. Finally, attacks against the Serbian Army in Bosnia and Russian troops in Chechnya (for example), were more analogous to defensive jihad than Islamist terrorism, and drew on the ideology and experience gained fighting the Soviet military occupation in 1980s Afghanistan.

The Post-Afghan Jihad Landscape

The post-Afghan jihad environment was considered a melting pot of radical beliefs, particularly in the bazaars of Peshawar, situated on the Pakistan-Afghanistan border. According to Brynjar Lia, 'Peshawar around 1990 seemed a fertile ground for new ideas about jihadism',[110] in particular the near and far enemy debate, but also debating other jihads, such as in Kashmir in the early nineties. In his diary entry of 28 August 1992, Abu Zubaydah recalled that 'in the past we thought there were only simple differences among jihadist parties, but now the communist regime has collapsed in Afghanistan, it has resulted in fierce fighting amongst the Arab jihadists'.[111] According to Mohammed Hafez, after the Soviet withdrawal the new Afghan Arabs became exposed to a:

> range of political beliefs along the Islamist spectrum. Invariably, some were attracted to the more radical factions. Peshawar was truly an open market place of ideas without bounds or censors, and young men had plenty of time on their hands to read, discuss, and argue the finer points of jihadi politics.[112]

The more radical factions were generally those Afghan Arabs who had known pre-existing terrorist links. They appeared to dominate the post-jihad landscape, despite their relatively small numbers. Extracted from the dataset, only 14 per cent (fifty-one) of Afghan Arabs had known pre-existing terrorist links, whilst 86 per cent had no documented linkage. It appeared that the Egyptians with pre-existing terrorist links had a disproportionate influence upon the less experienced Afghan Arabs,[113] possibly because in Egypt, 'Islamist movements were at their most militant'.[114] Particularly notable Afghan Arab members of Egyptian Islamic Jihad (EIJ) include Ayman al-Zawahiri, the current leader of Al Qaeda; Abu Khabab al-Misri (d. 2008) who became responsible for the Al Qaeda biological and chemical weapons programme; and five members involved in the 1998 East Africa embassy attacks.[115] Notable Afghan Arab members of the Egyptian Islamic Group (EIG) include Omar Abdul Rahman (d. 2017) and Mahmood Abu Halima, who were both involved in the 1993 WTC attack, and Mustafa Hamza who was involved in the 1997 Luxor massacre.

The next feature of the post-Afghan jihad landscape was the possible effects of the brutalisation of the Afghan jihad, perhaps akin to post-traumatic stress disorder (PTSD). Some accounts suggest that many Afghan Arabs were 'transformed by the baptism of blood and fire',[116] to the degree that many were 'hardened and radicalized by the experience'.[117] It is difficult to recreate the 'context of violence' within the Afghan jihad, however personal involvement in it appeared to affect some participants. One veteran Syrian Afghan Arab Muhammad Loay Bayazid (aka Abu Rida al-Suri), reflected on his experience:

> I went to Afghanistan with a blank mind and a good heart ... everything was totally strange. It was like I was born just now, like I was an infant, and I have to learn everything new. It was not so easy after that to leave and go back to your regular life.[118]

The first anomaly however, is that many Afghan Arabs did not actually engage in close combat with the Soviet army. The literature[119] is broadly united in agreeing that 'only a fraction had significant exposure to ... combat',[120] whilst 'the vast majority of volunteers did not go inside Afghanistan, let alone fight there'.[121] One Afghan *mujahhideen* leader, Commander Akhtarjhan, held a similar view: 'We had some Arabs who were with us for jihad credit. They had a video camera and all they wanted to do was to take videos. They were of no value to us'.[122] That is not to say that the Afghan Arabs did not fight; indeed the dataset has documented 212 fatalities (53.8 per cent of the Afghan Arab dataset), however most had been involved in administrative, logistical or charitable positions during the Afghan jihad.

The third feature of the post-Afghan jihad landscape facing veteran Afghan Arabs was the realisation that their regimes were banning them from returning home,[123] thus making them stateless with no place back in their wider society. This was acknowledged in the diaries of Abu Zubaydah, who recognised that 'many of them could not go back to their home countries because they had been documented as terrorists in every state without exception'.[124] The situation of Egyptian veteran Afghan Arabs is revealing. In the early 1990s, the Egyptian regime fully appreciated the possible threat posed by returning Afghan Arabs, particularly those who had prior terrorist links with the EIG or EIJ, and were now 'ready to move their armed operations to Egypt to fight the regime'.[125] This left many veteran Afghan Arabs rootless, sure in the knowledge that 'returning to their home countries meant certain arrest, torture, and likely death'.[126] Veteran Arab foreign fighter Nassir al-Bahri remembered Osama bin Laden himself explaining 'that the Egyptians were obliged to stay in Afghanistan ... they simply had no other place to go since they were wanted men back home in Egypt'.[127] Looking at the dataset, it is worth briefly examining the future trajectories of the thirty-eight Egyptian veteran Afghan Arabs. First, twenty-one had pre-existing terrorist links, thus justifying in part the Egyptian regime's concern about Afghan Arab returnees. Interestingly, none of those twenty-one Egyptians with pre-existing terrorist links returned to Egypt voluntarily[128] after the Afghan jihad, with the vast majority (76 per cent) joining Al Qaeda.[129] Of those who joined Al Qaeda, five were involved in the East Africa embassy bombings (three of whom were also involved in planning the 9/11 attacks), and two were involved in the 1993 WTC attack. Out of the remaining seventeen Egyptian veteran Afghan Arabs, who despite having had no known prior terrorist links, were now known to the Egyptian authorities and could not return to Egypt, ten subsequently joined Al Qaeda (two of whom were involved in the 1998 East Africa embassy bombings), and five were later killed participating in defensive jihad in Bosnia and/or Chechnya.[130] Such a policy of refusing re-entry to a nation's citizens has interesting (and often violent) ramifications including 'deflecting the problem onto others',[131] particularly concerning the returning Arab foreign fighters (and Islamist terrorists) from Syria and Iraq in 2018, and this is discussed further in Chapter 4.

The final feature of the post-Afghan jihad landscape was the existence of 'comradeship ties' that had developed during the jihad. Earlier in this chapter it was noted that kinship or friendship ties contributed to the initial involvement of Afghan Arabs in the Afghan jihad, yet it is suggested that comradeship ties appeared to supplant those pre-Afghan jihad ties (friendship and kinship) – less perhaps for those with pre-existing terrorist links. The new friendships that developed and blossomed during the Afghan jihad appeared to be based on shared hardships in a hostile environment that produced a military form of comradeship. Useful examples of comradeship ties that developed during various defensive jihads are those of veteran Saudi Afghan Arab Abdul Rahim al-Nashiri, who planned the 2000 USS *Cole* attack. He developed comradeship ties with 9/11 hijacker Hamza al-Ghamdi[132] and USS *Cole* conspirator Walid Muhammad bin Attash[133] in 1992 (in Tajikistan), Abu Zubaydah[134] in 1993 (in Afghanistan), and Osama bin Laden in 1994 (in Afghanistan).[135] Then, in 1998, he formally joined Al Qaeda 'after learning of his cousin Jihad Harazi's suicide bombing of the US Embassy in Kenya'.[136] These examples perhaps suggest that the broad socialisation (involving comradeship ties) that occurs during jihad appears to contribute to subsequent involvement in terrorist-related activities. The idea of comradeship ties, developed as a result of situational circumstances in a war zone, is not unprecedented in military history. One veteran German soldier, Guy Sajer, recounted his experience during World War II on the Russian Front, explaining how 'friendships counted for a great deal . . . consolidating men on the same side in friendships which never would have broken through the normal barriers of ordinary peacetime life'.[137] Former British officer Brigadier Fitzroy Maclean also recounted how, during World War II with Tito's Partisans in Yugoslavia, the 'common experience of hardships and dangers had overcome all differences of class or race or temperament and forged between them lasting bonds of loyalty and affection'.[138]

Before examining the three main post-Afghan jihad trajectories, it is worth quickly understanding the figures extracted from the dataset. First (as noted earlier), out of the 394 Afghan Arabs, 212 were killed in Afghanistan, leaving a surviving cohort of 182. The post-jihad trajectories of this cohort are the focus of the remainder of this chapter. Out of the 182 veteran Afghan Arabs, 107 (59 per cent) initially remained in defensive jihad (generally moving to Bosnia); sixty-one (33.5 per cent) became involved in global Islamist terrorism; forty-three (23.6 per cent) became involved in religious nationalist terrorism; ten appeared to hang up their Kalashnikov (AK–47) rifles; and the trajectories of twenty-six (14.3 per cent) are unknown. It should be noted from these figures that many veteran Afghan Arabs continued to participate in further defensive jihads (for example, Bosnia and Chechnya), but eventually became involved in Islamist terrorism (against the far and/or near enemy).

Defensive Jihad in Support of Persecuted Muslims (Post-Afghan Jihad)

One of the post-Afghan jihad trajectories of veteran Afghan Arabs included further participation in another foreign jihad defending co-religionists. Their enemies were regimes and countries that were deemed to be persecuting fellow Sunni Muslims, such as the Serbs in the Bosnian war and Russian troops in the Chechen conflict. In deciding on this choice, veteran Afghan Arabs appeared to eschew the more extremist Islamist ideology that supported terrorism and remained focused on the broad ideological tenets of Abdullah Azzam – defending fellow Sunni Muslims. The incidence of veteran Afghan Arabs' involvement in further defensive jihads is presented in Figure 2.2.

A short explanation of Figure 2.2 is warranted. First, the high number of Afghan Arabs going to Bosnia may be explained by the fact that many were

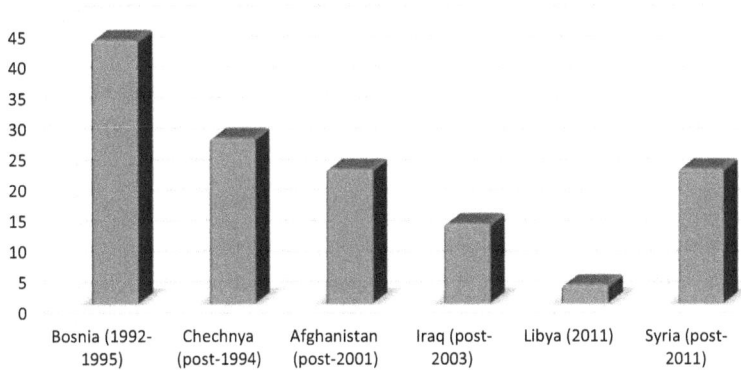

Figure 2.2 Veteran Afghan Arab subsequent involvement in further defensive jihads (n=107).

prevented from returning home (by their regimes), and also by the fact that Pakistani authorities had begun to arrest Afghan Arabs who had remained in Peshawar after the April 1992 collapse of the Afghan communist regime. Involvement in the Bosnian jihad which started on 6 April 1992 coincided with this collapse, so in many ways it was the next logical jihad in which to participate. Second, all the conflicts were deemed to be defensive in nature: in Chechnya the jihad was to defend Chechen Muslims against Russian invaders; in Afghanistan (post-2001) the jihad was to defend (again) Afghan Muslims from the US-led coalition; in Iraq (post-2003) the jihad was to defend Iraqi Muslims (initially Sunni and Shi'a) from the US-led coalition occupation; and in Libya and Syria the jihads were fought to defend the Muslim populations from the autocratic despotic regimes of Gaddafi and Assad, respectively. It is also important to acknowledge that both the Libyan opposition, which had Arab foreign fighters in their ranks, enjoyed the support of NATO, and the Free Syrian Army (FSA), which also had Arab foreign fighters in their ranks (see Chapter 4), also enjoyed US support. However, there is a contradiction in that if countries subsequently label Arab foreign fighters as Islamist terrorists, this would mean that NATO and the United States supported terrorism.

Whilst 107 (59 per cent) veteran Afghan Arabs involved in further defensive jihads is a substantial number, there were quite a few who became 'career' Arab foreign fighters travelling from one jihad to another. The dataset reveals that the 107 veteran Afghan Arabs were subsequently involved in an accumulative figure of 130 defensive jihads. Two good examples of the phenomenon are presented below. First, there was Saudi Arab Afghan Abu Turab al-Najdi, who fought in

Bosnia in 1992, in Somalia in 1993 (against the United States); in Chechnya in 1999 and alongside the Taliban in 2000. He was killed by US forces at Khoja Ghar in November 2001. Second, there was Saudi Afghan Arab Fahd Mahdi al-Shehri, who had fought in Bosnia, Tajikistan, and later in Iraq (post-2003), where he was last seen in 2006.

Finally, it is instructive that many veteran Afghan Arabs were to become 'military commanders who would lead future struggles in places like Algeria, Egypt, Bosnia, Chechnya and Iraq'.[139] Thus, having served in the Afghan jihad, many veteran Afghan Arabs became esteemed and venerated, allowing for charismatic authority to be bestowed upon them. This resulted in them commanding new and less experienced Arab foreign fighters in other jihad theatres. This is corroborated by the dataset that finds Saudi veteran Afghan Arabs, Abdul Aziz Barbaros (aka Abdul Rahman al-Dosari) and Khalid al-Harbi (aka Abu Sulaiman al-Makki) became the leaders of the Arab foreign fighter contingent in Bosnia;[140] Saudi veteran Afghan Arab Thamir al-Suwailam (aka Khattab) became the leader of Arab foreign fighters in Chechnya; Jordanian veteran Afghan Arab Abu Musab al-Zarqawi became the initial leader of Arab foreign fighters in Iraq; and Syrian veteran Afghan Arab Abu Firas al-Suri became the official spokesman for *Jabhat-al-Nusrah* in Syria. The last two examples bring out a key point. Having been involved in one or more defensive jihads, many eventually became involved in Islamist terrorism, including joining groups such as Al Qaeda in Iraq or *Jabhat al-Nusrah* in Syria. This may be due to the asymmetric nature of many contemporary insurgencies and civil wars, but such a continuum is a security concern, particularly with the number of Arab (and Western) foreign fighters departing Syria in 2018.

Religious Nationalist Terrorism Against the Near Enemy

The next post-jihad trajectory of veteran Afghan Arabs was involvement in Islamist terrorism in their home countries, targeting their autocratic regimes – the near enemy. This was paradoxically just the scenario that many of the regimes had tried to prevent by originally sending many of their violent Islamists to Afghanistan in the hope that they would be killed, or by preventing their re-entry. Many veteran Afghan Arabs tried to spin their involvement in religious nationalist terrorism as defensive in nature, along the lines of Abdullah Azzam. As Nelly Lahoud succinctly states, many veteran Afghan Arabs saw 'themselves to be engaged in *defensive warfare* in the defensive sense of the word … under attack by their own leaders'.[141] In addition, ideologically, Ayman al-Zawahiri felt that jihad against the near enemy must take priority over the far enemy – particularly the Egyptian regime of President Hosni Mubarak, on which he wrote a book, *The Black Book: Torturing Muslims under Hosni Mubarak*.[142] As Professor Martha Crenshaw argued, 'if terrorists perceive the state as unjust, morally corrupt, and violent, then terrorism may seem legitimate and justified'.[143] Certainly, this perception was prevalent among the veteran Afghan Arabs and was summed up by Abu Zubaydah: 'The truth is that all the rulers of the Islamic and Arab, especially Arab states, are traitors who work against their religion. That's the reason there are fundamentalists who demand for Islamic law to rule'.[144] According to veteran Afghan Arab Mustafa Hamid, 'armed jihad against rulers of these countries began to rise to the primary interest for trainees and Arab camps'.[145]

The appeal of attacking the near enemy is demonstrated within the dataset, which shows that forty-three (23.6 per cent) of the 182 Afghan Arabs who survived the Afghan jihad (and who had no known prior terrorist links), became religious nationalist terrorists. They came from six countries: Algeria, Libya, Syria, Jordan, Saudi Arabia and Tunisia, as represented in Figure 2.3.

These statistics should not come as a surprise, as during 'the Afghan-Soviet war, these Arabs were also preparing themselves for jihad in their own countries'.[146] For example, the dataset reveals that the majority (68 per cent) of Algerian veteran Afghan Arabs returned home and established the Groupe Islamique Armée (GIA),[147] a finding supported by other scholars.[148] In addition, the dataset also highlights that 50 per cent of the Libyan veteran Afghan Arabs,

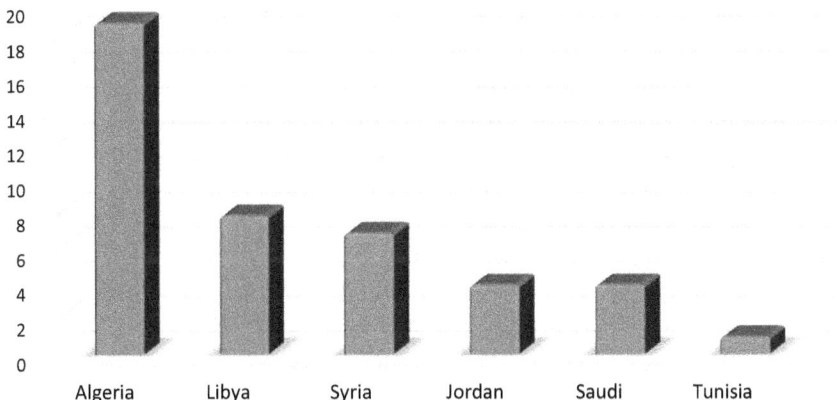

Figure 2.3 Afghan Arab involvement in religious nationalist terrorism (n=43).

returned home and established the Libyan Islamic Fighting Group (LIFG), with the intention of overthrowing the regime of Muammar Gaddafi and establishing an Islamic country ruled by *Shariah* law. Interestingly, the majority of Algerian Afghan Arabs who returned to Algeria had arrived in Afghanistan after the Soviet withdrawal, with the express desire of gaining training prior to returning to Algeria. The path taken by these individuals suggests that they may not necessarily have been radicalised in Afghanistan, but may have had some pre-existing links to Islamist (although not necessarily terrorist) groups.

A key question in the analysis is that considering 14 per cent (fifty-one) of the Afghan Arabs had arrived in Afghanistan with known pre-existing terrorist links, did those who survived the Afghan jihad, later return to their home countries to continue their involvement in Islamist terrorist-related activities? The evidence from the dataset suggests that in fact, the vast majority (who had known pre-existing terrorist links) did not return to their countries to continue a religious nationalist agenda.[149] This was in large part due to their regimes banning them from returning, with the most effective being Egypt. It appears that it was those Afghan Arabs who had arrived in Afghanistan with no known pre-existing terrorist links who were able to return to their countries to engage in religious nationalist terrorism. Again, it seems that many Afghan Arabs who went to Afghanistan (particularly latterly) were more focused on terrorist training, than participating in defensive jihad. This desire for terrorist training in Afghanistan, particularly by religious nationalist terrorists, is discussed later in this chapter.

A good example of a religious nationalist terrorist attack by veteran Afghan Arabs[150] against the near enemy was the November 1995 car bombing against a Saudi-US joint facility in Riyadh, Saudi Arabia. At the time of the Riyadh attack, Saudi Arabia was clamping down on the reformist political opposition (the *Sahwa*) in the Kingdom. This led to a lot of arrests and widespread torture in prisons. In response to such brutality, a veteran Afghan Arab named Shaykh Abdullah al-Hudhayf, 'threw acid in the face of a police officer to avenge the arrest of the leaders of the [*Sahwa*]'.[151] Al-Hudhayf was subsequently arrested and 'tortured to death by vengeful security officers, a suspicion that is probably not unfounded, for his body was never returned to his family'.[152] Four friends of al-Hudhayf, three of them veteran Afghan Arabs (Riyad al-Hajiri, Muslih al-Shamrani and Khalid Sa'id), decided to avenge his untimely demise. According to a former bodyguard of Osama bin Laden, Nassir al-Bahri, the motivation behind the 1995 Riyadh attacks was solely because 'Muslih al-Shamrani called to avenge the death of Shaykh Abdullah al-Hudhayf'.[153]

The notion of revenge is an interesting concept and has been identified by many terrorism scholars as one of many possible motivations for terrorist violence.[154] According to Professor Andrew Silke, the 'desire for revenge and retribution is an extremely common motive for joining terrorist groups'.[155] Although it appears that the motivations behind the 1995 Riyadh bombing included grievances against the Saudi regime, an ideology of anti-Americanism and a desire for vengeance, it does raise the question of why, in particular, veteran Afghan Arabs perpetrated the attack. There is little publicly available evidence because the Saudi regime promptly executed the alleged perpetrators after they gave a televised confession, 'no doubt under duress'.[156] Nevertheless, the common denominator was that three of the alleged terrorists were veteran Afghan Arabs. This strongly suggests that previous comradeship ties that were developed during the Afghan jihad played a role, as did prior explosive training in order to construct the car bomb. In addition, their experience during the jihad in Afghanistan may also have played a part – the brutalisation of close combat resulting in an increased propensity for violence.

Global/Transnational Islamist Terrorist Attacks Against the Far Enemy

The last post-jihad trajectory of veteran Afghan Arabs was involvement in global Islamist attacks targeting the far enemy, which accounted for sixty-one (33.5 per cent) of the surviving cohort. Many were involved Al Qaeda franchises (for example, AQAP, AQIM and the Algerian Six Cell), but there were other global non-Al Qaeda Islamist terrorist cells including the one involved in the 1993 World Trade Centre (WTC) attack and the 'Bojinka plot'.[157] Perhaps the four most infamous global Islamist terrorist attacks, involving eighteen veteran Afghan Arabs, are represented in Figure 2.4.

It is revealing from Figure 2.4 that eighteen veteran Afghan Arabs (with no known prior terrorist links) were involved in the global Islamist attacks amounting to 37 per cent of the overall forty-eight perpetrators, and arguably their involvement was qualitatively greater due to their leadership and organisational positions. Whilst the 1993 WTC attack was not linked to Al Qaeda, the other three were directly linked. It should also be recognised that other veteran Afghan Arabs were also involved in many of these attacks (for example, Ayman al-Zawahiri), but they had known pre-existing links to Islamist terrorism, thus their post-Afghan jihad trajectory was perhaps more predictable,

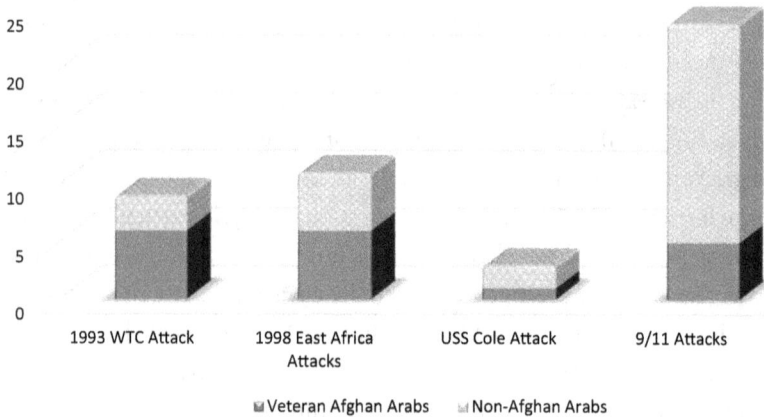

Figure 2.4 Veteran Afghan Arab involvement in global Islamist terrorist Attacks (n=18).

in that they returned to being terrorists. Each Islamist terrorist attack from Figure 2.4 deserves a short explanation.

The first global terrorist attack, a vehicle bombing of the WTC in New York, occurred on 26 February 1993, killing six and injuring 1,042 civilians.[158] It was quickly established by the US Joint Terrorism Task Force that 'a disparate group of Afghan Arabs ... formed the bulk of the group behind the bombing'.[159] Yet why did they do it? According to the perpetrators themselves, the sentiment was entirely anti-American, to punish them, to seek revenge, and challenge their perceived invincibility. In the words of Egyptian Omar Abdul Rahman,[160] the spiritual leader of the 1993 WTC bombing, 'America is the worst enemy of Islam';[161] she 'has surrounded Iraq and they have starved its Muslim people';[162] she 'preserves Israel';[163] and she 'loved President Mubarak'.[164] According to veteran Afghan Arab and the 1993 WTC chief strategist Khalid Shaykh Muhammad, the motivation for the 1993 WTC attack was 'to make US citizens suffer, especially economically, which would put pressure on the US government to change its policies'.[165] Finally, Ramzi Yusuf, the leader and perpetrator of the WTC bombing itself, explained that the motivation for the attack was 'against the United States Government and against Israel, because [these countries] are more than terrorists'.[166] What is illuminating is that Ramzi Yusuf had developed comradeship ties with Mahmood Abu Halima and Ahmad Ajaj in a training camp in Afghanistan, that US investigators later believed led directly to their involvement in the 1993 WTC attack.[167]

The next global terrorist attacks in August 1998, involved two near simultaneous bombings of the US embassies in Kenya and Tanzania, killing 213 and 11 civilians, respectively.[168] In the intervening years since the 1993 WTC attack,[169] Osama bin Laden had been evicted from Sudan (in May 1996);[170] he had issued his August 1996 declaration[171] declaring war against the Americans; and had issued his 1998 declaration[172] calling on Muslims to 'kill the Americans and their allies'. Out of the nineteen Arabs[173] involved in the East Africa attacks, six were veteran Afghan Arabs with no known prior links to terrorism; five were veteran Afghan Arabs with known pre-existing terrorist links;[174] and eight were Arabs (with no foreign fighter experience).[175] Nassir al-Bahri (a veteran Arab foreign fighter and former bodyguard to Bin Laden) recounted that the motivation behind the 1998 East Africa US embassy attacks was based on Bin Laden's conspiratorial perception that:

> the two American embassies … were just big American detention centres in Africa. They were the plotting minds behind the events that took place in Rwanda, where more than 80,000 Muslims were killed [and] they were feeding that struggle.[176]

The motive therefore appears to be one of revenge based on a conspiratorial world view, but conducted primarily by veteran Afghan Arabs. Finally, it is interesting that Wadih al-Hajj (involved in the East Africa embassy bombings) and Mahmud Abu Halima (1993 WTC terrorist) had comradeship ties from Afghanistan which were rekindled in 1989 at an Islamic conference in Oklahoma City,[177] eventually contributing to Wadih al-Hajj's role in the 1998 East Africa embassy attacks.

The third global Islamist terrorist attack occurred in October 2000 in the Yemeni port of Aden. According to the 9/11 Commission Report, 'al Qaeda operatives in a small boat laden with explosives attacked … the USS *Cole* … killing 17 members of the ship's crew and wounding at least 40'.[178] Again, a veteran Afghan Arab Abdul Rahim al-Nashiri,[179] was considered 'the field commander' of the attack.[180] The motivation behind the USS *Cole* attack, according to Nassir al-Bahri, was 'to damage the USA's reputation in the naval arena, to raise the morale of the Muslims, and to prove to the Islamic nation that its sons are capable of striking the nation's enemies wherever they may be'.[181] At a strategic level, it appeared to have been conducted in order to provoke 'US military retaliation',[182] which was never forthcoming. It was only after the 9/11 attacks that the United States retaliated militarily. The 9/11 attacks, perpetrated just under a year after the attack on the USS *Cole*, involved five veteran Afghan Arabs[183] who acted as the planners and ideologues. Although no veteran Afghan Arab physically participated in the 9/11 attacks, four veteran Arab foreign fighters from other jihads were 9/11 hijackers: two appeared to have participated in the defensive jihad in Bosnia[184] and two in Chechnya.[185] This again suggests some form of linkage exists between participation in defensive jihad and subsequent involvement in Islamist terrorist-related activities.

Although many of these terrorist motivations appeared to be based on real and perceived grievances against the United States, it is instructive that the US Department of State predicted correctly 'the likelihood that US interests increasingly will become targets for violence from former mujahidin'.[186] The report added that such attacks may happen 'should the US appear to be supporting the increasingly repressive policies of these [Arab] regimes'.[187] This is corroborated by Fawaz Gerges, who argued that it was the failure of Islamist terrorists to topple their own 'pro-Western Muslim regimes' that led them to attack Western interests (the far enemy).[188] In addition, whilst it is easy to disregard the words of Osama bin Laden or his lieutenants as conspiratorial world views (as in the case of the 1998 US embassy attacks), or perceived grievances, some grievances are arguably more genuine than simply perceived. For example, Bin Laden articulated his grievances against 'the Zionist-Crusader alliance' that included American-led UN sanctions on Iraq. In his 1996 declaration, he states that '[m]ore than 600,000 Iraqi children have died due to lack of food and medicine and as a result of the unjustifiable aggression imposed on Iraq and its nation. The children of Iraq are our children'.[189] Whilst easy to dismiss, former US Ambassador to the UN, Madeleine Albright acknowledged a figure of 'half a million children',[190] whilst other studies also resonate with Bin Laden's claim.[191] Thus when asking why Islamist terrorists attacked Western targets in the late nineties, the question can ring slightly hollow. However, more pertinent to this chapter is why there were so many veteran Afghan Arabs involved in these global Islamist attacks?

From Veteran Afghan Arabs to Global Islamist Terrorists

Earlier in this chapter the post-Afghan jihad landscape was discussed and included: exposure to more radical beliefs, particularly from Afghan Arabs who had prior terrorist links; the fact that many Afghan Arabs were rootless having being forbidden re-entry to their home countries; and the fact that some veterans had been brutalised by fighting in the jihad. However, perhaps there is a piece of the jigsaw still missing: the presence of terrorist training and indoctrination. Central to the increased extremist beliefs of some Afghan Arabs was the existence of terrorist training camps, which often existed alongside camps where the training was still focused on defensive jihad, often labelled 'open fronts such as Chechnya'.[192] In the terrorist training camps, the recruits 'underwent four important and interlinked processes: violence acculturization, indoctrination, training and relations-building'.[193] The presence of terrorist training camps in Afghanistan appears to undercut the very ideology enshrined within defensive jihad. If it is true, then the Afghan jihad was used partially as a pretext for future terrorist training, rather than defending co-religionists. Mohammed Hafez makes a compelling argument to suggest that 'by 1989, after the complete withdrawal of Soviet forces, Pakistan and Afghanistan were flooded with Arab volunteers seeking training in guerrilla warfare'.[194] Certainly, Abu Zubaydah admitted in his diary (6 January 1991) that he had specifically gone to Afghanistan 'to receive training', while Libyan Afghan Arab Noman Benotman went 'to develop our fighting skills in anticipation of the day we would return to Libya to fight the Gadhafi regime'.[195] The terrorist training included 'urban sabotage, car bombings, anti-aircraft weapons, sniper rifles and land mines',[196] which according to veteran Afghan Arab Mustafa Hamid, 'were not needed by Arab *mujahideen* in Afghanistan'.[197]

Evidence from US court transcripts given by veteran Algerian Afghan Arab Ahmad Ressam,[198] confirmed that training in Khaldan Camp[199] in Afghanistan included explosives and sabotage against 'electric plants, gas plants, airports, railroads' and assassinations,[200] which is corroborated by Abu Zubaydah in his diary (5 February 1990). In the Darunta Camp the terrorist training involved 'making explosives and electronic circuits'.[201] According to veteran Egyptian Afghan Arab Mustafa Hamid, the existence of terrorist training camps in Afghanistan was due to a 'power vacuum' that formed after the battle of Jalalabad in 1989, resulting in the formation of a 'Jalalabad School of jihad . . . characterised by impetuous youth with extreme Salafi thoughts'.[202] The so-called Jalalabad School 'pioneered attacking America and planted the idea of 9/11 with Bin Laden',[203] and that some former 'students' were involved in the 1995 Riyadh attack.[204] It is illuminating that the alumni of the 'Jalalabad School' also included Ramzi Yusuf and Khalid Shaykh Muhammad (involved in the 1993 WTC attack); Osama Azmarai (involved in the 1995 'Bojinka' plot in Asia); and Abu Musab al-Zarqawi (the former leader of Al Qaeda in Iraq).[205]

Second, the dataset also demonstrates that, for example, the three main 1993 WTC bombers Ramzi Yusuf, Mahmood Abu Halima and Ahmad Ajaj all travelled to Afghanistan in order to receive terrorist training (in Khaldan Camp) between 1988 and 1992. It has been established that Ahmad Ajaj 'went to

Afghanistan in April 1992, specifically for militant training'.[206] Also, many of the Arabs (as opposed to Africans) involved in the 1998 East Africa attacks were trained in Afghanistan in the 1990s. For example, Jerrold Post testified in Muhammad Odeh's (the 1998 Nairobi bomber) defence in 2001, that 'he went to Afghanistan for training, but also ideological conditioning, which meant that Muhammad was indoctrinated beyond his first inchoate ideas to help suffering Muslims'.[207] Thus, although Muhammad Odeh's initial ideology may have been more consistent with the tenets of defensive jihad, it was only after he had arrived in Afghanistan that he received training and 'lectures more sophisticated than those ... heard previously'.[208] 'Sophisticated' is rather a loose term and is more accurately conceptualised by Mohammed Hafez as being part of the 'ideological socialization' whereby Afghan Arab trainees were subjected to 'Islamic history, theology and politics from an extremist point of view'[209] – in effect indoctrination.

The existence of indoctrination in the Afghan training camps is fairly well documented. It is also clear that many Arab volunteers were 'diverted from their desire to get training or undertake armed jihad at an open front, to join al-Qaeda',[210] whose 'radicalisation program [included] convincing people to become martyrdom operatives'.[211] For example, the 9/11 pilots who had initially gone to Afghanistan for training in order to 'wage jihad in Chechnya' in defence of fellow Muslims, never eventually went to Chechnya as 'al Qaeda quickly recognized their potential and enlisted them in its anti-US jihad'.[212] This also happened to Egyptian Afghan Arab Sabri-al-Attar, who 'considered going to Chechnya but his mentors opposed the idea [and instead he] received extensive indoctrination in their radical ideology'.[213] Thomas Hegghammer also found that many Saudis, 'having been indoctrinated in training camps' in Afghanistan, returned to Saudi Arabia 'with a more global, anti-American and intransigent ideological vision'.[214] Finally, although beyond the scope of this book, terrorist training and recruitment continued well after the April 1992 collapse of the Soviet-backed communist regime, indicating that unstable countries (and failed states) such as Afghanistan after 1992, provided and continue to provide, safe havens for Islamist terrorist training.

Hanging Up the Kalashnikov Rifle – The Reintegration of Veteran Afghan Arabs

Finally, the last post-jihad trajectory of veteran Afghan Arabs was reintegrating back into society, whether that be Arab society (assuming they were able to return), or gaining political asylum in a Western country. In both contexts, these veteran Afghan Arabs hung up their Kalashnikov (AK-47) rifles and disengaged themselves from involvement in defensive jihad (and indeed Islamist terrorism). It is worth examining briefly ten veteran Afghan Arabs who appeared to hang up their Kalashnikovs in order to explore why, given the same situational circumstances, these individuals chose to reintegrate back into society and disengage from defensive jihad. The first, Saudi veteran Afghan Arab Musa al-Qarni, returned to Saudi Arabia in 1992. According to Al-Qarni, he had been a fighter and a *Shariah* law ideologue but left Afghanistan before the Taliban took over. However, despite reintegrating back into Saudi society, he retained very strong views on the need for defensive jihad in Iraq (post-2003) in order to defeat the 'infidel occupying armies of the US and other countries.'[215] He stressed 'that the jihad waged by Muslims in Iraq in order to drive out the enemies from among the Jews and the Christians … is legal.'[216] What is clear from Al-Qarni's own narrative is that whilst he resettled back in his native country, his ideology (whilst not appearing to support Islamist terrorism) appeared to continue to support defensive jihad.

The second, Jordanian/Palestinian Afghan Arab Abu Muhammad al-Maqdisi, departed Afghanistan and returned to Kuwait, in time to be evicted (with all other Palestinians) by the Kuwaiti government at the end of the 1991 Gulf War (for Palestinian support of Iraq). He moved back to Jordan, where due to his political agitation, he was imprisoned from 1994 until 1999. Al-Maqdisi famously scolded Abu Musab al-Zarqawi (a veteran Afghan Arab and the late leader of Al Qaeda in Iraq) in 2004, for his employment of indiscriminate self-sacrificial ('martyrdom/suicide') attacks against civilians and non-combatants in Iraq – in effect Islamic terrorist tactics. Whilst al-Maqdisi currently remains (in 2018) engaged in non-violent Islamist politics (the Salafi-jihadi movement) and continues to agitate the Jordanian government (resulting in prison sentences), he has broadly reintegrated back into Jordanian society and has been consistently critical of the so-called Islamic State. The third veteran Afghan Arab to reintegrate back into society is Abdullah Anas, an Algerian who was granted political asylum to live in London. As recorded earlier in this chapter, he continues to hold views that support defensive jihad, but is consistently opposed to Islamist terrorism and the targeting of civilians and non-combatants. Although he has clearly hung up his Kalashnikov, his sentiments remain close to the ideology of defending fellow Muslims, through the use of defensive jihad against both invading foreign forces and forces loyal to autocratic despotic regimes.

The fourth veteran Afghan Arab, Huthaifa Azzam (son of Abdullah Azzam), is perhaps an interesting enigma. Introduced earlier in this chapter, he fought in

Afghanistan as a young man and, after his father was assassinated in 1989, he moved back to Jordan. He had also hung up his Kalashnikov but remained involved in Islamist circles, returning to prominence after the 2003 invasion of Iraq by proclaiming that the resistance by Sunni rebels was a defensive jihad, based on the same Islamist philosophy as his father twenty years previously. Huthaifa Azam had tried to return to the battlefield to fight the US-led invasion of Iraq but was detained at the Jordanian-Iraqi border. Yet he publicly condemns all forms of Islamist terrorism, particularly by groups associated with Al Qaeda, which is anathema to his late father's ideology. What seems apparent is that Huthaifa Azzam had disengaged, attempted to re-engage in jihad, and by 2014 was condemning the actions of ISIS and Jabhat al-Nusrah in Syria. The fifth veteran Afghan Arab is a Libyan called Nomen Benotman, who was also a former member of the LIFG which was a proscribed Islamist terrorist organisation. He appears to have successfully reintegrated back into society, albeit having been granted political asylum to live in London. In 2018, he became the President of Quilliam, a UK-based 'counter-extremism organisation'.[217]

Lastly, five Syrian veteran Afghan Arabs returned home to Syria at the end of the Afghan jihad. Whilst there is little information about their intervening years, they became deeply involved with armed groups in the Syrian jihad (post-2011). Abu Farris al-Suri (d. 2016) was the spokesman for *Jabhat al-Nusrah*; Muhammad Ayman Aboul-Tout was an ideologue for *Ahrar ash-Shaam*; while both Baha Mustafa al-Jughl and Muhammad Haydar Zammar are/were members of *Ahrar ash-Shaam*. Finally, Abu Basir al-Tartusi was an ideologue during the Syrian conflict, particularly concerning martyrdom. What is instructive about these five Syrian Afghan Arab veterans is that whilst they appeared to reintegrate back into Syrian society in the early 1990s, it also appears that their ideology of defensive jihad remained dormant, only to resurface over twenty years later. This somewhat begs the question whether a veteran Arab foreign fighter ever completely readjusts to civil society, or ever really disengages.

Conclusion

This chapter has uncovered that, for the most part, Afghan Arabs (who had no known pre-existing terrorist links) were not necessarily radicalised prior to their involvement in the Afghan jihad, nor did they employ terrorist tactics against civilians and non-combatants, having arrived in Afghanistan. In addition, their notion of martyrdom was dying on the field of battle, *fee sabeel Allah* (in the path of God), against the Soviet military invaders, and not as a result of self-sacrificial ('martyrdom/suicide') attacks, against civilians and non-combatants. Additionally, despite the relatively small research sample, it is also illuminating that the ten veteran Afghan Arabs who appeared to have reintegrated back into their societies, all retained the ideology of defensive jihad to some degree.

The main findings of this chapter have established that the primary motivation for the initial mobilisation of the Afghan Arab cohort was the centrality of religion and the prevailing ideological narrative supporting defensive jihad. Next, the situational environment within the country of origin played a role in encouraging and pushing ordinary Arabs to travel to Afghanistan. In parallel, the situational environment of the country of residence (as an Arab expatriate) also played a role in pushing many Arabs to depart for Afghanistan. Finally, kinship and friendship ties were influential in joining the Afghan jihad providing moral support, companionship and trust. With the collapse of the communist regime in April 1992, other situational factors also played a role in their subsequent post-jihad trajectories.

These subsequent post-jihad trajectories involved identifying new enemies. The first were the West in general and the United States in particular (the far enemy); the second were Arab regimes (the near enemy); and the third were any invading foreign troops or forces loyal to autocratic despotic regimes, that required the defence of fellow Sunni Muslims employing the tactic of defensive jihad. This chapter has established that out of the surviving cohort of 182 veteran Afghan Arabs, 107 (59 per cent) initially remained in defensive jihad; 61 (33.5 per cent) became involved in global Islamist terrorism; 43 (23.6 per cent) became involved in religious national terrorism; 26 (14.3 per cent) are unknown; while ten eventually appeared to hang up their Kalashnikovs but retained ideological leanings consistent with defensive jihad. It is difficult to establish why some veteran Afghan Arabs subsequently became involved in Islamist terrorism against the West or Arab regimes, while others opted to defend their co-religionists in other defensive jihads, however what is clear from the dataset is that the majority of veteran Afghan Arabs remained involved in violent Islamist activities, with some oscillating between involvement in defensive jihad and that of Islamist terrorism.

The main factors that may have led veteran Afghan Arabs to adopt a certain post-jihad trajectory involved one or all of four situational circumstances. The first factor was the influence of Afghan Arabs who had known prior links to Islamist terrorism, particularly the Egyptian cohort, whose extremist narrative found fertile ground in the post-jihad landscape in the markets of Peshawar and the mountains of Afghanistan. Second, many veteran Afghan Arabs were unable to return to their home countries and were thus left in limbo – stateless and embittered fighters who were now susceptible to new beliefs and new adventures. Third, the comradeship ties that had developed in Afghanistan, appeared in many cases, to be stronger than their original kinship and/or friendship ties – they had become a band of brothers. Aligned with comradeship ties, were the shared experiences of the brutalisation of combat in the Afghan jihad perhaps akin to PTSD, which only fellow Afghan Arabs would understand. Finally, the existence of training camps offered the Afghan Arabs a variety of military courses in line with their preferred trajectory: Islamist terrorism or defensive jihad. Naturally, in parallel with the training provided was the existence of ideological indoctrination. One of the many Islamist terrorist training camps in Afghanistan, near the western Afghan city of Heart, was run by the Jordanian veteran Afghan Arab, Abu Musab al-Zarqawi, who was to emerge as the leader of the defensive jihad in Iraq.

Iraq: The Unintended Cultivation of a New Generation of Terrorists

To describe the resistance as led by terrorists, fanatics and foreigners is neither convincing nor helpful.

A letter from 52 former senior British diplomats to
Tony Blair, *The Guardian*, 27 April 2004.[1]

Introduction

This chapter, the second of three case studies, explores the complexion of the (non-Iraqi) Arab foreign fighters who participated in the defensive jihad in Iraq (post-2003), and examines why and how some of them subsequently became involved in Islamist terrorist-related activities. However, the defensive jihad in Iraq was uniquely different to the Afghan jihad. First, unlike the veteran Afghan Arabs whose subsequent involvement in Islamist terrorism was distinct from the Afghan jihad in both time and space,[2] the Arab foreign fighters in Iraq became involved in defensive jihad and/or Islamist terrorism during the same time and in the same space. In many ways, such overlaps represent a textbook insurgency, often defined as 'a hybrid form of conflict that combines subversion, guerrilla warfare and terrorism ... [in] an internal struggle in which a disaffected group seeks to gain control of a nation'.[3] Identifying and then separating Arab foreign fighters (involved in defensive jihad) from Islamist terrorists, despite the obvious overlaps present in an insurgency, was largely predicated on their targeting (of civilians and non-combatants) and their tactics. Second, as noted in Chapter 2, Islamist terrorism directed against the far enemy had, until the invasion of Iraq, been conducted in distant places such as East Africa, Yemen and the US mainland. These attacks had required planning, travel, money and logistics. In Iraq, the far enemy had arrived on near enemy territory, thus greatly reducing the challenges of attacking the far enemy. However, this chapter rejects the assertion, often characterised in the media and in politics, that the Arab foreign fighters who went to Iraq (post-2003) were all Islamist terrorists, portrayed as radicalised extremists, uneducated and originating from impoverished backgrounds. Whilst not sympathetic in any way, this chapter provides a more empathetic human face to many of these individuals, and offers a more nuanced picture of their initial and subsequent motivations. This is achieved by leveraging a dataset compiled for this book of 721 Arab foreign fighters (representing between 14 and 23 per cent of the total foreign fighter cohort),[4] not including indigenous Iraqis.

The dataset is based on primary and secondary sources. Primary Arabic sources include *maloomaat shakhseeya khaasa bil-muhaajjireen* (Special Personal Information of the Immigrants) from *dawlat al-Iraq al-Islameeya* (the Islamic State of Iraq) – sometimes known as the 'Sinjar Records',[5] *shuhada' fi zaman al-ghurba* (Martyrs in a Time of Alienation), and martyrdom biographies published by *Al Furqan* Media Foundation (the Islamic State in Iraq and later the ISIS media wing). Secondary sources include previous studies[6] and the Chicago Project on Security and Threats (CPOST) Suicide Attack Database.[7] The research net was cast far and wide in order to attempt to dilute any biases in particular datasets,[8] such as Anthony Cordesman's dataset that only examined Saudi foreign fighters, in order to produce a broad and representative sample. Also by including individuals within the dataset who died as a result of self-sacrificial ('martyrdom/suicide') attacks, the analysis could appear skewed towards the notion of 'martyrdom'. It is acknowledged that 'martyrdom' biographies do not necessarily have the bandwidth to explain an individual's intentions, motivations and ideology, as they often include *post hoc* interpretations of the motivations of dead men. For example, it is possible that the attacker is not necessarily in a position to decide what kind of target (civilian or military) to attack. That said, such biographies offer a start point for further research, and indeed they populate less than 18 per cent of the Iraqi jihad dataset. Finally, the dataset covers a research period starting from the invasion of Iraq (23 March 2003) by US-led coalition troops until December 2009, by which time all UK troops had departed and US casualties were at an all-time low.[9]

This chapter is broken down into two broad sections. The first section offers a brief overview of the Iraqi jihad and analyses the broad backgrounds of the Arab foreign fighters, including their geographic origin, education and age, as well as the influence of religion (as perceived by those involved); the influence of veteran foreign fighters and/or Islamist terrorists; and any kinship or social ties to other foreign fighters and/or terrorists. These factors appeared to contribute to the Arab foreign fighters' initial involvement in defensive jihad in Iraq, against the US-led coalition. The second part of this chapter examines the situational circumstances experienced by the Arab foreign fighters having arrived in Iraq that influenced their subsequent behavioural trajectories (including involvement in Islamist terrorism). These circumstances include the influence of competing ideologies, targeting preferences, terrorist training and indoctrination, which are used to illuminate the trajectory between defensive jihad and Islamist terrorism.

Background to the 2003 Iraq War

A short background brief to the 2003 Iraq War and the subsequent involvement of Arab foreign fighters and Islamist terrorists is essential, in order to give the Iraqi insurgency meaning and context. The contemporary history of Iraq includes the rise to power of the late President Saddam Hussein and his Sunni-orientated Ba'ath Party in 1979, and a continuation of the trend of a Sunni Muslim minority (32–37 per cent) governing a Shi'a Muslim majority (60–65 per cent).[10] In 1980, Saddam Hussein led his country into an inconclusive eight-year war with Iran, whilst in the latter stages of that war, he also led a campaign (sometimes labelled the 'Anfal Campaign') against his own Kurdish population. In particular, in March 1988, chemical weapons were used against the Kurdish village of Halabja, killing an estimated 4,000 people.[11] The man responsible for employing such weapons was Ali Hassan al-Majid (aka 'Chemical Ali').[12] Less than two years later, Saddam Hussein took his country to war again, this time by invading Kuwait in August 1990. Aware that a Western and Arab coalition were amassing their forces on the Saudi-Kuwaiti border, in early January 1991 he changed the national flag of Iraq to include the *takbeer*[13] (in his handwriting) of *Allahu Akbar* (God is greatest), in an attempt to demonstrate his Sunni religiosity and to court Islamists worldwide.[14] In February 1991, the US-led coalition forced the withdrawal of Iraqi forces from Kuwait, with two repercussions. First, after the Gulf War the United States was invited to station troops in Saudi Arabia, a decision that later contributed to Osama bin Laden's 1996 *Declaration of War against the US*.[15] The second repercussion (as noted in Chapter 2) was the post-Gulf War UN sanctions (Resolution 687) against Iraq, which resulted in the death of an estimated 500,000 Iraqi children.[16] This death rate was not disputed by US administration officials and subsequently provided a genuine grievance and the ideological justification for much of the anti-American sentiment amongst many Islamists in the Arab world.[17]

After the collapse and withdrawal of Iraqi forces from Kuwait, Saddam Hussein later established an organisation called *Fidayeen* Saddam, a loyal Sunni paramilitary force originating from the predominantly Sunni triangle in Iraq,[18] and separate from his armed forces. The label *fidayeen* is often confused with 'suicide bombers', but this is not entirely accurate. First, they are defined in the Hans Wehr Dictionary as 'fighters who risk their lives recklessly, soldiers prepared to sacrifice their lives; commandos, shock troops',[19] or more broadly as 'men of sacrifice, someone who gives up his life for a cause'.[20] Second, Iraqi documents captured in 2003 demonstrate that permission was required for members of *Fidayeen* Saddam to become involved in martyrdom. An example is an Iraqi document (dated 25 March 2002) entitled *Request to Carry Out Martyrdom Duties* (*talib tanfeedh waajib istishhaadi*) for three '*fidayeen* compatriots' (*ar-rafeeq al-fidaa'i*)[21] from Anbar province in the Sunni triangle. Thus, whilst the *fidayeen* were willing to sacrifice their lives defending Saddam Hussein's regime, the explicit concept of martyrdom required permission from the Chief of Staff *Fidayeen* Saddam. The whole idea of martyrdom, suicide and sacrifice within an Islamist context are examined in further detail later in this chapter, but as in Chapter 2, the terms self-sacrificial ('martyrdom/suicide') attack or simply self-sacrificial attack are more broadly adopted.

After the 9/11 attacks and the subsequent dismantling of the Al Qaeda network in Afghanistan, Iraq became the next country of interest in the rather badly labelled 'war on terror'.[22] Conspiracy rumours aside, quite why Iraq became the target of attack is still unclear. Despite Iraq being an assertive and belligerent country, with an autocratic and despotic ruling regime which was willing to use chemical munitions against its own people, its links to Sunni-inspired terrorism were tenuous and anecdotal at best. For example, three veteran Afghan Arabs, Jordanian national Abu Musab al-Zarqawi, his Jordanian brother-in-law Khalid Mustafa al-Aruri (aka Abu Qassam) and Iraqi (Kurdish) national Wirya Salih (aka Abu Abdullah al-Shafi'i), were all part of a Sunni Islamist group called *Ansar al-Islam*. The group (numbering about 100) were based in Kurdistan (beyond the reach of Saddam Hussein due to the 1991 imposition of a no-fly-zone).[23] Despite possible comradeship ties to fellow Afghan Arabs who were linked to Al Qaeda, the Islamist ideology of *Ansar al-Islam* was religious nationalist, and as a group they lacked both the ability and reach to adopt a transnational terrorist agenda. It is also instructive that whilst CIA analysts had located Abu Musab al-Zarqawi in northern Iraq in 2002 and had planned his demise, they were allegedly prevented from attacking him by Vice President Cheney. This allowed the United States to continue to insist on a linkage between al-Zarqawi, Al Qaeda and Saddam Hussein, in order to justify the Iraq War.[24] When this linkage eventually became so tenuous as to become unbelievable, the United States (aware of the need for political legitimacy), changed tack and decided an attack on Iraq could be justified by the country's alleged possession of weapons of mass destruction (WMD). However, despite the lack of credible evidence of WMD in Iraq,[25] the lack of a legal basis for invading Iraq[26] and that any invasion would be considered 'a serious violation of international law',[27] the United States and the United Kingdom still decided on regime change.

Whatever the actual intentions or legality of the US-led invasion of Iraq, what was important was the perception of such an invasion by Arab governments, and perhaps more importantly, their people. Whether situated within mainstream and moderate Islam, or on the Islamist fringes, the US-led coalition invasion of Iraq resulted in 'a textbook case of defensive jihad. Foreign military forces occupied Muslim territory after what was widely perceived as an unjustified aggression'.[28] It was perhaps the overall illegality of the Iraq War, and the seemingly 'unjustified aggression' that provided the motivation for the initial cohort of Arab foreign fighters to travel to Iraq. What is equally clear is that there was no Al Qaeda organisation in Iraq prior to the US-led coalition invasion; arguably the invasion itself generated and cultivated a new generation of Arab foreign fighters and Islamist terrorists. However, before examining in detail the new generation, what was the influence of the older generation of veteran Afghan Arabs and Islamist terrorists on the jihad in Iraq?

The Influence of Veteran Arab Foreign Fighters and Islamist Terrorists

Naturally there were some veteran Arab foreign fighters and individuals with known pre-existing Islamist terrorist links who were also involved (externally from and/or internally) in Iraq. Despite any overlaps, these two groupings numbered only sixteen non-Iraqi Arabs, yet their influence in the initial defensive jihad in Iraq was proportionally greater than their small number suggests. These influences included positions of leadership, ideological support, the production of Islamist training material and recruitment. Both groupings were connected by comradeship ties established during their previous involvement in defensive jihad and/or Islamist terrorist-related activities. Arguably the most influential group were those known Islamist terrorists who were involved internally in the Iraqi jihad. Perhaps the best-known Islamist terrorist involved in the Iraqi jihad was the former Jordanian Afghan Arab Abu Musab al-Zarqawi. Unlike Abdullah Azzam, who in the 1980s Afghan jihad focused on defeating the Soviet occupation forces, Abu Musab al-Zarqawi hijacked the defensive jihad in Iraq, and fairly quickly adopted terrorist tactics that explicitly targeted Iraqi civilians and non-combatants. It appeared a total contradiction of the basic ideological tenets of defensive jihad, and although initially commanding *Jama'at Tawhid wal-Jihad* (The Monotheism and Jihad Group), in October 2004 he renamed the group *Tanzim Qaedat al-Jihad fee Bilad al-Rafidayn* (aka Al Qaeda in Iraq).[29] His influence was entirely counter-productive to defending co-religionists from foreign occupation forces, and he will be remembered as the epitome of a particularly sadistic Islamist terrorist, who brought death and wanton destruction to Iraq and the wider *Shaam* (Levant) region. He was killed by a US airstrike in June 2006, but his ideology survived which, whilst totally at odds with the concept of defensive jihad, continued to support the targeting of predominantly Iraqi Shi'a Muslims. His successor, an Egyptian named Abu Ayoob al-Misri (aka Abu Hamza al-Muhajjir or Abu Munim al-Badawi) was a member of both Al Qaeda and EIJ. His link to al-Zarqawi was through Ayman al-Zawahiri (then deputy leader of Al Qaeda) in 1999 in Afghanistan. He continued al-Zarqawi's ruthless terrorist campaign in Iraq targeting Shi'a Muslims, and in October 2006 on the establishment of the Islamic State in Iraq (ISI), he became the influential 'war minister' under a local Iraqi leader, Abu Omar al-Baghdadi.

Other known Islamist terrorists involved internally in the Iraq jihad include Omar Yusuf Juma (aka Abu Anas al-Shami), who was a veteran Jordanian Afghan Arab who had also been involved in the jihad against the Serbs in Bosnia, defending Bosnian Muslims. He was close to veteran Jordanian Afghan Arabs, Abu Muhammad al-Maqdisi and Abu Musab al-Zarqawi. Prior to travelling to Iraq in 2003, he went to Mecca (Saudi Arabia) to perform the *umra* (a small pilgrimage), and later served on the influential *Shura* (consultative) council of Abu Musab al-Zarqawi. Interestingly, according to his father Yusuf Juma, Omar Yusuf 'believed Islam was about love and peace [however the] Americans came to Iraq to kill Muslims, and they had a right to defend themselves',[30] which is entirely consistent with the tenets of defensive jihad. However, having arrived in Iraq to defend fellow Sunni Muslims, Omar Yusuf subsequently supported the indiscriminate killing of Shi'a Muslims. He was killed by US forces in September 2004. Lastly, al-Zarqawi's brother-in-law, Khalid al-Aruri, was also involved in the Iraqi jihad, although his influence is unknown, as he fled to Iran but absconded from prison in July 2005.

The next influential group of Islamist terrorists were those involved externally from Iraq, who exerted an influence on the ideology and tactics employed by Arab foreign fighters and Islamist terrorists in Iraq. This group included Osama bin Laden (as head of Al Qaeda); Ayman al-Zawahiri (as deputy head of Al Qaeda); Yusuf al-Uyayri and Abdul Aziz al-Muqrin who were both clerics in Al Qaeda in the Arabian Peninsula (AQAP); Abu Faraj al-Libi (who managed Al Qaeda operations in Iraq after the arrest of Khalid Shaykh Muhammad); and finally, Abu Muhammad al-Maqdisi and Abu Musab al-Suri who were both Islamist ideologues. These individuals, despite not being based in Iraq, provided much of the advice and ideological guidance, which perhaps counter-intuitively, was often at odds with the Arab foreign fighters/Islamist terrorists who were fighting in Iraq. For example, the use of *takfir*[31] and the employment of self-sacrificial ('martyrdom/suicide') attacks against Iraqi civilians (adopted by Abu Musab al-Zarqawi) were not supported by Ayman al-Zawahiri or Abu Muhammad al-Maqdisi, and are covered later in this chapter. Yusuf al-Uyayri, an AQAP member, wrote an influential book, *The Future of Iraq and the Arabian Peninsula After the Fall of Baghdad*, that provided advice on how to resist the US-led coalition. In his book, he hailed 'the destruction of Ba'athism in Iraq', yet warned his readership that 'there are only two sides ... we have a clash of two visions of the world and the future of mankind. The side prepared to accept more sacrifices will win'.[32] Out of all the Islamist terrorists situated outside Iraq, he was the most cited and referenced author.[33] The other AQAP ideologue (and veteran Afghan Arab), Abdul Aziz al-Muqrin, wrote an influential book (published after his death in 2004), *dawrat at-tanfeedh wa-harb al-'isaabaaat* (*A Practical Course for Guerrilla War*), and whilst its influence in the Iraqi jihad is difficult to assess, his ideas have appeared within the Iraqi jihad.[34]

The next outside Islamist terrorist influence on Arab foreign fighters in Iraq was Abu Musab al-Suri, who was the author of a popular book, *The Call for a Global Islamic Resistance*, which was released in late 2004, where he labels the Iraq insurgency 'an open front jihad'. Perhaps counter-intuitively, Al-Suri states that 'in the word terrorist, we do not find any negative meaning when we use it to characterise the resistance fighters or the *mujahhidoon* ... [who] are repelling their enemies and the enemy's terror through a defensive jihad'.[35] It is an interesting position to take, as most Islamists shun the term *irhaabi* (terrorist) due to it being a pejorative label. However, in line with the tenets of defensive jihad, Al-Suri did not support the killing of co-religionists, except for 'senior apostate leaders who are allied to the American invader campaigns'[36] and 'the security forces and political and military forces directly collaborating with the occupation'.[37] Finally, Abu Bakr al-Naji[38] authored his 2004 *idaarat at-tawahhush* (*The Management of Savagery*), translated by McCants,[39] which has often been considered the blueprint for the doctrine and tactics of Al Qaeda in Iraq, although this is debateable. For example, al-Naji's guidance to 'lighten the severity of the violence against reasonable people amongst the enemy'[40] was arguably not reflected on the ground in Iraq. Perhaps most surprising is that there was no explicit inclusion of *takfir*, with al-Naji noting only that 'the rules governing the killing of [Muslim] tyrants are conflicting'.[41] In summary, whilst it is difficult to really assess the impact of the external Islamist terrorist influence on the tactics adopted by Arab foreign fighters in Iraq, it appears to have been more superficial than defining. The headstrong Abu Musab al-Zarqawi as head of Al Qaeda in Iraq, appeared to reject the advice from those based outside of Iraq, perhaps feeling that he understood the situation better, living with the *mujahhideen* on the battlefield in Iraq.

The third influential cohort comprised of veteran Arab foreign fighters who operated inside Iraq. From the dataset, perhaps counter-intuitively, there were only three veteran Afghan Arabs (who had not embraced the ideology of Al Qaeda), and who were also veterans of Bosnia and Chechnya. The veteran Afghan Arabs included Saudi national Abu Raghd al-Jazrawi and Lebanese national Mustafa Ramadan Darwish, who both established the Rawa Training Camp in Anbar province (in Iraq) in 2003. Here they drew on their knowledge, experience and comradeship ties gained during the Afghan jihad, which afforded them credibility in the eyes of the new trainees. They were both subsequently killed by US forces in 2003 and 2004 respectively. Finally, Saudi national Suhail al-Sahli was a 'career' Arab foreign fighter who had been involved in defensive jihads in Afghanistan, Tajikistan, Bosnia and Chechnya. In February 2003, aware that the Iraq invasion was looming, he performed the annual Islamic pilgrimage, the *Hajj* (9–14 February 2003), before going to Iraq in preparation to fight the Americans. He died in Iraq, leaving behind a very proud family who believed that he had been 'defending Islam and Arab causes'.[42]

The last influential cohort were veteran Arab foreign fighters involved externally from Iraq, whose influence is more academic, inasmuch as by 2003 they had eschewed support for Islamist terrorism but still retained the mainstream view of the ideology of defensive jihad. As touched on in the last chapter, perhaps unsurprisingly, veteran Afghan Arab (and son of Abdullah Azzam – the former leader of the Afghan Arabs) Huthaifa Azzam, viewed the jihad in Iraq in a purely defensive manner. In 2006, in an interview with a journalist from the *Irish Times*, Mary Fitzgerald, he makes clear that 'if I find the way, I would go today to fight jihad in Iraq because it is compulsory for me as a Muslim, but it can only take place inside the borders of Iraq, you cannot bring it outside'. He expands on his view by stating:

> If I saw an American or British man wearing a soldier's uniform inside Iraq I would kill him because that is my obligation. If I found the same soldier over the border in Jordan I wouldn't touch him. In Iraq he is a fighter and an occupier, here he is not. This is my religion and I respect this as the main instruction in my religion for jihad.[43]

Azzam's view appears not to be radical in the sense of supporting terrorism that predominantly targets civilians and non-combatants. His view is more consistent with the tenets of defensive jihad, defending co-religionists against a foreign occupation force. In some respects, Azzam's view is analogous to US Catholic support (NORAID) for the Provisional Irish Republican Army and the broader Catholic community, against a perceived British military occupation of Northern Ireland during the 1970s and 1980s. Taken to the international level, Azzam's view still appears relatively normal, if put alongside the idea of collective defence that underpins the North Atlantic Treaty. Perhaps the defensive jihad in Iraq resembles a 'non-state' version of Article 5 of the North Atlantic Treaty, whereby:

> an armed attack against one or more ... shall be considered an attack against them all and consequently they agree that, if such an armed attack occurs, each of them, in exercise of the right of individual or collective self-defence ... will assist the Party or Parties so attacked by taking forthwith, individually and in concert with the other Parties, such action as it deems necessary, including the use of armed force.[44]

The idea of a collective defence in the Arab and wider Muslim world is sometimes referred to as 'pan-Islamism', defined by Thomas Hegghammer as 'an ideology based on the view that all Muslims are one people who [have] a responsibility to help each other in times of crisis'.[45] Although the ideology and concept of defensive jihad may be considered little more than a non-state treaty for collective defence, in reality, the Iraqi jihad enjoyed considerable Arab state political and religious support, and again perhaps more analogous to the North Atlantic Treaty than some pundits may like to imagine. Covered in greater detail later in this chapter, most Arab states supported the involvement of their nationals in the defensive jihad in Iraq – that is until the initial defensive jihad turned terroristic.

Finally, Saudi veteran Afghan Arab Musa al-Qarni, now an academic living in Riyadh, was interviewed in 2005 and 2006 about the legitimacy of the Iraqi jihad. He was unequivocal about the nature of such a jihad: 'I want to stress that the jihad waged by Muslims in Iraq in order to drive out the enemies ... who are attacking both land and honour – this jihad is legal. It is jihad for the sake of Allah and in defence of Muslim lands, honour, and sanctities'.[46] In 2006, he continued with the same message:

> I think that fighting the Americans on the land of Iraq is jihad, that the Americans are aggressors, and that the [fighting] of Iraqis and Muslims against the Americans in Iraq constitutes a legitimate and obligatory defence. The Americans are the aggressors.[47]

Despite being of a different generation, the over-arching message of veteran Afghan Arabs (particularly Huthaifa Azzam and Musa al-Qarni) was the normality of involvement in jihad, the defensive and legitimate nature of the Iraqi jihad, and the obligatory duty to become involved in it. It appears devoid of an extremist tone, offering a persuasive message for a new generation of Arab foreign fighters. This generation would broadly, but not exclusively, consist of ordinary, non-radicalised Arab youth, who had no known previous links to Islamist-related activities (including defensive jihad and/or Islamist terrorism). The Iraqi jihad appeared to be attracting rather ordinary and unremarkable Arab youth who were broadly representative of the social *mores* of their home countries. This position is adopted notwithstanding the fact that despite 'the numerous endeavours in academia ... no metrics exist to gauge radicalisation'.[48]

The Concept of Ordinary Arab Foreign Fighters in Iraq

The idea that many of the Arab foreign fighters arriving in Iraq were ordinary non-radicalised youth seems counter-intuitive, and challenges the numerous accounts of those who subsequently became involved in terrorism in Iraq. To be clear, the apparent disparity is more one of timing than of substance, in that having mobilised and arrived in Iraq with good intentions, many Arab foreign fighters did subsequently engage in Islamist terrorist attacks, particularly against Iraqi civilians and non-combatants. One may ask – so what? The distinction is important because by automatically labelling Arab foreign fighters as terrorists (or extremists), it prevents any nuanced understanding of their initial motivations. In addition, it also arguably hides the situational factors experienced in Iraq that actually influenced many of them to become terrorists. It is often implicit in the scholarly literature that individuals who depart their country of residence in order to participate in defensive jihad, in defence of their co-religionists, are somehow already radicalised and/or already Islamist terrorists,[49] however this should not go unchallenged. In addition, just because the United Nations Security Council[50] labels such individuals as 'foreign terrorist fighters' does not mean that they actually are. It is a subtle argument and amounts to 'what in the West is commonly defined as terrorist activity is regarded in the Arab world, including in Iraq, as national resistance against an occupying power.'[51] It is perhaps time to view the individual trajectories of all foreign fighters (Arab and Western) with a view to identifying the common push and pull factors that feed initial involvement in defensive jihad, and subsequent involvement in Islamist terrorism. In a nutshell, the West needs a greater understanding of the Arab and wider Islamic world, due to the influence it has on Western Muslims.

In the specific case of the Iraqi jihad, there is broad academic consensus that most Arab foreign fighters were ordinary citizens prior to travelling to Iraq, and this chimes with the findings in this book. In his seminal monograph, *The Far Enemy*, Professor Fawaz Gerges noted that far 'from being Al Qaeda-type fanatics, these young men had not been politicized before the American-led invasion and had not joined any Islamist, let alone paramilitary, organization.'[52] In a leading study of Saudi foreign fighters in Iraq conducted by US national security analyst Anthony Cordesman, one of his primary conclusions was 'the unsettling realization that the vast majority of Saudi militants who ... entered Iraq were not terrorist sympathizers before the war.'[53] In Great Britain, there was also broad diplomatic consensus concerning the resistance in Iraq, demonstrated in a 2004 letter reprimanding the Prime Minister, arguing that '[t]o describe the resistance as led by terrorists, fanatics and foreigners is neither convincing nor helpful.'[54] Finally, even in the media, journalist Abdel Bari Atwan 'discovered that the majority of foreign fighters were not jihadis before the war.'[55] These conclusions support the dataset, which indicates that over 98 per cent of Arab foreign fighters initially involved in the Iraqi jihad had no documented pre-existing terrorist links, perhaps suggesting that the repercussions of the invasion of Iraq included the establishment of a new generation of young Arab male fighters, and the subsequent unintended cultivation of a new generation of terrorists.

Looking in more detail at the dataset, Arab foreign fighters in Iraq were well represented educationally and career wise: ninety (12 per cent) of the 721 Arab foreign fighters had a university education, with five of them qualified as medical doctors. Whilst these findings are in harmony with those of the Afghan Arab cohort in Chapter 2,[56] they hide an interesting facet. Of those ninety with a university education, it is instructive to find that actually sixty-eight (76 per cent) were university students who cut short their education in order to go to Iraq and participate in defensive jihad, suggesting conviction rather than radicalisation as a motive. Deeper interrogation of the dataset also reveals that 42 per cent were Saudis and 21 per cent were Libyans, of which 32 per cent of Saudi students came from Mecca, and 50 per cent of Libyan students came from Durna (the importance of Mecca and Durna are discussed in detail later under geographic origin). Age wise, based on 283 Arab foreign fighters where data were available, they varied between fifteen and fifty-four years old, with 49 per cent of them aged twenty-three or under. The average age was twenty-four and the median was twenty-eight, which correlates well both with the Afghan Arab cohort in Chapter 2[57] and much of the scholarly literature.[58] Also, the fact that 49 per cent of Arab foreign fighters in Iraq were twenty-three-years old or under suggests (as with the Afghan Arabs) the 'absence of personal constraints ... such as marriage and family responsibilities',[59] and perhaps the presence of the idea of 'age-related vulnerabilities of community members'.[60] Whilst the first point indicates biographical availability, the second recognises that Arab youth may have been more susceptible to appealing narratives that encouraged them to travel to Iraq.

The Geographic Origin of Arab Foreign Fighters in Iraq

A brief overview of the nationalities of Arab foreign fighters in Iraq offers the opportunity to examine the broad social, political and religious context from where the individuals originated. The top three countries of origin were Saudi Arabia (44 per cent), Libya (16 per cent) and Syria (9 per cent). Interestingly, there was no evidence of involvement in the Iraqi jihad among citizens from four Gulf countries (the Sultanate of Oman, Qatar, Bahrain and the UAE). The breakdown of the geographic origin of Arab foreign fighters in Iraq from the dataset is presented in Figure 3.1.

Saudi Arabia being the predominant country of origin has been identified by many other scholars,[61] and is largely explained by Saudi government and clerical support for the defensive jihad in Iraq.[62] Saudi Arabia was more than simply a permissive environment – arguably it was an encouraging one, actually promoting the notion of defensive jihad in Iraq. It is fairly well documented that

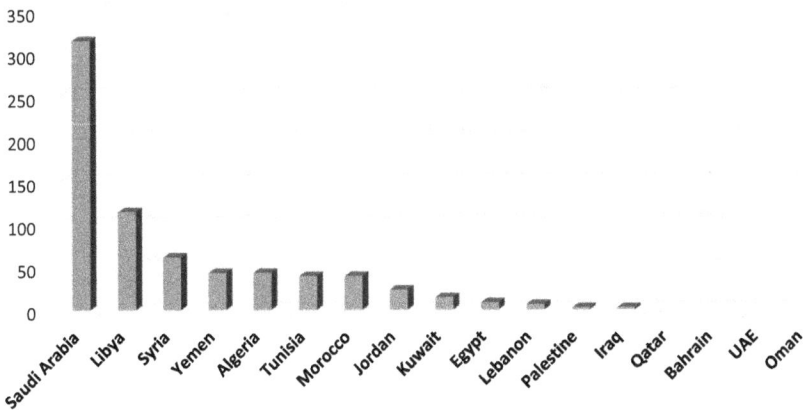

Figure 3.1 The geographic origin of Arab foreign fighters in Iraq (n=721).

the 'support for violent Jihad in Iraq against the Americans was encouraged by the Saudi Islamic establishment',[63] supported by evidence from 'interrogations of nearly 150 Saudis suspected of planning to join the Iraqi insurgency [that] indicate that they were heeding the calls of clerics and activists'.[64] Such evidence of support includes a religious *fatwa*[65] (albeit addressed to the Iraqi people) signed by twenty-six Saudi clerics, that stressed the legality of the resistance in Iraq, and as noted above, it was Saudi cleric (and veteran Afghan Arab) Yusuf al-Uyayri, who wrote *The Crusade in Iraq Series* advising Iraqi and Arab foreign fighters on how to fight the US-led coalition. It is also instructive that veteran Saudi Afghan Arab and now academic, Musa al-Qarni, argued in 2006 that:

> The Saudi youth are exceptional in their willingness to sacrifice. They long for jihad. Look at Iraq now – who are most of the young men there? Are they not Saudis? Despite the difficulties and obstacles, the Saudi youth do not listen to any authority or to any call [to refrain from] jihad for the sake of Allah.[66]

It is also worth briefly exploring whether religiosity[67] within Saudi Arabia was a factor that may explain the large contingent of Saudi foreign fighters in Iraq. According to the US Department of State, Saudi Arabia follows 'the rigorously conservative and strict interpretation of the Salafi . . . school of the Sunni branch of Islam',[68] often labelled *Wahhabism*. There appears to be a tentative link between Saudi Arabia and this 'puritanical sect of Islam'[69] and the suggestion that 'more religious societies do produce more jihadists'.[70] Understandably, there is not total agreement on this linkage, with a few scholars arguing (in the context of

Palestine) that the 'relationship between religion and support of political violence only holds true when mediated by deprivations and psychological resource loss'.[71] As will be demonstrated later, religiosity was a common motivating circumstance for many Arab foreign fighters, but in the specific case of Saudi Arabia, explicit state and clerical support for defensive jihad in Iraq appeared to be the dominant factor, at least in the early phases of the insurgency.[72]

Although Libya was the second most predominant country of origin, it actually had the highest involvement *per capita* (twenty per million). The explanation for the relatively large participation of Libyan foreign fighters is twofold. First, as noted in Chapter 2, there was a tendency for Arab regimes to either export militants abroad, or if already abroad, to prevent their return. In the case of Libya, 'local Salafi-jihadist movements [were] in conflict with their government ... forcing fighters to search for new havens'.[73] The second explanation is that the eastern towns of Durna and Benghazi have long been associated with Islamic militancy in Libya, particularly in the mid-1990s involving the Libyan Islamic Fighting Group (LIFG). Durna in particular had a 'local tradition of resistance and religious fervor'.[74] This is supported by the dataset that reveals that Libyan foreign fighters from either Durna or Benghazi made up 64 per cent of the total cohort of Libyan fighters, and 10 per cent of all Arab foreign fighters in Iraq.

Finally, the substantial involvement of Syrian foreign fighters has two possible broad explanations: regime support and geographic proximity. Syrian regime support was similar to that of Egypt during the Afghan jihad, getting 'rid of thousands of the most aggressive Salafists with a taste for jihad, packing them off to a foreign war from which many would never return to pose a threat'.[75] This was to lead to Syria being 'one of the leading state sponsors of both Baathist and Al Qaeda terrorism in Iraq'.[76] This support included arranging 'buses to ferry fighters ... the issuing of documentation ... discount on passport fees',[77] and also 'the chance to receive military training and fight against Coalition forces in Iraq'.[78] This level of Syrian regime support was recognised by the US-led coalition, resulting in the 2008 killing of the Syrian logistics manager for Al Qaeda in Iraq, Abu Ghadiya,[79] in the Syrian border town of Abu Kamal. The second point concerning the large involvement of Syrian Arab foreign fighters is the geographic proximity of Syria with Iraq, and their largely porous 599 km border that facilitated the movement of both Syrian and other Arab foreign fighters. This suggestion might however be countered in that Jordanian foreign fighters made up less than 3 per cent of the cohort of 721 Arab foreign fighters, yet Jordan and Iraq share a 181 km border. This point may indicate the lack of a permissive environment within Jordan,[80] but also more generally demonstrates the lack of a single reason why one nationality may be more involved in defensive jihad than another.

The apparent non-involvement in the Iraqi jihad of citizens from four Gulf countries (the Sultanate of Oman, Qatar, Bahrain and the UAE) deserves comment, all the more in that it is in stark contrast to their fellow Gulf neighbour, Saudi Arabia. Arguably a more moderate religiosity (than Saudi Arabia) may have played a part, although as noted earlier in some circles, religiosity and involvement in political violence requires an association with deprivations – deprivations that these four oil rich Gulf countries (and indeed Saudi Arabia) are generally not known to suffer. Perhaps the most plausible explanation is that these four Gulf countries have no notable history in Islamist militancy (including involvement in defensive jihad and/or Islamist terrorism), or links to organisations such as the Muslim Brotherhood. The apparent lack of involvement in the defensive jihad in Iraq by nationals from these four Gulf countries was also noted in Chapter 2 vis-à-vis their lack of involvement in the defensive jihad in 1980s Afghanistan. This trend demonstrated by these four Gulf countries is further explored in the Syrian jihad (post-2011).

Finally, it is instructive that while the majority of expatriate Afghan Arabs had been living in other Arab countries, the majority (90 per cent) of expatriate Arab foreign fighters in Iraq had been living in the West.[81] Although a small overall number, only 3 per cent out of 721, the fact that they mobilised from Western countries may be explained by the fact that it was a highly controversial Western-inspired invasion of an Arab country. It may have made them uncomfortable to remain living and working in the West, particularly in Muslim immigrant communities. France and Italy were the two Western countries from where the highest numbers were mobilised with, perhaps unsurprisingly, Arab migrants from mainly Algeria and Tunisia respectively. Anecdotally, Cherif Kouachi, a French national of Algerian parentage, who was arrested in Paris whilst attempting to go to Iraq in 2005, was later involved in the 2015 Charlie Hebdo terrorist attacks in Paris.[82]

The Influence of Religion

Whilst the religiosity of some Arab foreign fighters was discussed earlier in this chapter, it is time to look beyond the biographical data and examine evidence of the possible religious convictions that influenced their decisions to travel to Iraq. Such evidence would support the finding by Professor Ahmed Hashim that 'many of the volunteers were deeply religious'.[83] Extracted from the dataset, it is possible to demonstrate that religiosity did play a role in the travelling date of Arab foreign fighters to Iraq. During the twelve-month period from September 2006 to August 2007, 55 per cent of the 291 Arab foreign fighters travelled to Iraq during, or after, one of the four notable occasions in the Sunni Islamic calendar: the fasting month of *Ramadan* (23 September–22 October 2006); *Eid al-Fitr* (23–24 October 2006); the *Hajj* pilgrimage (28–31 December 2006); and *Eid al-Adha* (30–31 December 2006). By noting the travel dates of Arab foreign fighters, the three favourite travel months in 2006 correlate directly to these annual Islamic occasions, in effect periods of increased religiosity. The most prolific month (October 2006) corresponds to *Ramadan*, the second most prolific month (January 2007) corresponds to the *Hajj* and *Eid al-Adha*, and the third (November 2006) relates to *Eid al-Fitr*. This is presented in Figure 3.2.

Many Arab foreign fighters appeared to travel to Iraq only after having participated in one of these Islamic events, except for *Ramadan*, where the evidence shows that they often deployed throughout the fasting month. Fasting during *Ramadan* is one of the five pillars of Islam, and compliance is rewarded. In the *Hadeeth Bukhari*,[84] it is said that 'whoever observes fasts during the month of *Ramadan* out of sincere faith ... all his past sins will be forgiven'.[85] This may help explain a keenness to participate in all or some of *Ramadan*, prior to involvement in defensive jihad in Iraq. In effect, participation appeared to offer a form of absolution or self-purification. Although this appears to be the first empirical study to explicitly highlight this phenomenon linking religiosity with

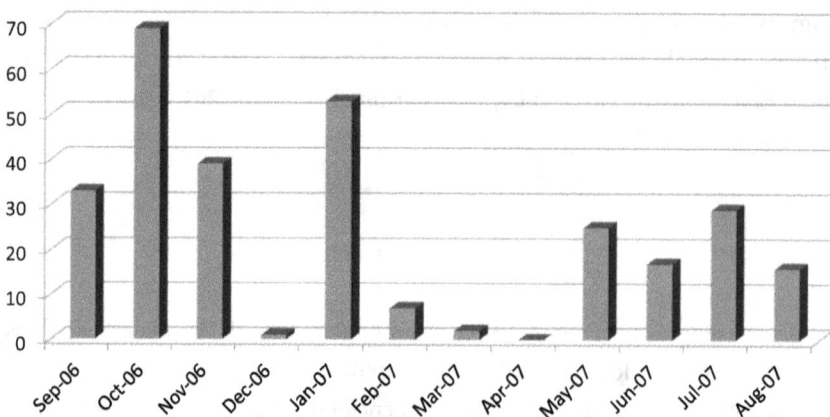

Figure 3.2 Arab foreign fighter deployment months to Iraq: 2006–2007 (n=291).

involvement in defensive jihad, Thomas Hegghammer had also recognised that 'a striking number of people travelled [to Iraq] during or around the month of *Ramadan*'.[86] With the greater granularity of data collected for the Syrian jihad, this phenomenon is again revisited.

The *umra* and the annual *Hajj* pilgrimage in Mecca (Saudi Arabia) also featured in the accounts of Arab foreign fighters. The *umra* is considered 'the lesser pilgrimage',[87] a rite that requires only a few hours to accomplish, whereas the *Hajj* is another of the five pillars of Islam, and attendance offers a similar form of absolution. In the *Hadeeth Bukhari* it narrates that the Prophet Muhammad said that 'whoever performs *Hajj* for Allah's pleasure ... then he will return (after the *Hajj*) free from all sins as if he were born anew'.[88] The influence of the *Hajj* pilgrimage appears to have been twofold. First, it was used by those already committed to participating in defensive jihad in Iraq, as a form of absolution (for past sins). Second, it appears that some young Arab nationals were targeted and recruited by individuals whom they met during the *Hajj*.[89]

Whilst the three-day *Hajj* pilgrimage is in the Islamic calendar, the *umra* is a shortened pilgrimage (in Mecca, Saudi Arabia) that can be performed in only a few hours, at any time of the year. Individuals who performed the *umra* also appeared to do so as a form of absolution (for past sins) prior to travelling to Iraq. Anecdotally, the few that did perform the *umra* appeared to be already committed to Islamist terrorist-related activities including the use of self-sacrificial ('martyrdom/suicide') attacks. Examples include Jordanian national Raa'id al-Banna, who having performed the *umra*, blew himself up one month later (on 28 February 2005) in Iraq, killing 120 civilians. Fellow Jordanian and radical ideologue Omar Yusuf Juma, a veteran Arab foreign fighter of 1980s Afghanistan and Bosnia, also insisted on performing the *umra* before travelling to Iraq and serving alongside Abu Musab al-Zarqawi. The fact that the *umra* can be performed at any time of the year as noted above, suggests that there was a degree of urgency and an unwillingness to wait for the next *Hajj* or *Ramadan*.

Whilst this book is not proposing a cause–effect relationship, it is striking that 55 per cent of Arab foreign fighters in 2006–2007 travelled during, or after, one of these Islamic practices. From this it can be deduced that involvement in these annual events in the Sunni Islamic calendar may have stimulated their feelings towards their co-religionists in Iraq, whilst at the same time gaining a degree of solace, aware of the possible realisation that they may not return alive. Such a belief may be equated to British soldiers attending

Christian services in the Kuwaiti desert, prior to the invasion of Iraq in March 2003. As a journalist embedded with the Royal Marines, Tim Butcher, noted 'the unit's chaplain has been a particularly busy man. The number of soldiers attending his services has grown steadily over the past few weeks as the seriousness of what many of them might face in the coming days steadily became apparent'.[90]

Anecdotally, religiosity influenced the mobilisation of individuals such as Tunisian foreign fighter Walid Muhammad al-Masmoodi, who 'readily admitted that the ... exhortations of clerics were the primary influences on his decision to go to fight in the jihad'.[91] It is also instructive that the father of one Saudi foreign fighter (Muqrin al-Utaybi), who was killed in Fallujah in November 2004, blames the clerics who 'corrupted the minds of young men' by calling for 'jihad against the occupiers as a duty for all who are able'.[92] The concept of religiosity is not necessarily realised in Western societies, yet for the Arab world it is not considered radical to travel to a foreign country and defend fellow Muslims. To be automatically labelled an Islamist terrorist based on travelling to Iraq to resist the US-led invasion appears largely to be a Western political conceptualisation, one that has become conventional wisdom. However, such labelling is not scientific and/or evidence-based, and only focuses on those Islamist terrorists who attack civilians and non-combatants, ignoring the many other Arabs who are fighting only the US-led coalition. In many ways, it is analogous to labelling every English football fan as a hooligan, simply based on the behaviour of some, whether a minority or a majority. The uncomfortable and perhaps inconvenient truth is that religiosity played a major role in the initial mobilisation of many ordinary Arab foreign fighters to Iraq – Muslim land was being occupied by non-Muslims, and this necessitated the need to fight in defence co-religionists.

The Epitome of an Ordinary Arab Foreign Fighter in Iraq – Ahmad Abdullah al-Shaya

The biography of Ahmad Abdullah al-Shaya is perhaps the epitome of an ordinary Arab foreign fighter. He had no known pre-existing links to any Islamist groups (violent or non-violent), yet he was motivated to fight defensive jihad in Iraq. He was born in 1984 in the town of Buraidah in central Saudi Arabia, known to be 'a pietist community characterised by an extreme social conservatism' and 'the heartland of the Saudi Islamist landscape'.[93] Educationally, he dropped out of school 'where half the classes were in religious subjects' and domestically he had endured an abusive father.[94] After a short time in a gang in an area where 'at least half of all men under twenty-five were unemployed', al-Shaya and notably his cousin and close friend, Adil, both turned to religion and started attending their local mosque.[95] Their increased religiosity happened to coincide with the 2003 US-led invasion of Iraq, and a resultant environment in Saudi Arabia where 'both local imams and some senior clerics were encouraging participation in the Iraqi resistance'.[96] The narrative was for the need for *jihad ad-difaa* (defensive jihad) and *fard ayn* (an individual duty) of all able-bodied Muslims to travel to defend their co-religionists against a non-Muslim force who were occupying Muslim territory. A year later (April 2004) the Abu Ghraib prison abuses became public knowledge, and appeared to be the 'final straw'[97] for both al-Shaya and his cousin. In October 2004 during the Islamic fasting month of *Ramadan*, al-Shaya and Adil decided to travel to Iraq in order to 'to fight the Americans on Noble Jihad'.[98] From a transcript of his subsequent interrogation (conducted in Saudi Arabia), his 'objective was to kill the Americans, policemen, national guards and the American collaborators'.[99]

However, having arrived in Iraq, his immediate environment involved training and indoctrination, which included further references to the Abu Ghraib prison abuses, revenge and the benefits of martyrdom. The leader of their group in Iraq demanded to know: 'How many of you will die to avenge Abu Ghraib? Those most blessed among you in God's eyes are noble *shaheeds* [martyrs][100] ready to go to heaven on a martyrdom mission for Allah Almighty'.[101] Within less than two months of his arrival, on 24 December 2004, al-Shaya carried out a vehicle-borne self-sacrificial ('martyrdom/suicide') attack outside the Jordanian Embassy in Baghdad, which killed twelve Iraqi civilians.[102] He, however, survived (although badly burnt and missing fingers) and after a series of interrogations, he became the 'poster boy' of the Saudi rehabilitation programme denouncing Islamist terrorism in all its forms.[103] Al-Shaya's motivation to travel to Iraq appears rather unremarkable, devoid of extremist rhetoric, but driven mainly by his own sense of religious duty. His biography appears ordinary. He was a young single male, originating from a religious community in a traditionally conservative Arab country; he was influenced by his cousin, Adil, through kinship ties; and was motivated to defend his co-religionists in Iraq. His stated enemy included the Americans but interestingly (accepting that it was a *post hoc* rationalisation), he also included the Iraqi police which suggested a sectarian (anti-Shi'a) motivation. The key aspect in his account is that he departed to Iraq to defend his co-religionists, yet less than two months after his arrival, he was targeting them. Why?

The Trajectory from Defensive Jihad to Islamist Terrorism in Iraq

Introduction

To empirically test the argument that the original rationale behind many Arab foreign fighters' involvement in defensive jihad in Iraq was largely to fight the US-led coalition, it is worth examining their targeting patterns in Iraq from 2003 onwards. The challenge to such research, however, is that the data on conventional attacks (shootings, mine and IED attacks) that targeted coalition troops rarely mention the perpetrator, let alone record whether he/she was an Iraqi national or an Arab foreign fighter. Such a challenge may be overcome by examining self-sacrificial ('martyrdom/suicide') attacks instead, which often identify both the targets and the perpetrators. Despite the existence of overlaps and the challenge of defining civilians and non-combatants (as noted in Chapter 1), research that includes the disaggregation of targets may offer a more nuanced understanding of the targeting rationales (military and/or civilian targets), and the perpetrators (Arab foreign fighters and/or Islamist terrorists) who adopted them. This concept is not entirely new; for example, one study on 'suicide bombers' in Iraq conducted by Katherine Seifert and Clark McCauley argued that 'suicide attacks must be disaggregated by target in order to understand these attacks as the expression of different insurgent priorities'.[104]

Whilst Seifert and McCauley argued for the disaggregation of targets of 'suicide attacks', perhaps they were responding to Martha Crenshaw who first recognised the 'over-aggregation' of the tactic of suicide attacks:

> The tactic is usually treated as though it were a single unified method of violence.
> All types of suicide attacks are merged together, despite their serving different
> instrumental purposes: destroying military targets . . . killing enemy civilians, or
> massacring co-religionists in factional struggles. For instance, why do some
> groups target civilians and others military assets or individual officials? Why
> should the manner of violence matter more than the target or the purpose?[105]

Such support for the disaggregation of targets offers academic ballast to the suggestion that, whilst both tactics in Iraq involved an attacker who 'does not expect to survive the mission',[106] labelling all self-sacrificial attacks as 'suicide attacks' regardless of the intended target, is not scientific. Assaf Moghadam makes a nuanced (albeit controversial) argument suggesting that a suicide attack should 'not be labelled a terrorist attack if it is targeted against members of an army, because attacks are ordinarily labelled terrorist attacks when they are aimed at non-combatants'.[107] This argument suggests a more subtle approach is needed to understand non-state self-sacrificial attacks, with a greater emphasis on the intended target, rather than the likelihood that the perpetrator will die. For example, the self-sacrificial ('martyrdom/suicide') attack against the USS *Cole* in October 2000 was intended as a symbolic act of terrorism to elicit an over-reaction by the United States, and not an act of jihad or guerrilla warfare intended to whittle down the US Navy's fighting capability. Therefore, aware of the 'lack of a common definition of the concept of suicide terrorism',[108] at least focusing on the intended target and why it was attacked, offers a greater degree of conceptual clarity when trying to understand the perpetrators.

This concept is perhaps somewhat provocative, in that it is easier to comprehend the pejorative sound-bite of 'suicide attack' regardless of the actual intent of the mission (as outlined above with the USS *Cole* attack). Perhaps in the post-9/11 landscape it has become conventional wisdom to adopt the label 'suicide' despite the lack of nuance, yet prior to the 9/11 attacks such use was less widespread. For example, take the IRA terrorists in the Maze Prison outside Belfast in 1981, the most infamous amongst them being Bobby Sands, who went on a 'hunger strike' with the explicit intention of putting pressure on the British Government to grant IRA prisoners a return to 'special category status'.[109] In the post-9/11 landscape, their 'hunger strikes' would probably be labelled 'suicide starvation' and they would be labelled 'suicide starvers', yet whilst their action did result in the deaths of ten of them, this was not their primary intention, it was a by-product.[110] The same arguably applies to self-sacrificial ('martyrdom/suicide') attacks by non-state actors, where the intended target and overall intention is a more tangible variable, rather than the fact that they died as part of the attack. For example, the Viet Minh conducted multiple sacrificial attacks against the French strongpoint during the battle of Dien Bien Phu in French Indo-China (now Vietnam). According to Jules Roy, 'every [Vietminh] soldier's ambition was to sacrifice himself',[111] permitting Vietminh battalions to ensure that attacks were 'preceded by a group of dynamiters with orders to make openings in the barbed-wire defences and destroy the blockhouses, blowing themselves up with them'.[112] Again it is clear that the intent of the Vietminh soldiers was not to commit suicide *per se*, but to lead the advance against a foreign army of occupation. Arguably, they were also participating in their version of a defensive jihad and were using self-sacrificial attacks against military strongpoints. Although many self-sacrificial ('martyrdom/suicide') attacks in Iraq targeted civilians and non-combatants, many did not, and therefore the phenomenon deserves more nuanced analysis.

The Data

Based on the idea that the defensive jihad in Iraq was a struggle to defend fellow Muslims from subjugation, it would be reasonable to expect that the primary target for engagement by Arab foreign fighters would be US-led coalition forces. The casualty statistics for coalition forces and Iraqi civilians, extracted from *iCasualties* and *Iraq Body Count* respectively, whilst identifying casualties, unfortunately do not allow for a disaggregation of the perpetrators, in order to identify Arab foreign fighters.[113] However, using data on self-sacrificial ('martyrdom/suicide') attacks, permits analysis of the actors (Arab foreign fighters or Islamist terrorists) and the opportunity to examine the trajectory between them. It is assumed that as Arab foreign fighters 'constituted the bulk of suicide bombers',[114] the majority of self-sacrificial ('martyrdom/suicide') attacks were conducted by Arab foreign fighters/Islamist terrorists, and not Iraqis.[115] This was confirmed by Ahmed Hashim, who recognised that Iraqi nationalist insurgents were reluctant to engage in 'suicide attacks', and disliked 'the barbaric and provocative behaviour of the foreigners'.[116] One explanation offered by Abu Musab al-Zarqawi, was that 'the Iraqi brothers still prefer safety and returning to the arms of their wives, where nothing frightens them'.[117]

Extracted from the dataset, Figure 3.3 suggests that the initial targeting by Arab foreign fighters was aimed at US-led coalition forces involving self-sacrificial ('martyrdom/suicide') attacks, however the targeting soon switched to Iraqi civilians and non-combatants.

The reliability of the data in Figure 3.3 is supported by other academic studies: the peak in 2005 is also present in the analysis conducted by Mohammed Hafez,[118] while both peaks in 2005 and 2007 are present in the findings by Katherine Seifert and Clark McCauley.[119] Also, the use of the data on the number of actual attacks as opposed to the number of casualties, removes a potential distortion in the analysis, as civilian casualties were vastly higher than coalition and Iraqi troops, due to their lack of protection and hence viewed as 'soft targets'.[120] What was apparent in Iraq from 2005 onwards was that civilians, mainly Shi'a Muslims, were the target of choice. The 2005 spike broadly coincides with the Iraqi elections, where the once ostracised Shi'a were about to take over control of the Iraqi parliament (leading to Sunni fears of disenfranchisement), while the 2007 spike appears to have been a reaction to the US troop surge. The increased targeting of Iraqi civilians as a response to the US troop surge appears incongruous, in that one may reasonably have expected an increase in US casualties. However, US forces had fortified their bases and adopted enhanced

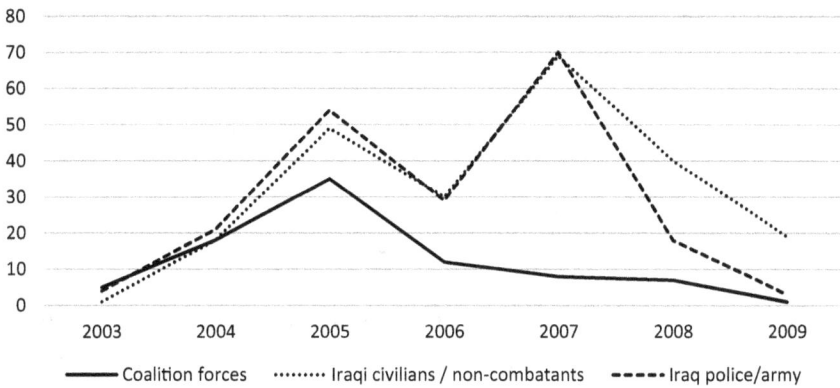

Figure showing a line graph with y-axis from 0 to 80 and x-axis years 2003 to 2009. Legend: —— Coalition forces ········ Iraqi civilians / non-combatants ----- Iraq police/army

Figure 3.3 Targeting comparison of self-sacrificial ('martyrdom/suicide') attacks in Iraq (2003–2009). n1=86 self-sacrificial attacks perpetrated by Arab foreign fighters targeting the US-led coalition troops. *Source*: Book dataset (incorporating CPOST, iCasualties, and GTD); n2=226 self-sacrificial attacks (by unknown perpetrators, but assumed non-Iraqi Sunni Arabs) targeting Iraqi civilians and non-combatants. *Source*: GTD database;[121] n3= 200 self-sacrificial attacks perpetrated by Arab foreign fighters targeting Iraqi police and army units. *Source*: GTD database.

force protection measures,[122] often leaving the Iraqi military to guard many of the static roadblocks and checkpoints, which were more vulnerable to attack. The question therefore is why were Iraqi civilians targeted? Was it just because they were 'soft targets'?

Figure 3.3 shows the point of inflection (in late 2004) that resulted in the strategic shift to increase self-sacrificial ('martyrdom/suicide') attacks against Iraqi civilians/non-combatants and Iraqi police/soldiers, with a corresponding reduction (in 2005) of such attacks against coalition troops. It suggests that the initial targeting of coalition troops was consistent with the notion of defensive jihad, whilst the later targeting of Iraqi civilians and non-combatants was consistent with the notion of *takfir*, within the context of Islamist terrorism. It is also suggested that whilst the almost parallel targeting of Iraqi police/soldiers and Iraqi civilians/non-combatants was consistent with the notion of *takfir*, the targeting of Iraqi police/soldiers was still more akin to defensive jihad. Regarding Iraqi civilians and non-combatants, the Islamist ideological pendulum had swung from defensive jihad to Islamist terrorism, although for the Arab foreign fighters and Iraqi Sunni fighters, it remained framed under the rubric of a defensive jihad. It appears that the shift in targeting was more as a result of ideological factors, rather than the fact that hardened military targets were more difficult to attack. What is also demonstrated in Figure 3.3 is the coexistence and overlaps of defensive jihad and Islamist terrorism, which may also explain their widespread conflation, intentional or not, in academia, the media and among policy makers.

A further extraction from Figure 3.3 produces Figure 3.4, which specifically disaggregates the targets that involved self-sacrificial ('martyrdom/suicide') attacks.

Figure 3.4 represents the targets that were killed by each self-sacrificial attack, rather than the possible intended target, which would have been largely speculative. In a study of 'suicide attacks' in Iraq, Seifert and McCauley claimed to have 'identified the intended target of each suicide attack' and coded accordingly.[123] The research conducted for this book found such identification is, in reality, largely subjective. At best, research can generally only identify the cluster of targets, a policy adopted by GTD, for example Government (General); Military; Private Citizens and Property; or Religious Figures/Institutions.[124] Despite such clusters of targets and the obvious overlaps, the research reveals that 37 per cent of attacks involved Iraqi civilians and non-combatants including Shi'a religious figures; 24 per cent involved Iraqi government and businesses; 28 per cent involved Iraqi police and troops; and only 11 per cent involved foreign troops.

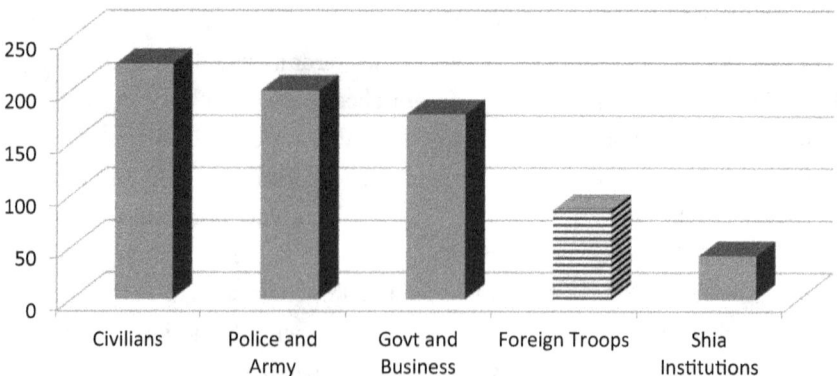

Figure 3.4 Targeting comparison of 731 self-sacrificial attacks in Iraq (2003–2009). n1=86 self-sacrificial attacks targeting foreign troops. *Source*: Book dataset (incorporating CPOST, iCasualties, and GTD); and n2=645 self-sacrificial attacks targeting Iraqi police and army, Iraq civilians and non-combatants, Iraqi government, Iraqi businesses, and Shi'a institutions. *Source*: GTD database.

Although touched on in Chapter 1, it is worth clarifying that Iraqi police or military 'recruits' are considered civilians and/or non-combatants, and that attacking them is an act of Islamist terrorism. For example, the GTD database records that on 11 February 2004, a 'suicide bomber driving a car targeted Iraqi military recruits waiting outside an army recruitment centre in Baghdad'.[125] However, the label 'recruit' is potentially misleading as they were in fact simply 'job-seekers'.[126] This would also apply to Iraqi police recruitment centres where individuals are 'recruits in the process of signing up to work for the Iraqi police'.[127] This disaggregation (between civilians looking for work and members of Iraq's armed forces) also conforms to the International Committee of the Red Cross (ICRC), in that civilians are defined 'as persons who are not members of the armed forces'.[128] Iraqi volunteers outside army or police recruitment centres would thus be considered civilians, and attacking them would reasonably be considered a terrorist act. It is this more nuanced picture of the Iraqi jihad that allows researchers to conduct greater in-depth analysis in order to produce findings that are more scientifically based and empirically grounded.

Accepting that most Iraqi government posts including the police and army were made up of Iraqi Shi'a,[129] research suggests that 89 per cent of all self-sacrificial ('martyrdom/suicide') attacks in Iraq targeted Iraqi Shi'a Muslims – in effect confirming the *takfiri* ideology of the perpetrators. The ideology supporting the attacks that targeted Iraqi businesses (24 per cent) and civilians and non-combatants (37 per cent), is best understood as *takfiri* in nature in that it justified terrorist self-sacrificial ('martyrdom/suicide') attacks against fellow Muslims (amounting to 61 per cent of attacks). The ideology supporting the attacks against the remaining 28 per cent (Iraqi army and police forces) is also *takfiri* in nature, but is complicated by the fact of being more consistent with the notion of defensive jihad, in that they were military targets, on duty and operating against the Iraqi Sunni insurgents and Arab foreign fighters. Overlaps notwithstanding (particularly *takfiri* self-sacrificial ('martyrdom/suicide') attacks against the Iraqi police and military), this conceptualisation permits the disaggregation of Arab foreign fighters and Islamist terrorists in the unique context of the Iraq insurgency. Using the data gathered for this book and working within the conceptual parameters outlined above, the Arab foreign fighters who crossed the threshold from defensive jihad to Islamist terrorism, by targeting Iraqi civilians and non-combatants, appeared to be driven by many situational factors having arrived in Iraq. This included exposure to Al Qaeda in Iraq's ideology and subsequent indoctrination and training.

Grievances and Ideology

The notion of grievances and ideology are nestled together due to their relationship with radicalisation and extremism, in that they appear to have been central to the more extreme positions taken by many Arab foreign fighters having arrived in Iraq. The two macro-level factors embedded within Islamist doctrine include the concept of *takfir* and the employment of self-sacrificial ('martyrdom/suicide') attacks against Iraqi civilians and non-combatants. Noted earlier in this chapter, *takfir* is the practice of declaring a fellow Muslim an 'unbeliever' (*kafr*) and is often used to sanction violence against Arab regimes who are judged insufficiently religious. Importantly, these macro-level factors are broadly consistent with Salafi-jihadism, an ideology that supports 'violence and revolution'.[130] According to Assaf Moghadam, Salafi-jihadis 'engage in *takfir* ... condone the targeting of civilians ... and support the use of suicide operations'.[131] The label Salafi-jihadis (whilst often used by themselves) is more akin to Islamist terrorists, despite it being a pejorative term. The linkage between the *takfir* and self-sacrificial attacks in Iraq is that having been designated a *kafr*, the employment of self-sacrificial attacks is a tactical choice of the method of attack. However, overlaps notwithstanding, *takfir* and the use of self-sacrificial attacks (against Iraqi civilians and non-combatants) are disaggregated in this chapter in an attempt to gain a more nuanced understanding of the situational circumstances that inspired Arab foreign fighter involvement in Islamist terrorist-related activities in Iraq.

Takfir against Iraqi Shi'a Muslims

The grievances against Iraqi Shi'a Muslims became more pronounced after the transfer of sovereignty to an Iraqi interim government in June 2004. This led to an ideological switch from targeting the far enemy (the US-led coalition) to the near enemy (Iraqi Shi'as)[132] and is supported by the 2004 inflection point in Figure 3.3. The grievances against the Shi'a, articulated by Abu Musab al-Zarqawi, included their 'control of the institutions of the state'; their 'reign over the army and police apparatus'; and their desire to 'establish a Shi'a state stretching from Iran through Iraq, Syria and Lebanon'.[133] These grievances were perceived by al-Zarqawi as a threat entailing the 'suppression' and 'liquidation' of the Iraqi Sunni Muslims.[134] His ideological solution was *takfir* against the Shi'a in that 'fighting against the Shi'a is the way to drag the *ummah* into the battle',[135] involving local Iraqi Sunnis and Sunni foreign fighters. On the battlefields in Iraq (as demonstrated in Figure 3.3), this led to an almost parallel upsurge in violence directed against Iraqi Shi'a civilians, non-combatants (including those who were in the process of signing up to work in Iraq's security forces), and operational Iraqi police and army units. This became the watershed or point of inflection of the Iraq insurgency where the defensive jihad against the US-led coalition, whilst now including Iraqi forces, also began to morph into Islamist terrorism by targeting civilians and non-combatants, under the overarching Islamist ideology of *takfir*.

It is illuminating that even al-Zarqawi's former radical ideological mentor, Abu Muhammad al-Maqdisi, expressed his concerns about the 'indiscriminate violence and *takfir* of entire groups of people because it is wrong to do so and hurts the image of Islam'.[136] Unperturbed, al-Zarqawi later announced the establishment (in May 2005) of the *Al-Baraa bin Malik Brigade* comprising of a 'suicide brigade' within Al Qaeda in Iraq,[137] and issued a religious *fatwa* in order to 'clarify the position of the *Shari'a* regarding such incidents in which Muslims are killed incidentally'. Al-Zarqawi argued that:

> The legitimacy of ... killing a number of Muslims even if it is known that they are likely to be there at the time ... is justified under the principle of *daroorah* [necessity], due to the fact that it is impossible ... to distinguish between them and those infidels against whom war is being waged ... it is permissible to commit this evil ... in order to ward off a greater evil, namely, the evil of suspending jihad.[138]

At first glance it appears difficult to fully comprehend the logic behind this *fatwa*, and it arguably supports the view that al-Zarqawi was 'theologically illiterate'[139] and possessed 'few intellectual inclinations'.[140] Yet on closer inspection, al-Zarqawi's use of the Arabic word *daroorah* is in complete harmony with the 'doctrine of necessity', whereby according to H.H.A. Cooper, terrorism may be 'justified as a response to something even more unsavoury',[141] which in al-Zarqawi's case was the 'evil of suspending jihad'. As Cooper further argued, an 'understanding of this viewpoint, whether acceptable or not, is essential to an understanding of the terrorist'.[142] The result, as Figure 3.3 demonstrates, was that Iraqi Shi'a civilians and non-combatants were heavily targeted in 2004 and 2005 by Islamist terrorists leading to concern within Al Qaeda. In July 2005, Al Qaeda's deputy Ayman al-Zawahiri, wrote to Abu Musab al-Zarqawi concerned that 'many of your Muslim admirers amongst the common folk are wondering about your attacks on the Shi'a ... what loss will befall us if we did not attack the Shi'a?'[143] The main concern articulated by Ayman al-Zawahiri was losing 'the popular support of the Muslim masses in Iraq'.[144]

The book dataset has information on how 143 Arab foreign fighters and/or Islamist terrorists died in Iraq.[145] It finds that seventy-seven died in self-sacrificial ('martyrdom/suicide') attacks although their intended target was unknown. Out of the remaining sixty-six individuals for whom data were available, 77 per cent died fighting the US-led coalition (in gun battles or self-sacrificial ('martyrdom/ suicide') attacks), while the remaining 23 per cent died targeting Iraqi civilians and non-combatants. This finding however conflicts with the earlier finding that 61 per cent of attacks targeted Iraqi businesses, civilians and non-combatants. It is suggested that these figures perhaps expose the challenges of terrorism research, where the perpetrators are often intentionally anonymous. The view taken in this book is that despite the apparent anonymity of many of the attackers, as noted earlier in this chapter, it is reasonably assumed that they were (non-Iraqi) Arab foreign fighters, turned Islamist terrorists. Thus, the 23 per cent of identified Arab foreign fighters who died targeting Iraqi civilians and non-combatants may therefore be considered representative of the larger cohort of Islamist terrorists responsible for the 61 per cent of terrorist attacks that targeted Iraqi businesses, civilians and non–combatants.

The Ideology Supporting 'Suicide Attacks' against Shi'a Civilians and Non-Combatants

There have been many studies examining the motivations and circumstances of individuals who perpetrate self-sacrificial ('martyrdom/suicide') attacks in Iraq,[146] but despite the inclusion of impressive data and evidence of academic rigour, they still tend to aggregate military targets (coalition and Iraqi forces) and civilians and non-combatants. One study authored by Mohammed Hafez, argued that the circumstances behind the 'suicide bombings' in Iraq were the 'humiliation of Muslims at the hands of foreigners, impotence of official Muslim governments in the face of hegemonic powers, and redemption through faithful sacrifice'.[147] Another study by Assaf Moghadam, believed the circumstances included 'anger at the United States ... a belief in the need to defend a religion that is perceived to be under attack ... and reaping the benefits of martyrdom'.[148] In both findings, the common grievance is against a foreign occupation and an ideology of action underpinned by martyrdom and redemption, yet the grievance(s) and ideology do not explain satisfactorily why Iraqi Muslim civilians and non-combatants were targeted. What appears particularly contradictory is how the need to defend a religion translated on the ground in Iraq into attacks targeting co-religionists. This is answered by acknowledging that within the sectarian (Sunni–Shi'a) context in Iraq, the Shi'a were often not considered co-religionists. Perhaps therefore, there is a need to defend Sunni Islam, rather than a religion, that is perceived to be under attack.

The ideology supporting self-sacrificial ('martyrdom/suicide') attacks against Shi'a civilians and non-combatants appears to have been adopted more readily by Saudi foreign fighters,[149] yet as Anthony Cordesman noted correctly, 'the vast majority of Saudi militants who have entered Iraq were not terrorist sympathizers before the war'[150] (as noted earlier). Again, whilst it is broadly accepted that 'most Saudi recruits genuinely did hold a deep belief in and desire for martyrdom',[151] this desire for martyrdom should not necessarily be conflated with a desire to conduct self-sacrificial ('martyrdom/suicide') attacks against Iraqi civilians and non-combatants. First, by examining the dataset, although Saudi foreign fighters were overrepresented among 'suicide bombers' on a numerical basis, they were not on a *per capita* basis (2.16 per million), trailing for example Kuwait at 5.13 per million. Second, by disaggregating the targets for self-sacrificial attacks conducted by Saudi foreign fighters, 54 per cent of attacks targeted Iraqi civilians, with the remaining 46 per cent targeting coalition troops. This paradox returns to the pejorative labelling of all self-sacrificial attacks being 'suicide attacks', and hides the much deeper motivations, ideologies and targeting rationales. It raises the question that attacking a well-fortified coalition base may only be possible by using a vehicle-borne improvised explosive device (VBIED), resulting in a convergence of both the ideology of martyrdom and tactical necessity. This paradox also highlights the issue of conflating the notions of *istishhaad* (martyrdom) and *intihaar* (suicide).

Istishhaad or Intihaar in Iraq

The academic discourse on martyrdom (operations) and suicide (attacks) is measured and cautious. Noted in Chapter 1, some preeminent scholars including David Cook, place the term 'martyrdom operations' inside quotation marks, due to a declared unwillingness 'to take a stand on the question of whether people who die during the course of these actions [suicide attacks] are actually martyrs or not'.[152] Karin Fierke takes a slightly different tack, and chooses to adopt the term 'suicide/martyrdom [in order] to highlight the tension in the relationship between the two concepts'.[153] It is therefore instructive that some Islamist ideologues also have a similar debate. One in particular, a Syrian ideologue and veteran Afghan Arab Shaykh Abu Basir al-Tartusi, published a *fatwa* (*Suspicions of Sin in Martyrdom or Suicide Attacks*) making the distinction between 'suicide attacks' and 'martyrdom operations'. Al-Tartusi argued that suicide 'attacks are closer to suicide [*intihaar*] than to martyrdom [*istishhaad*] and they are forbidden because of sins they may potentially entail ... which sow discord between Muslims and their '*ulama*'. However, al-Tartusi supported the notion of martyrdom gained through *inghimasi* operations (covered in detail in Chapter 4), conducted by 'plunging into enemy lines ... not to kill one's self, but rather to enter into situations where one is killed by the enemy'.[154] Implicit in his view is the notion of martyrdom gained by militarily plunging into the enemy lines, although he (unhelpfully) fails to disaggregate the targets of 'suicide attacks', leaving open the prospect of such attacks being employed against both military and civilian targets.

One influential study on Arab foreign fighters in Iraq, which also appeared to conflate the notion of 'martyrdom' and 'suicide', was authored by the US Combating Training Center (CTC) staff, Joseph Felter and Brian Fishman, *Al Qaeda's Foreign Fighters in Iraq: A First Look at the Sinjar Records*.[155] Despite the written records in Arabic showing *istishhaadi* – 'one who desires martyrdom',[156] the authors 'coded all such individuals "suicide bombers" in an effort to avoid confusion'.[157] Based on this arguably reductionist coding, Felter and Fishman found that '85.2 per cent ... of Libyan fighters listed "suicide bomber" as their work in Iraq',[158] and concluded that 'Libyan fighters were much more likely than other nationalities to be listed as suicide bombers'.[159] Perhaps equally surprising is that other scholars have referenced and regurgitated these findings uncritically.[160] Based on the data collected on 110 confirmed self-sacrificial ('martyrdom/suicide') attacks in Iraq,[161] Libyans do not appear to feature so strongly, appearing only ninth equal in comparison with other Arab countries, as presented in Figure 3.5.

Examined another way, one would also expect Libyans as a percentage of the overall Libyan cohort to be more strongly represented as perpetrators of self-sacrificial ('martyrdom/suicide') attacks, in line with the finding of Felter and Fishman. Again, this appears not to be the case. Using the data on the perpetrators of self-sacrificial ('martyrdom/suicide') attacks in Figure 3.5, and the data on the geographic origin of all 721 Arab foreign fighters in Iraq (in Figure 3.1), the country of origin of perpetrators of self-sacrificial ('martyrdom/suicide') attacks as a percentage of each national cohort may be calculated, as presented in Figure 3.6.

Naturally, caution is required when interpreting the dataset. For example, the high Lebanese position may be due to greater publicity of their biographies as a direct result of their involvement in self-sacrificial attacks, or because many

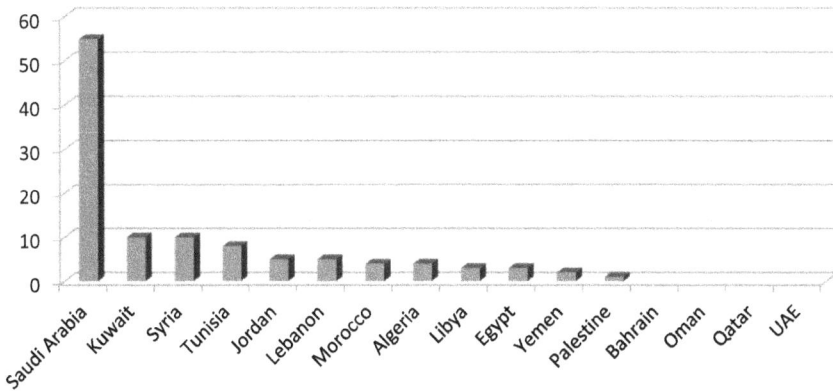

Figure 3.5 Country of origin of perpetrators of self-sacrificial ('martyrdom/suicide') attacks (n=110).

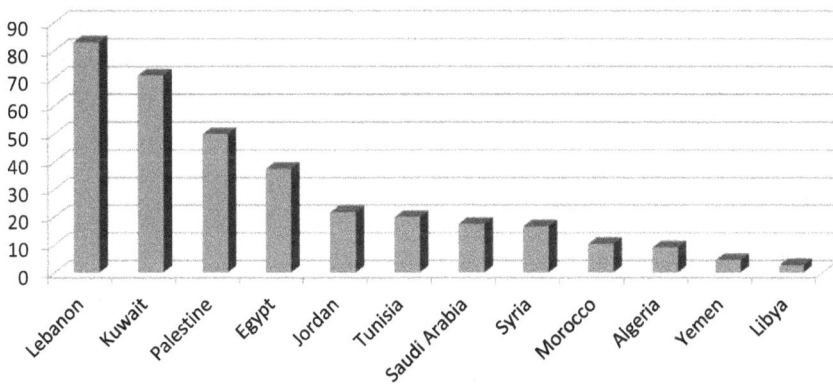

Figure 3.6 Country of origin of perpetrators of self-sacrificial attacks as a percentage of each national cohort (n=110)

Palestinian refugees in Lebanon often used the pseudonym of al-Labnani. In the same light, a lack of publicity may also partially explain the findings from Figures 3.5 and 3.6, which suggest that Libyan fighters were much less likely than other nationalities to be perpetrators of self-sacrificial ('martyrdom/suicide') attacks. Be that as it may, an interesting corollary to the Felter and Fishman report is that two of the Libyan so-called 'suicide bombers'[162] were languishing in an Iraqi prison by 2012.[163]

Again, the point to be made here is perhaps the need for a more nuanced understanding amongst academics, the media and policy makers of *istishhaad* (martyrdom) leading to more contextualised analysis of such data. In Chapter 4, this dichotomy reoccurs in another CTC report analysing Islamic State personnel records that directly translates *istishhaadi* as a 'suicide bomber',[164] without even contemplating the complexities of the meaning and context of martyrdom in both Islamic and Islamist ideology. It is interesting that there remains, even with the backdrop of the Syrian jihad, a lack of consensus amongst scholars concerning the concepts of self-sacrificial ('martyrdom/suicide') attacks, as there was in Iraq between al-Zarqawi and both al-Zawahiri and al-Maqdisi. To address this disharmony in Iraq and to encourage Arab foreign fighters to also target civilians and non-combatants, there appears to have been terrorist training and indoctrination that helped to reinforce al-Zarqawi's ideology pertaining to self-sacrificial ('martyrdom/suicide') attacks.

Terrorist Training and Indoctrination

The existence of indoctrination and training is viewed as a 'more recent trend' that is nestled within the 'ideology and structure of terrorist groups',[165] and arguably reflects the nexus between defensive jihad and Islamist terrorism. Once an individual decided to participate in defensive jihad in Iraq, unless they had received prior military training (possibly as conscripts in their home countries), they entered training camps established in either Syria or Iraq. One Syrian foreign fighter, Abu Ibrahim, recalled how his group was transported 'across the border and then into villages on the Iraqi side; and from there the Iraqi contacts would take the *mujahhideen* to training camps'.[166] According to Thomas Hegghammer, these 'training camps generated an ultra-masculine culture of violence which brutalized the volunteers and broke down barriers to the use of violence'.[167] Some Arab foreign fighters were trained to be *shuhada* (martyrs) leading to their subsequent involvement in self-sacrificial ('martyrdom/suicide') attacks, aimed at both military and civilian targets, although at the group (Al Qaeda in Iraq) level, the targeting distinction appeared to be over-ridden by tactical and strategic necessities. The tactical necessities often involved attacking hardened and fortified military bases or vehicles, whilst the strategic necessities included the overarching requirement to topple the Shi'a-led government of Iraq.

A unique insight into the training of perpetrators of self-sacrificial ('martyrdom/suicide') attacks in Iraq was obtained in a rare 2005 interview for *Time* magazine by Aparisim Ghosh. Although the perpetrator was an Iraqi (not a foreign Arab), Marwan Abu Ubaydah's story is instructive. According to Ghosh, Marwan admitted to having undergone a programme to discipline the mind and cleanse the soul. The training, 'supervised by field commanders and Sunni clerics was mainly psychological and spiritual'. They were 'expected to immerse themselves in spiritual contemplation and prayer'. In addition to reading the Quran, they also read about the history of defensive jihad, in particular the stories of Afghan Arab martyrdom, written by Abdullah Azzam.[168] Noting from Chapter 2 that no Afghan Arabs were understood to have committed self-sacrificial ('martyrdom/suicide') attacks during the Afghan jihad,[169] it is instructive that Sunni clerics in Iraq had relied on such stories of martyrdom gained through conventional fighting against Soviet military forces, in order to motivate their 'suicide bombers' to attack Iraqi women and children in the markets of Baghdad. It appears to be a total ideological distortion, disingenuous in the extreme, and by hijacking the original notion of martyrdom extolled by Abdullah Azzam, Al Qaeda in Iraq demonstrated their inability to construct 'a theological argument justifying such attacks'.[170]

Indoctrination

As mentioned earlier, Islamist terrorism in Iraq was uniquely different from the Islamist terrorism undertaken (after the Afghan jihad) by veteran Afghan Arabs, in that in Iraq, defensive jihad and Islamist terrorism coexisted in the same time and space. The trajectory in Iraq from involvement in defensive jihad to subsequent participation in Islamist terrorism did not require travel to, or training in, another country; it all took place within the war zone of Iraq. However, much of the literature on domestic Islamist terrorism presupposes correctly that a lot of the recruitment, possible indoctrination and radicalisation prior to involvement in Islamist terrorism, occurs in an individual's home country. This nevertheless appears not to be true concerning Iraq, where individuals had already left their home countries and committed themselves to participate in defensive jihad, and as suggested earlier in this chapter, the majority of Arab foreign fighters arriving in Iraq appeared to be ordinary men, and were not (yet) necessarily radicalised. This implies that most radicalisation that led to subsequent involvement in Islamist terrorism in Iraq actually took place, in Iraq. With this in mind, scholarly literature explaining the involvement of foreigners in terrorism in Iraq, may (in some cases) have been better situated had it more fully acknowledged the context and situational environment of the Iraqi battlefield, that included indoctrination, training and the brutalising effects of combat.

The notion that some Arab foreign fighters were indoctrinated (and arguably radicalised) in Iraq to become perpetrators of self-sacrificial ('martyrdom/

suicide') attacks targeting Iraqi civilians and non-combatants is worthy of examination, as it challenges the conventional wisdom that most foreign fighters arrived in Iraq, somehow already indoctrinated. The term 'indoctrination' is understood to mean the teaching of 'a person or group systematically to accept partisan or tendentious ideas uncritically'.[171] A distinction needs to be drawn between indoctrination and brainwashing, in that brainwashing involves 'the surrender of strongly held beliefs and the adoption of new beliefs often diametrically opposed to them'.[172] Therefore, whilst indoctrination involves a gentle transition to more immoderate ideas, brainwashing suggests a conversion involving a complete U-turn in beliefs. Mohammed Hafez argues correctly that 'volunteers for suicide attacks are not brainwashed victims of opportunistic recruiters, nor are they manipulated individuals who are fooled by calculating terrorists',[173] yet this book argues that many were *indoctrinated*. By volunteering for defensive jihad in Iraq, most Arab foreign fighters possessed feelings of martial fervour, yet volunteering for self-sacrificial attacks would require some degree of indoctrination, rather than brainwashing. Quintan Wiktorowicz adopts the alternative label of 'culturing' to portray the transmission of 'information to persuade audiences to change attitudes, preferences, and values'.[174] Implicit in the notion of indoctrination is the assumption that individuals lack personal agency and are simply vessels swept along with the ideological current. Had they had personal agency, any choice they made would be underpinned by the academic belief (in some circles) that they can personally 'alter conditions or policies through collective action'.[175] The dataset suggests that the presence of personal agency is more noticeable in their decision making prior to travelling to Iraq, rather than after having arrived when arguably they are more vulnerable.

There appears to be a link between the notions of vulnerability and indoctrination, in this case a vulnerability to a certain ideology, narrative or message. Although within a Western domestic context, the reality of 'vulnerable people being drawn into terrorism' is recognised by the UK Government in various official documents.[176] John Horgan implicitly links the notions of vulnerability and indoctrination, but argued that it 'might be more appropriate if not useful to consider [vulnerability] more in terms of how the individual may be more open to influence at any juncture'.[177] This may be as a result of 'a sense of disillusionment with alternative avenues'[178] or 'a provocative event'.[179] Possible examples of Arab foreign fighters who may have been potentially 'more open to influence' include Saudi national Abdul Aziz al-Gharbi, who had tried to join the Imam Mohammad ibn Saud Islamic University in Al-Ahsa, but was rejected.

This rejection contributed to his decision to go to northern Iraq and conduct a self-sacrificial ('martyrdom/suicide') attack on a checkpoint in March 2003.[180] There was also Tunisian national Abdul Halim Badjoudj, an unemployed second-generation immigrant living in France, who 'saw no future for himself' and conducted a self-sacrificial ('martyrdom/suicide') attack against a US military patrol.[181] The two main factors identified that contributed to Arab foreign fighters becoming involved in self-sacrificial attacks were the existence of a short training or incubation period conducted after arrival, and the young age of many Arab foreign fighters.

First, the short training period after their arrival in Iraq, away from family and friends, suggests that they may have been at their most vulnerable or impressionable, and hence 'more open to influence'.[182] Training for self-sacrificial attacks involved 'the creation of a point of no return' in order to make sure that individuals did not change their minds.[183] There are many examples of individuals who conducted self-sacrificial attacks after only a short incubation period in Iraq. They include Saudi foreign fighter Muhammad al-Halil, who 'less than a month later ... detonated his car beside an American Humvee' vehicle;[184] Saudi foreign fighter Abdullah al-Shimri, who had only been in Iraq for two months before he conducted a self-sacrificial ('martyrdom/suicide') attack against German contractors;[185] and Jordanian foreign fighter Raa'id Mansur al-Banna, who conducted a self-sacrificial ('martyrdom/suicide') attack within a month of arrival, killing 120 Iraqi civilians.[186] Also noted earlier in this chapter, it was less than two months after Ahmad Abdullah al-Shaya had arrived in Iraq that he carried out his self-sacrificial ('martyrdom/suicide') attack killing twelve Iraqi civilians in Baghdad. Naturally in the earlier examples, there may be competing explanations including that some individuals may have arrived in Iraq already intent and committed to conduct a self-sacrificial attack. Additionally, it is interesting that while all the perpetrators only had a short incubation period having arrived in Iraq, they conducted self-sacrificial attacks that targeted both military and civilian targets. This indicates that the training for such missions was perhaps more focused on the overall merits of martyrdom, and that the trainers did not necessarily make any targeting distinctions for such operations.

Second, as noted earlier, the United Nations Security Council acknowledged the notion of 'age-related vulnerabilities',[187] and thus it is worth briefly exploring whether there was an age difference between the participants of self-sacrificial ('martyrdom/suicide') attacks who targeted coalition and Iraqi forces, and those who targeted civilians and non-combatants. In the literature, John Horgan recognised 'the emotional responsiveness of people at a younger age and the increased susceptibility towards greater involvement this might bring'.[188] In Iraq, according to Fawaz Gerges, many young Arab foreign fighters were 'ideologically transformed by their experience ... coupled with socialization with hard-core jihadis'.[189] Extracted from the dataset (n=19), the average age of Arab foreign fighters who targeted Iraqi civilians and non-combatants was only twenty-one years old, while the average age of those who targeted coalition and Iraqi forces was twenty-five years old. This may tentatively suggest that, those slightly more mature Arab foreign fighters were committed to defensive jihad that included self-sacrificial ('martyrdom/suicide') attacks targeting the US-led coalition, while the younger cohort may have been more open to influence concerning the targeting of civilians and non-combatants.

Conclusion

By drawing on a dataset of 721 biographies of Arab foreign fighters in Iraq, albeit often fragmentary and propagandistic, this chapter has illuminated the initial motivational factors supporting their involvement in defensive jihad. This chapter found that many, if not most of them, were ordinary Arab male citizens whose primary motivational factor was religious conviction, rather than the rather ill-defined label of radicalisation. The religious conviction, often heightened during annual Islamic practices such as the *Hajj* pilgrimage, was in response to foreign aggression and the need to defend their co-religionists. The Arab foreign fighters were largely young men, many with a university education, with the vast majority having no known previous militant or terrorist links. Of course, there were other considerations, including the political and religious environment of their geographic origin, and the influence of kinship and friendship ties. However, having arrived in Iraq, it appeared that Arab foreign fighters faced a different set of circumstances and factors that led many to become involved in terrorist-related activities, including self-sacrificial ('martyrdom/suicide') attacks that targeted Iraqi civilians and non-combatants.

The trajectory to involvement in Islamist terrorist-related activities appears to have been underpinned by grievances (against Iraqi Shi'a Muslims) and a corresponding extremist ideology that invoked the notion of *takfir*. Although this excommunication of fellow Muslims lacked a coherent theological justification, research showed that Al Qaeda in Iraq employed self-sacrificial ('martyrdom/suicide') attacks targeting Iraqi civilians and non-combatants (61 per cent) and Iraqi military forces (28 per cent).[190] The spreading of this extremist ideology appeared to have been primarily conducted in Iraq through training and indoctrination. There is evidence that the training included strong exhortations towards martyrdom, and whilst not brain-washing *per se*, was a form of indoctrination that often resulted in self-sacrificial ('martyrdom/suicide') attacks. The targeting distinction between attacking military forces and civilian and non-combatants was generally blurred by Abu Musab al-Zarqawi, although the practice was contested by both Al Qaeda's deputy (al-Zawahiri) and the radical Jordanian Islamist ideologue (al-Maqdisi).

Lastly, it is perhaps instructive that in 2004, Abu Musab al-Zarqawi made an important prophecy, about the prospect of jihad in Syria (involving a town called Dabiq). He proclaimed that 'the spark has been lit in Iraq and its flames will blaze, God willing, until they consume the Armies of the Cross in Dabiq'.[191] Linking the Iraqi jihad with a future jihad in Syria also has other subscribers. Introduced earlier in this chapter, Ahmad Abdullah al-Shaya, the Saudi 'suicide bomber' who survived his 2004 attack in Baghdad and was repatriated back to Saudi Arabia, reappeared again in November 2013 on the (now defunct) Arabic language Facebook account (www.shaghor.com). Dressed in khaki fatigues and holding a Kalashnikov rifle, he announced that he was 'honoured to be a soldier's soldier of the Islamic State of Iraq and al-Sham (ISIS), having pledged allegiance to [its former, now deceased leader] Shaykh Abu Bakr al-Baghdadi'. At the same time, he opened up a now deleted Twitter account (@ja3fr) to explain his reasons for joining ISIS.

4

4

Arab Foreign Fighters and Islamist Terrorists in Syria

Not all fighters going to Syria are extremists, says former UK minister.
Shahid Malik.[1]

Introduction

This chapter, the last of the three case studies, examines the involvement of (non-Syrian) Arab foreign fighters who participated in the defensive jihad in Syria (post-2011), and why and how some of them subsequently became (and continue to become) involved in Islamist terrorist-related activities in Syria. Similar to the Iraqi jihad where overlaps developed between defensive jihad and Islamist terrorism, the conflict in Syria is also perhaps best understood as an insurgency in that it 'combines subversion, guerrilla warfare and terrorism ... [in] an internal struggle in which a disaffected group seeks to gain control of a nation'.[2] These overlaps were correctly identified by Randy Borum and Robert Fein, who recognised that the Syrian insurgency appeared to 'blur the lines between civil war and terrorism, pushing many of the foreign fighters aggressively towards terrorist tactics'.[3] However, unlike the Iraqi insurgency that initially witnessed a defensive jihad against US-led coalition troops (the far enemy), the Syrian insurgency initially involved defensive jihad against Syrian regime forces (the near enemy). Despite the Syrian insurgency becoming entangled with the prolonged Iraqi insurgency due to the cross-border influence of groups such as the Islamic State,[4] this chapter specifically examines the insurgency in Syria and the (non-Syrian) Arab foreign fighters who participated in defensive jihad and who subsequently became involved in Islamist terrorist-related activities. The research period is from 29 August 2011, which marked the first documented death of an Arab foreign fighter (Saudi national Hussam al-Mutayri)[5] in

Damascus, until 6 December 2017 when the Russian government declared that Syria had been completely liberated from ISIS.

This chapter leverages a dataset of 2,252 (non-Syrian) Arab foreign fighters, compiled mostly from Arabic language social media sites, most of which are no longer available due to the suspension of many Islamist (violent and non-violent) accounts by Facebook, Twitter and Instagram.[6] In addition, there is information obtained from ISIS documents including General Border Administration personal files on arriving and departing Arab foreign fighters. Despite ISIS being in Iraq and Syria, this chapter is about Arab foreign fighters in the Syrian jihad, and hence Iraqis who were fighting in Syria are included in the dataset, as are foreign Arabs in *Jabhat al-Nusrah* (JN) and the Free Syrian Army (FSA).[7] The bar for inclusion in the dataset was set at all non-Syrian Sunni Arab fighters who were (or continue to be) involved physically or ideologically[8] in the Syrian insurgency and who were (or continue to be) aligned with a non-state armed group. The dataset includes but is not limited to their names, nationalities, age and date of involvement, previous jihad experience, group(s) joined and date and method of death. In many cases, it offers a through-life account of 2,252 Arab foreign fighters in Syria, starting with their arrival data and finishing with their martyrdom eulogies.

The dataset represents about 13 per cent of the overall cohort of Arab foreign fighters based on figures published by Professor Alex Schmid.[9] It is arguably the most comprehensive and complete dataset on Arab foreign fighters based on open-source information in that it is not time specific,[10] group specific[11] or action specific.[12] There is no known comparable dataset. Researching Sunni Arab fighters (as opposed to Western fighters) is largely predicated on the reality that 'Arabs dominate the list of foreign jihadists . . . in Syria, and nine of the top ten countries represented are from the Arab world'.[13] Naturally, there were research challenges dealing with such data, including authenticity, source reliability, triangulation of data, the transliteration of thousands of Arabic names, and whether the content of the data was largely propagandistic. Each case was dealt with individually and a subjective judgement taken. Where there was genuine doubt, individuals were not included in the dataset.

This chapter is broken down into two component sections. First, there is a short introduction to the Islamist terminology in use in Syria followed by a brief overview of the Syrian insurgency.[14] Next, there is an examination of the biographical data on Arab foreign fighters to determine their broad motivations and the influences upon them, in order to contextualise their initial involvement in defensive jihad in Syria. This includes their ages, geographic origins, friendship and kinship ties, signs of religiosity, and any previous experience in defensive jihad and/or Islamist terrorism. The second section explains why and how some Arab foreign fighters subsequently became involved in Islamist terrorist-related activities. It examines the targeting of groups such as ISIS, *Jabhat al-Nusrah* and the Free Syrian Army (FSA), and the cause of death of their fighters as a result of conventional combat or self-sacrificial ('martyrdom/suicide') attacks. For example, if an Arab foreign fighter was killed fighting against the Syrian Arab Army (SAA), this is broadly conceptualised as being in harmony with the notion of defensive jihad. However, if an Arab foreign fighter was killed whilst detonating an explosive vest amongst civilians and non-combatants, this is interpreted as an act of Islamist terrorism. This section explores the grievances against the al-Assad regime and the ideology of the various groups, leading some to continue defensive jihad while others became involved in Islamist terrorism. In particular, this section dissects the use of 'martyrdom/suicide' attacks and examines the role of religiosity in their adoption. Finally, terrorist training and indoctrination within the groups in Syria are examined in order to further explain the subsequent behavioural choices of Arab foreign fighters.

Terminology

The Syrian insurgency has spawned and resurrected a Sunni Arab terminology that warrants a brief explanation, as the labels are present in much of the Sunni anti-Shi'a rhetoric.[15] They include Alawite, *nusairi, rafidah, murtadd* and *taghoot*. The first term, Alawite, is understood to represent a subset of the Shi'a denomination that, even during the Arab revolt in 1917, was perceived by 'Lawrence of Arabia' as 'clannish in feeling and politics'.[16] The word *nusairi* is generally understood to be another disparaging term for Alawites. In some English language Islamist magazines, the label is constructed as '*nusairi* Alawite'.[17] Due to the many variations in spelling and for clarity, this chapter will use the labels *nusairi* and Alawite interchangeably. The next term *rafidah* is also disparaging and commonly used within the Syrian insurgency; it refers to 'dissenters, defectors, a Shiitic sect',[18] in effect, yet another term for Alawites. Its frequent use is confirmed by its appearance 173 times in the Islamic State magazine *Dabiq* 13. The term *murtadd* refers to an 'apostate'[19] (someone who renounces his religion) within both Sunni and Shi'a Islam, and again its wide use is demonstrated by its appearance fifty-nine times in the Islamic State magazine *Dabiq* 13. Finally, the label *taghoot* (plural *tawagheet*) is a Quranic term, defined as 'an idol, tyrant, oppressor',[20] which is largely used by rebel groups in Syria to denote al-Assad and his regime (*tawagheet*). The former chief ideologue for ISIS, a Bahraini foreign fighter named Turki al-Binali (d. 2017), defined *taghoot* as a 'despot ruler who assails the rulings of God'.[21] The widespread use of such derogatory and dehumanising terms underpins the deep-seated sectarian hatreds held by the combatants on all sides of the Syrian insurgency.

Background to the Syrian Insurgency

The contemporary history of Syria includes 'the arbitrary partition of the Arabic-speaking provinces of the Ottoman Empire by Britain and France after World War I',[22] and the creation of the modern Syrian state as a French mandate. In 1928, British traveller Dame Freya Stark, who travelled through Syria, observed the absence of any 'national feeling: it is all sects and hatreds and religions'.[23] This sectarian division continued and arguably became more pronounced in 1970 when the al-Assad family came to power in a bloodless coup, led by Hafez al-Assad, father of the current President Bashar al-Assad. After the coup, Hafez al-Assad immediately increased Alawite dominance of the security and intelligence sectors to a near-monopoly,[24] resulting in a Shi'a Alawite minority (13 per cent) presiding over a Sunni Muslim majority population of 73 per cent.[25] This arguably is a reverse of the situation in pre-2003 Iraq where as noted in Chapter 3, a Sunni Muslim minority (under Saddam Hussein) governed a Shi'a Muslim majority.

The autocratic rule of Hafez al-Assad was challenged, particularly by Syrian Islamists in Hama in 1982, but was crushed when 'the Syrian army massacred thousands of civilians'.[26] The next major challenge to the al-Assad dynasty (now controlled by Bashar al-Assad) was the Arab Spring,[27] led by pro-democracy movements in Daraa in March 2011, but quickly spreading to other parts of Syria. According to Human Rights Watch, the Syrian 'security forces responded brutally, killing at least 3,500 protesters and arbitrarily detaining thousands, including children under age eighteen, holding most of them incommunicado and subjecting many to torture'.[28] The level of Syrian regime violence against Syrian civilians and non-combatants was noted at the United Nations, prompting a draft resolution (S/2014/348 dated 22 May 2014), vetoed only by China and Russia, referring Syria to the International Criminal Court. The Syrian Network for Human Rights (2018) estimated that over the period from March 2011 to May 2018, Syrian government forces have been responsible for a 'civilian death toll' of 217,764. Taking a snap shot of the year 2016, the Syrian Network for

Human Rights established that 'the Syrian-Iranian-Russian regime was responsible for 76 per cent of civilian deaths. It is this level of unequivocal violence directed against fellow Muslim civilians and non-combatants that provided the basis for genuine grievances against the al-Assad regime, resulting in the largest documented Arab foreign fighter mobilisation in history.

There are numerous accounts by relatives of victims of Syrian regime atrocities, including the widespread use of torture, however, a short account based on a BBC documentary[29] is included here, as the victim called Khalid survived to tell the tale. Prior to the revolution, Khalid was a young Syrian man living in Raqqa who considered himself to be 'a bit religious, but not too strict' and was employed as an organiser for religious pilgrimages (to Mecca, Saudi Arabia), including the annual *Hajj*. In 2011, he got caught up in the anti-government protests and felt 'an amazing feeling of freedom mixed with fear of the regime'. His feelings of fear were well founded, as he was soon arrested at his home and taken to the Criminal Security Department in Damascus. There he was severely tortured by one of the guards who would:

> hang me from my arms with chains to the ceiling. He would force me to strip . . . and whip my back. I left his prison paralysed, and when they moved me to the Central Prison inmates were crying when they saw me . . . I couldn't walk . . . they brought me in on a stretcher.

He was released from the Central Prison after a month, and immediately took up arms against the Syrian regime. Whilst his story is anecdotal, it appears to represent the environment in Syria in 2011 and the wider context for involvement in the revolution, by both Syrians and Arab foreign fighters.

Biographical Data on Arab Foreign Fighters Travelling to Syria

As in the previous case study chapters, this chapter explores the biographical data on Arab foreign fighters who travelled to Syria, including their age, geographic origin, religiosity, and any previous experience in defensive jihad and/or Islamist terrorism. As highlighted in Chapters 2 and 3, the notion of age facilitates examination of the influence of biographic availability,[30] and 'age-related vulnerabilities of community members'.[31] The inclusion of geographic origin offers examination of the influence of state support and the sometimes complex relationship governments have with their citizens. Finally, examining any previous experience in defensive jihad and/or Islamist terrorism of Arab foreign fighters facilitates research on their later influence (as charismatic leaders and/or ideologues) on other Arab foreign fighters, and how that may have affected the subsequent trajectories of some newly arrived fighters in Syria.

Age of Arab Foreign Fighters in Syria

Age wise, based on 361 Arab foreign fighters in Syria where ages were available, they ranged from sixteen to sixty-five years old with 52 per cent of them twenty-four years old or under. The average age was twenty-six-and-a-half years old and the median was thirty-three. Again, these findings correlate fairly well with Arab foreign fighters in Iraq (post-2003),[32] the Afghan Arab cohort,[33] and other reports on Arab foreign fighters in Syria,[34] although they do raise two points. First, the slightly higher average age of twenty-six-and-a-half (compared to those Arab foreign fighters who fought in 1980s Afghanistan and Iraq) is probably due to the number of older Arab foreign fighters, with the dataset revealing twenty-two veteran Afghan Arabs who vary between forty-nine and sixty-five years old.[35] Second, even when removing the older cadre of Arab foreign fighters, the average age only lowers to twenty-five years old. This suggests that their involvement in defensive jihad may be less as a result of vulnerability to indoctrination, and more due to the notion of personal agency.[36] Covered in more detail later, it is also revealing that the average age of 130 documented ISIS *istishhaadi* (martyrdom volunteers) was 25.8 years old, whilst the average age of known perpetrators of self-sacrificial ('martyrdom/suicide') operations was 25.5 years old.[37] Again, this perhaps demonstrates the rationality and maturity of many Arab foreign fighters who travelled to Syria, but also that anyone of any age can be indoctrinated (if such a process is required).

Finally, it is worth noting that the reasons for going to Syria may have changed after the announcement of the establishment of the so-called Islamic Caliphate (29 June 2014) by the former leader of ISIS, Abu Bakr al-Baghdadi (d. 2019). The lure (or pull factor) of living in a Caliphate may have trumped the initial reasons for wanting to wage defensive jihad against the al-Assad regime. Although care needs to be taken with these figures, based on 372 Arab foreign fighters, pre-Caliphate volunteers were aged 25.5 years old whilst post-Caliphate volunteers (or aspiring dwellers) were 22.7 years old. Perhaps the slightly younger individuals were more taken by the notion of living in a so-called Caliphate with all its spiritual meaning and the material attractions of a house, car, wife and salary, which to many young Arab men (particularly Tunisians) were largely beyond reach in their home countries.[38]

The Geographic Origin of Arab Foreign Fighters in Syria

A brief overview of the nationalities of Arab foreign fighters in Syria offers the opportunity to examine the broad social, political and religious context from where the individuals originated. The geographic origin of Arab foreign fighters in Syria from the dataset is presented in Figure 4.1.

Figure 4.1 shows the top three countries of origin being Saudi Arabia (29 per cent), Tunisia (18 per cent) and Libya (15 per cent). At the other end of the scale, the Sultanate of Oman had only two known nationals participating in defensive jihad in Syria. It also appears to suggest that there were very few Iraqi foreign fighters in Syria, arguably due to them having been more focused on battles in Iraq.

Saudi Arabia being the predominant country of origin[39] is best explained by the structural influences within Saudi Arabian *Wahhabi*[40] society, aware that ISIS relied heavily on the ideology of Muhammad Abdul Wahhab (d. 1792). First, Saudi Arabia appears to conform to the observation that some 'national governments ... [are] enabling foreign fighters to arrive on the battlefield ... by providing material resources or turning a blind eye when recruits leave the country to fight' in Syria.[41] This may be understood within the context of Saudi-Iranian geo-strategic regional hostilities, generally predicated on Sunni-Shi'a rivalries. In many ways, the Saudi state sees itself as the defender of Sunni Muslims in the region, against the perceived threat from Shi'a Muslims. Yet the Saudi position is arguably a contradiction: on the one-hand they gave 'open support for the Syrian revolution from the summer of 2011',[42] while on the other

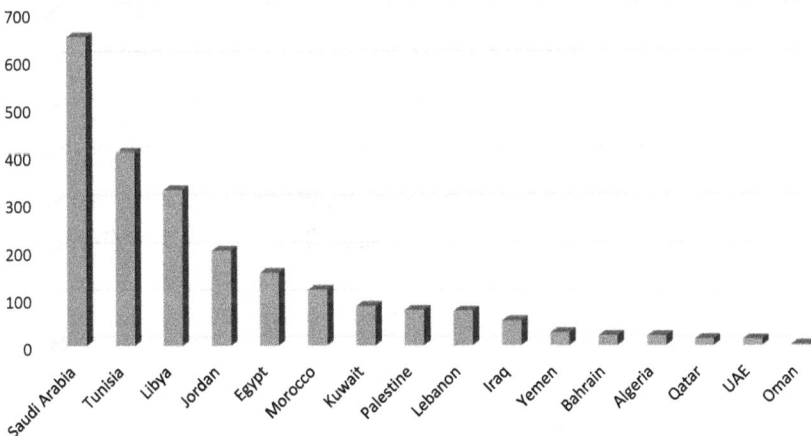

Figure 4.1 The geographic origin of Arab foreign fighters in Syria (n=2,252).

hand, in 'early February 2014, the Saudi government issued a royal order declaring that any citizen who fights in conflicts abroad will face three to twenty years of jail'.[43] According to Nawaf Obaid, despite this royal order, Saudi Arabia's 'ultimate objective in Syria is to take on ... al-Assad and the Iran-created Shi'a militias, which are the source of as much, if not more, regional terror than ISIS and Al Qaeda'.[44] It is not known whether this royal order was enforced, although in 2015 the Saudi Ministry of Interior arrested '431 people suspected of belonging to ISIL cells'.[45]

The second point, for why Saudi Arabia appears to be the predominant country of origin of Arab foreign fighters is that Saudi 'Islamic scholars do wield a considerable amount of power in the political system'.[46] An example of this power is demonstrated in a 2013 statement by seventy-two prominent Saudi shaykhs supporting the need for defensive jihad in Syria and the creation of the Islamic Front.[47] Of particular influence was Saudi Shaykh Abdullah al-Muhaysani, who in September 2015 gave a speech in Idlib (Syria) emphatically declaring that the defensive jihad in Syria was an existential battle 'between the Sunnah and the *Nusayri Alawites* and the *rafidah*'.[48] Thus, despite the Saudi regime's belated opposition to Saudi nationals participating in defensive jihad in Syria, Saudi clerical backing[49] for involvement in the Syrian jihad had 'huge support amongst the Saudi population, and was seen as a just uprising against a dictatorial ... Shiite Alawite regime'.[50] The third point is that some areas of Saudi Arabia embrace(d) a more politicised version of Islam (Islamism) than others. For example, according to Thomas Hegghammer, the central Najd region consisting of Riyadh, al-Qaseem and Ha'il is considered to be 'the heartland of the Saudi Islamist landscape'.[51] It is, therefore, perhaps no surprise that 20 per cent (129) of the 649 identified Saudi foreign fighters in Syria originated from the Nejd region, including Shaykh Abdullah al-Muhaysani. Even historically, 22 per cent (thirty-one) of the original 139 Saudi detainees in Guantanamo Bay prison originated from the Nejd region.[52] The significance of an Islamist region is not suggesting a direct cause–effect relationship, but rather that individuals (due to their geographic origin) may be more pre-disposed to Islamist activities, which include participating in defensive jihad. This Islamist pre-disposition should not however be confused with religiosity, inasmuch as many Saudi foreign fighters had only a 'simple' grasp of Islamic *Shariah* law, including those originating from the Nejd.

The explanations for the high number of Tunisian and Libyan fighters are probably more complex. Both countries had recently experienced revolutions, Tunisia through broadly peaceful means and Libya through a violent jihad. In many ways, the youth of the two countries had been operationalised and having tasted freedom (not necessarily democracy), felt pre-disposed to export the feeling to other Arab countries. In addition, perhaps with the Libyans, they had tasted the success of jihad over an autocratic dictator and believed the same model could be applied in Syria. That said, from the dataset, only nine Libyan fighters from the 2011 Libyan revolution were positively identified as participating in the Syrian jihad. It is also instructive that ISIS defectors who were interviewed by Anne Speckhard and Ahmet Yayla, suggested that Tunisian fighters travelled to Syria 'because they are unemployed and too poor to be married at home'.[53] Another former ISIS member, Abu Ahmad, stated that many Tunisians join ISIS 'to cleanse themselves of their previous sins'.[54] Finally, one Tunisian foreign fighter, Abu Muadh al-Tunisi, admitted that he was motivated by the new Islamist current in Tunisia after the revolution, and by watching 'clips, where they were burning and torturing people'.[55] Of course, these are three amongst many reasons why an individual would travel to Syria to wage defensive jihad, but they do offer an insight into the more mundane human reasons that make individuals more open to mobilisation.

Finally, it is worth briefly mentioning expatriate Arab foreign fighters, those who were living, working or studying outside their country of birth, away from home and family ties. It is arguably whilst living in those foreign countries that such fighters decided to travel to Syria. Interestingly, there were only fifty-one (2.26 per cent) out of the dataset of 2,252 who were identified as expatriates. Out of these fifty-one expatriates, thirty-three (65 per cent) were living in Western countries, with the vast majority living in the EU. These individuals were not first- or second-generation immigrants, but economic migrants with no meaningful support base and who were likely to experience discrimination by the host societies.[56] The attraction of living in a so-called Islamic Caliphate would likely be appealing to many disenfranchised expatriates, who would regain some form of identity, status and power. The push factors (due to discrimination) and pull factors (due to the lure of a Caliphate) experienced as an Arab expatriate living in Western Christian heritage societies, offer some explanation as to why they travelled to Syria. The same could possibly be applied to first, second or third-generation Arab migrants living outside mainstream society in the West.

The Influence of Veteran Arab Foreign Fighters and Islamist Terrorists

The last 'past contextual influence',[57] namely previous experience as an Arab foreign fighter and/or Islamist terrorist, is arguably of great significance. According to one report, 'relationships formed as far back as Afghanistan in 1979 directly influence[d] the brutality we see in Syria'.[58] Noting from Chapter 2 that many veteran Afghan Arabs remained involved in defensive jihad (such as in Bosnia or Chechnya), one might reasonably expect to see a plethora of fighters in Syria with similar background experiences. This, however, is not the case, with only 3.3 per cent (seventy-four) identified from the dataset,[59] although their influence and impact appears to be a more qualitative than quantitative issue. The dataset breakdown of prior experience of defensive jihad by Arab foreign fighters in Syria is presented in Figure 4.2.

There is a general convergence between these findings and those of other scholars, particularly the prominence of veterans from the defensive jihads in Afghanistan (post-2001), Libya[60] and Iraq (post-2003). The number of veteran Iraqi foreign fighters should come as no surprise, particularly from the perspective of geographical proximity (between Iraq and Syria), and ideological synergy (AQI and ISI are forefathers of the Islamic State). In addition, there have been copious reports linking involvement in the Iraqi jihad to the emergence of the Islamic State,[61] and indeed former UK Prime Minister Blair went on record admitting that 'you can't say that those of us who removed Saddam in 2003 bear no responsibility for the situation' in Syria.[62] Particularly prominent and influential veterans of the Iraqi jihad include Abu Bakr al-Baghdadi (former leader of ISIS; d. 2019); Abdul Rahman al-Qaduli (deceased, deputy leader of IS); Abu Muhammad al-Adnani (deceased, former Emir of IS in Syria and director of external operations); Abu Muhammad al-Gholani (leader of *Hayat Tahrir al-Sham*); Hashim al-Shaykh (current 2019 Shura head of *Hayat Tahrir al-Sham*); and Abu Hammam al-Suri (deceased, former leader of military wing

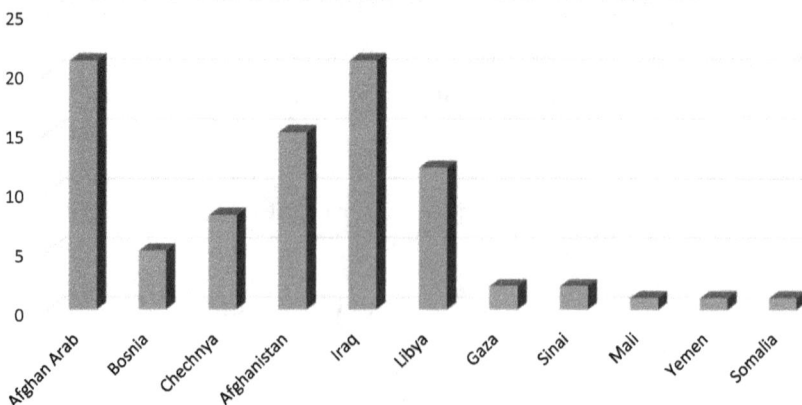

Figure 4.2 Prior jihad experience of Arab foreign fighters in Syria (n=74).

of *Jabhat al-Nusrah*). The positions of authority and overall influence of these Iraqi jihad veterans are self-evident concerning the direction of the Syrian jihad (particularly involving ISIS and *Jabhat al-Nusrah / Hayat Tahrir al-Sham*).

A further important observation to make is that many of the groups in Syria were founded by veteran Arab foreign fighters and formed largely on their geographic (national) origins. Examples would be *Kateebat al-Battar* and *Jaysh Muhammad fee Balad ash-Shaam* established by Libyan foreign fighters,[63] and *Harakat Shaam al-Islam* established by three Moroccan foreign fighters from the defensive jihad in Afghanistan (post-2001).[64] Thus, although small in number (only 3.3 per cent of the book dataset), veteran Arab foreign fighters arguably had a disproportionate influence over the Syrian insurgency.

Overlaps notwithstanding between veteran Arab foreign fighters and Islamist terrorists, it is also important to identify the presence and influence of veteran Islamist terrorists (thirty-five) within the Syrian conflict, mostly those linked with Al Qaeda (nineteen) and HAMAS (seven).[65] According to Mubaraz Ahmed et al., the 'leaders of *Jabhat al-Nusrah* and ISIS today can be linked through personal contacts over generations to the forefathers of global jihad [Islamist terrorism]'.[66] The overlaps include eighteen Islamist terrorists who were also veteran Arab foreign fighters from previous conflicts, supporting the argument that many Arab foreign fighters do eventually become involved in Islamist terrorist-related activities. Notable veteran Islamist terrorists involved in the Syrian insurgency include Ayman al-Zawahiri (leader of Al Qaeda, linked to *Jabhat al-Nusrah* until July 2016); Abu Firas al-Suri (deceased, former Al Qaeda Shura council member and spokesman for *Jabhat al-Nusrah*); Abu Khalid al-Suri (deceased, former Al Qaeda member and former leader of *Ahrar al-Shaam* in Aleppo); and Muhammad Haydar Zammar (a veteran Syrian Afghan Arab and an Al Qaeda inspiration for the 9/11 pilots), who joined ISIS in Raqqah and was later arrested by Kurdish militia in April 2018.

Again, the point to be made is that veteran Arab foreign fighters and Islamist terrorists appear to have had a disproportionate influence over the Syrian conflict. This is corroborated by Mubaraz Ahmed et al., who concluded that while the majority of Arab foreign fighters were inexperienced with no prior experience of defensive jihad or Islamist terrorism, once in Syria 'on the battlefield, jihadi novices are being introduced to seasoned veterans' in the form of 'an ideologue or a top-level operative'.[67] Whilst perhaps unsurprising, it does lend a degree of credence to the existence of charismatic leaders and ideologues, and their influence through indoctrination on those arriving in Syria, which is covered later in this chapter.

How Ordinary were Arab Foreign Fighters in Syria?

This section of the chapter continues to make the case that the majority of Arab foreign fighters who travelled to Syria were more 'ordinary' than 'radicalised' prior to their decision to participate in defensive jihad. It is often implicit in the scholarly literature on Arab foreign fighters in Syria, that individuals who depart their country of residence in order to participate in defensive jihad in defence of their co-religionists are somehow already radicalised and/or already Islamist terrorists.[68] J.M. Berger and Jessica Stern go further to suggest that ISIS 'sought recruits ... who were further down the path toward ideological radicalization or more inclined by personal disposition toward violence'.[69] Even at the international level, the 'Arab foreign fighters' who populate the dataset compiled for this book are labelled by the United Nations Security Council as 'foreign terrorist fighters'.[70] Those who do recognise that not all foreign fighters in Syria are necessarily radicalised, include Thomas Hegghammer, Jennifer Cafarella and the EU's Director of Justice and Home Affairs, Gilles de Kerchove.[71] This idea that Arab foreign fighters are somehow already radicalised (based on their international volunteerism), whilst compelling, is not persuasive. Nathan Patin, an investigative journalist, researched the motivations of 108 foreign fighters in Syria. Citing the exact words of the foreign fighters themselves, the circumstances supporting their personal (not group) involvement included:

> the killing of innocent people that couldn't even defend themselves;' 'religion is a major one;' 'I'm going to have an adventure;' 'to fight on my terms against an enemy I know is evil ... it is redemption, in a sense;' and 'governments weren't doing [anything] about it – by God we will.[72]

The circumstances highlighted above appear to lack the notion of radicalisation and perhaps more accurately demonstrate a certain compassion towards victims, a mild religious fervour to act, and the need of many young men – that of adventure and excitement. What is particularly striking about Nathan Patin's study is that it was actually investigating 'American volunteers travelling to Iraq and Syria to fight *against* the Islamic State',[73] not alongside the Islamic State. Interestingly, in a separate study conducted by Emman El-Badawy et al., *Inside the Jihadi Mind*, the 'system of ideas' that attracted recruits to ISIS and *Jabhat al-Nusrah* (and AQAP), broadly mirrored the study by Patin, and included the influence of 'creedal values', 'the enemy', 'nobility of jihad', and 'allies of God'.[74] The synergy between the two reports is striking and their findings have an uncanny resemblance, yet the subjects of research were (in theory) complete opposites.

Therefore, were the Americans fighting against ISIS also 'foreign terrorist fighters' and were they also assumed to have been radicalised? The conclusion by Patin was that the American foreign fighters were motivated by 'a sense that something needed to be done in the face of IS's continuing barbarity'.[75] This chimes with the motivations of Arab foreign fighters – that something needed to be done 'in the face of al-Assad's continuing barbarity'.[76] Such a convergence of motivations despite being on opposing sides, suggests more the presence of moral rationality, rather than radicalisation.

By 2014, US policy 'chose to stand by those advocating "jihad only in Syria" [but was] against the regional and global jihadist trend represented by ISIS'.[77] This implicitly acknowledged that defensive jihad (against the al-Assad regime) was different from global Islamist terrorism. Perhaps it signalled an embryonic awareness and realisation of the distinction between Arab foreign fighters and Islamist terrorists, going back to the 1980s. This drawing of distinctions was further demonstrated by the use of the term 'moderate' in statements made by the US White House and Department of State, in relation to those forces opposing al-Assad's regime and the Islamic State. Such terms included 'moderate opposition forces'[78] and 'moderate groups',[79] however, what is meant by 'moderate groups'? Are they 'un-radicalised' fighters and followers of 'moderate Islam'? Certainly, according to journalist Mowaffaq Safadi, it is 'virtually impossible to bracket these fighters into distinct moderate or non-moderate categories'.[80] The point to be made is that painting every Arab foreign fighter with the label of being 'radicalised' or 'moderate' is not helpful in trying to gain a nuanced understanding of their motivations and circumstances. The actions of the few should not define them all.

Finally, it is illuminating that the US Treasury Department issued a waiver authorising the provision of logistical and financial support to the Free Syrian Army.[81] This presupposes that the Free Syrian Army was considered a moderate conglomeration of opposition groups in Syria, despite their loose alliances and shifting allegiances. Yet the book dataset identifies 126 Arab foreign fighters within the Free Syrian Army, arguably resulting in them being supported by the US Treasury Department whilst at the same time being labelled 'foreign terrorist fighters' by the United Nations Security Council. Arguably more worrying is that the book dataset also reveals that ten out of the 126 Arab foreign fighters in the Free Syrian Army conducted self-sacrificial ('martyrdom/suicide') operations against Syrian army units;[82] attacks that would be labelled by most governments and academics, as 'terrorist attacks'.[83] This leads to the contradiction of being both supported by the United States, whilst also being labelled 'suicide bombers'.

This inconsistency appears to demonstrate an overall misunderstanding and misrepresentation of many Arab foreign fighters in Syria and their *modus operandi*. Therefore, whilst it is impossible to prove definitively that the majority of Arab foreign fighters were not necessarily radicalised based on their decision to travel to Syria, there is little convincing empirical evidence to suggest otherwise. Nonetheless, the absence of evidence is not evidence of absence, however having arrived in Syria it is accepted that some 'will become radicalised as they spend time in the trenches'.[84]

The Influence of Religion

Measuring religiosity is singularly difficult and even individuals who appear seemingly devout and pious, can act in a way that does not necessarily reflect their religion, be it Christianity, Islam or Judaism. That said, it seems possible to infer a degree of religiosity based on 'religious practices' and behaviour.[85] For example, Chapter 3 examined the travel dates to Iraq of 291 Arab foreign fighters in 2006 and 2007, and noted that more volunteers travelled during annual Islamic practices and festivals, suggesting that religiosity may have played a part. The same research was conducted on the travel dates for 133 Arab foreign fighters crossing into Syria, and in particular 2014 showed a spike in travelling during *Ramadan*. In 2014, the average movement into Syria was eighteen Arab foreign fighters a month, yet during the period of *Ramadan* and the subsequent *Eid al-Fitr* festival (28 June to 31 July) the flow increased to thirty-four fighters. Perhaps not only related to the religiosity associated with *Ramadan*, but the increase coincided with the establishment of the so-called Islamic Caliphate, again something of religious significance. The increased movement of Arab foreign fighters over this period in 2014 is shown in Figure 4.3.

To further support the case that increased religiosity may have influenced the travel dates of many Arab foreign fighters, of the thirty-four who arrived in Syria during *Ramadan* 2014, twenty decided to leave only weeks later. This information is gleaned from the rather bureaucratic book-keeping skills of ISIS, who monitored departures at the border crossing out of Syria. Perhaps it was a case of failed expectations having been caught up in the euphoria of the holy fasting month of *Ramadan*, to arrive in Syria to find the reality that many Islamist groups and fighters were not as religious as their propaganda suggested. The majority of the twenty fighters who subsequently departed stayed less than two weeks, with one fighter staying only three days.[86] Their reasons varied from

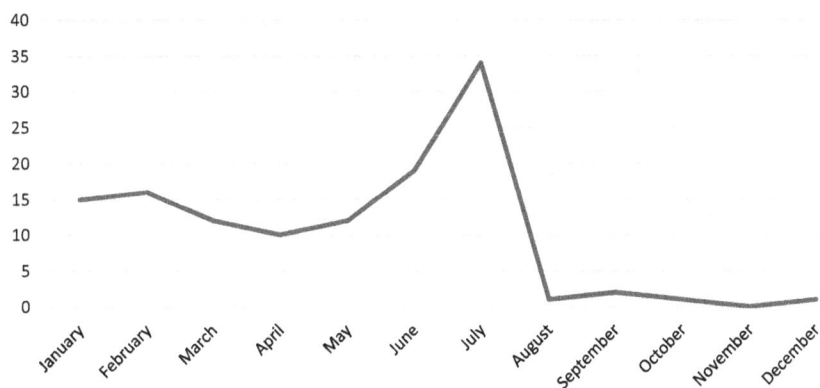

Figure 4.3 Arab foreign fighter travel months to Syria in 2014 (n=133).

'family circumstances', 'he does not want military life and jihad',[87] to 'he claims to be sick'.[88] It is instructive that a Syrian ISIS fighter named Ibn Ahmad recalled that 'Arab foreign fighters really thought it was a true Islamic state and jihad',[89] and felt deceived once they witnessed the irreligious nature of ISIS. This may be true, in that 246 ISIS General Border Administration forms show that 68 per cent of Arab foreign fighters had only a simple (*baseet*) 'level of knowledge' of Islamic *Shariah* law, and hence were deceived by the narrative of 'an Islamic state and jihad'. A further Syrian ISIS fighter named Abu Zafir, also admitted that 'Islam and jihad are not as *ad-Dawlah* [ISIS] tells you',[90] yet their religious narrative was compelling enough to influence many individuals from the Arab (and Western) world to travel to Syria. During Islamic festivals, it would be reasonable to expect many Muslims to experience increased feelings of religiosity, a greater sense of belief and perhaps increased openness to a religious narrative that called for the defence of their co-religionists in Syria.

The Islamist recruiting narrative is a fairly well-worn record used by groups' religious ideologues, preachers and leaders. Yet at the individual fighter level, their religious narrative also had a compelling, almost persuasive tone, a good example being that from a young university-educated Egyptian fighter named Saif Allah al-Muhajjir. In his video posting on Facebook in July 2013[91] (well before the Caliphate was declared by al-Baghdadi), he calls on his fellow Muslims to come to Syria. He questions 'how can we remain in our homes secure, while our sisters are raped, our children killed, and our youth are slaughtered? How can you be pleased with standing back while the Shi'a rape our Muslim sisters?' He explained that 'we did not emigrate [to Syria], except to rush to aid our Muslim brothers and sisters, implement *Shariah* law, even if we sacrifice our souls and blood'. Al-Muhajjir cleverly framed the Syrian jihad as defensive in nature, sectarian in context and invoked the need for martyrdom. He also however gently threatens prospective fighters that 'Allah will humiliate you and not relieve you of this humiliation, until you return to your religion ... we want to return the honour of this *ummah*, and stop this Shi'i *Nusairi* assault ... we must emigrate to Sham'. His words were a clever mix of pull and push factors, but the underlying tone appeared sectarian drawing on Sunni religiosity within the Syrian conflict. Interestingly, he later appears to slightly go off-script and asks his viewers 'how can you be pleased with living in humiliation under the rule of the *taghoots*, such as those of Egypt, Tunisia and Libya?' Again, the religious undertone was there, hinting that the lack of *Shariah* law in these North African countries was another reason to emigrate to Syria.

The notion that religiosity played a part in the recruitment and travel of Arab foreign fighters is potentially contentious as many scholars (with some exceptions),[92] chose to eschew linking Islam and violence. This chapter contends however, that heightened religiosity did appear to influence some Arab foreign fighters to travel to Syria, and indeed it appeared that it was religiosity that also gave them the strength to depart. This chapter does not support the notion that Islam is in any way responsible for terrorism (as defined by Professor Alex Schmid), yet it would be naïve to suggest that religion played no part in supporting Arab foreign fighter involvement in defensive jihad in Syria. Defensive jihad, defending fellow Sunni Muslims from external or internal attack, has a moral quality attached to it along with an increased sense of religious identity. In addition, what is often omitted from the literature is what the individual fighters believe themselves. Whether what they believe is scripturally correct is immaterial; it is what they believe. As noted earlier, these beliefs can be misguided, leading some who travelled to Syria to promptly return, while others appeared to accept an increasingly violent and extremist interpretation of Islam. The notion of religiosity will be revisited later in this chapter to explore whether it may have influenced volunteers for self-sacrificial ('martyrdom/suicide') operations.

The Epitome of an Arab Foreign Fighter in Syria

Hamza al-Awani (Abu Hajjar al-Tunisi) was born in the popular seaside town of Sousse in Tunisia on 10 July 1986. This town was later to become infamous after the 2015 Islamist terrorist attack that left thirty-eight civilians dead, including thirty Britons. Although all individuals have unique characteristics, Al-Awani's story appears broadly representative of many Arab foreign fighters who travelled to Syria. He was raised within a conservative working-class family who were practising Muslims and whose father worked in a local factory in Sousse. Throughout his childhood, he had listened to discussions of jihad and in particular the atrocities against Muslims in Bosnia and Chechnya, and by the age of sixteen, he attempted unsuccessfully to join the jihad in Chechnya against the Russians. He later attended the Higher Institute of Applied Science and Technology in Sousse, where he graduated with a Media Engineering degree in 2011, and quickly found employment earning 1,000 Tunisian dinars a month. However, despite job opportunities in Europe, by early September 2012 Hamza al-Awani felt obliged to participate in jihad against the Syrian regime, and was content to join the Free Syrian Army or the *Jabhat al-Nusrah* group.

At the time of his arrival, *Jabhat al-Nusrah* was not considered a terrorist organisation (it was proscribed only on 11 December 2012) and ISIS had not yet been established in Syria; thus Al-Awani appeared to be getting involved in a legitimate jihad defending fellow Sunni Muslims. Even when ISIS was established in April 2013, it is interesting that Al-Awani saw no difference between the *Jabhat al-Nusrah* and ISIS as they both appeared to be defending co-religionists against the Syrian regime. During his time in Syria, he observed first-hand the tactic of self-sacrificial ('martyrdom/suicide') operations and the military advantage this had over the Syrian military, and hence he decided that this would be his chosen path. Just under ten months after arriving in Syria, on the first day of the Holy Month of *Ramadan* (10 July 2013) and coincidentally his twenty-seventh birthday, he executed his own self-sacrificial ('martyrdom/suicide') operation. His target was not identified and has never appeared in the media or on CPOST or GTD databases.[93] His death was posted on Facebook on 16 July 2013,[94] and later his obituary was posted by *Shamookh al-Islam* on a Syrian Islamist website *shaghor.com*.[95] Hamza al-Awani was the first Arab foreign fighter to appear in a series called the *Flags of Martyrs in the Levant*. By all accounts, it appears that he was an ordinary Tunisian man, perhaps above average in intelligence, moderately pious, but with no known links with any Tunisian Islamist groups (such as *Ansar al-Shariah*). The question, therefore, that must be asked is why and how did some fairly unremarkable Arab foreign fighters, such as Hamza al-Awani, subsequently become involved in Islamist terrorist-related activities in the Syrian jihad?

How Arab Foreign Fighters Become Islamist Terrorists

Much of the academic literature on Islamist fighters in Syria makes no distinction between Arab foreign fighters and Islamist terrorists, which is not surprising due to the overlaps between defensive jihad and terrorism, particularly within the context of a civil war. However, there are a few rare scholars who do make the distinction by identifying the subsequent 'pathways' of those foreign fighters having 'already arrived in Syria ... and joined one of the fighting parties'.[96] One such report by Alastair Reed et al. identified three 'pathways': 'fighting, supporting terrorist activity, or leaving the jihadi group'.[97] These three pathways more broadly represent participating in defensive jihad, involvement in Islamist terrorism, or withdrawing from militant activities. The following section focuses on those Arab foreign fighters who subsequently opted for 'supporting terrorist activity' in Syria, and the factors that influenced their behaviour: Islamist ideology, training and indoctrination.

Islamist Ideology in Syria

In the context of the insurgency in Syria, the underlying Islamist ideology of ISIS and *Jabhat al-Nusrah* was based on Salafi-jihadism, a point corroborated by Fawaz Gerges.[98] This was largely predicated on both groups' emphasis on *takfir*, their justifications for targeting civilians and non-combatants, and the permissibility of 'suicide attacks'.[99] Using a reduced dataset of 305 Arab foreign fighters where the influence of Islamist ideology may be inferred, this section explores ideological issues and circumstances in order to help explain why some fighters subsequently became involved in Islamist terrorist-related activities. Whilst this book broadly agrees that 'ISIS is a creature of accumulated grievances [and] ideological and social polarization',[100] identifying their content and impact is central to this chapter. With increased access to fine-grained data on Arab foreign fighters in Syria, it is now possible to analyse them by identifying their respective groups (FSA, ISIS, or *Jabhat al-Nusrah*); their adopted method of attack (conventional or self-sacrificial); their intended target (military or civilian/non-combatant); and their cause of death (fighting the Syrian army, internecine warfare, terrorism, or coalition bombing). Using this empirical data, inferences may be made concerning the individual motivations and group ideology that supported the method of attack against a particular target.[101]

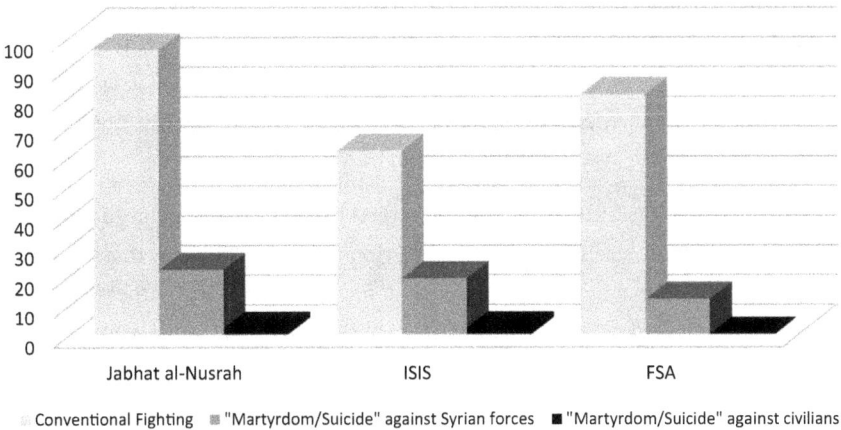

Conventional Fighting ▨ "Martyrdom/Suicide" against Syrian forces ■ "Martyrdom/Suicide" against civilians

Figure 4.4 Cause of death of Arab foreign fighters within rebel groups in Syria (n=305). August 2011–May 2018.

An interesting and evidence-based finding of the cause of death of Arab foreign fighters within rebel groups in Syria is presented in Figure 4.4.

Figure 4.4 offers inferences that indicate that the primary ideology held by Arab foreign fighters in the three major non-state groups (*Jabhat al-Nusrah*, the FSA or ISIS) included *takfir* against *nusairi* Alawites; the tactic of 'martyrdom/ suicide' operations primarily targeting Syrian army and militia units; and the lack of recorded 'martyrdom/suicide' operations that targeted civilians and non-combatants. Thus, despite the UN listing of ISIS and *Jabhat al-Nusrah* as terrorist organisations,[102] the evidence suggests that their targeting ideology is more directed towards military targets than civilians and non-combatants. Arguably, it is the ISIS targeting ideology employed against Europe (inspired and actual) rather than in Syria, that is often more visible and terroristic in nature, particularly in the attacks in Paris, Brussels and Nice.[103] In Syria, the terroristic nature of ISIS and *Jabhat al-Nusrah* may be better understood by examining their atrocities against civilians and non-combatants off, rather than on, the battlefield.

The ideology of *takfir* against all *nusairi* Alawites appears to guide much of the targeting in Syria, in that it fuels the insurgency against forces aligned with the al-Assad regime (the Syrian army, Iranian militias, Russian mercenaries and Lebanese Hezbollah). The reasons for this are well documented and include cases of Syrian regime extrajudicial killings, detainee abuses and the widespread use of barrel bombings on civilian areas. One investigation conducted in 2012 by the UN Commission of Inquiry on Syria concluded that:

> Syrian Government forces ... have committed crimes against humanity, war crimes and gross human rights violations. These crimes included murder, summary execution, torture, arbitrary arrest and detention, sexual violence, violations of children's rights, pillaging and destruction of civilian objects – including hospitals and schools.[104]

This 2012 report has (unfortunately) remained timeless, although arguably with the Syrian regime's use of chemical munitions against civilians, the atrocities have become even worse. It appears that having physically witnessed these 'crimes against humanity, war crimes and gross human rights violations', many Arab foreign fighters began to seek revenge. It is illuminating, therefore, that a later report (2016) commissioned by the UNHRC revealed that although cases of 'torture and other ill-treatment by armed opposition groups occurred in isolated incidents in the early phase of the conflict ... this phenomenon appears to be on the rise'.[105] It is suggested that this increase in torture and ill-treatment by rebel groups was in part, driven by the need to reciprocate in kind. The whole situational environment in Syria involving a civil war superimposed upon an insurgency appears to have generated increased acts of violence on all sides, which are ideologically justified. For example, the notion of revenge is firmly established in the Quran,[106] and its link to terrorism more generally is well documented in the literature.[107]

The Islamist Ideologues

Before going into greater detail on the specific aspects of the ideology of Arab foreign fighters in Syria, it is worth briefly touching on the ideologues and scholars who promote it. The main ideologues based in Syria include, but are not limited to, a Bahraini named Turki al-Binali (ISIS, d. 2017), a Jordanian named Sami al-Uraydi (*Jabhat al-Nusrah*) and a Saudi named Shaykh Abdullah al-Muhaysani (unaffiliated Islamist ideologue). Those outside Syria include Jordanian ideologue Abu Muhammad al-Maqdisi and Ayman al-Zawahiri (Al Qaeda's leader). It is revealing that Joas Wagemakers contends that in the Syrian insurgency, it is a 'question of who speaks for jihad: scholars with their theoretical knowledge of Islamic law, or fighters, with their practical knowledge of actual combat'.[108] This point was brought out during the Iraqi jihad that witnessed the ideological clash between Abu Musab al-Zarqawi, the AQI leader physically leading fighters in Iraq, and his former mentor Abu Muhammad al-Maqdisi, who was safely ensconced in Jordan. There appears to be a tension between the credibility of an ideologue based on where he is situated, and the reliability of his jurisprudential narrative. As Shiraz Maher noted, 'fighters in the field are driven by a real-time, *ad hoc* form of jurisprudence that is borne of both the privations and exigencies of war'.[109] It is suggested, as with Osama bin Laden who lived amongst the Afghan Arabs in the caves of Afghanistan, that the credibility of ideologues is predicated on the shared experiences of combat and danger in Syria, regardless of the reliability of their narrative. It appears that the credibility and reputation of Islamist ideologues are key attributes, particularly concerning their powers of persuasion[110] and in operationalising their charismatic authority.[111]

The Islamist Ideology Supporting *Takfir*

The ideology of *takfir* against *nusairi* Alawites arguably originated from the 'extremist ideas brought to Iraq by al-Qaeda after 2003'.[112] Whilst Vera Mironova et al. suggest that in Syria 'Islamist group leaders appear to be better at using religion to channel collective sectarian grievances',[113] arguably it is not the religion of Islam *per se*, but a politicised version of Islam often labelled 'political Islam'. Fawaz Gerges argued that the operationalisation of *takfir* is the result of 'the instrumentalization of religion for political purposes'.[114] This appears a more accurate portrayal and one that has broad academic support.[115] Evidence from the dataset and from Figure 4.4 supports the notion of *takfir* against Alawite soldiers and other Sunnis who warrant being labelled a *kufr* (particularly other Sunni rebel groups). This *takfiri* ideology has led to 'the largest religious cleansing strategy that has ever been planned in human history',[116] which is tantamount to genocide, and is discussed later in this chapter.

It is interesting that Abu Muhammad al-Maqdisi who is considered 'one of the most important ideologues of Jihadi-Salafism',[117] and once 'the true spiritual father of the Islamic State',[118] is now labelled a 'donkey of knowledge' by the Islamic State in their magazine *Dabiq* 10.[119] This was largely due to al-Maqdisi 'denouncing the Islamic State upon rumours of excess in violence and *takfir*'.[120] In a religious *fatwa*, al-Maqdisi labelled ISIS 'a deviant organisation from the path of truth … which leans towards extremism (*ghuluw*) … and who have become embroiled in the unlawful spilling of blood';[121] a position he reaffirmed in June 2015.[122] In essence al-Maqdisi, whilst supportive of *takfir* against the 'Alawite regime', believes the ideology of *takfir* against other Sunni groups (particularly *Jabhat al-Nusrah*) to be wrong. It is, however, revealing that whilst labelling al-Maqdisi a 'donkey of knowledge', a dispute had already 'emerged among senior theorists within the Islamic State over the practice of *takfir*', leading to the arrest of some Arab foreign fighters.[123] This lack of overall ideological cohesion appears to have led to varying shades of *takfir* within ISIS – creating what Hassan Hassan labels 'a culture of *takfirism* within *takfirism*'.[124]

The Islamist Ideology Supporting 'Martyrdom/Suicide' Operations

The ideology supporting the tactic of self-sacrificial ('martyrdom/suicide') operations in Syria first needs to be put into context. Kenneth Pollack, who conducted an assessment of the strengths and weaknesses of conventional Arab militaries, established that 'the majority of Arab military personnel demonstrated impressive degrees of self-sacrifice and personal bravery'.[125] This suggests that the notion of sacrifice and martyrdom in battle *fee sabeel Allah* is not an aberration in the Arab world. The parallel to be drawn is that these conventional Arab militaries were in combat against other conventional militaries (either Iranian or Israeli), in the same way that the Free Syrian Army, ISIS and *Jabhat al-Nusrah* were initially against the Syrian army. This section makes the argument that the employment of 'martyrdom/suicide' operations by Arab foreign fighters against the Syrian military (or other rebel combatants) is ideologically more akin to defensive jihad, rather than Islamist terrorism. It continues to develop the argument made in Chapter 3 that in Iraq (post-2003), Arab foreign fighters often conducted 'martyrdom/suicide' operations against US-led coalition troops under the auspices of a defensive jihad; while Islamist terrorists conducted 'martyrdom/suicide' operations against civilians and non-combatants under the auspices of Islamist terrorism. One of the leading texts legitimising the use of 'martyrdom/suicide' operations was authored by a veteran Egyptian Afghan Arab and currently (2018) a member of ISIS, Abu Abdullah al-Muhajjir. In his treatise, *Masaa'il min Fiqh al-Jihad* (Issues from the Jurisprudence of Jihad), he draws parallels with the notion of bravery and 'martyrdom operations',[126] and yet he fails to distinguish between military and civilian targets. Aware that there is scholarly agreement that most 'martyrdom/suicide' operations in Syria appear to be conducted by foreigners,[127] it is essential to disaggregate their targeting in order to understand both the group and individual motivational ideology and intentions supporting such attacks.

The Influence of Islam as an Ideology in 'Martyrdom/Suicide' Operations

As mentioned in Chapter 3, the religion of Islam does not sanction 'martyrdom/ suicide' attacks or the act of suicide itself. It does however condone, to the extent of encouragement, martyrdom *fee sabeeel Allah*, and there are many verses in the Quran that lend such support.[128] It remains, however, a contested and controversial topic and is difficult to prove or disprove. That said, with the growing use of social media by Islamists (violent and non-violent), it is becoming increasingly possible to test the hypothesis that Islam in some way influences the willingness of some fighters to become involved in self-sacrificial ('martyrdom/ suicide') operations. It must be reiterated that the key thing is what Arab foreign fighters believe, rather than any relevant theological prohibition against it. Such an argument draws on the William and Dorothy Thomas dictum: 'If men define situations as real, they are real in their consequences'.[129] For example, examining the monthly death rate of 985 known Arab foreign fighters in Syria in 2013, it is possible to establish whether more were killed during heightened periods of religiosity, such as the fasting month of *Ramadan* and the subsequent celebration *Eid al-Fitr* (9 July to 10 August 2013). Research shows that eighty-two Arab foreign fighters were involved in 'martyrdom/suicide' attacks in 2013, with the average monthly death-rate being 6.8. However, during *Ramadan* this figure rose to nineteen Arab foreign fighters, an increase in nearly 280 per cent. In addition, eighty-two fighters a month were 'martyred' *fee sabeeel* Allah in conventional fighting, whereas during *Ramadan* it was 175.

Figure 4.5 tentatively demonstrates that over *Ramadan* and the subsequent celebration *Eid al-Fitr* in 2013, there was a spike in 'martyrdom/suicide' attacks that were not connected to any specific battle or campaign over that period.[130] The influence of religiosity is suggestive and not definitive and great care needs to be applied to interpreting such data. For example, whilst the spike in deaths over *Ramadan* also holds for 2014, such spikes were not visible in 2012 or 2015. Returning to the 2013 (and indeed 2014) 'martyrdom/suicide' attacks, it is suggested that many Arab foreign fighters were likely to be more willing to sacrifice themselves *fee sabeeel Allah* during *Ramadan*, and that they were more spiritual and felt they were closer to God. Whilst there may be many other competing explanations for such spikes, it does seem that increased religiosity related to *Ramadan* made them more open to the notion of 'martyrdom' in the sense of a greater willingness to die in a defensive jihad. Other scholars and journalists have also commented on Islamist spikes in violence during *Ramadan*,

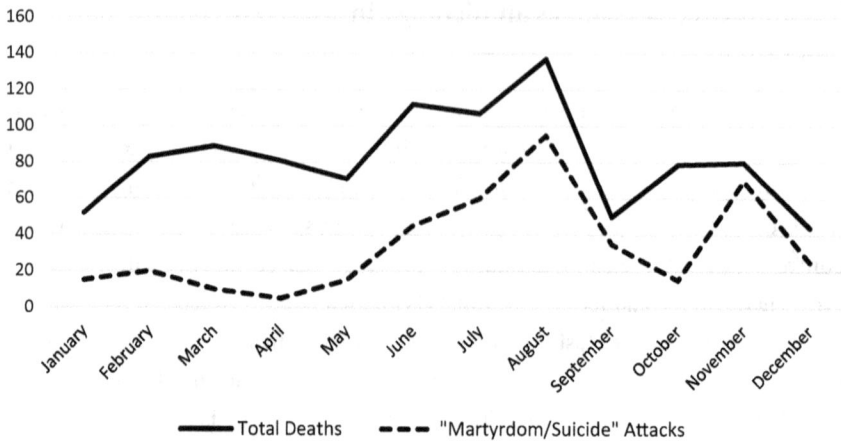

Figure 4.5 Monthly Arab foreign fighter deaths in 2013 (n=985) including eighty-two 'martyrdom/suicide attacks' (x5).

including by Sunni insurgents in Iraq (in 2006),[131] by Boko Haram in Nigeria (from 2011–2017),[132] and by ISIS in 2016.[133] However, other scholars deny the existence of such spikes, arguing that in fact Islamist violence actually decreases during *Ramadan*.[134] Whatever the truth, there is irrefutable evidence of spikes in 'martyrdom/suicide' attacks perpetrated by Arab foreign fighters in Syria during *Ramadan* in 2013 and 2014, and hence perhaps the lack of scholarly agreement is more one of interpretation and explanation of those spikes.

Volunteering for 'Martyrdom/Suicide' Operations

The willingness to die in a defensive jihad is recorded on the ISIS General Border Administration in-processing forms, by volunteering to be an *istishhaadi* (one who seeks martyrdom). However, due to the increased availability of data from social media, it appears that it is an unreliable indicator to subsequent behaviour. For example, taking the Arab nationalities of 126 documented ISIS martyrdom volunteers and establishing the rate per 100 fighters (from the dataset of 2,252), it appears from Figure 4.6 that Morocco, Egypt and Tunisia are the top three countries (per 100 fighters) volunteering to be an *istishhaadi*.

However, when examining 225 confirmed and documented 'martyrdom/ suicide' operations perpetrated by identifiable Arab foreign fighters, the results are different. For example, although Saudi and Iraqi fighters were placed fifth and twelfth respectively as volunteers for 'martyrdom/suicide' operations, they

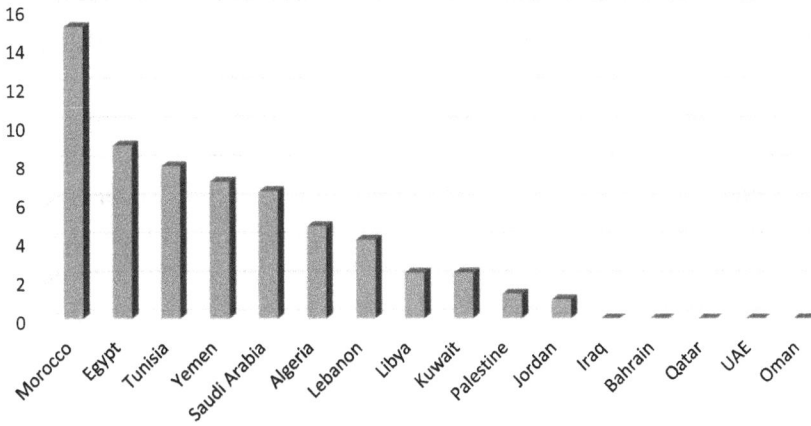

Figure 4.6 Desire for martyrdom (from ISIS Files) per 100 fighters (n=126)

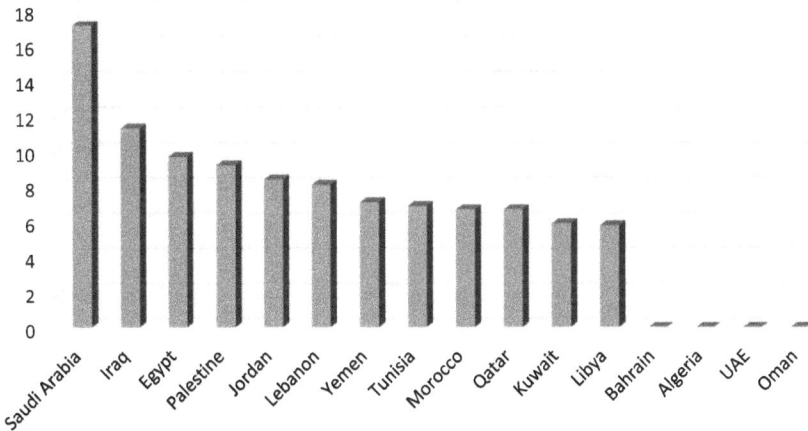

Figure 4.7 Confirmed 'martyrdom/suicide' bombers (targets not identified) per 100 fighters (n=225).

moved to first and second place respectively as actual perpetrators of such attacks, as demonstrated in Figure 4.7.

This raises four interesting points. First, research and subsequent analysis on terrorism is inherently difficult, and without the data for Figure 4.7 the data from Figure 4.6 could be interpreted to suggest that Moroccan, Egyptian and Tunisian fighters are the most willing to become involved in 'martyrdom/suicide' operations. Second, it could be suggested that Moroccan and Tunisian foreign fighters arrived with more bravado, thinking that martyrdom was a most noble role to fulfil and was expected of them. However, once the reality of what that really entailed became apparent, their enthusiasm waned. Third, Figures 4.6 and 4.7 may suggest that after training and indoctrination, the more easily persuaded were Saudi and Iraqi fighters. Iraq having suffered violent militancy since 2003, may have contributed to Iraqi fighters' eventual decision-making. Finally, the word *istishhaadi* does not necessarily mean 'suicide bomber', although in some circles it may imply it. As noted in Chapter 3, *istishhaadi* is a martyrdom seeker, whilst a suicide bomber is a *shakhs intihaari*. The broad distinction concerns the targeting of the attackers, and in the Syrian civil war it appears that the majority of 'martyrdom/suicide' operations were directed against the Syrian army, Iranian militias, Lebanese Hezbollah and other Sunni Arab fighters. As such, targeting appears to be a critical variable in determining the behaviour of Arab foreign fighters in Syria.

Targeting

Data extracted from the Chicago Project on Security and Threats (CPOST) Suicide Attack Database,[135] suggest that 'martyrdom/suicide' operations in Syria appear to target primarily Syrian military units, and not civilians and non-combatants. This is demonstrated in Figure 4.8.

The CPOST data from Figure 4.8 ostensibly reveal that 75 per cent (125) of 'martyrdom/suicide' attacks targeted the Syrian military, whilst only 25 per cent (forty-three) were classified as targeting civilians (and non-combatants). Yet closer examination, using content analysis of supporting media articles, reveals

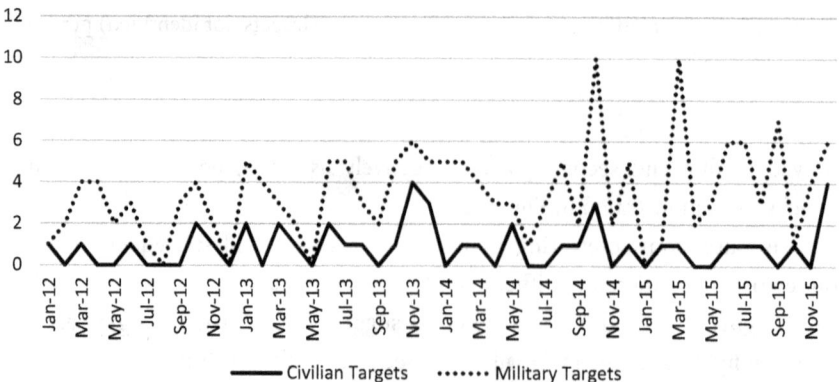

Figure 4.8 Comparison of 'martyrdom/suicide' attacks (targets and fighters identified) in Syria (n=168).

that although the 'target' may be documented by CPOST as 'civilian', this often appears to have been inaccurate. Examples include an attack on the 'al-Kindi hospital' that was not occupied by civilian staff or patients, but was occupied and being defended by Syrian army units,[136] hence it was attacked. This analysis resulted in establishing that out of the forty-three 'suicide attacks' listed by CPOST as attacks against civilian targets, actually only twenty-eight could reasonably be considered as targeting civilians and non-combatants,[137] with the remaining twelve attacks targeting enemy combatants. Therefore, out of the 168 'martyrdom/suicide' operations in Syria, actually 82 per cent (137) targeted military personal, suggesting that the ideological motivation of most Arab foreign fighters was in support of defensive jihad and seeking to gain a military advantage. This is also corroborated by Charlie Winter, who analysed 923 Islamic State suicide operations between 1 December 2015 and 30 November 2016, and concluded that '84 per cent ... were geared towards achieving military goals ... [while] just 16 per cent of the time, IS used suicide attacks to target civilians.'[138] This independent corroboration of the book findings suggests the dawn of more nuanced academic appraisals of 'martyrdom/suicide' operations in Syria.

In their own words, Arab foreign fighters and Islamist terrorists appear to offer conflicting views over the employment of 'martyrdom/suicide' operations in Syria. For instance, according to Saudi foreign fighter Ayachi Abdul Rahman (aka Abu Hajar), 'killing the innocent along with the enemy is not acceptable. If my target is military and I knowingly kill even one innocent, this is terrorism.'[139] Yet Iraqi foreign fighter Ibrahim Ammar Ali al-Khazali admitted that 'it was about hitting as many people as possible – especially police officers, soldiers and Shi'as ... they are infidels'[140] (unbelievers). Despite the vagueness in defining Shi'as, which could reasonably include civilians and non-combatants, it raises an interesting question whether 'infidels' are perceived as belonging to the 'civilians and non-combatants' category. Tentative evidence from Figures 4.4 and 4.8 suggests otherwise – the targeting priority appears to be focused on 'infidel' Syrian soldiers and police officers. In a separate interview, al-Khazali also admitted that whilst 'most people who died were valid targets ... those who were caught up in the attacks will be accepted by God'[141] – in other words collateral damage. Finally, albeit anecdotally, Libyan fighter Akram Fathi al-Saaliheen crossed into Syria in July 2013 and volunteered to be an *istishhaadi*, yet in the remarks column on his ISIS General Border Administration in-processing form it states: 'Tell his family about his death without mentioning the process of martyrdom'. This offers a rare glimpse into the mind of an Arab foreign fighter who, whilst a 'martyrdom' volunteer, was aware that such 'martyrdom' would not be approved of by his family.

The evidence that the majority of Arab foreign fighters targeted only Syrian regime forces and other armed combatants raises three issues. First, it reinforces the argument (initially discussed in Chapter 3) made by Assaf Moghadam, that an attack should 'not be labelled a terrorist attack if it is targeted against members of an army, because attacks are ordinarily labelled terrorist attacks when they are aimed at non-combatants'.[142] Second, it supports the personal view of Thomas Hegghammer, that maybe 'the Syrian rebel cause is just and that some of the foreign fighters leave with noble intentions'[143] – normative arguments notwithstanding. Lastly, it challenges Professor David Cook's view that 'suicide attacks for the most part ... rarely occur against truly military targets',[144] a position that now appears (understandably) increasingly obsolete and unrepresentative of the realities on the battlefields in Syria since 2011.

Inghimasi Operations

The last point drawing distinctions between 'martyrdom/suicide' operations in Syria, is the use of the term *inghimasi*,[145] which has re-surfaced in media releases from both ISIS and *Jabhat al-Nusrah*.[146] In the scholarly literature the term *inghimasi* is often conflated with suicide attacks and/or more vague labels such as 'fully committed',[147] 'suicidal',[148] 'commando'[149] or 'suicide fighter'.[150] Probably the most contextualised definition of *inghimasi* from among the many scholars,[151] refers to 'special operations involving fighters ... distinct from suicide bombers ... that willingly put themselves in harm's way, maximising the risk of their deaths in order to cause as much damage as possible'.[152] The broad constituent parts of an *inghimasi* operation appear to involve the target being 'an enemy position' (implicitly military); the offensive employment of light weapons and bombs (not just an explosive vest); and that the likelihood of survival is low, although not impossible.[153] The idea that *inghimasi* combatants are necessarily terrorists, whilst comforting and even compelling, should not go unchallenged, especially when they are not 'targeting mainly civilians and non-combatants', a key tenet in Alex Schmid's 'revised academic consensus definition of terrorism'.[154]

The term *inghimasi* is, however, a contested term, perhaps less amongst ideologues but certainly between groups. Ideologically, according to Rebecca Molloy, Ibn Taymiyya (d. 1328) justified *inghimasi* operations under the pretext of 'a soldier on a battlefield deciding to carry out an attack that will likely result in his death'.[155] Contemporary Syrian ideologue Abu Basir al-Tartusi, supported *inghimasi* operations 'even if it leads to one being killed by the enemy ... so long as there is benefit to jihad, to Islam, and to Muslims'.[156] The ideological emphasis is military in nature and appears to be the position adopted by the Islamic State, but not by Al Qaeda-affiliated groups.

The Islamic State interpret *inghimasi* operations as a military tactic, against enemy combatants who are generally labelled 'apostate soldiers';[157] '*murtaddeen* officers and soldiers';[158] or 'PKK and FSA *murtaddeen*'.[159] In an August 2015 ISIS video,[160] the targets identified as suitable for *inghimasi* operations included 'well protected targets with barricades, solid buildings or enemy commanders'. The ISIS video also specified that an *inghimasi* volunteer must be of *hasan al-khuluq* (good moral disposition) and *hubb at-tadh-heeya fee sabeel* Allah (like sacrificing in the path of God). A typical ISIS report of an *inghimasi* operation found in magazines such as *Dabiq* would include:

> *inghimasi* soldiers of the Khilafah armed with light weapons and explosive belts,[161] 'plunging into the enemy ranks'[162] and 'following the clashes, the two *inghimaasiyyeen* detonated their explosive belts in the midst of the *murtaddeen*, killing a number of the officers and commanders.[163]

Al Qaeda-affiliated groups appear to adopt a different interpretation. In Al Qaeda's magazine *Inspire*, it defines an *inghimasi* as 'an individual or a small group immersing themselves within a large army of non-believers in search of martyrdom and causing damage to them'.[164] Al Qaeda cited examples of *inghimasi* operations including the 2008 attacks in Mumbai; the 2009 attack by Major Nidal Hassan in Fort Hood; and the 2013 attack in Nairobi's Westgate Mall.[165] The Islamist terrorist ideology of these examples, involving civilians and non-combatants, is unmistakable. It appears that such nuances and subtleties between Islamist groups in general, and in Syria in particular, limit our current understanding of *inghimasi* operations.

To conclude, there is a compelling case to conceptualise Arab foreign fighters, who attack military targets in a war zone, as being more analogous with Kamikaze pilots and Viet Minh fighters, rather than being simplistically labelled 'suicide bombers'. As noted in Chapter 3, Professor Karin Fierke recognised the tension in the relationship between 'suicide terrorism' and 'martyrdom operations', and uses 'the term "suicide/martyrdom" when pointing to it'.[166] There appears to be a need to distinguish between 'martyrdom/suicide' and *inghimasi* operations, as there is a tension between the various labels largely based on the differences in targeting. It is suggested that the ideology supporting the tactic of 'martyrdom/suicide' operations against military targets is consistent with the more general trend of martyrdom *fee sabeel Allah*, rather than supporting 'martyrdom/suicide' attacks against civilians and non-combatants. This leads to the suggestion that Arab foreign fighters who conducted 'martyrdom/suicide' operations against the Syrian regime units, should not necessarily be considered 'suicide bombers', let alone Islamist terrorists. After all, there is no known documentary evidence that Kamikaze pilots or the Communist Viet Minh were ever labelled terrorists. This suggestion clearly challenges much of the existing literature on suicide terrorism, and is addressed in Chapter 5.

The Ideology Supporting the Targeting and Killing of Civilians

The ideology (enshrined within Salafi-jihadism) supporting the killing of civilians and non-combatants by Arab foreign fighters in Syria appears to manifest itself as much in the form of genocidal atrocities (based on *takfir* as noted earlier), as it does as a result of Islamist terrorism. Although the scale of ISIS atrocities is small compared with that of the al-Assad regime, their atrocities against Shi'a, Sunni, Christian and Yazidi civilians have been well documented.[167] This lends support to the argument that the atrocities could be conceptualised ideologically through the prism of genocide (that includes ethnic cleansing),[168] as well as through the prism of Islamist terrorism. To support this argument, 'the legal definition of genocide', is defined under Article II of the United Nations (1948) *Convention on the Prevention and Punishment of the Crime of Genocide* as:

> any of the following acts committed with intent to destroy, in whole or in part, a national, ethnical, racial or religious group, as such: killing members of the group; causing serious bodily or mental harm to members of the group; deliberately inflicting on the group conditions of life calculated to bring about its physical destruction in whole or in part; imposing measures intended to prevent births within the group; [and] forcibly transferring children of the group to another group.[169]

In March 2016, five years after the conflict in Syria had erupted, the then US Secretary of State, John Kerry, publicly went on record and acknowledged that ISIS 'is genocidal by self-proclamation, by ideology, and by actions – in what it says, what it believes, and what it does'.[170]

It is therefore illuminating that Ervin Staub in his 1989 seminal book, *The Roots of Evil*, found that 'perpetrators change, as individuals and as a group, as they progress along a continuum of destruction that ends in genocide'.[171] This perhaps is a key finding that has wider applicability to help explain the subsequent behaviour of some Arab foreign fighters in Syria. It supports the argument that despite not necessarily being radicalised prior to their arrival in Syria, over time they can change as individuals and groups, and later embrace a more violent ideology. Therefore, although perhaps not currently on the scale of the genocide in Rwanda,[172] many of the crimes committed by Arab foreign fighters were perhaps analogous to genocide (including ethnic cleansing), rather than Islamist terrorism. It is worthy of inclusion to note that some Islamist ideologues, including Shaykh Abdullah al-Muhaysani,[173] posted tweets that use the Arabic verb 'to exterminate, eradicate, or annihilate' (*ibaada*)[174] on their Twitter accounts. These ideologues were not necessarily invoking the virtues of martyrdom 'gained' in 'martyrdom/suicide' operations, but dehumanising Alawite civilians and non-combatants, and legitimising genocide against them. This again suggests that simply labelling Arab foreign fighters as Islamist terrorists, due to their often-unrestrained violence off the battlefield, is not necessarily helpful in trying to understand them.

Finally, some academics believe that the ideology supporting the killing of civilians is underpinned by Abu Bakr al-Naji's (2004)[175] treatise, *The Management of Savagery (idaarat at-tawahhush)* – translated by William McCants.[176] It deserves inclusion, as according to Fawaz Gerges, it provides the 'intellectual and ideological motivation and inspiration for Abu Bakr al-Baghdadi [d. 2019] and his ideologues';[177] and according to the Islamic State magazine *Dabiq*, it 'describes very precisely the overall strategy of the *mujahhideen*'.[178] However, it raises two points. First, whilst McCants's translation of *at-tawahhush* as 'savagery' is eye-catching and sensational, a degree of caution is required as *Dabiq* 1 and 5 translates *at-tawahhush* as 'mayhem';[179] whilst *Dabiq* 8 and McCants also translate *at-tawahhush* as 'chaos'.[180] Whilst savagery may cause chaos, they are not synonymous. Second, whilst *The Management of Savagery* discusses 'the path for establishing an Islamic state',[181] it arguably does not necessarily provide the 'rationale for how the movement behaves today', as Shiraz Maher proposed.[182] This is primarily due to the many contradictions between the behaviour, tactics and *modus operandi* of the Islamic State and what is recommended in *The Management of Savagery*.

For example, despite the guidance of al-Naji to 'lighten the severity of the violence against reasonable people amongst the enemy',[183] and 'to focus on economic targets, particularly petroleum',[184] it appears that this has not been embraced by the 'foreign fighters ... [who] have been among the worst perpetrators of ... serious abuses including indiscriminate attacks, extrajudicial executions, kidnapping, and torture'.[185] In addition, reference to 'the *rafidah* Shia' appears only once,[186] and perhaps most surprising is that there is no explicit inclusion of *takfir*, with al-Naji noting only that 'the rules governing the killing of [Muslim] tyrants are conflicting'.[187] This final point was also raised in *Dabiq* 12, which claimed that 'al-Naji fell into some errors in his discussions on issues related to the *takfir* of parties who forcefully resist the *Shariah* laws'.[188] Similar to the broad ideological current of Salafi-jihadism, relying on Abu Bakr al-Najdi's treatise to explain the ideology of the Islamic State is overly simplistic. It offers little in the way of nuance and despite the importance of ideology when selecting targets,[189] al-Naji's treatise has little explanatory value as to why some Arab foreign fighters in Syria may have adopted certain ideologies analogous with Islamist terrorism.

To conclude, the ideology that appeared to support the targeting of civilians and non-combatants in Syria may be better understood as a form of genocide off the battlefield. This is based on the toxic mixture of *takfir*, the 'situational circumstances'[190] Arab foreign fighters experienced in combat in Syria; the grievances and need for revenge against the Shi'a; and the notion of 'a continuum of destruction'.[191] Using a historical military example for context, Guy Sajer, an Alsatian Wehrmacht soldier on the Russian front in World War II, recalled that the brutality both on and off the battlefield often induced 'the most innocent of youths on whatever side to commit inconceivable atrocities'.[192]

Terrorist Training and Indoctrination

Introduction

As in the previous chapters, the notion of terrorist training and indoctrination are present in both academic and governmental literature, including a British Security Service (MI5) webpage devoted to *Terrorist Training and Indoctrination*.[193] This section explores the philosophy of the structural influences of such training and indoctrination in Syria, and how it may have facilitated the subsequent adoption of Islamist terrorism by some Arab foreign fighters. It includes the need for obedience to those in authority; the near absence of traditional terrorist training in preference for conventional military training needed in the insurgency; and the existence of indoctrination.

The need for obedience to those in authority appears central to the Islamic State and other groups, and follows the doctrine of Abdul Aziz al-Sharif (aka Dr Fadl).[194] On the ISIS General Border Administration forms, aspiring fighters were assessed on their 'level of hearing and obedience' (*mustawa' sama' wa aT-Taa'a*), and the subject is widely discussed in the Islamic State magazine, *Dabiq*. For example, in *Dabiq* 1, obedience (to those in authority) contributed to the 'roadmap towards an Islamic Caliphate for the *mujahhideen*'.[195] This particular emphasis on obedience and training was reiterated in *Dabiq* 12, which directed newly arrived Arab foreign fighters 'to listen to and obey those whom Allah has given authority over the affairs of the *mujahhideen*',[196] and that it 'is obligatory to yield to the opinion he has chosen and submit to his order'.[197] The level and degree of obedience demanded by Islamic State leaders is illustrated by the confessions of an Islamic State defector (Muhammad Khweis), an American-born fighter descended from Palestinian immigrants:

> we were supposed to just obey. If they tell you to slay others, you have to do it. Even if they tell you to behead your own father you have to do it. Whatever the Sheikh tells you to do, you have to do. When we hear the order we have to execute it.[198]

This notion of obedience to authority during both training (and in combat) has explanatory value as to why some Arab foreign fighters became involved in terrorist related and/or genocidal activities. Obedience to authority was scientifically explored by Stanley Milgram[199] and later confirmed by Ervin Staub.[200] Specifically, Milgram in his infamous 'obedience to authority experiment' uncovered 'the sheer strength of obedient tendencies ... to hurt another person'.[201] This contention is buttressed by Staub's own finding that a 'strong respect for authority and strong inclination to obedience are other predisposing characteristics for mass killing and genocide',[202] and that the ability of those in authority to 'repress dissent ... enhances the potential for evil'.[203] This demand for obedience helps to partially explain the trajectory from involvement in defensive jihad to subsequent participation in Islamist terrorist-related activities. It appears to be the case that, having arrived in Syria, Arab foreign fighters were required to obey orders without hesitation, regardless of the content or legitimacy of such an order.

Training

The ability of Arab foreign fighters to train in Syria is similar to 1980s Afghanistan in that rebel groups held and controlled territory within Syria, allowing for the establishment of training camps, with the necessary infrastructure to practise basic and more advanced military drills and exercises. According to Arie Perliger and Daniel Milton, 'training camp attendance ... [for] members of Islamic State [occurred] in 96% of cases',[204] demonstrating the 'nearly obligatory part of the experience of all foreign fighters entering Syria'.[205] Evidence of ISIS and *Jabhat al-Nusrah* training is widely available on the Internet,[206] but perhaps counter-intuitively, it generally concentrates on conventional military training required for an insurgency. In an ISIS Arabic language training video, released in January 2016, the training included *al-idaad al-badani* (physical preparation), *tadreeb asliha* (weapon training), *al-iqtihamaat al-layliya* (night raids), *fikaak al-asra* (freeing of POWs) and *tafaadi al-kumaa'in* (anti-ambush drills). Although there is an obvious propagandistic nature to these videos, they do demonstrate a solid training infrastructure and a well-developed training regime.[207] Despite the military training overlaps between defensive jihad and Islamist terrorism, training for 'martyrdom/suicide' operations was notably absent from this training video, although such omissions are arguably compensated for by 'martyrdom' videos that often show the training, preparation, farewell statements and post-attack results.[208]

According to journalist Hassan Hassan, who personally conducted interviews with members of ISIS, he discovered that the ISIS training regime was heavily influenced by religious instruction that included Islamist ideology. He recalled a young Arab man, Hamid Ghannam, who had trained in an ISIS camp near Deir Ezzor. In Ghannam's own words: 'they test you first ... they check your knowledge of religion ... they discuss with you everything. They talk to you about the *nusairi* regime and ... all the misguided groups'.[209] Hassan also established that 'new recruits join training that ranges from two weeks ... up to one year. Inside the camps, students receive a mix of military, political and *Shariah* orientation, usually given by around five instructors'.[210]

The Islamist ideological current is demonstrated in the Islamic State Training Camp Textbook, *Curriculum in Monotheism* (*muqarrar fee tawhid*), particularly within the *Shariah* chapter, which was authored by Bahraini cleric Shaykh Turki al-Binali, and translated by Aymenn al-Tamimi.[211] The curriculum is heavily reliant on the writings and ideology of both Ibn Taymiyya (d. 1328) and Muhammad Abdul Wahhab (d. 1792). The continual referencing to bygone Islamist ideologues adds to the legitimacy of the ISIS narrative, and helps prevent any challenge to it. A major section of the curriculum exposes the aspiring ISIS recruits to 'the ten nullifiers of Islam' written by Muhammad Abdul Wahhab, which 'outlines ten things that automatically expel someone from the religion' of Islam.[212] As al-Tamimi observed, inclusion of the ten nullifiers is 'a distinctly Wahhabi concept, and provides a very fertile basis for the *takfir* tendencies' of the Islamic State.[213] The most central (fourth) nullifier which undergirds the Syrian insurgency is when Muslims prefer the ruling of a *taghoot* (tyrant) over Allah's ruling. This leads to those Muslims being labelled disbelievers who require *takfir* (excommunication), which in Syria results in death. The common thread of *takfir* throughout much of this chapter does appear to be a central component of the ideology of both ISIS and *Jabhat al-Nusrah*.

However, there is evidence that ISIS are selective in their references in that whilst relying heavily on Muhammad Abdul Wahhab, he is not referenced concerning martyrdom, due in part to the fact that 'at no point in any of his writings does he promote the concept of martyrdom or encourage Muslims to seek it'.[214] The existence of training for 'martyrdom/suicide' operations in Syria is largely anecdotal, and whilst such individuals are eulogised after conducting such attacks, as noted earlier, these 'martyrdom' videos do often show the training and preparation, in particular the preparation of the vehicle-borne improvised explosive devices.[215] It is suggested, that whilst such training does take place, because the majority of 'martyrdom/suicide' operations appear to be woven into the *modus operandi* of the Islamic State and *Jabhat al-Nusrah* and employed against military targets, arguably they are more reliant on bravery, bravado and brazenness, rather than formal military training. This is arguably applicable within conventional armies too, where the notion of bravery is not necessarily gained through military training, but rather that 'a man of character in peace becomes a man of courage in war'.[216]

Brynjar Lia, a Norwegian historian and professor, identified 'four leading jihadi scholars' who wrote 'about principles for training and preparation in some depth'.[217] They were Abdullah Azzam (covered in Chapter 2),[218] Abdul Aziz al-Sharif (aka Dr Fadl),[219] Abu Bakr al-Naji (covered earlier in this chapter) and Abu Musab al-Suri.[220] According to Lia, whilst these four individuals (who incidentally were all veteran Afghan Arabs) agreed on the importance of training, they also stressed 'that ideological indoctrination and spiritual preparation should take precedence over physical and military training'.[221] It is perhaps instructive therefore, that according to Hassan Hassan, 'in some cases, new members who struggle with the brutality of the Islamic State's acts will be sent back to receive more training to "strengthen" their faith'.[222] The notion of strengthening their faith has many of the hallmarks of ideological indoctrination, which Abdul Aziz al-Sharif claims 'compensates for numerical inferiority and lack of resources'.[223] Overlaps notwithstanding, it is suggested that the transition between involvement in defensive jihad and Islamist terrorism in Syria likely included exposure to 'ideological indoctrination and spiritual preparation', as argued by Lia.[224]

Ideological Indoctrination

The indoctrination argument[225] proposed in this chapter has academic ballast[226] and builds on the findings in Chapter 3. The ultimate aim of indoctrination is to 'produce battle-hardened, martyrdom-seeking fighters, whose primary strength lies in their spiritual determination, their patience, and a willingness to employ savagery against the enemy'.[227] Again, the notion of indoctrination is underpinned by the concepts of vulnerability and peer pressure, experienced by Arab foreign fighters who left their home countries and found themselves involved in an insurgency in Syria, where 'the rebel group' became their new family, upon which they became reliant for everything. Although the notion of 'age-based vulnerabilities' was largely discounted earlier in this chapter, more promising perhaps are 'the experiences of violence, displacement, trauma and loss' in Syria.[228]

It is suggested that the situational circumstances 'of violence, displacement, trauma and loss' were likely to increase the 'vulnerability' of Arab foreign fighters to the ideological indoctrination within rebel groups. Noted in Chapter 3, but worth repeating again, vulnerability should be considered 'in terms of how the individual may be more open to influence at any juncture'.[229] The juncture perhaps most relevant to Arab foreign fighters was the time they arrived in Syria, where they were 'isolated from the other members, their passports are taken away and they attend meetings in which they are brainwashed'.[230] Despite the rather loose terminology (the use of 'brainwashed'),[231] this reception on arrival in Syria was likely to have exposed any vulnerabilities to indoctrination.

Evidence of the notion of indoctrination in Syria was apparent in the 'textbooks, guidance literature, and indoctrination methods of the Islamic State'.[232] Specifically, according to Jacob Olidort the Islamic State had 'a deliberate strategy it [could] apply systematically to indoctrinating its followers',[233] and 'an indoctrination program for areas under its control'.[234] The result of this strategy was witnessed by a journalist, Jürgen Todenhöfer, who conducted a rare visit in 2014 to meet Arab and other foreign fighters of the Islamic State, in areas under its control including Raqqah (Syria) and Mosul (Iraq). At the end of his visit, he summarised the fighters as 'completely brainwashed; I've never in my life met people like this'.[235] As noted earlier, this first-hand observation chimes with the importance placed on ideological indoctrination and spiritual preparation, and also confirms the finding in a year-long study of over 350 FSA and *Jabhat al-*

Nusrah fighters, that 'many fighters are aggressively socialised and exposed to religious preaching once inside the group'.[236]

According to Fawaz Gerges, Arab foreign (and Syrian) fighters who decided to join the Islamic State had 'to undergo religious re-education to indoctrinate them with the group's theology'.[237] This appeared to include religious stories, often taken out of context, in order 'to help Islamic State members who struggle with committing acts of extreme violence'.[238] This gradual acceptance of more extreme violence may underpin the transition from Arab foreign fighter to Islamist terrorist – a point raised by journalist Nagieb Khaja, who noted that fighters in the Islamic State became more ideologically motivated over time, especially having been exposed to the combat environment of Syria, and attended additional courses.[239]

The other main Islamist group in Syria, *Jabhat al-Nusrah*, also appeared to adopt a strategy to indoctrinate Arab foreign (and Syrian) fighters. One, albeit a Syrian fighter, Muhammad Amin al-Abdullah, explained that '*Jabhat al-Nusrah* leaders kept "brainwashing" him and others about the need for jihad and the rewards that good Muslims get in the Hereafter'.[240] It is also instructive that if a 'suicide bomber' did have a 'last minute' change of mind (as happened with Saudi suicide bomber Muhammad al-Owhali in the 1998 Nairobi US Embassy attacks), the attack coordinator could remotely blow up the explosive-laden vehicle. In a double 'martyrdom/suicide' operation against a Syrian Intelligence building in Damascus on 10 May 2012,[241] Jordanian foreign fighter Abu Musab and Palestinian foreign fighter Muhammad al-Ghazi were both monitored. According to Al-Abdullah 'there was a remote detonator controlled by the leader, who if the suicide bombers failed to blow up the vehicles for any reason, he would detonate the vehicles from a distance'.[242] This is an interesting revelation that perhaps challenges the notion (highlighted earlier) suggested by Todenhöfer that each and every fighter is 'completely brainwashed'.

Finally, this leads to the notion of deception, given that there is evidence that some Arab foreign fighters were deceived. Muhammad Azzam, a journalist for *The New Arab*, documented many cases where Arab foreign fighters were duped by the Islamic State into participating in 'a suicide mission targeting Syrian army soldiers', that later proved to be other 'Syrian opposition groups [including] the al-Nusrah Front'.[243] In addition, Muhammad Azzam cited Arab foreign fighter, Abu Musab al-Tunisi, who posted a video on YouTube, accusing the Islamic State of 'using religious rhetoric in order to convince them their targeted attacks would not harm women or children', which was untrue. Perhaps more alarmingly, Muhammad Azzam also established that Arab foreign fighters who did not volunteer for 'martyrdom/suicide' operations were bound by their pledge of obedience and allegiance to the group.[244] A good example, uploaded to YouTube,[245] showed a weeping and reluctant Uzbeki foreign fighter Jaffar al-Tayyar, who was 'ordered to drive an armoured vehicle packed with explosives into the besieged villages of Fua and Kafriyeh' in Syria.[246] Whilst the frequency of such orders is unknown, as is the use of attack coordinators who can remotely blow up an explosive laden vehicle (as noted earlier), it does perhaps demonstrate that in some cases, there may have been a lack of successful indoctrination and/or a lack of 'martyrdom/suicide' volunteers.

Conclusion

The research undertaken for this chapter suggests that the majority of Arab foreign fighters, with no known prior terrorist links, were more ordinary than radicalised, but went to Syria to participate in a defensive jihad in response to the indisputable Syrian regime violence against fellow Sunni co-religionists. Once in Syria, it appeared that the majority of Arab foreign fighters remained intent on participating in a defensive jihad, fighting in conventional battles against the Syrian regime elements and other rebel combatants. There appears to be a motivational difference between travelling to Syria to become involved in defensive jihad, and travelling there with the intention of joining a terrorist group. In addition, terrorist self-sacrificial ('martyrdom/suicide') attacks against civilians and non-combatants appear infrequent, and the actions of the few should not define the majority. That said, some Arab foreign fighters did subsequently get involved in Islamist terrorist-related activities, although arguably they gained more publicity when such activities were conducted in Europe, rather than in Syria. Those terrorist-related activities that did take place in Syria appeared to be closer to genocide, including crimes against humanity and ethnic cleansing. It seems that over time, being exposed to the realities of defensive jihad on the battlefields of Syria, involving exposure to a more extreme *takfiri* ideology, and undergoing training and indoctrination, many Arab foreign fighters became aligned with Islamist terrorists. It is suggested that many of the Arab foreign fighter excesses in Syria may be better understood as a result of 'obedience to authority' and 'toxic situational forces', consistent with the research findings of Stanley Milgram and Philip Zimbardo, respectively. Arab foreign fighters and Islamist terrorists are not monolithic groupings and thus there will be a need for tailored and nuanced rehabilitation and reintegration programmes for returnees.

Analysis and Reflection

Introduction

The three case study chapters, which were supported by a dataset involving 3,367 Arab foreign fighters, established a series of findings that suggested the need for a more contextualised approach to understanding Arab foreign fighters and Islamist terrorists. Specifically, the three major findings were that Arab foreign fighters who participated in defensive jihad should not necessarily be conflated with Islamist terrorists; that self-sacrificial ('martyrdom/suicide') attacks targeting civilians and non-combatants are not necessarily synonymous with those targeting military forces; and those Arab foreign fighters who subsequently became involved in Islamist terrorist-related activities were largely influenced by variables (or factors) of the *Lucifer Effect*. The *Lucifer Effect* is understood as 'processes of transformation at work when good or ordinary people do bad or evil things [and] may be traced to factors outside the actor, to situational variables . . . unique to a given setting'.[1] These variables involved situational factors unique to defensive jihad including, but not limited to, the personal experience of close combat in a war zone; being subjected to ideological indoctrination; being exposed to charismatic leadership; and operating under a rigid code of obedience to authority. These findings constitute a significant and original contribution to knowledge insofar as they challenge much of the existing literature on Arab forcign fighters, Islamist terrorists and the nexus between them. This chapter analyses these three major findings and enters into a philosophical debate about their relevance and relationship to political violence.

Analysis of Case Study Findings

The Conflation of Arab Foreign Fighters and Islamist Terrorists

Introduction

The first major finding of this research was that Arab foreign fighters who participated in defensive jihad should not necessarily be conflated with Islamist terrorists, in that conflation of the two groups, overlaps notwithstanding, is misleading and represents a form of sociological essentialism. By this it is meant that governments see the two cohorts as having the same set of social characteristics, a view which is simplistic and lacking any meaningful depth. Noted in Chapter 1, such conflation is apparent at all levels of government, including the United Nations Security Council who passed Resolution 2178 in 2014:

> *expressing grave concern* over … foreign terrorist fighters, namely individuals who travel to a State other than their States of residence or nationality for the purpose of the perpetration, planning, or preparation of, or participation in, terrorist acts …[2]

Based on the research conducted for this book, this resolution is not evidence-based – there is no research to support it – to the degree that (as noted in Chapter 1), Professor Alex Schmid argued that 'a distinction ought to be made between a "Foreign Fighter" and a "Foreign *Terrorist* Fighter".'[3] This conflation of violent Islamist activities (defensive jihad and Islamist terrorism) appears to demonstrate a lack of a nuanced understanding, and may ultimately lead to flawed policies concerning foreign fighter returnee programmes. Perhaps such labelling should not come as a surprise, inasmuch as Professor Andrew Silke maintained, 'governments and security agencies are extremely quick to try to label their enemies as terrorists in the hope that this will undermine international sympathy for the organisation and deflect criticism away from any policies used to fight the group'.[4] Although beyond the scope of this book, it is instructive to note that governments and the media often embrace and use other inaccurate labels, for example the term *jihadi*. Whilst the label *jihadi* is also used by Islamist terrorist groups, such linguistic collaboration is not extended to the label *martyrdom operation* (used by most Islamist terrorist groups) where a *suicide attack* is deemed a more appropriate and pejorative term. Therefore, whilst this book fully acknowledges the potential threat posed by some returning Arab (and Western) foreign fighters, labelling them all as 'foreign terrorist fighters' is compelling but not persuasive, and appears to be a politically inspired mischaracterisation.

At the academic level, the conflation of foreign fighters and terrorists is also more the norm than the exception, as noted in Chapter 1. It is illuminating for example, that whilst scholars justify using the label *jihadi-salafi* (or *salafi-jihadi*) because 'it has been employed by the Islamist actors themselves',[5] such synergy between academics and non-state actors is not extended when it comes to the labels *mujahhideen* (those who partake in defensive jihad) and *irhaabiyeen* (those who conduct terrorist acts).[6] It is also revealing that Western governments have supported *mujahhideen* directly or indirectly, for example in 1980s Afghanistan, Libya (2011),[7] and in Syria (post-2011)[8] – yet they often retrospectively label those they supported as terrorists. Perhaps most striking is the term *global jihad* used by scholars, which implicitly conflates the notion of jihad with Islamist terrorism, and has now become conventional wisdom.[9] In this instance, the term *global terrorism* would be the most accurate label.

Finally, there is a need to contextualise Islamist violence; comparisons need to be made by reference to historical military conflicts. Islamist violence is not *sui generis*; the motivations for involvement in defensive jihad are not unique to Islamists or to Muslims in general. Examples would include the International Brigade in the Spanish Civil War and British expatriates at the outbreak of World War I. This may be seen in the reflections of Sir Philip Gibbs which for completeness, are quoted in full:

> Some instinct of a primitive savage kind for open-air life, fighting, killing, the comradeship of hunters, violent emotions, the chance of death, surged up into the brains of quiet boys, clerks, mechanics, miners, factory hands. The shock of anger at frightful tales . . . women foully outraged; civilians shot in cold blood – sent many men at a quick pace to the recruiting agents.[10]

It his book, *Realities of War*, Gibbs was portraying the motivations of young British volunteers who enlisted to fight in World War I, yet arguably these same motivations could also apply to Arab foreign fighters and their motivations to become involved in the defensive jihads in 1980s Afghanistan, Iraq (post-2003) and Syria (post-2011). The emotional narrative that included the need to defend women and civilians appeared a strong motivating factor in all three defensive jihads. Abdullah Azzam had preached that 'Afghan children are being slaughtered, women are being raped, the innocent are killed and their corpses scattered'.[11]

Abu Musab al-Zarqawi had spoken of conditions in Iraq where 'thousands of young boys and old men have been killed, many of the women raped and many houses burnt'.[12] Finally, Saif Allah al-Muhajjir had made an emotional call for fighters to travel to Syria because 'our sisters are raped, our children killed, and our youth are slaughtered'.[13] This suggests a degree of synergy (however unpalatable) between the emotional rationales of World War I British volunteer soldiers and that of many Arab foreign fighters who mobilised to defend their co-religionists, beyond national borders. In order to support such an argument and help differentiate between Arab foreign fighters and Islamist terrorists, this section will discuss the targeting and radicalisation of both transnational Islamist mobilisations.

Targeting and Collateral Damage

At the most basic level, the intentional targeting of either military forces, or civilians and non-combatants, helps to distinguish Arab foreign fighters participating in defensive jihad from Islamist terrorists. Although ideology may not be the sole driver of targeting, it does provide Arab foreign fighters and Islamist terrorists with 'an initial range of legitimate targets ... as a means by which ... to justify attacks'.[14] Put into historical context, ideologically during 'World War II, the civilian became the legitimate target'.[15] In the defensive jihads in 1980s Afghanistan, Iraq (post-2003) and Syria (post-2011), the research found that the targeting by Arab foreign fighters was predominantly directed against Soviet troops, the US-led military coalition and Syrian regime forces, respectively. In 1980s Afghanistan and Iraq (post-2003), Arab foreign fighters were participating in defensive jihad targeting foreign occupation forces – occupations that lacked full international support.[16] Perhaps this lack of full international support underpinning the invasions made resistance to them all the more legitimate in the eyes of Arab foreign fighters. Arguably the same logic could apply to the Syrian insurgency vis-à-vis the perceived lack of support for the Syrian regime in the eyes of the international community.[17] The philosophy of targeting predominantly military forces during defensive jihad contrasts sharply with terrorists targeting predominantly civilians and non-combatants. For example, targeting a British military patrol in Basrah is entirely different (philosophically, ideologically, morally, tactically and strategically) from targeting fellow Muslim women and children shopping in a Basrah market.

Islamist terrorism that involves the intentional targeting of civilians and non-combatants appears altogether different. After the 1980s Afghan jihad, some of the veteran Afghan Arabs switched from targeting Soviet troops to involvement in Islamist terrorist attacks that targeted civilians and non-combatants. As noted in Chapter 2, these included the US embassies in Kenya and Tanzania, and the World Trade Centre attacks in 1993 and 2001. In Iraq, the point of inflection that signalled the move from defensive jihad to Islamist terrorism was the targeting switch, away from US-led coalition troops and onto Iraqi civilians and non-combatants, as shown in Figure 3.3. Unlike the clear delineation between defensive jihad in 1980s Afghanistan and the subsequent Islamist terrorism in the 1990s, the Iraqi insurgency blurred the distinctions[18] somewhat in that Iraqi police and army units (because they were mainly Shi'a) were also targeted. The sectarian overlay within the Iraqi insurgency certainly complicated the overall picture, however relying on Professor Alex Schmid's 'revised academic consensus definition of terrorism'[19] and similar definitions,[20] attacks on trained Iraqi police and army units[21] remain more akin to defensive jihad, than Islamist terrorism. Finally, in Syria, those attacks that did intentionally target civilians and non-combatants could reasonably be considered acts of terrorism, and perhaps part of a wider strategy of genocide.[22]

In Syria, there were numerous attacks against the military apparatus of the Syrian regime that also caused civilian casualties (collateral damage), but as noted in Chapter 4, they often appeared to be misdiagnosed in some academic databases as attacks against civilians. The permissibility of collateral damage has ideological support based on a *fatwa* (*Majmua al Fatawa* 28/537) issued by Ibn Taymiyya (d. 1328). Within the context of human shields ('when the *kaffir* takes Muslims as human shields') according to Ibn Taymiyya, it becomes permissible to fire at civilians and non-combatants.[23] There is also further theological support for the inevitability of collateral damage, with Islamists drawing on the words of the Prophet Muhammad, who sanctioned the use of a rock throwing catapult during the 630 siege of Taif (in Saudi Arabia), where enemy fighters were mixed with a civilian population. Despite any cries of 'no moral equivalence', collateral damage is an accepted and indeed planned for consequence of combat, perpetrated by both state and non-state actors,[24] the only real difference being that the non-state actor is normally employing a less conventional method of attack.

The notion of collateral damage comes down to assessing the intention behind the attack(s). Invariably, civilians that are killed unintentionally are labelled collateral damage. Collateral damage is addressed by conventional militaries using the Law of Armed Conflict (LoAC) that 'stipulates that anticipated civilian or non-combatant injury or loss of life ... incidental to attacks must not be excessive in relation to the expected military advantage to be gained'.[25] The incidence of civilian casualties as a result of Arab foreign fighters attacking a military target has manifested itself particularly in Iraq and Syria. As noted in Chapter 3, collateral damage in Iraq was addressed by Abu Musab al-Zarqawi, who whilst acknowledging the prohibition of killing 'those who are not intended as targets, such as women and children', justified collateral damage 'under the principle of *daroorah*[26] . . . in order to ward off a greater evil, namely, the evil of suspending jihad'.[27] A similar theological justification was also proffered by the late ISIS spokesman, Abu Muhammad al-Adnani, who argued that 'whether the disbeliever is civilian or military . . . both of them are disbelievers . . . the only things that make blood illegal and legal to spill are Islam and an Islamic covenant'.[28] Yet these opinions are not universally supported, as other Arab foreign fighters and Islamist terrorists hold more philosophical views towards collateral damage. In Syria for example, as noted in Chapter 4, Iraqi bomb maker Ibrahim al-Khazali, argued that 'those who were caught up in the attacks will be accepted by God';[29] while Saudi foreign fighter Ayachi Abdul Rahman argued that 'killing the innocent along with the enemy is not acceptable'.[30] The point to be taken away is that, by examining the targeting patterns of the two transnational mobilisations despite the existence of collateral damage, it is possible to start distinguishing between Arab foreign fighters participating in defensive jihad, and those involved in Islamist terrorist-related activities.

Radicalisation

The second method to help differentiate between Arab foreign fighters and Islamist terrorists was by using the concept of radicalisation. This was not unproblematic, in that radicalisation is 'a contentious term vulnerable to subjective and retroactive application',[31] and despite 'the numerous endeavours in academia . . . no metrics exist to gauge radicalisation'.[32] That said, radicalisation is a widely used term, which this book defines as an ideological process whereby groups or individuals begin to embrace views and beliefs of a more extremist nature, which may subsequently cross a threshold that leads to acts of illegal violence of varying degrees of brutality and immorality. As noted in the three case study chapters, there was no compelling evidence to suggest that most Arab foreign fighters (with no known prior links to Islamist terrorism) were necessarily radicalised. This finding is largely predicated on the available data that included geographical origin, age, religiosity, friendship and kinship ties, political and religious ideology, and by comparison with conventional militaries. This finding is not uncontroversial, in that INTERPOL believe that 'terrorist groups work to radicalize individuals and incit[e] them to leave their homes to become foreign terrorist fighters'.[33] Whilst this may apply to some Western foreign fighters, the evidence based on 3,367 Arab foreign fighters suggested that most were not radicalised prior to leaving their homes. Using the conceptualisations advanced by Professor Peter Neumann,[34] this suggests that most Arab foreign fighters did not initially hold extremist beliefs (cognitive radicalisation), or exhibit extremist behaviour (behavioural radicalisation) – a typology empirically supported by other academics.[35] The last point, the apparent lack of behavioural radicalisation, is perhaps the most counter-intuitive finding, in that many Arab foreign fighters clearly demonstrated martial fervour whilst participating in defensive jihad. However, national standing armies also exhibit martial fervour in war zones but are not considered radicalised, hence warranting a greater discussion.

The three case study chapters found that the Arab foreign fighters were largely volunteers who engaged in defensive jihad, often employing unconventional tactics against a militarily superior force. The fact that the militarily superior force was representing a government or governments (for example, the US-led coalition in the Iraqi jihad), to label those foreign fighters opposing the aggression as 'radicalised' is an extremely dubious assertion, suggesting political expediency. There is some academic consensus that the 'conventional wisdom' on radicalisation has been sapped of its 'scientific value',[36] in that it 'is believed to serve political agendas [and] is inherently context-dependent'.[37] In many ways governments, the media and some scholars have conflated Arab foreign fighters and Islamist terrorists by linking them together through the notion of radicalisation, yet perhaps it is the notion of radicalisation that separates the two mobilisations.

It was noteworthy that Chapter 4 found a lack of radicalisation amongst Western (mainly American) foreign fighters who were fighting *against* ISIS in Syria, and also amongst Arab foreign fighters who were fighting against Syrian regime forces. Both cohorts were not necessarily radicalised in the sense of cognitive or behavioural radicalisation but were fighting their respective combatant enemies whilst largely eschewing violence against civilians and non-combatants. They both had deeply held beliefs that innocent people were being killed on a large scale, and that something needed to be done. Arguably it may have been a sense of righteousness (despite the normative value attached to it), rather than radicalisation, which motivated both cohorts. The notion of extreme radicalisation appears to be more applicable to those Arab foreign fighters who became involved in Islamist terrorism that included atrocities tantamount to genocide. The three case study chapters found that over time, in some cases, there appeared to be a greater acceptance of both extremist beliefs (cognitive radicalisation) and extremist behaviour (behavioural radicalisation). Yet despite this perceived state of extreme radicalisation, are all Islamist terrorists actually radicalised? Are there historical military examples involving national standing armies attacking civilians and non-combatants, and if so, were they considered radicalised? This conundrum is re-visited later in the chapter.

The Lack of Nuance Involving Self-Sacrificial ('Martyrdom/Suicide') Operations

Introduction

The second major finding of this research was the uncritical analysis of self-sacrificial ('martyrdom/suicide') attacks, largely due to the lack of nuance concerning the intention of the attacker and the targeting rationale (civilians/non-combatants and military targets). Such analysis continues to dominate the academic literature and hinders conceptual understanding. As noted in Chapter 1, few scholars are willing to recognise this disparity apart from Professors David Cook and Karin Fierke. Cook places 'martyrdom operations' inside inverted commas, being unwilling 'to take a stand on the question of whether people who die during the course of these actions are actually martyrs or not';[38] while Fierke places 'suicide/martyrdom' inside inverted commas in order 'to highlight the tension in the relationship between the two concepts'.[39] This book also adopts a similar position by employing interchangeably the labels self-sacrificial attacks and/or 'martyrdom/suicide' attacks.

The three case study chapters identified self-sacrificial ('martyrdom/suicide') attacks that intentionally targeted civilians and non-combatants, and others that intentionally targeted military forces, often due to military inferiority.[40] As noted in Chapter 4, the tactic of employing *inghimasi* attacks has (re)surfaced in Syria, despite clear ideological differences between ISIS and Al Qaeda concerning appropriate targets.[41] Based on the research undertaken for this book that included 187 identified Arab foreign fighters who conducted self-sacrificial attacks,[42] there is a tactical, conceptual and ideological divide between those attacking a military target (within the context of an insurgency), and those attacking civilians and non-combatants (whether as part of an insurgency or within a peacetime environment). To lump together all attacks that generally involve the death of the attacker as 'suicide attacks' is simplistic if not misleading, and lacks nuance as regards the underlying intentions, targeting rationale and circumstances. In order to support such an argument, the next section will discuss the typology of self-sacrificial ('martyrdom/suicide') attacks, the importance of targeting and finally leverage historical military examples that involved such attacks.

The Typology of Self-Sacrificial ('Martyrdom/Suicide') Attacks

The research conducted for this book found that, based on conventional wisdom, the broadly agreed academic definition of a 'suicide attack' appears to be unreliable, and is at best a platitude. Noted in Chapter 1, many notable academics seem to regurgitate uncritically the explicit theme that 'the perpetrator's death is a precondition of a successful attack', while ignoring the physical targets of such attacks. This raises two issues. First, the success of Japanese kamikaze pilots in World War II was measured by the US military on how 'effective [they were] in hitting ships' and not on 'the perpetrator's death'.[43] Second, the definitional focus on 'the perpetrator's death' also fails to take into account instances when perpetrators of self-sacrificial attacks do survive.[44] For example, Saudi foreign fighter Ahmad Abdullah al-Shaya (discussed in Chapter 3) intentionally conducted a self-sacrificial ('martyrdom/suicide') attack in Iraq killing eleven Iraqi civilians in 2004, but still survived. Based on current academic definitions, al-Shaya's attack would not be labelled a 'suicide attack' – although it still appears in suicide attack databases.[45] This is a recurring and constant theme within the literature on suicide terrorism, yet it is not necessarily an accurate typology and appears at odds with this book's findings that are based on empirical evidence. The only known scholar identified who disputed the academic definition was Professor Ariel Merari, who argued correctly that 'the assertion that the attacker's death is essential for the success of the operation is not always true'.[46]

One of the definitions of suicide is 'a self-destructive action',[47] therefore a suicide attack may reasonably be considered 'an attack that involves a self-destructive action'. However, it is notable that the 1981 Irish Republican Army (IRA) hunger strikes, which resulted in ten deaths, were never labelled (for example) 'suicide starvation', despite being a self-destructive action involving starvation, albeit with a wider political objective (against the UK government). It is therefore important to identify the actual intent of a self-sacrificial attack, which is normally to attack a target consisting of military personnel, or civilians and non-combatants, or a combination of the two, that will likely result in the attacker's own demise. Whilst suggesting the disaggregation of non-state actor self-sacrificial ('martyrdom/ suicide') attacks, even these terms fail to really capture the essence and intent of their missions, when compared with historical military examples. For instance, a former member of the Hitler Youth, Hannsjoachim Koch, noted that due to 'the demand for unselfish self-sacrifice' placed upon the Hitler Youth,[48] when 'cornered they frequently fought to the last child'.[49] This suggests the need for an overarching category of 'self-sacrificial action' or 'self-destructive action', that could then be subsequently categorised to include state and non-state actions involving a variety of intended targets (including oneself as a hunger striker).

As a result of the three case studies, there appears to be a need to more accurately label and define attacks where an individual or a group initiate an explosive device that is being driven or carried, intentionally targeting civilians/non-combatants, even if the individual survives. This requirement should also be extended to include those attacks that intentionally target military forces in a combat zone, in line with the argument of Assaf Moghadam.[50] To label them all simply as suicide attacks is as much political expediency as it is a shamelessly dubious academic assertion. Whilst it may perhaps appear contrived, distinguishing between targets (civilian or military) underpins much of the Law of Armed Conflict and international humanitarian law (as outlined in Chapter 1), which are adopted by most Western governments. Any new definition of a self-sacrificial attack should recognise the predicted demise of the attacker as a means to an end (to kill civilians/non-combatants or military forces), rather than an end in itself. It is suggested that the label 'self-sacrificial ("martyrdom/ suicide") operation' would suffice as long as the intended target was included in the narrative, for reasons that are set out below.

Targeting

Despite the limitations of some academic databases in accurately identifying the intended target of self-sacrificial attacks, careful analysis of supporting documents has revealed that the intended targets appeared to relate broadly to group ideology, identity and strategy. Whilst this is in harmony with Charles Drake,[51] analysis of the employment of self-sacrificial attacks in Iraq is instructive. In Iraq, Figure 3.3 demonstrated that out of the 512 identified self-sacrificial attacks, 17 per cent (eighty-six) targeted US-led coalition troops; 39 per cent (200) targeted Iraqi police and army units; and 44 per cent (226) targeted Iraqi civilians and non-combatants. These figures correlate well with the changing ideology and strategy of Abu Musab al-Zarqawi and draw out three points.

First, al-Zarqawi initially sought to resist the US-led invasion, by targeting coalition forces employing self-sacrificial ('martyrdom/suicide') attacks. Although the US-led coalition labelled them all suicide attacks, such tactics are often employed by the militarily weaker party[52] when combating a numerically superior force. Despite the US-led coalition's armoured vehicles, it was an effective tactic (killing 118 coalition troops) and arguably well within the arsenal of Arab foreign fighters participating in defensive jihad. As noted earlier, the Arab foreign fighters in Iraq were resisting a hugely contentious invasion of Arab territory, which did not enjoy the full support of the UN Security Council, or the international community. Such resistance, including the use of self-sacrificial ('martyrdom/suicide') attacks, appeared to be viewed by Arab foreign fighters as a legitimate defence of Arab land. As Chapter 3 found, the evidence from the biographies of those Arab foreign fighters who conducted such attacks against US-led coalition troops, suggested that they were not necessarily radicalised. Devout, incensed, humiliated and vengeful appeared to be a more accurate portrayal of their motivational circumstances.

Second, the switch in targeting of self-sacrificial ('martyrdom/suicide') attacks from US-led coalition forces to Iraqi police and army personnel, continued to remain under the rubric of defensive jihad, due to their military and paramilitary posture. Despite the Iraqi military personnel being predominantly Shi'a and thus drawing on the (often terroristic) notion of *takfir*, the employment of self-sacrificial ('martyrdom/suicide') attacks, suggests military necessity, tactical efficiency, sacrifice and the 'promise' of a life hereafter. The pejorative labelling of such attacks as suicide attacks is misleading and problematic, in that it ignores the ideology and context of the violence. Third, the switch in targeting of self-sacrificial ('martyrdom/suicide') attacks from US-led coalition forces to Iraqi civilians and non-combatants, whilst reflecting the prevailing ideology of al-Zarqawi,[53] is better situated under the rubric of Islamist terrorism. It is interesting from Chapter 3, that those Arab foreign fighters who targeted US-led coalition troops had no known previous terrorist links; they originated from various Arab countries and had an average age of twenty-five. In comparison, assuming that the dataset is representative in both instances, those Arab foreign fighters who targeted Iraqi civilians and non-combatants had a lower average age of twenty-one, with 46 per cent of them originating from Saudi Arabia. This perhaps suggests that those individuals who targeted Iraqi civilians and non-combatants may have been more open to conduct such attacks due to their age, and who also originated from countries where 'children are exposed to the most extreme cases of intolerance and calls to violence during their education'.[54]

In Syria, relying on the assumption that the majority of self-sacrificial ('martyrdom/suicide') attacks were conducted by Arab foreign fighters,[55] out of the 168 self-sacrificial attacks (from Figure 4.8), 82 per cent targeted Syrian military targets, while only 18 per cent targeted civilians and non-combatants. This is a reliable finding[56] in that out of the known seventy-seven attacks that identified both the Arab foreign fighter and his intended target, 84 per cent (sixty-five) targeted Syrian military targets. This suggests that self-sacrificial attacks were primarily a military tactic in order to provide what Mohammed Hafez referred to as 'strategic advantages in the context of asymmetrical warfare'.[57] At the individual level, such attacks against Syrian military targets appear appropriate within the realm of a defensive jihad where they are conducted *fee sabeel Allah* (in the path of God).

As noted in Chapter 4, whilst ISIS was understandably first proscribed as a terrorist organisation (on 13 December 2011), the terroristic nature of the group appeared less apparent through its use of self-sacrificial ('martyrdom/suicide') attacks, which were infrequent. It appeared that ISIS involvement in Islamist terrorist-related activities was more visible in Western countries, whilst in Syria it was arguably more visible off the battlefield (in the form of atrocities and genocide including ethnic cleansing). Yet the terrorist label is still not clear cut, with academics such as Andrea Beccaro arguing that 'too often, media, research papers, essays and books refer to ISIS as a terrorist group, but this definition is misleading ... insurgent groups have always used guerrilla tactics and terrorism interchangeably because insurgency includes both'.[58] Concerning Syria, whilst controversial, this may also be true, however the call for terrorist attacks targeting Western countries was promoted by the now deceased ISIS spokesman, Abu Muhammad al-Adnani in 2014. He issued a *fatwa* calling on followers of ISIS to 'kill a disbelieving American or European ... including the citizens of the countries that entered into a coalition against the Islamic State'.[59] It is arguably this targeting rationale against the West that gave ISIS its terrorist designation, whereas in Syria its *modus operandi* appears more genocidal and apocalyptic within the context of an insurgency.

Historical Military Examples Involving Self-Sacrificial Attacks

According to Professor Ariel Merari, 'suicide attacks by individuals or small groups of soldiers of many nations have been carried out before and after World War II'.[60] There are numerous historical military examples of ideologically supported self-sacrificial ('martyrdom/suicide') attacks, including Japanese kamikaze pilots in World War II, and Communist Viet Minh forces in the French-Indochina war. There has been some literature drawing analogies and similarities between Japanese kamikaze pilots and Islamist 'suicide bombers',[61] notwithstanding kamikaze pilots 'were acting on behest of a state at war'.[62] However in Syria (and Iraq), the Islamic State ideologue Turki Binali announced that 'the Islamic State is a sovereign polity with courts and a legal system',[63] suggesting it too was a state at war. According to Shiv Malik, 'leaked documents show how ISIS [was] building its state'[64] and were keen 'to demonstrate [that] the Islamic State [was] not a state in name only, but really [was] a state'.[65] After the establishment of the Islamic State in June 2014, some scholars suggested that it could be conceptualised as 'a quasi-state entity',[66] and that it was not 'only a terrorist organization'.[67] Insofar as ISIS self-sacrificial ('martyrdom/suicide') attacks targeted primarily enemy combatants, there appear to be certain similarities with Japanese kamikaze pilots who targeted the American military in the Pacific. The parallels are noteworthy in the sense that 'Japanese suicide attackers seemed to be motivated more by a desire to protect their country'.[68] In a similar vein, Saudi foreign fighter Ayachi Abdul Rahman argued that 'it is not terrorism to defend your country, whether it is Iraq, Afghanistan, Chechnya, Syria'.[69] To label such defence as terrorism and the combatants as terrorists is not entirely persuasive, an argument echoed by Eline Gordts who recognised that many Arab foreign fighters were 'certainly Islamists, but they were not necessarily full-blown jihadi terrorists'.[70] A more nuanced understanding includes the notion of an 'intra-Sunni solidarity norm [involving] young men ... who go to Syria, [who] see its people as their own and feel a more moral and religious obligation to defend them'.[71]

The second historical military example of ideologically supported self-sacrificial attacks involves the Communist Viet Minh forces in the 1954 battle of Dien Bien Phu in French-Indochina. According to Bernhard Fall, the Viet Minh often employed 'Communist death volunteers loaded with explosives'.[72] Those in the French Foreign Legion who witnessed these attacks recalled 'death volunteers carrying satchel charges for the French machine-gun posts';[73] and that 'death volunteers ... with twenty pounds of TNT strapped to their chests, came out of the trenches and threw themselves at the French blockhouses'.[74] It is illuminating to draw parallels between the militarily inferior Arab foreign fighters in Syria, and the militarily inferior Viet Minh fighters at Dien Bien Phu, who were compelled to adopt self-sacrificial attacks in order to defeat the well-defended French strongpoints. This chimes with Smhuel Bar who argued that 'jihadis' conduct self-sacrificial attacks against armies because they 'do not have the military power of their adversaries',[75] therefore self-sacrificial attacks by Arab foreign fighters are, as Bruce Hoffman claimed, a 'weapon of the weak'.[76] A further classic example would also be the Viet Cong 'suicide cells' who attacked US forces during the Tet offensive in Vietnam in 1968.[77] These historical military examples demonstrate that, despite sometimes being labelled 'suicide bombers'[78] or 'death volunteers', self-sacrificial attacks are not unique to defensive jihad, and are more generally 'to do with gaining military advantage'.[79]

Why do some Arab Foreign Fighters Become Involved in Islamist Terrorism?

Introduction

Having tentatively established from the three case study chapters that many Arab foreign fighters were not necessarily radicalised prior to their involvement in defensive jihad, the next logical step would be to examine any radicalisation process that may have influenced those who subsequently participated in Islamist terrorist-related activities. Does membership of a terrorist group mean you are radicalised? For example, can 'a fighter who ... was coerced into joining ISIS, be said to have been radicalized',[80] a question first raised by Eleanor Beevor. As the case study chapters' findings also suggested, not all Arab foreign fighters who subsequently became members of proscribed Islamist terrorist groups appeared to exhibit signs of being radicalised, although the book findings varied across the three case study defensive jihads. For instance, many of the Afghan Arabs who later became Islamist terrorists clearly demonstrated an increased commitment to an extremist political or religious ideology (i.e. radicalised), by exporting their Islamist terrorism to the far enemy. Yet it is not so clear-cut concerning the Arab foreign fighters in Iraq (post-2003) and Syria (post-2011). Here, they were engaged in defensive jihad within an insurgency, where according to Ariel Merari, the 'mode of struggle ... is dictated by circumstances rather than choice' resulting in the adoption of terrorism, 'which is the easiest form of insurgency'.[81] This suggests that the Arab foreign fighter 'mode of struggle' involving terrorism may be better understood by examination of the circumstances and environment of the insurgencies, and how these circumstances may have influenced their subsequent terroristic behaviour. As noted earlier, Jonathan Githens-Mazer and Robert Lambert questioned the 'conventional wisdom on radicalisation'[82] within a Western context, and perhaps the book findings also challenge the 'conventional wisdom on radicalisation' concerning Arab foreign fighter involvement in defensive jihad, that sometimes employs terrorism as part of an insurgency.[83]

The trajectory for those Arab foreign fighters who transited through initial involvement in defensive jihad to subsequent participation in Islamist terrorist-related activities appeared to involve situational variables (or factors) of the *Lucifer Effect* experienced during defensive jihad. These situational variables unique to defensive jihad included, but were not limited to, the personal experience of close combat in a war zone; being subjected to ideological indoctrination; being exposed to charismatic leadership; and operating under a rigid code of obedience to authority. These factors were not necessarily autonomous or discreet, but overlapped and intersected with one another, each contributing to an overall *Lucifer Effect*.

The Lucifer Effect

The overarching factor that appears to help explain the trajectory of some Arab foreign fighters to subsequently participate in Islamist terrorist-related activities, is the influence of the *Lucifer Effect* – understood as 'processes of transformation at work when good or ordinary people do bad or evil things'.[84] The notion of the *Lucifer Effect* is based on psychological research conducted by Professor Philip Zimbardo at Stanford University in 1971, whereby students acted out the roles of either prison guards or prisoners within a prison setting. Zimbardo concluded that individuals' actions can be 'traced to factors outside the actor, to situational variables and environmental processes unique to a given setting',[85] rather than dispositional qualities of 'genetic makeup, personality traits, character, free will and other dispositions'.[86] It is important to recognise that Zimbardo is not alone in his thesis, others scholars have drawn similar conclusions whilst studying terrorism and/or genocide.[87]

It is worth briefly discussing the notion of *ordinary people*, a term used by both Philip Zimbardo and Stanley Milgram,[88] insofar that it is a relational concept with normative connotations. The adjective *ordinary* is understood to mean 'regular, normal, customary, usual, commonplace',[89] and in the context of political contestation may be considered as being 'far removed from extremism'.[90] In the context of terrorist-related activities, Mitchell Silber and Arvin Bhatt used the adjective *ordinary* when describing individuals prior to their involvement in Western home-grown terrorist attacks. They concluded that 'the majority of the individuals involved in these plots began as "unremarkable"'

– they had "ordinary" jobs, had lived "ordinary" lives and had little, if any criminal history'.[91] In the context of the Arab world, as noted in Chapter 1, Asef Bayat defined 'ordinary people' as 'the globalizing youth and other urban grass roots'.[92] Finally, again as noted in Chapter 1, Fred Katz used the label *ordinary people* while Christopher Browning used the label *ordinary men*.[93] The book dataset reveals how ordinary, normal and unremarkable most of the Arab foreign fighters appeared to be: they held ordinary jobs, they lived ordinary lives, they had not been imprisoned, nor had they been involved in prior Islamist activism including terrorism.

The notion of the *Lucifer Effect* (although not the label) was identified by a German-born American philosopher named Hannah Arendt, who followed the 1961 trial of one of the notorious Holocaust perpetrators, Adolf Eichmann. According to Arendt, Eichmann appeared 'neither perverted nor sadistic … [just] terribly and terrifyingly normal'.[94] She summed Eichmann up as 'the banality of evil',[95] having simply been caught up in the situational environment of 1930s National Socialism in Germany. According to Stanley Milgram, Arendt's findings come 'closer to the truth than one might dare to imagine'.[96] Although psychological assessments are rare, it is sobering that the now declassified US Central Intelligence Agency 'psychological assessment of Abu Zubaydah'[97] found that his 'background did not indicate … a history of disturbance or other psychiatric pathology'.[98] This chimes with the view of forensic psychiatrist Marc Sageman who also concluded that Abu Zubaydah was 'frighteningly normal'.[99] The notion of being 'terrifyingly' or 'frighteningly' normal is of course a normative argument, and thus may be better conceptualised as being 'ordinary' – as defined earlier in this chapter. Such assessments mirror the ordinariness portrayed by most of the 3,367 Arab foreign fighters in the book dataset.

The findings from Chapter 2 established that the majority of Afghan Arabs possessed an idealised notion of defending co-religionists in the defensive jihad in 1980s Afghanistan, and (again the majority) had no known prior links to Islamist terrorism. Yet it was found that the environment that evolved in Afghanistan after (and not necessarily during) the defensive jihad, nurtured an ideology that was terroristic in nature.[100] Perhaps it is no surprise that much of the later ideological influence originated from Egyptian Islamist terrorist groups (EIG and EIJ) who effectively hijacked the original notion of defensive jihad. This resulted in some 'terrifyingly or frighteningly normal' men becoming involved in Islamist terrorist-related activities. The overarching notion of the *Lucifer Effect* – involving 'situational variables … unique to a given setting',[101] appears to help explain why some veteran Afghan Arabs from the book dataset (who had no known pre-existing terrorist links) eventually became involved in Islamist terrorist-related activities.

As noted in Chapter 3, the defensive jihad in Iraq (post-2003) soon developed into 'a civil war' that resulted in an insurgency involving Islamist terrorist activity, which was broadly based on the ideology of *takfir* against Shi'a Muslims who were dehumanised as 'crafty and malicious scorpion[s]'.[102] This explicit identification and dehumanisation of the enemy again chimes with the findings of Zimbardo, who suggested that 'war engenders cruelty and barbaric behaviour against anyone considered the Enemy, as the dehumanized, demonic Other'.[103] The notion of dehumanisation (and other 'situational factors') was also recognised by Christopher Browning, who found it 'was sufficient to turn "ordinary men" into "willing executioners"' in Poland in World War II.[104] Returning to Iraq, the influence of the *Lucifer Effect* on Arab foreign fighters included combat in a (civil) war zone; a *takfiri* ideology that dehumanised Shi'a Muslims; being constantly targeted by Western and Iraqi troops; and the requirement of swearing allegiance to al-Zarqawi (resulting in obedience to authority). These factors, which were 'outside the actor'[105] offer a persuasive explanation as to why some Arab foreign fighters in Iraq subsequently became involved in Islamist terrorist-related activities, involving self-sacrificial ('martyrdom/suicide') attacks against civilians and non-combatants.

The 'situational variables and environmental processes'[106] in the defensive jihad in Syria (post-2011) had many similarities with those in Iraq (post-2003); indeed ISIS, their leadership and their ideology spawned from Iraq after the US withdrawal of troops[107] and expanded into parts of Syria. As Chapter 4 established, most of the Arab foreign fighters had no known previous links to terrorism or defensive jihad, yet some were subsequently involved in Islamist terrorist-related activities including genocide, primarily against Shi'a (*Alawite*) Muslims and Yazidi Christians. The identification of a dehumanised 'out-group' is part of the situational environment that contributes to the *Lucifer Effect*, creating 'a hostile imagination . . . embedded deeply in their minds by propaganda that transforms those others into "The Enemy"'.[108]

Combat Experience in a War Zone

It is widely accepted that 'wounds and death [are] the currency of war'[109] and hence involvement in war is unlikely to leave a participant unaffected. However, unlike a nation's standing army that operates under the auspices of the Geneva Convention and Law of Armed Conflict, Arab foreign fighters participating in defensive jihad within a war zone (that involved insurgency, guerrilla tactics and terrorism in a civil war setting), arguably operated in a less humane and legal framework. They did not necessarily enjoy the privileges afforded to prisoners of war under the Geneva Convention, particularly during an inter-group and internecine conflict (such as in 1980s Afghanistan, Iraq and Syria), where torture and death appeared possible outcomes.[110] Poignantly, Professor Richard Holmes found that 'the stresses of the battlefield are so severe as to be totally different from the stresses which an individual might encounter in the course of his everyday life'.[111] It is revealing therefore, that a British foreign fighter in Syria, Abu Salman al-Britani, reflected that 'no one can feel the reality of a battle regardless of how many movies . . . one watches until he has actually been there', recalling that in his 'first battle . . . lay a brother with the majority of his head missing and the whole of his brain exposed'.[112] This is arguably the reality of involvement in defensive jihad, where in Syria '98% of fighters . . . had some direct exposure to'.[113]

Such combat experience in a war zone appeared to push some Arab foreign fighters further along a trajectory to more extreme violent behaviour, including atrocities and acts of Islamist terrorism. Broader research on armed conflict, however, suggests that such behaviour is often more the norm than the exception: Michael Bilton and Kim Sim posited that 'war is hell . . . atrocities are inevitable';[114] while Christopher Browning was more specific, arguing that 'war, and especially a race war, leads to brutalization, which leads to atrocity'.[115] Therefore, according to Stephen Ambrose, 'atrocity is part of war that needs to be faced and discussed'.[116] There are many instances of nations' standing armies committing atrocities against civilians and non-combatants (in effect war crimes). A particularly infamous example would be the 1968 My Lai massacre in the Vietnam War, which according to American psychiatrist Robert Lifton, was 'an atrocity-producing situation'.[117]

This massacre in South Vietnam involved the killing of 504 unarmed civilians by US Marines. According to Hugh Thompson, a helicopter pilot during the massacre, 'there was a lot of evil . . . five hundred and four people were murdered. It was a massacre, and civilians were murdered, not killed'.[118] Thompson believed that the massacre was due to 'revenge, prejudice, negative peer pressure, and bad leadership'. Although perhaps not a common occurrence in Vietnam,[119] the parallels with the *modus operandi* of ISIS and *Jabhat al-Nusrah* are striking. The notion of dehumanisation directed against the Vietnamese population appears tantamount to *takfir*[120] – indeed Thompson in his own words recalled that 'our training had dehumanized the enemy'. The negative peer pressure on individuals away from home fighting in Syria has parallels with US Marines in South Vietnam, vis-à-vis vulnerabilities, the demand for obedience to authority, indoctrination, and mixing with peers who were perhaps more experienced, or in the words of Thompson 'hoodlums, renegades disguised as soldiers'. The point to be made is that the killing of civilians and non-combatants is not the sole preserve of Islamist terrorists, and highlights the parallels of involvement in atrocities (war crimes) by conventional militaries. Within the context of a 'normality of excess', according to Professor Max Taylor, 'at My Lai, a group of otherwise perfectly normal soldiers engaged in a series of horrific acts'.[121]

Although perpetrated by 'a group of otherwise perfectly normal soldiers', Professor Kendrick Oliver argued that 'the crimes of war ... committed by US servicemen in Vietnam were primarily a product of the conflict itself'[122] – in effect the situational environment in which the soldiers operated. Specifically, Professor Richard Holmes identified that the 'road to My Lai was paved, first and foremost, by the dehumanisation of the Vietnamese'.[123] Together at My Lai, these situational factors led to 'a culture of violence, of brutality, with people around you doing the same thing ... there came a point when nothing mattered anymore'.[124] This 'culture of violence' in Vietnam appeared to occur as a result of the 'action-reaction syndrome',[125] whereby 'violence becomes cyclical, ratcheted by corresponding strike and counter-strike'.[126] It appears that 'the permissive structural environment'[127] in which US soldiers found themselves in Vietnam generated a certain psychology, perhaps a culture, of violence where even the Geneva Conventions and the LoAC were sometimes flouted. Renowned military historians have repeatedly identified lapses in military discipline during combat that have resulted in the killing of prisoners and the execution of civilians.[128] As renowned military historian Anthony Beevor noted in his seminal book *Ardennes 1944: Hitler's Last Gamble*, the 'shooting of prisoners of war has always been a far more common practice than military historians in the past have been prepared to acknowledge'.[129]

With this in mind, perhaps Western society should not be surprised that non-state actors including Arab (and Western) foreign fighters also commit atrocities in war zones. All nations' standing armies draw from the same pool of young citizens within society; some enlist to become regular combatants, whilst a small minority may become non-state actors. Authors Michael Weiss and Hassan Hassan made the same point about Arab foreign fighters in Syria: 'these are the same guys that militaries around the world have been counting on forever to be privates or infantrymen. They are knucklehead nineteen-year-olds looking to do something in their life'.[130] This book is not suggesting the conflation of state and non-state combatants, however both cohorts experience the violence of close combat, except that Arab foreign fighters generally operate(d) in a less regulated environment, with less oversight and less accountability. It is suggested that the longer Arab foreign fighters remained in a war zone, the more predisposed they became to committing increasingly violent atrocities (as recognised by German soldier Guy Sajer in World War II),[131] including acts of Islamist terrorism. This suggestion does need qualifying, however, insofar as some Arab foreign fighters had a very short incubation period in defensive jihad, before executing acts of terrorism. Research suggests that these cases invariably involved some form of training and ideological indoctrination.

Ideological Indoctrination

The second situational factor that appeared to influence the trajectory of some Arab foreign fighters to subsequently participate in Islamist terrorist-related activities was the notion of ideological indoctrination, often within a training environment. In Chapter 3, it was agreed that indoctrination entailed 'the teaching of a person or group systematically ... to accept ideas uncritically'.[132] This suggestion is not without its detractors, including Professor Andrew Silke, who argued that 'you don't have to teach, you don't have to brainwash, you don't have to push, you don't have to pressure, it goes around by osmosis'.[133] The notion of osmosis perhaps compliments the overall findings of this book, in that the two factors are not mutually exclusive – perhaps the notion of ideological indoctrination simply reinforces the process of osmosis.

One interesting empirical study conducted by British psychiatrist William Sargant demonstrated 'how beliefs, whether good or bad, false or true, can be forcibly implanted in the human brain; and how people can be switched to arbitrary beliefs altogether opposed to those previously held'.[134] He concluded that 'it is quite possible to indoctrinate people with ideas ... or even deliberate lies; and keep them fixed in these beliefs'.[135] Across the three case study chapters, the incidence of indoctrination appeared to vary, particularly concerning the employment of self-sacrificial ('martyrdom/suicide') attacks that targeted civilians and non-combatants. As Chapter 2 established, many Afghan Arabs remained in Afghanistan after the Soviet withdrawal[136] and became exposed to a 'range of political beliefs along the Islamist spectrum',[137] particularly involving 'the Jalalabad School of jihad'.[138] This created the conditions for the ideological indoctrination of many Afghan Arabs,[139] who subsequently returned to their countries to attack the near enemy (for example, Algeria and Libya), or became involved in terrorist attacks that were undergirded by a new ideological emphasis that targeted the far enemy (for example, the 9/11 attacks). In many cases, training camps were established based on nationalities (for example, Algerians and Jordanians),[140] where the ideological indoctrination involved either a religious nationalist agenda or a transnational global agenda.

The subsequent Islamist terrorism witnessed in Iraq (post-2003), occurring as it did in parallel with insurgent violence, was in part due to the presence of ideological indoctrination propagated by Abu Musab al-Zarqawi. The Islamist terrorism in Iraq was largely sign-posted by self-sacrificial ('martyrdom/suicide') attacks that targeted Iraqi civilians and non-combatants, yet the ideological indoctrination was underpinned by *takfir* against all Shi'a Muslims in Iraq, which included the country's military and police forces. This ideology blurred the targeting distinctions (between military and civilians) and consequently blurred the distinctions between defensive jihad and Islamist terrorism. That said, the results of the analysis conducted for Chapter 3 suggested that the ideological indoctrination was primarily aimed at two groups of Arab foreign fighters: those newly arrived in Iraq and arguably quite impressionable and more susceptible to being influenced, and those who may have had 'age-related vulnerabilities'.[141] It should be noted that the notion of vulnerability does not necessarily supplant the agency held by youth, however there is a growing body of evidence to suggest that 'terrorist groups prey upon the vulnerabilities of young persons . . . and in some cases, youth have been . . . tricked into participating in terrorist activities, including suicide bombings'.[142] To buttress this argument, Professor John Horgan also recognised 'the emotional responsiveness of people at a younger age and the increased susceptibility towards greater involvement this might bring'[143] – a position further reinforced by Christopher Browning.[144]

Finally, the ideological indoctrination that supported Islamist terrorism in Syria (post-2011) occurred within the context of insurgent violence. As Chapter 4 suggested, much of the Islamist terrorism perpetrated by ISIS was more representative of genocide, rather than specific terrorist attacks employing self-sacrificial ('martyrdom/suicide') operations. The ideological current of ISIS, with its particular emphasis on the establishment of an Islamic caliphate, the promotion of *takfir* and the staunchly anti-Shi'a rhetoric, seemed to have been embraced through indoctrination as well as by osmosis by socialisation. What appeared apparent in the case of Arab foreign fighters arriving in Syria was the presence of an identifiable process of formal ideological indoctrination.[145] The key question is, how influential was this ideological indoctrination in encouraging acts of terrorism in Syria? The answer appears that it was a necessary but not a sufficient cause for such acts, and that 'the phenomenon is far more complex than the superficial appeal of jihadist ideology'.[146] This is supported by veteran Egyptian Afghan Arab Mustafa Hamid, who argued that 'Arabs follow a leader not an idea; they find a person they trust and then they follow him – not the idea'.[147] Hamid's argument thus warrants an examination of the influence of charismatic authority.

The Influence of Charismatic Authority/Leadership

The third situational factor that appeared to influence the trajectory of some Arab foreign fighters to subsequently participate in Islamist terrorist-related activities was the influence of charismatic authority. According to the famous German sociologist Max Weber (d. 1920) charismatic authority involves a leader who 'is personally recognized as the innerly "called" leader of men. Men do not obey him by virtue of tradition or statute, but because they believe in him'.[148] This understanding is further advanced by David Hofmann and Lorne Dawson, who opined that 'charismatic authority is a form of legitimate domination exercised by an individual who is perceived to possess divinely given or inspired abilities',[149] and 'is something that is *attributed* to a leader, and not something the leader possesses'.[150] There is broad academic consensus as to the centrality and importance of charismatic authority in the birth of Islamist movements, both violent and non-violent.[151] In particular, Quintan Wiktorowicz stressed the centrality of 'reputation and sacred authority' of Islamic scholars, but 'also other characteristics, like charisma'.[152] It appears that much of the scholarly role was 'to transform widespread grievances and frustrations into a political agenda for violent struggle'.[153] It should be emphasised however that these scholars were examining a rather different cohort – a home-grown Western 'bunch of guys'[154] – rather than Arab foreign fighters who had already mobilised and become involved in defensive jihad.

As noted in Chapter 4, according to Hofmann and Dawson, the notion of charismatic authority is 'a potentially critical element of the process of radicalization'.[155] In particular, according to Jamie Bartlett and Carl Miller, this is engendered by 'previous conflict experience abroad, or the perception of "battle hardiness", including the charisma and gravitas derived from such experiences'.[156] Particular examples of individuals who possess(ed) charismatic authority from the case study chapters included Abdullah Azzam,[157] Osama bin Laden,[158] Shaykh Omar Abdul Rahman,[159] Abu Musab al-Zarqawi[160] and Abu Bakr al-Baghdadi.[161] Regarding ISIS, Eleanor Beevor also argued persuasively that the group practises 'coercive radicalisation' through 'charismatic authority' once they capture territory, noting that some may be 'initially unwilling subjects'.[162] This book extends Eleanor Beevor's finding by suggesting that some Arab foreign fighters, who having mobilised to participate in defensive jihad, appeared to be lured into ISIS on their arrival in Syria, regardless of which group they had originally intended to join. This resulted in some Arab foreign fighters getting involved (some, somewhat involuntarily) in Islamist terrorist-related activities, and subsequently defecting from ISIS, as recorded in the ISIS General Border Administration forms and also identified by Professor Peter Neumann.[163]

The Influence of Obedience to Authority

In tandem with the notion of charismatic leadership, is the notion of obedience to authority, defined by Professor Stanley Milgram as 'a situation in which a person gives himself over to authority and ... no longer regards himself as responsible for his actions'.[164] It is clear from the evidence presented in the case study chapters that Islamist terrorist groups demanded unquestioning obedience, and in many cases, required the pledging of allegiance (*baya*) to a charismatic leader. As noted in Chapter 4, the ISIS magazine Dabiq 12 reminds its readership that it 'is obligatory to yield to the opinion [Allah] has chosen and submit to his order'.[165] The impact of obedience to authority was tested by Milgram at Yale University in 1961, whereby 'a person ... [was] told to carry out a series of acts that come increasingly into conflict with conscience'.[166] Milgram established that:

> ordinary people ... can become agents in a terrible destructive process. Moreover, even when the destructive effects of their work become blatantly clear, and they are asked to carry out actions incompatible with fundamental standards of morality, relatively few people have the resources needed to resist authority.[167]

It is interesting that the findings of Milgram's study[168] were validated thirty-five years later by American psychologist Jerry Burger (in 2009), providing perhaps renewed reason to draw on Milgram's findings on the influence of authority.[169] Milgram made an important point concerning 'legitimate authority' and concluded that a 'substantial number of people do what they are told to do, irrespective of the content of the act and without limitations of conscience, so long as they perceive that command comes from a legitimate authority'.[170] The content of the act is important and could reasonably include terrorism and/or genocide, which according to Ervin Staub, requires a 'strong respect for authority and strong inclination to obedience.[171] For context, this also appeared to be the case in the 1968 My Lai massacre, in that the US Marines involved in the massacre 'were following orders in a context in which they had been trained to follow orders'.[172] Scientifically, this chimes with the research of Milgram, who also established that 'orders from a man with epaulets, and men are led to kill with little difficulty',[173] thus the results of his research arguably go some way to also explain why some Arab foreign fighters subsequently became involved in terrorism.

Conclusion

The analysis conducted for this book established three major findings. First, Arab foreign fighters who participate in defensive jihad should not necessarily be conflated with Islamist terrorists; overlaps notwithstanding, they tend to have different intentions, objectives and targeting rationales. Second, self-sacrificial ('martyrdom/suicide') attacks that targeted civilians and non-combatants are not necessarily synonymous with those aimed at military targets – again the intentions, objectives and targeting rationales tend to be different. Third, those Arab foreign fighters who subsequently became involved in Islamist terrorist-related activities were influenced by key situational factors that contributed to the *Lucifer Effect*, including, but not limited to, the personal experience of close combat in a war zone; being subjected to ideological indoctrination; being exposed to charismatic leadership; and operating under a rigid code of obedience to authority. These findings are important and hence the following chapter examines their implications on policy makers and academics, and offers an overall conclusion.

6

Implications and Conclusion

Introduction

This chapter draws on the analysis and reflections presented in Chapter 5, in order to suggest some implications relevant to these findings for policy makers and academia. It addresses the implications of conflating Arab foreign fighters and Islamist terrorists; it discusses the need to disaggregate self-sacrificial ('martyrdom/suicide') attacks based on the targeting rationale; and it explores the impact of the four situational factors (as part of the *Lucifer Effect*) on future reintegration programmes for returnees. The chapter closes by addressing the limitations of the study and offers an overall conclusion.

Implications for Policy

The first finding established the need to differentiate between Arab foreign fighters who participate(d) in defensive jihad, and Islamist terrorists, due to their differing intentions, objectives and targeting rationales. From a policy perspective, the implications are far reaching, but are perhaps most relevant to Arab governments assuming the eventual return of Arab foreign fighters. The assumption is that Arab foreign fighters 'who gain combat experience in Iraq and Syria ... come back as hardened veterans, steady in the face of danger and skilled in the use of weapons and explosives – ideal terrorist recruiting material'.[1] Arguably therefore, Arab (and indeed Western) governments need to develop individualised reintegration programmes (de-radicalisation programmes) that recognise that not all foreign fighters are automatically terrorists. This would entail a recalibration in the targeting and reintegration of those who partook in defensive jihad, and in particular the content of CT/CVE/PVE messaging,[2] which arguably should be crafted with respected and qualified Islamic scholars. This could assist in shaping the 'post-conflict behaviour' of veteran Arab foreign fighters (and terrorists) and in preventing Islamist terrorist attacks in both the Arab world and Europe.

The post-conflict behaviour of Arab foreign fighters is likely to include one or more of the following: reintegrating back into society; remaining involved in defensive jihad in another theatre; becoming (more) involved in religious nationalist terrorism in their home countries; or finally becoming involved in global terrorism. Aware that half of the above 'post-return behaviours' are violent in nature, some Arab foreign fighters returning from Syria are likely to pose a threat to their autocratic regimes. The threat is real, as already some Arab foreign fighters have returned from Syria and inspired or personally conducted terrorist attacks in their home countries including Saudi Arabia,[3] Tunisia,[4] Egypt,[5] Libya,[6] Kuwait[7] and Yemen.[8] However, what this book has established is that not all Arab foreign fighters or all former members of ISIS (for example) are necessarily terrorists. Treating all Arab foreign fighters and individuals returning from Syria as terrorists does not correlate with this book's findings, and lacks a nuanced understanding about the very nature of the phenomenon, and the threat returnees may, or may not, represent. If the aim of receiving governments is the reintegration and desistance of returnees, treating them all as terrorists will hinder such policies.

It is clear therefore that if Arab governments and regimes do not (or are unwilling to) prevent their citizens from getting involved in a foreign defensive jihad, they would benefit from establishing *post hoc* rehabilitation strategies. Whilst some Arab countries do have de-radicalisation programmes, for the most part they are particularly harsh models that also include the death penalty.[9] Examples include Saudi Arabia,[10] the United Arab Emirates (UAE),[11] Morocco,[12] Egypt,[13] Jordan,[14] Tunisia[15] and indeed Syria.[16] This approach is again problematic, in that 'returnees are likely to take up arms ... if the[y] are not being integrated into society'.[17] As Chapter 2 found, some veteran Afghan Arabs subsequently became involved in Islamist terrorism due in part to their inability to return home without being arrested and/or imprisoned. Perhaps this was a regime-strategic decision, as it resulted in Islamist terrorism being perpetrated beyond regime borders and thus beyond regime jurisdiction and responsibility – in effect implicitly exporting terrorism overseas. In most cases, Arab regimes are unelected officials who feel threatened by the thought of democratic elections for fear of being unseated. Their answer is to repress their citizens and any form of dissent. A typical example would be the so-called moderate United Arab Emirates (UAE), which, in 2013, convicted sixty-nine Emiratis whose only 'crime' was signing 'a petition calling on the Emirati government to institute a relatively modest set of democratic reforms'.[18] The likelihood of returning Emirati foreign fighters being fairly treated (legally, morally and/or humanely) is difficult to conceive, hence they, among many other Arab foreign fighters, are unlikely to return home and more likely to become part of a new generation of stateless Islamist terrorists. History appears to be repeating itself, where such obtuse and autocratic policies are likely to eventually 'come home to roost'.[19]

Second, self-sacrificial ('martyrdom/suicide') attacks that targeted civilians and non-combatants are not necessarily synonymous with those aimed at military targets. This finding is probably the most politically unpalatable, due in part to the monopoly states have on the application and use of violence. It appears that the state is always right, despite the autocratic or totalitarian tendencies of regimes and governments, particularly in the Arab world. Such a position makes any resistance to regime and government power illegitimate, creating the need to use pejorative terms for those who resist. It is also important to recognise the nature and intent supporting self-sacrificial ('martyrdom/suicide') attacks, that are primarily aimed at enemy combatants (whether state or non-state actors). It somewhat begs the question whether there is any moral, ethical or legitimate difference between a recklessly brave infantry attack on an ISIS position (that results in an infantryman's death), or an Arab foreign fighter's self-sacrificial ('martyrdom/suicide') attack on the same ISIS position (where the fighter also dies). ISIS is a recognised terrorist organisation, thus attacking a common enemy by whatever available military means has a degree of legitimacy.[20] Terminology notwithstanding, Professor David Cook succinctly noted that 'the line between bravery in battle and suicide is blurred'.[21] The converse is a self-sacrificial ('martyrdom/suicide') attack aimed at civilians and non-combatants, which has no legitimacy. Discussed in Chapter 5, but repeated again here, is that the intentional targeting of foreign forces in Iraq (conventionally or unconventionally), is entirely different (philosophically, ideologically, morally, tactically and strategically) than targeting women and children shopping in an Iraqi market.

Third, those Arab foreign fighters that subsequently became involved in Islamist terrorist-related activities were influenced by key situational factors contributing to the *Lucifer Effect*, including but not limited to, the personal experience of close combat in a war zone; being subjected to ideological indoctrination; being exposed to charismatic leadership; and the demand for obedience to authority. Looking first at the influence and impact of personal experience of close combat in a war zone within an insurgency suggests that the challenge is to recognise how this may have affected Arab foreign fighters on their return to their home country. Arguably, some returning individuals are likely to be suffering from mental illness, including post-traumatic stress disorder (PTSD),[22] and would most likely benefit from some form of decompression and rehabilitation, rather than simply being incarcerated in prison. Some Western countries, such as Denmark,[23] have recognised the presence of PTSD in foreign fighters and offered suitably tailored rehabilitation programmes. If the intent is to prevent future terrorist attacks, recognising and managing the impact of combat experience in an individual, post-conflict, could have tangible and long-term positive effects.

The influence and impact of being subjected to ideological indoctrination is similar to the personal experience of close combat in a war zone. The ideological overlaps would include enmity towards the 'out group', the moral, religious, 'legal' justifications for an armed conflict and the military necessity for the use of force. Again, foreign fighters' minds are likely to need time to readjust to a peacetime existence, and absorb more moderate ideological messaging from more moderate Islamic scholars and preachers. The Saudi rehabilitation model perhaps recognises this and focuses on three programmes, which include rehabilitation, counselling and aftercare.[24] In her edited book, *Trauma Rehabilitation After War and Conflict*, Professor Erin Martz stressed the importance of the 'psychological component of ... post-conflict rehabilitation'.[25] Additionally, many Arab regimes control the content of the sermons in mosques, and direct a less politicised message to the congregations. Western countries have yet to embrace such a policy, possibly due to feelings of over-reach and the secular nature of most governments.

The influence of charismatic leadership or authority was fairly central to both the initial mobilisation of Arab foreign fighters, and the subsequent involvement in terrorism by some of them. The implication of this suggests that governments should target those 'charismatic leaders' in order to eradicate that influence. However, history has revealed that with the deaths of Abdullah Azzam, Osama bin Laden and Abu Musab al-Zarqawi, their philosophy and ideology lived on. Arguably their 'martyrdom' invested them with increased charismatic authority. Decapitation strategies probably overlook 'the realities of the group dynamics inherent in the charismatization process, and assumes the charismatic leader is either difficult to replace or irreplaceable'.[26] The implication of this is perhaps the need for individuals with matching charismatic leadership who possess suitable credentials such as fellow reformed foreign fighters (for example, Abdullah Anas and/or Musa al-Qarni)), or highly respected (although arguably hugely controversial) religious authorities (for example, the Jordanian ideologue, Abu Muhammad al-Maqdisi) who are not perceived to be government officials.

Finally, the influence of operating under a rigid code of obedience to authority undoubtedly influenced the behaviour of many Arab foreign fighters. As noted in Chapter 5, a 'substantial number of people do what they are told to do, irrespective of the content of the act',[27] thus it appears to be a psychological weakness inherent in all humans. This leads to the conclusion that any post-conflict rehabilitation programme must acknowledge the notion of 'obedience to authority' and recognise how 'ordinary people . . . can become agents in a terribly destructive process'.[28] The implications of operating under a rigid code of obedience to authority appear inextricably linked to the notion of ideological indoctrination, thus rehabilitation programmes similar to the Saudi model that involves rehabilitation, counselling and aftercare, would best challenge the notion of obedience to authority.

Implications for Further Research

One of the many research challenges faced by terrorism scholars remains explaining why, given a large body of individuals exposed to the same environmental conditions (generally in their home countries), only a few become involved in terrorism. John Horgan addressed this challenge by advancing the concept of 'predisposing risk factors' – but these factors were considered most relevant at the juncture of '*initially becoming involved*' in terrorism.[29] This book, however, has examined a different part of their trajectory – that of already '*being involved*' in Islamist violence (that includes but is not limited to terrorism). The conundrum in this book is why, given the large number of Arab foreign fighters who travelled to Afghanistan, Iraq and/or Syria and had been exposed to the same situational factors, some but not others became involved in terrorism. This is probably best explained by the absence of an identifiable control group from which to conduct such analysis (i.e. Arab foreign fighters who were not exposed to the situational factors having arrived in a foreign conflict theatre). In many ways, the concept of an identifiable control group within a defensive jihad, whilst seductive, is arguably impractical. Perhaps the reason why some Arab foreign fighters attacked civilians and non-combatants while others attacked military targets is more consistent with the general idiosyncratic dynamics of human behaviour within the fog of war. That said, despite the current impracticalities, further research in this area may be achievable in the future by interviewing Arab foreign fighter returnees.

Second, future research could also include conducting a comparative study that examines how Western foreign fighters, who initially participate in defensive jihad subsequently become involved in Islamist terrorist-related activities. Do the situational variables (inherent within a defensive jihad context) affect Western and Arab foreign fighters in the same way? Are Western Islamist foreign fighters, who often lack knowledge of the Arabic language, more easily persuaded to commit atrocities including terrorism and genocide? There is anecdotal evidence to suggest that this is true.[30] Are there cultural dissimilarities? Do Arabs have a greater propensity for obedience to authority? Can both the Western and the Arab world learn from each other about rehabilitation programmes?

Third, the findings in this book are not exclusive of other theories or explanations. These findings are empirically based on the available evidence, however it is accepted that they do not necessarily represent the definitive answer. There are other very worthy theories including social movement theory, social identity theory and violent socialisation theory, and other factors including radicalisation, kinship and social ties, education, democracy, repression and education. These theories and factors all contribute to the debate on Islamist foreign fighters and terrorists, and whilst their appearance and influence were noted during the research, they appeared to possess less explanatory value compared to those presented in this book. Additionally, despite the continual quest by academics to derive a new theory that can explain the emergence of terrorism, it is instructive that whilst not decrying those endeavours, sometimes the older, tried and tested theories, in particular Zimbardo's *Lucifer Effect* and Milgram's obedience to authority theories continue to retain relevance in the twenty-first century. Lastly, it appears that War Studies, in particular the behaviour of men (and women) in battle, may offer a contextualisation of warfare and also help explain why some individuals become involved in defensive jihad, while others seek a more terroristic and morally unjustified trajectory.

Conclusion

This book has attempted to explain why many Arab foreign fighters became involved in defensive jihad, and why some subsequently became involved in Islamist terrorist-related activities that targeted civilians and non-combatants. The book drew on a unique dataset of 3,367 Arab foreign fighters who had been involved in one or more of three defensive jihads: 1980s Afghanistan, Iraq (post-2003) and Syria (post-2011). By using such tools, the book provides rigorous evidence-based research, and in doing so, has challenged some basic academic assumptions. Specifically, Arab foreign fighters who participate in defensive jihad should not necessarily be conflated with Islamist terrorists; overlaps notwithstanding, they often appeared as markedly different cohorts. This book has also established the need to disaggregate self-sacrificial ('martyrdom/ suicide') attacks, in order to better understand their intent and targeting rationale. Calling all such attacks 'suicide attacks' is simplistic, politically expedient and lacks any nuance. The widely accepted definition of a suicide attack that focuses on the demise of the perpetrator, rather than on the intended target, appears an extremely dubious assertion.

There appeared to be two different phases in the lives of Arab foreign fighters. The first phase took place in their country of residence, where their decision to travel abroad to engage in a defensive jihad was formulated. The notion of radicalisation struggled to explain their desire to travel, and the young Arab volunteers appeared to be largely unremarkable and ordinary young men. A second phase took place after their arrival in the conflict zone involving defensive jihad, and many Arab foreign fighters were influenced by variables (or factors) of the *Lucifer Effect*. Those that became involved in Islamist terrorist activities were largely influenced by the situational environment that included, but were not limited to, the personal experience of close combat in a war zone; being subjected to ideological indoctrination; being exposed to charismatic leadership; and the demand for obedience to authority. Aware that many Arab and Western foreign fighters from the Syrian insurgency have returned home, a greater understanding of their initial motivations (to travel) and their subsequent behaviour (in Syria) is vital in order to assess whether they may pose a threat to their country of residence.

Notes

Chapter 1

1   US Department of State, 'The wandering mujahidin: Armed and dangerous', Bureau of Intelligence and Research, *The Washington Institute*. Weekend Edition. 21–22 August 1993, p. 5. Available at www.washingtoninstitute.org/uploads/Documents/other/StateDept199308WanderingMujahidin.pdf (accessed 21 December 2014).
2   The pilots were an Egyptian, Muhammad Atta, a Lebanese, Ziad Jarrah and an Emirati, Marwan al-Shehhi.
3   Ken Ballen, *Terrorists in Love: The Real Lives of Islamic Radicals* (London, 2011), p. 7.
4   Steven Komarow and Sabah Al-Anbaki, 'Would-be suicide bomber angry at those who sent him', *USA Today*, 24 January 2005.
5   Erin Cunningham, 'In stark transformation, Egyptian rights activist dies fighting for the Islamic State', *The Washington Post*, 5 November 2014. Available at www.washingtonpost.com/world/in-stark-transformation-egyptian-rights-activist-dies-fighting-for-the-islamic-state/2014/11/05/d03d0339-203e-42f0-9e87-95cff45cd1cb_story.html (accessed 10 November 2014).
6   Thomas Hegghammer found 'that no more than one in nine foreign fighters returned to perpetrate attacks in the West'. See Thomas Hegghammer, 'Should I stay or should I go? Explaining variation in Western jihadists' choice between domestic and foreign fighting', *American Political Science Review*, February 2013b, p. 10. Also, Mubaraz Ahmed, Milo Comerford and Emman El-Badawy found that 76 per cent of their 'prominent jihadi' terrorists had been foreign fighters. See Mubaraz Ahmed, Milo Comerford and Emman El-Badawy, 'Milestones to Militancy: What the Lives of 100 Jihadis Tell us about a Global Movement', *Centre on Religion and Politics*, Tony Blair Faith Foundation, April 2016, p. 6.
7   The 9/11 Commission Report surmised that Ahmed al-Ghamdi and Saeed al-Ghamdi had fought in Bosnia (p. 233), while Khalid al-Mihdhar and Nawaf al-Hazmi had fought in Chechnya (p. 155). See *The 9/11 Commission Report* (London, 2005).
8   'Foreign terrorist fighters' were defined on 24 September 2014, in the United Nations Security Council (UNSC) Resolution (2178: 2) as 'individuals who travel to a state other than their states of residence or nationality for the purpose of the perpetration, planning, or preparation of, or participation in, terrorist acts or the providing or receiving of terrorist training, including in connection with armed

conflict'. See United Nations Security Council, 'Resolution 2178 (2014), 24
September 2014. Available at www.un.org/en/sc/ctc/docs/2015/SCR%20
2178_2014_EN.pdf (accessed 6 July 2016).

9   United Nations Security Council Counter-Terrorism Committee, 'Background
Note: Stemming the flow of foreign terrorist fighters', Madrid, 27–28 July 2015a.
Available at www.un.org/en/sc/ctc/docs/2015/0721Special%20Meeting%20
Madrid%20-%20General%20background%20Note.pdf (accessed 7 June 2016).

10   Ronald W. Reagan, Proclamation 4908. Afghanistan Day. By the President of the
United States of America, 10 March 1982. Available at www.reagan.utexas.edu/
archives/speeches/1982/31082c.htm (accessed 20 January 2014).

11   Anne Speckhard and Mubin Shaikh, *Undercover Jihadi: Inside the Toronto 18
Al Qaeda Inspired, Homegrown Terrorism in the* West (McLean, 2014), p. 244.
The 'freedom fighter versus terrorist' labelling is one of the reasons why it is still
impossible to arrive at a consensual definition of terrorism.

12   Alex P. Schmid, 'Foreign (terrorist) fighter estimates: Conceptual and data issues',
International Centre for Counter-Terrorism Policy Brief, October 2015, p. 5.

13   David Malet, 'Foreign fighter mobilization and persistence in a global context',
Terrorism and Political Violence 0 (2015), p. 5.

14   Thomas Hegghammer, 'The foreign fighter phenomenon: Islam and transnational
militancy', *Belfer Center for Science and International Affairs*, February 2011a, p. 2.

15   Fawaz A. Gerges, *The Far Enemy: Why Jihad went Global* (Cambridge, 2005), p. 161.

16   This book definition is adapted from Thomas Hegghammer to reflect the sectarian
(Sunni–Shi'a) nature of the contemporary conflicts in Iraq and Syria. Thomas
Hegghammer, 'The rise of Muslim foreign fighters: Islam and the globalization of
jihad', *International Security* 35/3 (2010a), p. 53.

17   Philipp Holtmann recognised that 'jihad can contain elements of terrorism – in
terms of ideology, strategy and tactics'. The most obvious overlap is where Arab
foreign fighters employ terrorist tactics, such as in Iraq and Syria. This is addressed
in Chapters 4 and 5 respectively. See Philipp Holtmann, 'Terrorism and jihad:
Differences and similarities', *Perspectives on Terrorism* 8/3 (2014), p. 140.

18   Philip G. Zimbardo, *The Lucifer Effect: How Good People Turn Evil* (London, 2007),
p. 8.

19   Ibid., p. 7.

20   The Concise Oxford Dictionary (Oxford, 1995), p. 960.

21   Asef Bayat, *Life as Politics: How Ordinary People Change the Middle East*
(Amsterdam, 2010).

22   See Fred E. Katz, *Ordinary People and Extraordinary Evil: A Report on the Beguilings
of Evil* (Albany, 1993), and Christopher R. Browning, *Ordinary Men: Reserve Police
Battalion 101 and the Final Solution in Poland* (New York, 1998).

23   Katz, *Ordinary People and Extraordinary Evil*, pp. 1–10.

24 Edward T. Hall, *Beyond Culture* (Garden City NY, 1976), p. 213.

25 John Horgan, *The Psychology of Terrorism* (London, 2005), p. 85.

26 According to David Malet the 'foreign contingent' in 1980s Afghanistan was
    500–2,000 Afghan Arabs; in Iraq the 'foreign contingent' was 3,000–5,000
    (in various jihadi groups); and in Syria the 'foreign contingent' was 10,000–16,000
    (in various jihadi groups). See Malet, *Foreign Fighter Mobilization and Persistence in
    a Global Context*, p. 10.

27 Biographies of foreign fighters killed in Afghanistan and Pakistan between
    2002 and 2006, involving fifteen veteran Arab foreign fighters from 1980s
    Afghanistan.

28 The 'Sinjar records' were captured by US forces in October 2007 near Sinjar, along
    the Iraq-Syrian border, and comprised of 707 foreign fighters, including 555 Arabs.
    See Joseph Felter and Brian Fishman, 'Al Qaeda's Foreign Fighters in Iraq: A First
    Look at the Sinjar Records', *Harmony Project* (2007).

29 According to Terry McDermott, the Abu Zubaydah diaries 'contain the most
    detailed portrait of the interior life of a dedicated jihadi that we have ever seen, and
    that we might ever see'. See Terry McDermott, 'Abu Zubaydah and the banality of
    "jihadism"', *Al Jazeera America*. 19 December 2013. See also Abu Abu Zubaydah,
    'The Diary of Abu Zubaydah 1991', *United States Department of Justice. Federal
    Bureau of Investigation*. Unclassified. *Al-Jazeera America*. Available at http://america.
    aljazeera.com/multimedia/2013/11/original-documentabuzubaydahdiariesvolumeo
    ne.html (accessed 12 February 2014).

30 See Zimbardo, *The Lucifer Effect: How Good People Turn Evil*; Stanley Milgram,
    Obedience to Authority: An Experimental View (London, 1974).

31 The ideology of political Islam includes defensive jihad and Islamist terrorism;
    martyrdom and suicide attacks; the employment of *takfir* (excommunication of
    Sunni and Shi'a Muslims); the adoption and imposition of *Sharia* law and the
    notion of an Islamic state.

32 See David Cook, *Understanding Jihad* (Berkeley, 2005), p. 93.

33 See Michael Bonner, *Jihad in Islamic History* (New Jersey, 2008), p. 13; and Cook,
    Understanding Jihad, p. 32.

34 See Charles W. Amjad-Ali, 'Jihad and Just War Theory: Dissonance and Truth',
    Dialog: A Journal of Theology, 48/3 (2009), p. 245.

35 For more on 'just war theory' and jihad see Amjad-Ali, *Jihad and Just War Theory*,
    pp. 239–247; and John Kelsay, *Arguing the Just War Theory in Islam* (London, 2009).

36 See Quintan Wiktorowicz, 'A genealogy of radical Islam', *Studies in Conflict and
    Terrorism* 28/2 (2005a), p. 83. Another definition of jihad includes an 'intense
    struggle or effort ... [a] defence against an armed conflict in consequence of foreign
    aggression'. See Manzar Zaidi, *A Taxonomy of Jihad*, Arab Studies Quarterly 41/3
    (2009), p. 21.

37 Mohammed M. Hafez, 'Jihad after Iraq: Lessons from the Arab Afghans', *Studies in Conflict and Terrorism* 32/2 (2009), p. 79.
38 Jessica Stern, 'How Terrorists Hijacked Islam', *USA Today*, 1 October 2001.
39 Cook, *Understanding Jihad*, p. 3.
40 Kelsay, *Arguing the Just War Theory in Islam*, p. 155.
41 Whilst true for most Arab foreign fighters, the late Abu Bakr al-Baghdadi (d. 2019 and the former ISIS leader) and Abu Muhammad al-Golani (Jabhat al-Nusrah) both compete(d) for Arab foreign fighters arriving in Syria.
42 Perhaps this religious obligation could be conceptualised as similar to the secular NATO Article 5 collective defence, where an attack against one ally is considered as an attack against all.
43 Charles Glasse, *The Concise Encyclopedia of Islam* (London, 2008), p. 151.
44 The singular of *mujahhideen* is *mujahhid*, defined as a 'fighter or warrior'. See Hans Wehr, *A Dictionary of Modern Written Arabic* (London, 1980), p. 143.
45 See Cerwyn Moore and Paul Tumelty, 'Foreign Fighters and the Case of Chechnya: A Critical Assessment', *Studies in Conflict and Terrorism* 31/5 (2008), p. 412. In addition, David Malet defines foreign fighters as 'noncitizens of conflict states who join insurgencies during civil conflicts'. See David Malet, *Foreign Fighters: Transnational Identity in Civic Conflicts* (Oxford, 2013), p. 10.
46 The seventeen Arab countries are the Sultanate of Oman, Kuwait, Qatar, Bahrain, Saudi Arabia, the United Arab Emirates (UAE), Yemen, Lebanon, Palestine, Jordan, Syria, Iraq, Morocco, Algeria, Libya, Tunisia, and Egypt.
47 Schmid, *Foreign (Terrorist) Fighter Estimates: Conceptual and Data Issues*, p. 3.
48 Glasse, *The Concise Encyclopedia of Islam*, p. 538.
49 Alex P. Schmid, *The Routledge Handbook of Terrorism Research* (Oxon: (2013a), p. 86.
50 Ibid., p. 86.
51 Section 2656f(d) of Title 22 of the United States Code defines terrorism as 'premeditated, politically motivated violence perpetrated against non-combatant targets by subnational groups or clandestine agents'.
52 Boaz Ganor identified 'three important elements' for a definition of terrorism: 'the essence of the activity – the use of, or threat to use, violence; the aim of the activity is always political; and the targets of terrorism are civilians'. See Boaz Ganor, 'Defining terrorism: Is one man's terrorist another man's freedom fighter?' *International Institute for Counter-Terrorism* (1 January 2010).
53 Horgan, *The Psychology of Terrorism*, p. 80; and Andrew Silke, *Terrorists, Victims and Society* (Chichester, 2009), p. 29.
54 Horgan, *The Psychology of Terrorism*, p. 81 and p. 137.
55 According to the US PATRIOT Act Section 2339B, material support is defined as 'attempting to provide, conspiring to provide, or actually providing material support

or resources, to a foreign terrorist organization, knowing that the organization, has been designated a foreign terrorist organization, or engages, or has engaged, in 'terrorism' or 'terrorist activity'.

56 See the International Committee of the Red Cross, 'International Humanitarian Law. Chapter 1, Rule 1 (The Principle of Distinction between Civilians and Combatants)', *International Committee of the Red Cross* (2015b).

57 See Youssef H. Aboul-Enein, *Militant Islamist Ideology: Understanding the Global Threat* (Annapolis, 2010), p. 2.

58 See Quintan Wiktorowicz, 'Anatomy of the salafi movement', *Studies in Conflict and Terrorism* 29/3 (2006), p. 207; and Joas Wagemakers, *A Quietist Jihadi: The Ideology and Influence of Abu Muhammad al-Maqdisi* (Cambridge, 2012), p. 57.

59 Katerina Dalacoura, 'Islamist terrorism and the Middle East democratic deficit: Political exclusion, repression and the causes of extremism', *Democratization* 13/3 (2006), p. 510.

60 Thomas Hegghammer, 'The ideological hybridization of jihadi groups', Hudson Institute, *Current Trends in Islamist Ideology*, 9 (2009b), p. 28.

61 Egyptian ideologue, Muhammad Abdul Salam Faraj (1954–1982) labelled 'apostate Muslim regimes' as the 'near enemy'. See Johannes J.G. Jansen, *The Neglected Duty: The Creed of Sadat's Assassins and Islamic Resurgence on the Middle East* (New York, 1986), p. 192.

62 Gerges, *The Far Enemy: Why Jihad went Global*, p. 151.

63 Thomas Hegghammer uses the label 'socio-revolutionary', while Fawaz Gerges uses the label 'religious nationalist'. See Thomas Hegghammer, *Jihad in Saudi Arabia: Violence and Pan Islamism since 1979* (Cambridge, 2010b), p. 6; and Gerges, *The Far Enemy: Why Jihad went Global*, p. 151.

64 According to Alex Schmid, the term 'non-combatants' would apply 'to terrorism in the context of armed conflict and 'civilians' to war – and peacetime terrorism'. See Schmid, *The Routledge Handbook of Terrorism Research*, p. 67.

65 International Committee of the Red Cross, 'International Humanitarian Law. Chapter 1, Rule 5 (Definition of Civilians)', *International Committee of the Red Cross* (2015a).

66 Ibid.

67 US Department of State, 'Country Reports on Terrorism 2014', June 2015. Available at www.state.gov/documents/organization/239631.pdf (accessed 15 December 2015).

68 See Schmid, *The Routledge Handbook of Terrorism Research*, p. 55 and p. 67.

69 David Cook, 'Suicide Attacks or "Martyrdom Operations" in Contemporary *Jihad* Literature', *Nova Religio: The Journal of Alternative and Emergent Religions* 6/1 (2002), p. 35.

70 Karin M. Fierke, *Political Self-Sacrifice: Agency, Body and Emotion in International Relations* (Cambridge, 2014), p. 207.

71 See J. Reid Meloy, 'The Operational Development and Empirical Testing of the Terrorism Radicalization Assessment Protocol (TRAP-18)', *Journal of Personality Assessment*, 21 June 2018.

72 Alex P. Schmid, 'Radicalisation, de-radicalisation, counter-radicalisation: a conceptual discussion and literature review', *International Centre for Counter-Terrorism Research Paper*, March 2013b, p. 18.

73 Jonathan Githens-Mazer and Robert Lambert, 'Why Conventional Wisdom on Radicalization Fails: The Persistence of a Failed Discourse', *International Affairs*, 86/1 (2010), pp. 889–901.

Chapter 2

1 Abdullah Anas, 'Jihad, then and now: The Majalla speaks to Abdullah Anas', *Al Majalla*, 8 February 2014.

2 Based on the figures by David Malet, of between 500 and 2,000 Afghan Arabs (1979–1989). See David Malet, 'Foreign fighter mobilization and persistence in a global context', *Terrorism and Political Violence* 0 (2015), p. 10.

3 Scholars who use the label 'Arab-Afghans' include Brynjar Lia in *Architect of Global Jihad: The Life of Al-Qaida Strategist Abu Mus'ab al-Suri* (New York, 2008b); and Mustafa Hamid and Leah Farrall in *The Arabs at War in Afghanistan* (London, 2015).

4 Although the majority of the Afghan Arabs came from the Arab world, the dataset includes 17 per cent (sixty-six) who were Arab expatriates living in a country other than their country of birth.

5 Yaroslav Trofimov, *The Siege of Mecca: The Forgotten Uprising in Islam's Holiest Shrine and the Birth of Al Qaeda* (New York, 2007), p. 33.

6 Robert Fisk, 'Freedom, democracy and human rights in Syria', *Independent*, 16 September 2010.

7 Gilles Kepel, *Jihad: The Trail of Political Islam* (London, 2008), p. 138.

8 See Montasser Al-Zayyat, *The Road to Al-Qaeda: The Story of Bin Laden's Right-Hand Man* (London, 2004); Fawaz A. Gerges, *The Far Enemy: Why Jihad went Global* (Cambridge, 2005); Muhammad A. Rana and Mubasher Bukhari, *Arabs in Afghan Jihad* (Lahore, 2007); Brynjar Lia, *Architect of Global Jihad*; Mohammed M. Hafez, 'Jihad after Iraq: Lessons from the Arab Afghans', *Studies in Conflict and Terrorism* 32/2 (2009), pp. 73–94; Camille Tawil, *Brothers in Arms: The Story of Al-Qa'ida and Arab Jihadists* (London, 2010); Thomas Hegghammer, *Jihad in Saudi Arabia: Violence and Pan Islamism since 1979* (Cambridge, 2010b); Alex Strick van Linschoten and Felix Kuehn, *An Enemy We Created: The Myth of the Taliban-Al-Qaeda Merger in Afghanistan* (London, 2012); and Hamid and Farrall, *The Arabs at War in Afghanistan*.

9   Gerges, *The Far Enemy*, p. 62.

10 Nasser Al-Bahri, *Guarding Bin Laden: My Life in al-Qaeda* (UK, 2013); p. 16.

11 Nasser Al-Bahri, Interview with Nassir al-Bahri (Abu Jandal). Part 1. *Al-Quds al-Arabi*, 20 March 2005a.

12 Abdullah Y. Azzam, *The Lofty Mountain* (1989). Available at https://ebooks.worldofislam.info/ebooks/Jihad/The%20Lofty%20Mountain.pdf (accessed 15 May 2015). Due to his later alleged Al Qaeda links, Wa'il Julaidan was listed on the 2002 Al Qaeda Sanctions List, but his name was removed in August 2014.

13 Marc Sageman, *Understanding Terror Networks* (Philadelphia, 2004).

14 Kepel, *Jihad: The Trail of Political Islam,* p. 279.

15 Mark N. Katz, 'Civil conflict in South Yemen', *Middle East Review*, Fall 1986, p. 8.

16 According to Darryl Li the 'Arabs travelled to Pakistan and Afghanistan to work as engineers, doctors, journalists, teachers, preachers, and fighters.' See Darryl Li, 'Afghan Arabs, real and imagined', *Middle East Report* 260, 41 (Fall 2011), p. 15.

17 Algerian national Adil Hadi al-Jaziri Hamlili was involved from the age of eleven, going to Afghanistan in 1986 with his father, brother and second cousin (JTF-GTMO Detainee Assessment. Adil Hadi al-Jaziri Hamlili. 8 July 2008). The oldest Afghan Arab was an Egyptian national Shaykh Abdul Aziz Ali (aka Abu Osama al-Misri) 'who went to Afghanistan during the late 1980s, even though by then he was sixty-five' (see Lia, *Architect of Global Jihad*, p. 42).

18 Doug McAdam, 'Recruitment to high-risk activism: The case of Freedom Summer', *American Journal of Sociology* 92/1 (1986), p. 70.

19 Andrew Silke, 'Holy Warriors: Exploring the Psychological Processes of Jihadi Radicalization', *European Journal of Criminology* 5/1 (2008), p. 105.

20 *The Concise Oxford Dictionary* (Oxford, 1995), p. 960.

21 Gilles Kepel and Jean-Pierre Milelli, *Al Qaeda in its Own Words* (London, 2008), p. 97.

22 The notion of 'charismatic authority' is understood to mean 'the accepted power to lead and command others stemming from recognition of this quality'. See David C. Hofmann and Lorne L. Dawson, 'The neglected role of charismatic authority in the study of terrorist groups and radicalization', *Studies in Conflict and Terrorism* 37/4 (2014), p. 349.

23 The fundamentals of Islamic jurisprudence.

24 Shaykh Kamal Sananiri (who was married to Sayyid Qutb's sister, Amina) was part of an Egyptian Muslim Brotherhood delegation that first visited Afghanistan in November 1980. See Strick van Linschoten and Kuehn, *An Enemy We Created*, p. 30.

25 Thomas Hegghammer, 'Deconstructing the myth about al-Qa'ida and Khobar', *CTC Sentinel*, 1/3 (2008a), p. 91.

26 Musa Al-Qarni, 'Saudi academic recounts experiences from Afghan war', *Al-Hayat*, 20 March 2006a. Available at www.e-ariana.com/ariana/eariana.nsf/allPrintDocs/60F915EE3E3AA61F8725713700594314?OpenDocument (accessed 7 June 2016).

27 Tamim al-Adnani was Palestinian Afghan Arab who died in London in 1989, who was considered the 'second in command' to Abdullah Azzam (Hegghammer, 'Deconstructing the myth about al-Qaʻida and Khobar', p. 95).

28 Benotman is an unusual phonetic pronunciation of Ben Uthman, as shown in his Twitter account (@nbenotmen).

29 Al Jazeera America released the diaries on 7 November 2013. See Abu Zubaydah, Abu Zubaydah, 'Original document: Abu Zubaydah diaries volume one', *United States Department of Justice. Federal Bureau of Investigation*. Unclassified. *Al-Jazeera America*, 5 November 2013. Available at http://america.aljazeera.com/ multimedia/2013/11/original-documentabuzubaydahdiariesvolumeone.html (accessed 12 February 2014), Abu Zubaydah, 'Original document: Abu Zubaydah diaries volume two', *United States Department of Justice. Federal Bureau of Investigation*. Unclassified. *Al-Jazeera America*, 26 November 2013. Available at http://america.aljazeera.com/multimedia/2013/11/original-documentabuzubaydah diariesvolumetwo.html (accessed 12 February 2014).

30 Strick van Linschoten and Kuehn, *An Enemy We Created*, p. 58.

31 *Kuffar* refers to the plural of 'an atheist' (Charles Glasse, *The Concise Encyclopedia of Islam* (London, 2008), p. 305.

32 It seems that Abdullah Azzam was echoing Egyptian Muhammad Abdul Salam Faraj's concept of 'the neglected duty' of jihad, but in the context of evicting 'the *kuffar*' from Muslim lands (as opposed to the prevailing current of the early 1980s which was focused on religious nationalist causes, against local Arab regimes).

33 Abdullah Y. Azzam, *Defense of Muslim Lands: The First Obligation After Imam*, 1983. Available at www.kalamullah.com/Books/defence.pdf (accessed 25 January 2012).

34 The concept of *fard ayn* was explained in Chapter 1.

35 Hegghammer, *Jihad in Saudi* Arabia, p. 41.

36 The concept of *fard kifayya* was explained in Chapter 1.

37 Shaykh Abdul Aziz bin Bazz (1910–1999) was the Grand *Mufti* of Saudi Arabia and the highest religious authority in the country. He proclaimed that 'jihad in Afghanistan an individual duty on every Muslim' (See Trofimov, *The Siege of Mecca*, p. 244.

38 Shaykh Muhammad bin Uthaymin was one of 'Saudi Arabia's most famous scholars' (see Brynjar Lia, 'Destructive doctrinarians': Abu Musaʼb al-Suri's critique of the Salafis in the jihadi current', in R. Meijer (ed.), *Global Salafism: Islam's New Religious Movement* (London, 2009), p. 284.

39 Azzam, *Defense of Muslim Lands*.

40 Ibid.

41 Egyptian foreign fighter, Saif Allah al-Muhajjir: 'I could not resist answering Allah's call; our sisters are raped, our children killed, and our youth our slaughtered; how can you watch the Shia rape our Muslim sisters?' See Saif Allah al-Muhajjir, 'Sharia 4 Sham', 11 July 2013, *Facebook* (no longer available).

42 Al-Bahri, *Guarding Bin Laden*, p. 18.

43 *Caravan of Martyrs*; Afghanistan 1989; Abu Tayyib Al-Maghrabi.

44 Rana and Bukhari, *Arabs in Afghan Jihad*, p. 145.

45 Hamid and Farrall, *The Arabs at War in Afghanistan*, p. 313.

46 Tamim Al-Adnani, 'Lawrence Islamic video presents an interview with Tamim Adnani, Director of the Afghan Mujahideen Service Office in Afghanistan', *Why Islam*, 1989.

47 Anas, 'Jihad, then and now'.

48 Al-Qarni, 'Saudi academic recounts experiences from Afghan war'.

49 Olivier Roy, *Islam and Resistance in Afghanistan* (Cambridge, 1990), p. 233.

50 Rana and Bukhari, *Arabs in Afghan Jihad*, p. 21.

51 Katerina Dalacoura, *Islamist Terrorism and Democracy in the Middle East* (Cambridge, 2011), p. 42.

52 Thomas Hegghammer, 'Jihadi-Salafis or revolutionaries? On religion and politics in the study of militant Islamism', in R. Meijer (ed.) *Global Salafism: Islam's New Religious Movement* (London, 2009a), p. 246.

53 The term 'non-state actors' is widely used in International Relations, generally understood to mean individuals or groups who have political influence (possibly through the use of political violence), although they are not aligned to any country or state.

54 See Kepel, *Jihad: The Trail of Political Islam*, p. 148; and Brian G. Williams, 'On the Trail of the "Lions of Islam": Foreign Fighters in Afghanistan and Pakistan 1980–2010', *Orbis* 55/2 (2011), p. 220.

55 Hamid and Farrall, *The Arabs at War in Afghanistan*, p. 168.

56 Abdullah Anas, 'Naheed Mustafa talks to Abdullah Anas, who fought alongside bin Laden', *CBC News*, 16 September 2015.

57 Examples in the academic literature of suicide terrorism include Robert A. Pape, *Dying to Win: The Strategic Logic of Suicide Terrorism* (New York, 2005), and Ami Pedahzur, *Suicide Terrorism* (Cambridge, 2005).

58 Al-Qarni, 'Saudi academic recounts experiences from Afghan war'.

59 Roy, *Islam and Resistance in Afghanistan*, p. 218.

60 Mohammed M. Hafez, 'Martyrs without borders: The puzzle of transnational suicide bombers' in M. Breen-Smyth (ed.), *The Ashgate Companion to Political Violence* (Surrey, 2012a).

61 Another example was *Virtues of Martyrdom in the Path of Allah*, both missives are undated.

62 Abdullah Y. Azzam (n.d.). Fi Dhilal Surat at-Tawbah [In the shade of the at-Tawbah chapter] (date, place, and publisher unknown). *In the Words of Abdullah Azzam* (date, place, and publisher unknown). Available at http://ahlulislam.com/books/words_azzam.pdf (accessed 15 May 2015).

63 Assaf Moghadam, 'Motives for martyrdom: Al Qaeda, Salafi Jihad, and the spread of suicide attacks', *International Security* 3/3 (2008), p. 59.

64　*Caravan of Martyrs*; Afghanistan 1985; Yahya Sanyor al-Jeddawi.

65　Qur'an, Surah 3:169.

66　*Caravan of Martyrs*; Bosnia 1992; Abu Zubair al-Madani.

67　Rana and Bukhari, *Arabs in Afghan Jihad*, p. 150.

68　Sarah Shah as cited in Williams, 'On the Trail of the "Lions of Islam"', p. 20.

69　Quintan Wiktorowicz, 'A genealogy of radical Islam', *Studies in Conflict and Terrorism* 28/2 (2005a), p. 92.

70　Hegghammer, *Jihad in Saudi Arabia*, p. 67.

71　Rana and Bukhari, *Arabs in Afghan Jihad*, p. 149.

72　Rana and Bukhari, *Arabs in Afghan Jihad*, p. 125.

73　*Caravan of Martyrs*; Afghanistan 1989; Salim Umar Salim Al-Haddad (aka Abu Abdullah al-Ma'ribi) was killed during battles against the communist forces in Jalalabad, Afghanistan, in 1989.

74　Al-Bahri, *Guarding Bin Laden*, p. 98.

75　Rana & Bukhari, *Arabs in Afghan Jihad*, p. 152.

76　Examples include Saudi ISIS fighters, Abdul Rahman Abood on 16 January 2014, and Mundhir al-Tameemi on 21 February 2014. Translated from original ISIS 'General Border Administration documents.

77　Recommendation to Retain under DoD Control for Guantanamo Detainee, Omar Ahmed Khader. ISN: US9CA-000766DP. *US Department of Defense*. Joint Task Force Guantanamo (JTF-GTMO), 24 January 2004, p. 2.

78　See Raymond H. Hamden, 'Psychology of Terrorists: 4 Types', *The Foundation of International Human Relations*, Washington, DC, 2006, p. 164), and Marc Sageman, *Understanding Terror Networks* (Philadelphia, 2004), p. 112.

79　Rana and Bukhari, *Arabs in Afghan Jihad*, p. 132.

80　Rana and Bukhari, *Arabs in Afghan Jihad*, p. 124.

81　Based on figures provided by Malet, 'Foreign fighter mobilization', p. 10.

82　United Nations Department of Economic and Social Affairs, Population Division (2013). World Population Prospects: The 2012 Revision: Estimates, 1950–2010. June 2013.

83　Rana and Bukhari, *Arabs in Afghan Jihad*, p. 119.

84　Hegghammer, 'The rise of Muslim foreign fighters', p. 71.

85　Rana and Bukhari, *Arabs in Afghan Jihad*, p.143.

86　Dalacoura, *Islamist Terrorism and Democracy*, p. 56.

87　Silke, 'Holy Warriors' p. 112.

88　Sageman, *Understanding Terror Networks*, p. 92.

89　US Central Intelligence Agency, 'Psychological Assessment of Zain al-'Abedin al-Abideen Muhammad Hassan, a.k.a. Abu Zubaydah', 31 January 2003. Available at www.thetorturedatabase.org/files/foia_subsite/pdfs/CIA000544.pdf (accessed 6 July 2014).

90 Abu Zubaydah, 'Original document: Abu Zubaydah diaries volume one', p. 3.

91 Ibid., pp. 12–13.

92 Ibid., p. 21.

93 The term religiosity is understood to mean 'the condition of being religious or excessively religious' (The Concise Oxford Dictionary, 1995: 1161).

94 Abu Zubaydah, 'Original document: Abu Zubaydah diaries volume one', p. 27.

95 Ibid., p. 21.

96 Ibid., p. 30.

97 Abu Zubaydah, 'Original document: Abu Zubaydah diaries volume two', p. 28.

98 Little is known about Amin al-Jamil, except that he was also an Arab immigrant living (studying?) in India, and that his family lived in Kuwait (Kuwaiti?).

99 Silke, 'Holy Warriors'.

100 Abu Zubaydah, 'Original document: Abu Zubaydah diaries volume two', p. 23.

101 See John Horgan, *The Psychology of Terrorism* (London, 2005), p. 84.

102 Abu Zubaydah, 'Original document: Abu Zubaydah diaries volume two', p. 36.

103 Ibid., p. 46.

104 Ibid., pp. 55–56.

105 Zayn Al Abidin Muhammad Husayn (2007). Verbatim Transcript of Combatant Status Review Tribunal Hearing for ISN 10016. *US Department of Defense*. Joint Task Force Guantanamo (JTF-GTMO), 27 March 2007, p. 9.

106 Abu Zubaydah, 'Original document: Abu Zubaydah diaries volume two', p. 37.

107 Ibid., p. 46.

108 See Robert Alun Jones, *Emile Durkheim: An Introduction to Four Major Works* (Beverly Hills, 1986).

109 Marc Sageman, 'A Frighteningly Normal Man', *Al-Jazeera*, 26 November 2013.

110 Lia, *Architect of Global Jihad*, p. 87.

111 Abu Zubaydah, 'Original document: Abu Zubaydah diaries volume three', *United States Department of Justice. Federal Bureau of Investigation.* Unclassified. *Al-Jazeera America*, 26 November 2013, p. 128. Available at http://america.aljazeera.com/multimedia/2013/11/original-documentabuzubaydahdiariesvolume three.html accessed 12 February 2014).

112 Hafez, 'Jihad after Iraq', p. 78.

113 According to Nasser al-Bahri, Egyptian Afghan Arabs with previous terrorist links held 'six out of the nine key Al Qaeda' posts. Other nationalities with prior terrorist links included Libyans (seven), Syrians (five), Jordanians (three), and Algerians (five). See Al-Bahri, *Guarding Bin Laden*, p. 213.

114 Kepel, *Jihad: The Trail of Political Islam*, p. 81.

115 Ayman al-Zawahiri, Saif al-Adil, Muhammad Atif (Abu Hafs al-Misri), Abdullah Ahmad al-Alfi, and Ibrahim Husayn Abdul Hadi Eidarous.

116 Gerges, *The Far Enemy*, p. 60.

117 Louise Richardson, *What Terrorists Want: Understanding the Enemy, Containing the Threat* (New York, 2007), p. 66.

118 Lawrence Wright, *The Looming Tower: Al-Qaeda and the Road to 9/11* (New York, 2006), pp. 109–110.

119 See Gerges, *The Far Enemy*, p. 84; Kepel, *Jihad: The Trail of Political Islam*, p. 147; Lia, *Architect of Global Jihad*, p. 78); Strick van Linschoten and Kuehn, *An Enemy We Created*, p. 57; and Hamid and Farrall, *The Arabs at War in Afghanistan*, p. 36.

120 Hegghammer, *Jihad in Saudi Arabia*, p. 47.

121 Hafez, 'Jihad after Iraq', p. 76.

122 Ali A. Jalali and Lester W. Grau, *The Other Side of the Mountain: Mujahideen Tactics in the Soviet-Afghan War*. The US Marine Corp Studies and Analysis Division (1998), p. 396.

123 Gerges, *The Far Enemy*; Abdel Bari Atwan, *The Secret History of Al Qaeda* (Los Angeles, 2006), p. 48; Lia, *Architect of Global Jihad*; and Al-Bahri, *Guarding Bin Laden*, p. 57.

124 Abu Zubaydah, 'Original document: Abu Zubaydah diaries volume three', p. 94.

125 Al-Zayyat, *The Road to Al-Qaeda*, p. 61.

126 Evan F. Kohlmann, 'The Mujahideen of Bosnia: Origins, Training, and Implications', in J.J.F. Forrest (ed.), *The Making of a Terrorist: Recruitment, Training, and Root Causes*. Volume II: Training (London, 2006), p. 197.

127 Al-Bahri, *Guarding Bin Laden*, p. 57.

128 Egyptian Abu Talal al-Qaseemi was a member of EIG, a veteran of the Afghan and Bosnian jihads. He was abducted in Bosnia by the CIA in September 1995 in a case of extraordinary rendition and involuntarily returned to Egypt. He was sentenced to death. See Evan F. Kohlmann, *Al-Qaida's Jihad in Europe: The Afghan-Bosnian Network* (New York, 2004), p. 150.

129 According to Nasser al-Bahri, Osama bin Laden admitted that 'most of the brothers around me are Egyptian' and that the majority of the 'al-Qaeda top brass' were Egyptian. The future of the remaining five Egyptians (without pre-existing terrorist links) included two killed in the Bosnian jihad; two were imprisoned and one (Abu Talal al-Qaseemi) sentenced to death in Egypt (noted above). See Al-Bahri, *Guarding Bin Laden*, p. 57 and p. 96.

130 The trajectories of the remaining two Egyptian Afghan Arabs are unknown after the Afghan jihad.

131 See Kyle W. Orton, 'Al-Qaeda in Syria and American Policy', *The Syrian Intifada*, 4 October 2016.

132 Hamza al-Ghamdi was one of the 9/11 hijackers on United Airlines Flight 175.

133 Walid Muhammad bin Attash is a Yemeni JTF-GTMO detainee, who was a senior AQ lieutenant. He participated in jihad in Tajikistan in 1996 (against the Russians)

and in Afghanistan (against the Northern Alliance). He was involved in supporting the attack on the USS *Cole* in 2000. He was to be a hijacker for the cancelled SW Asia portion of the 9/11 attacks.

134 Abu Zubaydah has been widely referenced (through his diaries) in this chapter.

135 JTF-GTMO Combat Status Review Tribunal (8 December 2006). Abdul Rahim al-Nashiri; p. 2.

136 JTF-GTMO Combat Status Review Tribunal (8 December 2006). Abdul Rahim al-Nashiri; p. 3.

137 Guy Sajer, *The Forgotten Soldier* (London, 1971), pp. 83–84.

138 Fitzroy Maclean, *Eastern Approaches* (London, 1950), p. 329.

139 Hafez, 'Jihad after Iraq', p. 82.

140 Abdul Aziz Barbaros (aka Abdul Rahman al-Dosari) was born in Saudi Arabia (1942), but was ethnically Indian, not actually Arab.

141 Nelly Lahoud, 'Jihadi recantations and their significance', in A. Moghadam and B. Fishman (eds), *Fault Lines in Global Jihad: Organizational, Strategic, and Ideological Fissures* (London, 2011), p. 140.

142 Ayman Al-Zawahiri, *Al-Kitaab al-Aswad: Qissaat Ta'dheeb al-Muslimeen fi Ahd Hosni Mubarak* (1992).

143 Martha Crenshaw, *Understanding Terrorism: Causes, Processes and Consequences* (Oxon, 2011), p. 44.

144 Abu Zubaydah, 'Original document: Abu Zubaydah diaries volume three', p. 94.

145 Hamid and Farrall, *The Arabs at War in Afghanistan*, p. 140.

146 Rana and Bukhari, *Arabs in Afghan Jihad*, p. 22.

147 Apart from one (Abu Musab) who died in Bosnia, the remaining 32 per cent of Algerians were later involved in Al Qaeda related activities, and subsequently ended up in Guantanamo Bay prison.

148 See James Bruce, 'Arab Veterans of the Afghan War', *Jane's Intelligence Review*, 7/4 (1995), pp. 175–180; Barnett R. Rubin, 'Arab Islamists in Afghanistan', in John L. Espositi (ed.), *Political Islam: Revolution, Radicalism, and Reform?* (Colorado, 1997), p. 199; and Abdelaziz Testas, 'The roots of Algeria's religious and ethnic violence', *Studies in Conflict and Terrorism* 25/3 (2002), p. 163.

149 This is caveated by noting that some veteran Libyan Afghan Arabs had been Islamist activists (but not necessarily involved in terrorism) prior to their arrival in Afghanistan. Many of these individuals did subsequently return to Libya and formed the LIFG.

150 Veteran Afghan Arabs (with no prior terrorist links) in the 1995 Riyadh attack involved Abdullah al-Hudhayf (who initiated a pre-attack), Khalid al-Sa'id, Riyadh al-Hajiri, and Muslih al-Shamrani.

151 Hegghammer, 'Deconstructing the myth about al-Qa'ida and Khobar', p. 20.

152 Hegghammer, *Jihad in Saudi Arabia*, p. 72.

153 Nasser Al-Bahri, Interview with Nassir al-Bahri (Abu Jandal). Part 8. *Al-Quds al-Arabi*, 31 March [*sic*] 2005d, p. 5.

154 See Alex P. Schmid and Albert J. Jongman, *Political Terrorism: A New Guide to Actors, Authors, Concepts, Databases, Theories, and Literature* (New Brunswick, 1988); Richardson, *What Terrorists Want*; Silke, 'Holy Warriors'; Clark McCauley and Sophie Moskalenko, 'Mechanisms of Political Radicalization: Pathways Toward Terrorism', *Terrorism and Political Violence* 20/3 (2008), pp. 415–433; and Alex P. Schmid, *The Routledge Handbook of Terrorism Research* (Oxon, 2013a).

155 Silke, 'Holy Warriors', p. 36.

156 Hegghammer, *Jihad in Saudi Arabia*, p. 73.

157 The 1995 'Bojinka' plot involved assassinating Pope John Paul II, blowing up eleven aircraft from Asia to the US, and crashing a plane into the CIA building in Virginia.

158 Veteran Afghan Arab (with no prior terrorist links) involvement in the 1993 WTC attack involved Omar Abdul Rahman, Ramzi Yusuf, Khalid Shaykh Muhammad, Osama Azmairi, and Ahmad Ajaj.

159 Simon Reeve, *The New Jackals: Ramzi Yousef, Osama bin Laden and the Future of Terrorism* (London, 1999), p. 55.

160 See Omar Abdul-Rahman, 'Sentencing Statement of Blind Sheikh Omar Abdel Rahman and the New York Terrorists', *Intelwire*, 1996. Available at http://intelfiles. egoplex.com/61HKRAHS-sentencing.htm (Link no longer working). He died (of natural causes) in a US jail on 18 February 2017.

161 Ibid., p. 16.

162 Ibid., p. 19.

163 Ibid., p. 16.

164 Ibid., p. 17.

165 Khalid Shaykh Muhammad (2006). Combatant Status Review Tribunal Input and Recommendation for Continued Detention Under DoD Control (CD) for Guantanamo Detainee, ISN: US9KU-010024DP(S). *US Department of Defense*. Joint Task Force Guantanamo (JTF-GTMO), 8 December 2006, p. 11.

166 Ramzi Yusuf, 'Statement by Ramzi Yousef at Sentencing', *The New York Times*, 9 January 1998.

167 Reeve, *The New Jackals*, p. 138.

168 Veteran Afghan Arab (with no prior terrorist links) involvement in the 1998 East Africa attacks involved Osama bin Laden, Wadih al-Hajj, Abu Faraj al-Libi, Muhammad Odeh, Muhsin Musa, and Musafa Hamood.

169 The only other major global terrorist attack was the June 1996 Khobar Towers attack in Saudi Arabia, 'carried out principally, perhaps exclusively, by Saudi Hezbollah' and not by Al Qaeda (The 9/11 Commission Report, 2005: 60).

170 The 9/11 Commission Report (2005), p. 63.

171   Osama Bin Laden, *Declaration of War against the Americans Occupying the Land of the Two Holy Places*. Published in Al Quds Al Arabi, August 1996. Public Broadcasting Service. Available at www.pbs.org/newshour/terrorism/international/fatwa_1996.html (accessed 15 May 2012).

172   Osama Bin Laden, *Jihad Against Jews and Crusaders*. World Islamic Front Statement, 23 February 1998. *Federation of American Scientists*. Washington: FAS. Available at www.fas.org/irp/world/para/docs/980223-fatwa.htm (accessed 15 May 2012).

173   In addition, there were three Kenyans, two Tanzanians, and one Sudanese.

174   The five were all EIJ members: Ayman al-Zawahiri, Muhammad Atif, Saif al-Adil, Abdullah Ahmad Abdullah, and Ibrahim Eidarous.

175   For example, Jihad al-Harazi – the cousin of Abdul Rahman al-Nashiri – was one of the self-sacrificial ('martyrdom/suicide') bombers involved in the attack on the US Embassy in Nairobi.

176   Nasser Al-Bahri, Interview with Nassir al-Bahri (Abu Jandal). Part 3. *Al-Quds al-Arabi*, 28 March 2005b.

177   Oriana Zill, 'A portrait of Wadih El Hage', *Frontline – Public Broadcasting Service*, 12 September 2001. Available at www.pbs.org/wgbh/pages/frontline/shows/binladen/upclose/elhage.html (accessed 12 November 2014).

178   The 9/11 Commission Report (2005), p. 190.

179   Due to his interest in maritime terrorism, al-Nashiri was nicknamed 'Prince of the Sea'. See Peter Lehr, '(No) Princes of the Sea: Reflections on Maritime Terrorism', in J. Krause and S. Bruns (eds), *Routledge Handbook of Naval Strategy and Security* (Oxon, 2016), p. 211.

180   The 9/11 Commission Report (2005), p. 190.

181   Al-Bahri, Interview with Nassir al-Bahri (Abu Jandal), Part 1.

182   The 9/11 Commission Report (2005), p. 191.

183   Despite having been involved in previous Islamist terrorist attacks (1993 WTC, 1998 Embassy attacks), the five were Osama bin Laden, Khalid Shaykh Muhammad, Abu Faraj al-Libi, Abdul Rahman al-Nashiri, and Muhammad Zammar, who had arrived in 1980s Afghanistan with no prior terrorist links.

184   Saudi nationals Khalid Muhammad Abdullah al-Mihdhar and Nawaf Muhammad Salim al-Hazmi. The 9/11 Commission Report (2005), p. 155.

185   Saudi nationals 'Ahmed al Ghamdi and Saeed al Ghamdi were identified by Cerwyn Moore and Paul Tumelty as 'two of the 9/11 hijackers' who had fought in Chechnya. See Cerwyn Moore and Paul Tumelty, 'Foreign Fighters and the Case of Chechnya: A Critical Assessment', *Studies in Conflict and Terrorism* 31/5 (2008), p. 423.

186   US Department of State, 'The wandering mujahidin: Armed and dangerous', Bureau of Intelligence and Research, *The Washington Institute*. Weekend Edition. 21-22 August 1993. Available at www.washingtoninstitute.org/uploads/Documents/other/StateDept199308WanderingMujahidin.pdf (accessed 21 December 2014).

187 Ibid., p. 4.

188 Gerges, *The Far Enemy*, p. 131.

189 Bin Laden, *Declaration of War against the Americans*.

190 This was arguably a genuine grievance, and as noted earlier, was also articulated by Omar Abdul Rahman concerning the 1993 WTC attack. On 12 May 1996, Madeleine Albright (then US Ambassador to the UN) was interviewed by Lesley Stahl (in 1996) on *60 Minutes*, and asked 'we have heard that half a million children have died ... you know, is the price worth it?' Albright replied 'we think the price is worth it'. See Lesley Stahl (Producer) 'Interview with Madeleine Albright', *60 Minutes*, 12 May 1996). Available at www.youtube.com/watch?v=FbIX1CP9qr4 (accessed 21 December 2012).

191 Richard Garfield, a Columbia University nursing professor, estimated there were 345,000 to 530,000 Iraqi deaths over the 1990–2002 UN sanctions period. See also the United Nations Children's Fund, *The Situation of Children in Iraq: An Assessment Based on the UN Convention on the Rights of a Child*, February 2002. Available at www.casi.org.uk/info/unicef0202.pdf (accessed 21 December 2012).

192 Felix Kuehn, Leah Farrall and Alex Strick Van Linschoten, 'Expert Report in US vs. Talha Ahsan; US vs. Babar Ahmad; Exhibit F', April 2014. Available at www.sacc.org.uk/sacc/docs/ba_expert_reports.pdf (accessed 10 May 2014), p. 34.

193 Thomas Hegghammer, 'Terrorist recruitment and radicalization in Saudi Arabia', *Middle East Policy*, VIII/4 (2006), p. 46.

194 Hafez, 'Jihad after Iraq', p. 76.

195 Mahan Abedin, 'From mujahid to activist: An interview with a Libyan veteran of the Afghan jihad', *The Jamestown Foundation*, Terrorism Monitor, 3/2 (2005).

196 Hafez, 'Jihad after Iraq', p. 77).

197 Mustafa Hamid as cited in Mustafa Hamid and Leah Farrall, *The Arabs at War in Afghanistan* (London, 2015), p. 136.

198 See Ahmad Ressam, 'United States of America v. Mokhtar Haouari', *United States District Court Southern District of New York*, 3 July 2001. Ahmad Rassam, nicknamed the 'Millennium bomber' was an Al Qaeda terrorist imprisoned for his role in planning to blow up Los Angeles International Airport on 31 December 1999.

199 According to Hamid and Farrall, Khaldan Camp recruited 'students who took a tighter doctrinal approach and a political path that was more violent in nature'. See Hamid and Farrall, *The Arabs at War in Afghanistan*, p. 166.

200 Ressam, 'United States of America v. Mokhtar Haouari', pp. 550–551.

201 Ibid., p. 555. See also Roland Jacquard, *In the Name of Osama Bin Laden: Global Terrorism and the Bin Laden Brotherhood* (London, 2002), pp. 263–267, which contains a declassified British Secret Intelligence Service (MI6) document on training camps in 1990s Afghanistan.

202 Hamid as cited in Hamid and Farrall, *The Arabs at War in Afghanistan*, p. 165.

203 Ibid., p. 322.

204 Ibid., p. 169.

205 Ibid., p. 301.

206 Reeve, *The New Jackals*, p. 138.

207 Jerrold Post as cited in Peter L. Bergen, *Holy War Inc. Inside the Secret World of Osama Bin Laden* (London, 2002), p. 111.

208 Marc Sageman, *Leaderless Jihad: Terror Networks in the Twenty-First Century* (Philadelphia, 2008), p. 70.

209 Hafez, 'Jihad after Iraq', p. 78.

210 Kuehn et al., 'Expert Report in US vs. Talha Ahsan', p. 60.

211 Ibid., p. 72.

212 The 9/11 Commission Report (2005), p. 160.

213 Hafez, 'Jihad after Iraq', p. 85.

214 Hegghammer, *Jihad in Saudi Arabia*, p. 189.

215 Musa Al-Qarni, 'Saudi Cleric Musa Al-Qarni on Iqra TV', *Middle East Media Research Institute*, 29 October 2004. Available at http://memritv.org/clip/en/339. htm (accessed 7 June 2016).

216 Musa Al-Qarni, 'Saudi Cleric Musa Al-Qarni on Iqra TV', *Middle East Media Research Institute*, 3 February 2005. Available at http://memritv.org/clip/en/523. htm (accessed 7 June 2016).

217 Quilliam. Available at www.quilliaminternational.com/about/ (accessed 14 August 2017).

Chapter 3

1   *The Guardian*, 'Doomed to failure in the Middle East: A Letter from 52 former senior British diplomats to Tony Blair', *The Guardian*, 27 April 2004. Available at www.theguardian.com/politics/2004/apr/27/foreignpolicy.world (accessed 5 January 2015).

2   The defensive jihad in Afghanistan broadly ended in April 1992, however the first veteran Afghan Arab terrorist act was not until 1993, in New York (the WTC bombing).

3   Thomas R. Mockaitis, *British Counterinsurgency 1919–1960* (London, 1990), p. 3.

4   David Malet estimated that there were about 3,000–5,000 foreign fighters (including non-Iraqi Arabs) in Iraq between 2003 and 2009. David Malet, 'Foreign fighter mobilization and persistence in a global context', *Terrorism and Political Violence* 0 (2015), p. 10.

5   Introduced in Chapter 1, the 'Sinjar records' comprised of 707 foreign fighters, including 555 Arabs.

6   See Anthony Cordesman, 'Iraq and foreign volunteers', *Center for Strategic and International Studies* (18 November 2005); Evan F. Kohlmann, 'The Foreign Martyrs of Iraq: 2003–04', *Global Terror Alert*, 2005a; Reuven Paz, 'Arab volunteers killed in Iraq: An analysis', *The Project for the Research of Islamist Movements* 3/1 (March 2005); Mohammed M. Hafez, 'Suicide terrorism in Iraq: A preliminary assessment of the quantitative data and documentary evidence', *Studies in Conflict and Terrorism* 29/6 (2006b), pp. 591–619; and Mohammed M. Hafez, *Suicide Bombers in Iraq: The Strategy and Ideology of Martyrdom* (Washington, 2007b).

7   Use of the CPOST Suicide Attack Database is made, aware that it employs a fairly loose definition of a suicide attack: 'an attack in which an attacker kills himself or herself in a deliberate attempt to kill others'.

8   Potential biases include data that largely reflect a single country (due to availability, an author's interest, or that certain nationalities – or groups – have greater access to social media).

9   Iraq Coalition Casualty Count for 2009 provided by *iCasualties*.org.

10 US Central Intelligence Agency, *The World Fact Book 2014 – Iraq*. Available at www.cia.gov/library/publications/download/download-2014 (accessed 8 April 2015).

11 Charles Tripp, *A History of Iraq* (Cambridge, 2002), p. 244.

12 'Chemical Ali' was later hanged for his involvement in the Anfal Campaign, in 2010.

13 *Takbeer* is the exclamation of *Allahu Akbar* (God is greatest).

14 It must be remembered that Osama bin Laden had offered Saudi Arabia the use of Islamist militants in the form of veteran Afghan Arabs, although his offer was rejected in favour of a US-led coalition.

15 Osama Bin Laden, *Declaration of War against the Americans Occupying the Land of the Two Holy Places*. Published in Al Quds Al Arabi, August 1996. Public Broadcasting Service. Available at www.pbs.org/newshour/terrorism/international/fatwa_1996.html (accessed 15 May 2012). In effect Bin Laden was calling on his followers to now attack the far enemy (the United States and the West), in preference to the near enemy (Arab regimes).

16 United Nations Children's Fund, *The Situation of Children in Iraq: An Assessment Based on the UN Convention on the Rights of a Child*, February 2002. Available at www.casi.org.uk/info/unicef0202.pdf (accessed 21 December 2012).

17 Osama bin Laden 'spoke of the suffering of the Iraqi people as a result of sanctions imposed after the Gulf War'. See the 9/11 Commission Report (2005), p. 49.

18 The Sunni triangle in Iraq was broadly a triangular area, north-west of Baghdad, that included Baghdad, Baqubah, Tikrit, Ramadi, Samarra and Fallujah, where the majority of Sunni tribes lived.

19 See Hans Wehr, *A Dictionary of Modern Written Arabic* (London, 1980), p. 701.

20 Charles Glasse, *The Concise Encyclopedia of Islam* (London, 2008), p. 157.

21 The named Iraqi *fidayeen* were Tahussein Hamid al-Fahdaawi, Jameel Arabi al-Shamri, and Yussef Dukhayl al-Mansoori. Available at www.docexdocs.com/ internetarchive/ISGQ-2003-00002783.pdf) (accessed 8 April 2018).

22 Conceptually a 'war on terror' is meaningless. What is a war on extreme fear? A 'war against terrorism' would have been more understandable.

23 Abu Musab al-Zarqawi was head of his organisation, *Tawhid wal-Jihad*.

24 Public Broadcasting Service (PBS). *The Secret History of ISIS*, Frontline, Season 34 (2018), Episode 10. Available at www.pbs.org/video/frontline-secret-history-isis/ (accessed 29 April 2018).

25 Iraq Survey Group, 'Comprehensive Report of the Special Advisor to the DCI on Iraq's WMD, with Addendums (Duelfer Report)', *US Government Publishing Office*, 25 April 2005. Accessed at www.gpo.gov/fdsys/pkg/GPO-DUELFERREPORT/ content-detail.html (accessed 31 January 2015).

26 In September 2004, UN Secretary General Kofi Annan, said of the Iraq invasion: 'from the UN Charter point of view, it was illegal'. See Kofi Annan, 'Iraq War Illegal, Says Annan', *BBC*, 16 September 2004.

27 In November 2008, UK former Lord Chief Justice Lord Bingham, described the war as 'a serious violation of international law'. See Tom Bingham, 'Lord Bingham delivers Annual Grotius Lecture on the Rule of Law in the International Order', *British Institute of International and Comparative Law*, 18 November 2008. Available at www.biicl.org/newsitem/109 (accessed 15 May 2012).

28 Thomas Hegghammer, 'Saudi militants in Iraq: Backgrounds and recruitment patterns', *Norwegian Defence Research Establishment* (FFI), 5 February 2007, p. 9.

29 On 13 October 2006, the name changed again to the Islamic State in Iraq.

30 Edmond Sanders, *War Blazed Imam's Path to Extremism*, *LA Times*, 27 September 2004.

31 Introduced in Chapter 1, *takfir* is the practice of declaring a fellow Muslim an 'unbeliever' (*kafr*). It is often used to sanction violence against Arab regimes and fellow Muslims who are judged to be insufficiently religious.

32 Yusuf Al-Uyayri, *The Future of Iraq and the Arabian Peninsula After the Fall of Baghdad*. 5 September 2003. Available at www.freerepublic.com/ focus/f-news/976932/posts (accessed 1 May 2018).

33 William McCants and Jarret Brachman, 'Militant Ideology Atlas – Executive Report', *Combating Terrorism Center West Point* (2006a), p. 13.

34 Norman Cigar, *'Abd Al-'Aziz Al-Muqrin's A Practical Course for Guerrilla War* (Dulles, VA, 2009), p. 53.

35 Extract taken from Brynjar Lia, *Architect of Global Jihad: The Life of Al-Qaida Strategist Abu Mus'ab al-Suri* (New York, 2008b), pp. 386–387.

36 Ibid., p. 403.

37 Ibid., p. 404.

38 Abu Bakr al-Naji (possibly also known as Muhammad Hassan Khalil al-Hakim) authored a 'blueprint' for the establishment of an Islamic State.

39 Abu Bakr al-Naji, The Management of Savagery: The Most Critical Stage Through Which the Umma Will Pass (2004). Translated by W. McCants. *John M. Olin Institute for Strategic Studies*, 23 May 2006.

40 Ibid. This call for moderation by al-Naji (p. 76) contradicts his earlier guidance that 'the ingredient of softness is one of the ingredients of failure for any jihadi action' (p. 72).

41 Ibid., p. 73.

42 Zaki Chehab, *Inside the Resistance: The Iraqi Insurgency and the Future of the Middle East* (New York, 2005), p. 53.

43 Mary Fitzgerald, 'The son of the father of jihad', *The Irish Times*, 7 July 2006. Available at www.irishtimes.com/news/the-son-of-the-father-of-jihad-1.1027271 (accessed 15 April 2018).

44 The North Atlantic Treaty, *The North Atlantic Treaty* 4 April 1949. Available at www.nato.int/cps/ic/natohq/official_texts_17120.htm (accessed 15 April 2018).

45 See Thomas Hegghammer, *Jihad in Saudi Arabia: Violence and Pan Islamism since 1979* (Cambridge, 2010b), p. 16.

46 Musa al-Qarni, 'Saudi Preacher Musa Al-Qarni: The Jews and Christians are Allah's Enemies . . . We Ask Allah to Strengthen the Jihad Fighters in Iraq', *Middle East Media Research Institute*, Special Dispatch No. 859, 8 February 2005b. Available at www.memri.org/report/en/0/0/0/0/0/0/1312.htm (accessed 18 December 2015).

47 Musa Al-Qarni, 'Saudi Cleric Musa Al-Qarni on Iqra TV', *Middle East Media Research Institute*, 18 March 2006b. Available at http://memritv.org/clip/en/1082.htm (accessed 7 June 2016).

48 Rik Coolsaet, *Jihadi Terrorism and the Radicalisation Challenge: European and American Experiences* (London, 2011), p. 260.

49 Barnett R. Rubin, 'Arab Islamists in Afghanistan', in John L. Espositi (ed.), *Political Islam: Revolution, Radicalism, and Reform?* (Colorado, 1997), pp. 179–206; David B. Edwards, *Before Taliban: Genealogies of the Afghan Jihad* (Berkeley, 2002), pp. 266–271; and Katerina Dalacoura, *Islamist Terrorism and Democracy in the Middle East* (Cambridge, 2011), p. 42.

50 See United Nations Security Council Counter-Terrorism Committee, 'Background Note: Stemming the flow of foreign terrorist fighters', Madrid, 27–28 July 2015a. Available at www.un.org/en/sc/ctc/docs/2015/0721Special%20Meeting%20Madrid%20-%20General%20background%20Note.pdf (accessed 7 June 2016). Professor Alex Schmid also disagrees with the label 'foreign terrorist fighter'. See Alex P. Schmid, 'Foreign (terrorist) fighter estimates: Conceptual and data issues', *International Centre for Counter-Terrorism Policy Brief*, October 2015.

51 Loretta Napoleoni, *Insurgent Iraq: Al Zarqawi and the New Generation* (New York, 2005), p. 132.

52 Fawaz A. Gerges, *The Far Enemy: Why Jihad went Global* (Cambridge, 2005), p. 268.

53 Cordesman, 'Iraq and foreign volunteers', p. 5.

54 *The Guardian*, 'Doomed to failure in the Middle East: A Letter from 52 former senior British diplomats to Tony Blair', *The Guardian*, 27 April 2004. Available at www.theguardian.com/politics/2004/apr/27/foreignpolicy.world (accessed 5 January 2015).

55 Abdel Bari Atwan, *The Secret History of Al Qaeda* (Los Angeles, 2006), p. 206.

56 Chapter 2 found that fifty-two (13 per cent) of the 394 Afghan Arabs had a university education, with nine qualified as medical doctors.

57 Chapter 2 found that the Afghan Arab cohort varied between eleven years old and sixty-five years old, with 51 per cent of them twenty-two years old or under. The average age was twenty-three years old and the median was twenty-four years old.

58 Marc Sageman, *Understanding Terror Networks* (Philadelphia, 2004), p. 92; Andrew Silke, 'Holy Warriors: Exploring the Psychological Processes of Jihadi Radicalization', *European Journal of Criminology* 5/1 (2008), p. 105.

59 Doug McAdam, 'Recruitment to high-risk activism: The case of Freedom Summer', *American Journal of Sociology* 92/1 (1986), p. 70.

60 United Nations Security Council Counter-Terrorism Committee, 'Background Note: Group I: Technical sessions on detection, intervention against, and prevention of incitement, recruitment and facilitation of FTF travel', Madrid, 27–28 July 2015b. Available at www.un.org/en/sc/ctc/docs/2015/0721Tehnical%20Session%20 Group%20I%20-%20background%20note.pdf (accessed 7 June 2016).

61 See Murad B. Al-Shishani, 'The Salafi-Jihadist movement in Iraq: recruitment methods and Arab volunteers', *Terrorism Monitor*, 3/23 (2005b), pp. 6–8; Joseph Felter and Brian Fishman, 'Al Qaeda's Foreign Fighters in Iraq: A First Look at the Sinjar Records', *Harmony Project* (2007), p. 7; and Christopher Hewitt and Jessica Kelley-Moore, 'Foreign fighters in Iraq: A cross-national analysis of jihadism', *Terrorism and Political Violence* 21/1 (2009), pp. 211–220. The only study to challenge these assessments was Anthony Cordesman who found that 'the number of Saudi volunteers in August 2005 was around 12 per cent of the foreign contingent'. This observation does not conform to the multitude of other studies on Arab foreign fighters in Iraq. See Anthony Cordesman, 'Iraq and foreign volunteers'.

62 A lesser factor was the spillover from a failed AQAP campaign, that was defeated by early 2006, freeing up a greater pool of politicised and militarised individuals. The Global Terrorism Database shows four confirmed AQAP attacks against the Saudi state in 2004, with the last confirmed attack on 24 February 2006.

63 Paz, 'Arab volunteers killed in Iraq', p. 5.

64 Anthony Cordesman, 'Iraq and foreign volunteers', p. 9.

65 Public Broadcasting Service (PBS), 'The fatwa of the 26 Clerics: Open sermon to the militant Iraqi people' (given on 5 November 2004), Frontline, 8 February 2005. Available at www.pbs.org/wgbh/pages/frontline/shows/saud/etc/fatwa.html (accessed 7 June 2016).

66 Musa Al-Qarni, 'Saudi Cleric Musa Al-Qarni on Iqra TV', *Middle East Media Research Institute*, 18 March 2006b. Available at http://memritv.org/clip/en/1082. htm (accessed 7 June 2016).

67 The term religiosity is understood to mean 'the condition of being religious or excessively religious'. See the Concise Oxford Dictionary (Oxford, 1995), p. 1161.

68 US Department of State, 'International Religious Freedom Report 2004', Bureau of Democracy, Human Rights, and Labor. Available at www.state.gov/j/drl/rls/irf/2004/35507.htm (accessed 18 December 2014). The report reflects the religious environment in Saudi Arabia at the time of the Iraqi jihad, highlighting Saudi 'denunciations of non-Muslim religions from government-sanctioned pulpits'.

69 International Centre for Religion and Diplomacy, *The State of Tolerance in the Curriculum of the Kingdom of Saudi Arabia*, 2013. Available at https://assets. documentcloud.org/documents/3022108/State-Dept-Study-on-Saudi-Textbooks. pdf (accessed 31 January 2015), p. 3.

70 Hewitt and Kelley-Moore, 'Foreign fighters in Iraq', p. 219.

71 Daphna Canetti, Stevan E. Hobfall, Ami Pedahzur and Eran Zaidise, 'Much ado about religion: Religiosity, resource loss, and support for political violence', *Journal of Peace Research* 45/5 (2010), p. 575.

72 It was only later that Saudi 'government-affiliated clerics such as Abdul Muhsin al-Ubaykan ... declared that the insurgency in Iraq amounts to *fitna* [sedition] and is illegitimate'. See Hegghammer, 'Saudi militants in Iraq', p. 9.

73 Al-Shishani, 'The Salafi-Jihadist movement in Iraq'.

74 Riaz Hassan, 'What motivates the suicide bombers? Study of a comprehensive database gives a surprising answer', *YaleGlobal*, 3 September 2009.

75 Peter R. Neumann, 'Suspects into collaborators: Assad and the Jihadists', *London Review of Books* 36/7 (2014), p. 19.

76 Michael Weiss and Hassan Hassan, *ISIS: Inside the Army of Terror* (New York, 2015), p. 25.

77 Ghaith Abdul-Ahad, 'From here to eternity', *The Guardian*, 8 June 2005.

78 Neumann, 'Suspects into collaborators', p. 20.

79 In addition, the Iraqi border town of Sinjar was an entry point for Arab foreign fighters coming from Syria, and the target for the October 2007 US raid that produced the 'Sinjar records'.

80 This may be due in part to a government reaction to the three suicide attacks in Amman, Jordan, on 9 November 2005, killing sixty and wounding over 100.

81 Out of the twenty-two Arab expatriates, twenty were living in the West, and two were uprooted Palestinians working in Jordan. In a separate study, Paz identified

that one Moroccan foreign fighter had been living in Spain, and one Lebanese foreign fighter had been living in Denmark. See Paz, 'Arab volunteers killed in Iraq'.

82 Rukmini Callimachi and Jim Yardley, 'From amateur to ruthless jihadist in France: Cherif and Said Kouachi's path to Paris attack at Charlie Hebdo', *The New York Times*, 17 January 2015.

83 Ahmed S. Hashim, *Insurgency and Counter-Insurgency in Iraq* (New York, 2006), p. 148.

84 *Hadeeth Bukhari* is one of the main authoritative sources of the sayings and doings of the Prophet Muhammad.

85 *Hadeeth Bukhari*. Book 2 (Belief). 1:36–1.37: Narrated by Abu Huraira.

86 See Hegghammer, 'Saudi militants in Iraq', p. 17. In addition, CNN reporter Jomana Karadsheh also reported that 'with the Islamic holy month of *Ramadan* under way, insurgent attacks in Iraq have risen in the past two weeks'. See Jomana Karadsheh, 'US: Iraq suicide attacks rising during *Ramadan*', *CNN*, 27 September 2006. Whether travelling to, or fighting in Iraq, the fasting month of *Ramadan* appeared to stimulate increased religiosity.

87 Glasse, *The Concise Encyclopedia of Islam*, p. 540.

88 *Hadeeth Bukhari*. Book 26 (*Hajj* Pilgrimage). 2.596: Narrated by Abu Huraira.

89 Examples include a twenty-one-year-old Saudi student Adil Mastoor Yahya al-Kaabi, a twenty-one-year-old Tunisian student Ali Omar al-Kuki, and a twenty-one-year-old Saudi national Ahmad Mustafa Mufleh al-Kaabi (al-Hazli), who were all motivated as a result of conversations during the *Hajj* pilgrimage.

90 Tim Butcher, 'Troops show true grit in desert storms', *The Telegraph*, 20 March 2003.

91 Hashim, *Insurgency and Counter-Insurgency in Iraq*, p. 144.

92 Brian Whitaker, 'Bereaved father to sue over jihad call', *The Guardian*, 22 November 2004.

93 Hegghammer, *Jihad in Saudi Arabia*, p. 89 and p. 121. Also, according to Toby Matthiesen the city of Buraidah 'lies in the historical heartland of ... dissident Islamist movements, including al-Qaeda'. See Toby Matthiesen, *Sectarian Gulf: Bahrain, Saudi Arabia, and the Arab Spring that Wasn't* (Stanford, 2013), p. 84.

94 Ken Ballen personally interviewed Ahmad Abdullah al-Shaya in 2008, at a Ministry of Interior Prison Care Centre in Saudi Arabia. Ken Ballen, *Terrorists in Love: The Real lives of Islamic Radicals* (London, 2011), p. 8.

95 Ibid., p. 19.

96 Hegghammer, 'Saudi militants in Iraq', p. 16.

97 A 'final straw' is alternatively conceptualised as a 'triggering event', defined as a 'significantly provocative event'. See John Horgan, *The Psychology of Terrorism* (London, 2005), p. 84.

98 Ballen, *Terrorists in Love*, p. 7.

99 Steven Komarow and Sabah Al-Anbaki, 'Would-be suicide bomber angry at those who sent him', *USA Today*, 24 January 2005.

100 Strictly speaking a *shaheed* is singular for martyr, while the plural (martyrs) is *shuhaada*.

101 Ballen, *Terrorists in Love*, p. 27.

102 Global Terrorism Database (GTD) ID:200412240004; Chicago Project on Security and Threats (CPOST) Attack ID: 1006327513.

103 Peter Beaumont, 'Living suicide bomb' rejoins al-Qaida after Saudi deprogramming', *The Guardian*, 18 January 2014.

104 Katherine R. Seifert and Clark McCauley, 'Suicide Bombers in Iraq, 2003–2010: Disaggregating Targets Can Reveal Insurgent Motives and Priorities', *Terrorism and Political Violence* 26/5 (2014), p. 803.

105 Martha Crenshaw, 'Explaining Suicide Terrorism: A Review Essay', *Security Studies* 16/1 (2007a), p. 162.

106 Robert A. Pape, *Dying to Win: The Strategic Logic of Suicide Terrorism* (New York, 2005), p. 10.

107 Assaf Moghadam, *The Globalization of Martyrdom: Al Qaeda, Salafi Jihad, and the diffusion of suicide attacks* (Baltimore, 2011), p. 5.

108 Crenshaw, 'Explaining Suicide Terrorism', p. 135.

109 Special Category Status recognised a political motive for paramilitary activity, and permitted prisoners to wear their own clothing. That status, once allowed in 1972, was withdrawn in 1976, and the hunger strike was intended to restore that status. See Ed Moloney, *A Secret History of the IRA* (London, 2002), p. 144.

110 Although the IRA hunger strikes were unsuccessful, Bobby Sands had been elected (by his republican supporters) as a UK Member of Parliament, before he died.

111 Jules Roy, *The Battle of Dienbienphu* (London, 1965), p. 72.

112 Ibid., p. 119.

113 For Iraqi civilian casualties, perpetrators are listed as: (1) any perpetrators; (2) US-led coalition, no Iraqi state forces; (3) US-led coalition, including Iraqi state forces; (4) Iraqi state forces without coalition, (5) anti-government/ occupation forces; (6) unknown actors. For US-led coalition casualties, the perpetrators are not identified.

114 See Assaf Moghadam, *The Globalization of Martyrdom*, p. 223. In addition, in May 2007 US General Petraeus also confirmed that '80 to 90 per cent of the suicide bombers come from outside Iraq'. See Joshua Partlow, 'An uphill battle to stop fighters at border', *Washington Post*, 5 May 2007.

115 Martha Crenshaw, 'Foreword by Martha Crenshaw', in M.M. Hafez (author), *Suicide Bombers in Iraq: The Strategy and Ideology of Martyrdom* (Washington, 2007b), p. ix.

116 Hashim, *Insurgency and Counter-Insurgency in Iraq*, p. 209.

117 This letter was captured by US forces in Iraq on 23 January 2004, and after translation, was released by the Coalition Provisional Authority in February 2004.

See Abu Musab Al-Zarqawi, 'February 2004 Coalition Provisional Authority English translation of terrorist Musab al Zarqawi letter obtained by United States Government in Iraq' (2004a). Available at http://2001-2009.state.gov/p/nea/rls/31694.htmhttp://2001-2009.state.gov/p/nea/rls/31694.htm (accessed 12 February 2012).

118 Hafez, *Suicide Bombers in Iraq*.

119 Seifert and McCauley, 'Suicide Bombers in Iraq'.

120 James A. Piazza, 'Is Islamist terrorism more dangerous?: An empirical study of group ideology, organisation, and goal structure', *Terrorism and Political Violence* 21/1 (2009), pp. 62–88.

121 GTD Search Criteria: 'Years: (between 2003 and 2009); all incidents regardless of doubt; including only suicide attacks; Country: (Iraq).' It is noted that the GTD does not include a definition of a 'suicide attack' in the 2015 GTD Codebook.

122 This included warning signs on all US vehicles: 'Danger. Keep back 100m. Authorised to use lethal force.'

123 Seifert and McCauley, 'Suicide Bombers in Iraq', p. 808.

124 For example, the 30 April 2005 suicide attack in Baghdad. GTD ID: 200504300006.

125 Conducted by Lebanese suicide bomber (Abbas Hassan) on 11 February 2004, in Baghdad (CPOST Attack ID 1225780728; GTD Database Incident ID 200402110004).

126 Marwan Ani and Caryle Murphy, 'Bombing in Kurdish City in Northern Iraq Kills 60', *Washington Post Foreign Service*, 5 May 2005.

127 For example, the 4 May 2005 suicide attack in Irbil (GTD Database Incident ID 200505040004).

128 International Committee of the Red Cross, 'International Humanitarian Law. Chapter 1, Rule 5 (Definition of Civilians)', *International Committee of the Red Cross*, 2015a.

129 Murad B. Al-Shishani, 'Al-Zarqawi's rise to power: Analyzing tactics and targets', *Terrorism Monitor*, 3/22 (2005a), pp. 5–7.

130 Quintan Wiktorowicz, 'Anatomy of the salafi movement', *Studies in Conflict and Terrorism* 29/3 (2006), p. 208.

131 Assaf Moghadam, 'Motives for martyrdom: Al Qaeda, Salafi Jihad, and the spread of suicide attacks', *International Security* 3/3 (2008), p. 62.

132 Thomas Hegghammer also recognised that initially in 'Iraq post 2003 ... the declared motivations of foreign fighters ... suggest that anti-Americanism was a much more important motivator than anti-Shiism'. See Thomas Hegghammer, 'Syria's foreign fighters', *The Middle East Channel*, 9 December 2013a.

133 al-Zarqawi, Abu Musab Al-Zarqawi, 'February 2004 Coalition Provisional Authority English translation of terrorist Musab al Zarqawi letter obtained by United States Government in Iraq'.

134 Ibid.

135 Ibid.

136 Joas Wagemakers, *A Quietist Jihadi: The Ideology and Influence of Abu Muhammad al-Maqdisi* (Cambridge, 2012), p. 47.

137 Hafez, *Suicide Bombers in Iraq*, p. 121.

138 Abu Musab Al-Zarqawi, 'The Return of Ibn Al-'Alqami's Grandchildren. 90-minute audio heard on the Internet on 18 May 2005', *The Middle East Media Research Institute,* Special Dispatch 917, 7 June 2005. *Fatwa* dated 18 May 2005.

139 Fawaz A. Gerges, *ISIS: A History* (Oxford, 2016), p. 90.

140 Jean-Charles Brisard and Damien Martinez, *Zarqawi: The New Face of al-Qaeda* (Cambridge, 2005), p. 11.

141 H.H.A. Cooper, 'What is a terrorist?: A psychological perspective', *Legal Medical Quarterly* 1/1 (1977), p. 26,

142 Ibid., p. 17.

143 Ayman M. Al-Zawahiri, 'Personal letter to Abu Musab al-Zarqawi 9 July 2005'. Available at www.ctc.usma.edu/posts/zawahiris-letter-to-zarqawi-english-translation-2 (accessed 12 September 2012).

144 Ibid.

145 These 143 Arab foreign fighters represent 20 per cent of the dataset. This is broken down to seventy-seven who died in self-sacrificial attacks (but critically their intended target was not identified). The remaining sixty-six Arab foreign fighters are broken down to thirty-three who died in conventional combat against US-led coalition forces; eighteen who died in self-sacrificial attacks against US-led coalition forces; and fifteen who died in suicide attacks against Iraqi civilians and non-combatants.

146 See Hafez *Suicide Bombers in Iraq*; Moghadam, *The Globalization of Martyrdom*; and Seifert and McCauley, 'Suicide Bombers in Iraq'.

147 Hafez, 'Suicide Bombers in Iraq', p. 95.

148 Moghadam, *The Globalization of Martyrdom*, pp. 230–231.

149 See Hegghammer, 'Saudi militants in Iraq', p. 4; Hafez 'Suicide terrorism in Iraq', p. 616; and Moghadam, *The Globalization of Martyrdom*, p. 225.

150 Anthony Cordesman, 'Iraq and foreign volunteers', p. 5.

151 Hegghammer, 'Saudi militants in Iraq', p. 14.

152 See David Cook, 'Suicide Attacks or "Martyrdom Operations" in Contemporary *Jihad* Literature', *Nova Religio: The Journal of Alternative and Emergent Religions* 6/1 (2002), p. 35. It was also noted in Chapter 2, that he used the term 'suicide/martyrdom' – in order 'to highlight the tension in the relationship between the two concepts'.

153 Karin M. Fierke, *Political Self-Sacrifice: Agency, Body and Emotion in International Relations* (Cambridge, 2014), p. 207.

154 Abu Basir Al-Tartusi, 'Suspicions of sin in martyrdom or suicide attacks', *Al-Tartosi Website*, 11 November 2005. Available at www.en.altartosi.com/suicide.htm#A (accessed 12 February 2012).

155 Felter and Fishman, 'Al Qaeda's Foreign Fighters in Iraq'.

156 Wehr, *A Dictionary of Modern Written Arabic*, p. 489.

157 Felter and Fishman, 'Al Qaeda's Foreign Fighters in Iraq', p. 18.

158 Ibid., p. 19

159 Ibid., p. 27. Even in their subsequent analysis of the Sinjar Records, Fishman et al. (2008: 6) still concluded that 'Libyan and Moroccan nationals registered as 'suicide bombers' at a higher rate than their Saudi counterparts'. This finding is only true on a *per capita* basis (which was not mentioned) for Libya (9.14 per million); Saudi Arabia second (3.03 per million); and Jordan third (1.47 per million).

160 Moghadam, *The Globalization of Martyrdom*, p. 227; David Malet, 'Foreign fighter mobilization and persistence in a global context', *Terrorism and Political Violence* 0 (2015), p. 14; and Brian Dodwell, Daniel Milton and Don Rassler, 'Then and Now: Comparing the Flow of Foreign Fighters in AQI and the Islamic State', *Combating Training Centre at West Point, United States Military Academy* (December 2016b), p. 22.

161 The data are extracted from various sources including the Chicago Project on Security and Threats (CPOST) Suicide Attack Database; Kohlmann, 'The Foreign Martyrs of Iraq: 2003–04'; and Hafez, *Suicide Bombers in Iraq*.

162 Adil Juma al-Shalali and Hamza Ali Awad.

163 Aaron Y. Zelin, 'The Ghosts of Sinjar in Tripoli and Benghazi', *Al-Wasat*, 10 January 2013a.

164 Brian Dodwell, Daniel Milton and Don Rassler, 'The Caliphate's Global Workforce: An Inside Look at the Islamic State's Foreign Fighter Payroll', *Combating Training Centre at West Point, United States Military Academy* (April 2016a), p. 28.

165 Alex P. Schmid, *The Routledge Handbook of Terrorism Research* (Oxon, 2013a), p. 4.

166 Abdul-Ahad, 'From here to eternity'.

167 Thomas Hegghammer, 'Global jihadism after the Iraq war', in F. Volpi (ed.) *Political Islam: A Critical Reader* (London, 2011b), p. 298.

168 Aparisim Ghosh, 'Inside the Mind of an Iraqi Suicide Bomber', *Time Magazine*, 28 June 2005.

169 A conclusion also reached by Muhammad Hafez: 'Afghan Arabs did not engage in suicide attacks *per se*'. See Hafez, 'Martyrs without borders'.

170 Quintan Wiktorowicz, 'A genealogy of radical Islam, *Studies in Conflict and Terrorism* 28/2 (2005a), p. 92.

171 The Concise Oxford Dictionary (Oxford, 1995), p. 693.

172 William Sargant, *Battle for the Mind: A Physiology of Conversion and Brain-washing* (London, 1959), p. xvii.

173 Mohammed M. Hafez, 'Martyrdom mythology in Iraq: How jihadists frame suicide terrorism in videos and biographies', *Terrorism and Political Violence* 19/1 (2007a), p. 112.

174 Quintan Wiktorowicz, *Radical Islam Rising: Muslim Extremism in the West* (Maryland, 2005b), p. 27.

175 Christina Hellmich, 'The physiology of al-Qaeda: From ideology to participation', in M. Ranstorp (ed.), *Understanding Violent Radicalization: Terrorist and Jihadist Recruitment in Europe* (Oxon, 2010), p. 75.

176 See the UK Government, 'Roots of violent radicalisation', *House of Commons Home Affairs Committee*. Nineteenth Report of Session 2010-2012. Volume 1 (6 February 2012). Available at www.publications.parliament.uk/pa/cm201012/cmselect/cmhaff/1446/1446.pdf (accessed 7 June 2014); and the UK Government, 'Channel Duty Guidance: Protecting vulnerable people from being drawn into terrorism', 2015. Available at www.gov.uk/government/uploads/system/uploads/attachment_data/file/425189/Channel_Duty_Guidance_April_2015.pdf (accessed 7 June 2016).

177 Horgan, *The Psychology of Terrorism*, p. 103.

178 Ibid., p. 95

179 Ibid., p. 84.

180 CPOST Attack ID 1230594988. Abdul Aziz Al-Gharbi used to lead prayers at the Imam Bukhari Mosque in Dammam 75 District. On 22 March 2003, he killed four people in a suicide attack in Kirkuk, including an Australian cameraman Paul Moran.

181 Kohlmann, 'The Foreign Martyrs of Iraq: 2003–04', p. 1. No GTD database details. This attack occurred on 20 October 2004.

182 Horgan, *The Psychology of Terrorism*, p. 103.

183 Diego Gambetta, *Making Sense of Suicide Missions* (Oxford, 2005).

184 Zaki Chehab, *Inside the* Resistance, p. 53.

185 CPOST Attack ID 2127396409. He belonged to Abu Musab al-Zarqawi's group *Jama'at al-Tawhid and Jihad*. He targeted a convoy of German contractors in Baghdad (14 June 2004), killing more than seventy-eight and injuring over fifty.

186 CPOST Attack ID 1214934544. The attack was in Hillah on 28 February 2005, considered 'the worst single massacre since the US invasion'. He had also made the Islamic pilgrimage (*umra*) prior to going to Iraq. See also Hafez, 'Suicide terrorism in Iraq', pp. 617–619.

187 United Nations Security Council Counter-Terrorism Committee, 'Background Note: Group I: Technical sessions on detection, intervention against, and prevention of incitement, recruitment and facilitation of FTF travel'.

188 Horgan, *The Psychology of Terrorism*, p. 102.

189 Gerges, *The Far Enemy: Why Jihad went Global*', p. 269.

190 As noted earlier in this chapter, the remaining 11 per cent of attacks were directed against US-led coalition forces.

191 Abu Musab Al-Zarqawi, 'Al-Zarqawi's message to the fighters of jihad in Iraq on September 11, 2004', *The Middle East Media Research Institute,* Special Dispatch 785, 15 September 2004b. According to *Hadeeth Muslim* 2897, as narrated by Abu Hurairah 'The Last Hour would not come until the Romans would land at Al-A'maq or Dabiq. An army consisting of the best (soldiers) of the people of the earth at that time will come from Medina … win and … be conquerors of Constantinople.' In effect, this signified a climactic battle involving a final Muslim victory over non-Muslims. Such a battle is now beyond reach, and is acknowledged by the Islamic State, who changed the name of their magazine *Dabiq* to *Rumiyah* (Rome), publishing *Rumiyah* Issue 1, on 5 September 2016.

Chapter 4

1 Malik, Shahid, 'Not all fighters going to Syria are extremists, says former UK minister Shahid Malik', *The Sydney Morning Herald,* 18 May 2014.

2 See Thomas R. Mockaitis, *British Counterinsurgency 1919–1960* (London, 1990), p. 3. Such disaffected groups would include the Free Syrian Army (FSA), *Ahrar al-Sham*, *Jabhat al-Nusrah* and the Islamic State in Iraq and al-Sham.

3 Randy Borum and Robert Fein, 'The psychology of foreign fighters', *Studies in Conflict and Terrorism* (2016), p. 10.

4 This chapter uses Islamic State, IS and ISIS interchangeably.

5 *Shamukh al-Islam* Jihadi Forum (17 February 2012). Now password protected.

6 Examples of suspended accounts are www.facebook.com/Strangers.Sy1 and www.Shaghor.com. By 5 February 2016, Twitter had 'suspended over 125,000 accounts for threatening or promoting terrorist acts, primarily related to ISIS'. Available at https://blog.twitter.com/2016/combating-violent-extremism (accessed 12 February 2017).

7 The FSA was established in July 2011, and JN in January 2012. JN was proscribed on 11 December 2012.

8 Prominent Arab foreign fighters who are not in Syria but are ideologically involved include Egyptian Al Qaeda chief, Ayman al-Zawahiri, and Jordanian ideologue, Abu Muhammad al-Maqdisi.

9 Alex Schmid determined there were 17,500 'from the Arab Middle East and North Africa's Maghreb region'. See Alex P. Schmid, 'Foreign (terrorist) fighter estimates: Conceptual and data issues', *International Centre for Counter-Terrorism Policy Brief*, October 2015, p. 3.

10 For example, Dodwell et al. examined fighters over a time period of only 2013–2014. See Brian Dodwell, Daniel Milton and Don Rassler, 'The Caliphate's Global Workforce: An Inside Look at the Islamic State's Foreign Fighter Payroll', *Combating Training Centre at West Point, United States Military Academy* (April 2016a). In their report, they analysed 'over 4,600 unique Islamic State personnel' (p. iv), and identified 4,188 foreign fighters (p. 3), of which only 1,880 were Arab foreign fighters (p. 9), not including the 120 Syrian ISIS fighters.

11 For example, *Jabhat al-Nusrah* in Charles Lister, 'Profiling Jabhat al-Nusra', *The Brookings Project on US Relations with the Islamic World*, Analysis Paper 24 (July 2016).

12 For example, 'suicide attacks' in Charlie Winter, 'War by suicide: A statistical analysis of the Islamic State's martyrdom industry', *International Centre for Counter-Terrorism – The Hague*. February 2017b.

13 Aaron Y. Zelin, 'Foreign Jihadists in Syria: Tracking Recruitment Networks', *The Washington Institute for Near East Policy*, Policy Watch 2186 (19 December 2013b).

14 Other scholars who have written on foreign fighters in Syria include Thomas Hegghammer, 'Syria's foreign fighters', *The Middle East Channel*, 9 December 2013a; Vera Mironova, Loubna Mrie and Sam Whitt, 'The motivations of Syrian Islamist fighters', *CTC Sentinel Terrorism Monitor* 7/10 (2014); Peter R. Neumann, 'Victims, perpetrators, assets: The Narratives of Islamic State defectors', *The International Centre for the Study of Radicalisation and Political Violence* (2015); Fawaz A. Gerges, *ISIS: A History* (Oxford, 2016); Dodwell et al., 'The Caliphate's Global Workforce'; C. Winter 'War by suicide'; and Elena Pokalova, 'Driving factors behind foreign fighters in Syria and Iraq', *Studies in Conflict and Terrorism* 0/0 (2018), pp. 1–34.

15 Chapters 1 and 3 briefly covered the roots of the Sunni-Shi'a divide. For more, see Nathan Gonzalez, *The Sunni-Shia Conflict: Understanding Sectarian Violence in the Middle East* (Mission Viejo, 2009).

16 Thomas E. Lawrence, 'Seven Pillars of Wisdom' (London, 1935), p. 329.

17 For example, Abdullah al-Adaam, *Do Not Consult Anyone in Killing the Alawites*, 12 July, 2012.

18 Hans Wehr, *A Dictionary of Modern Written Arabic* (London, 1980), p. 349.

19 Ibid., p. 334.

20 Ibid., p. 561.

21 Aymenn J. Al-Tamimi, 'Islamic State training camp textbook: Course in monotheism – complete text', *aymennjawad.org*, 26 July 2015. Available at www.aymennjawad.org/17633/islamic-state-training-camp-textbook-course-in (accessed 12 February 2016).

22 John McHugo, 'The roots of Syria's tragedy', *Al-Jazeera*, 5 October 2015.

23 A quote by Dame Freya Stark in 1928, as cited in Daniel Pipes, *Greater Syria: The History of an Ambition* (Oxford, 1990), p. 13.

24 See Raymond Hinnebusch, *Syria: Revolution from Above* (London, 2001), p. 65; Gerges, *ISIS: A History*, p. 171.

25 US Central Intelligence Agency, *The World Fact Book 2014 – Syria*. Available at www.cia.gov/library/publications/download/download-2014 (accessed 8 April 2015). The remaining 14 per cent includes Christians, Druzes, and Jews.

26 See Barnett R. Rubin, *The Tragedy of the Middle East* (Cambridge, 2002), p. 35. Also, a declassified US Defence Intelligence Agency (1982) report on Syria and the Muslim Brotherhood, estimated 'the total casualties for the Hama incident probably number about 2,000' (p. 7). See US Defence Intelligence Agency, '*Declassified Report: Syria and Muslim Brotherhood*, 1982. Released 2016. Available at https://syria360.files.wordpress.com/2013/11/dia-syria-muslimbrotherhoodpressureintensi fies-2.pdf (accessed 21 December 2016).

27 Literature covering the Arab Spring includes, but is not limited to, John R. Bradley, *After the Arab Spring: How the Islamists Hijacked the Middle East Revolts* (New York, 2012); Lin Noueihed and Alex Warren, *The Battle for the Arab Spring: Revolution, Counter-Revolution and the Making of a New Era* (New Haven, 2012); Carsten Wieland, *Syria – A Decade of Lost Chances: Repression and Revolution from Damascus Spring to Arab Spring* (Seattle, 2012); and M.E. McMillan, *From the First World War to the Arab Spring: What's Really Going on in the Middle East?* (New York, 2016).

28 United Nations Human Rights Council, 'Independent International Commission of Inquiry on the Syrian Arab Republic established pursuant to United Nations Human Rights Council Resolutions S-17/1, 19/22 and 21/26', 20 December 2012. Available at www.ohchr.org/Documents/Countries/SY/ColSyriaDecember2012.pdf (accessed 21 December 2012).

29 BBC, 'Islamic State assassin: How I killed more than 100 people', *BBC World News*, 4 May 2018. Available at www.bbc.com/news/world-middle-east-43881659 (accessed 5 May 2018).

30 Doug McAdam, 'Recruitment to high-risk activism: The case of Freedom Summer', *American Journal of Sociology* 92/1 (1986), pp. 64–90. Noted in Chapters 2 and 3, biographical availability refers to the 'absence of personal constraints that may increase the costs and risks of movement participation, such as full-time employment, marriage, and family responsibilities' (p. 70).

31 United Nations Security Council Counter-Terrorism Committee, 'Background Note: Group I: Technical sessions on detection, intervention against, and prevention of incitement, recruitment and facilitation of FTF travel', Madrid, 27–28 July 2015b. Available at www.un.org/en/sc/ctc/docs/2015/0721Tehnical%20Session%20 Group%20I%20-%20background%20note.pdf (link no longer working).

32 Chapter 3 found that based on the available data of 283 Arab foreign fighters in Iraq, they varied between fifteen and fifty-four years old with 49 per cent of them

twenty-three years old or under. The average age was twenty-four; the median twenty-eight.

33 Chapter 2 found that based on the available data of 102 Afghan Arabs, they varied between eleven and sixty-five years old, with 51 per cent of them twenty-two years old or under. The average age was twenty-three; the median twenty-four.

34 Dodwell et al., 'The Caliphate's Global Workforce', p. 12, found 'the average prospective fighter was 26–27-years-old'; Nate Rosenblatt, 'All jihad is local: What ISIS's files tell us about its fighters', *New America*, July 2016, p. 7, found 'the average age of a fighter . . . was approximately 26 or 27'; and Arie Perliger and Daniel Milton, 'From cradle to grave: The life cycle of foreign fighters in Iraq and Syria', *Combating Terrorism Center* (November 2016), p. 21, found the average age to be of twenty-four years old.

35 The veteran Afghan Arabs involved in the Syrian insurgency are an Algerian named Saif Areef (forty-nine years old), and the Al Qaeda chief, Ayman al-Zawahiri (sixty-five years old). Both hold command-level positions.

36 'Agency refers to the belief that one can alter conditions or policies through collective action.' See Christina Hellmich, 'The physiology of al-Qaeda: From ideology to participation', in M. Ranstorp (ed.), *Understanding Violent Radicalization: Terrorist and Jihadist Recruitment in Europe* (Oxon, 2010), p. 75.

37 Data extracted from ISIS General Border Administration files. The ages of only fifteen known self-sacrificial attackers could be determined and ranged between eighteen and thirty-eight years old. Ten of those attackers were targeting Syrian military installations (and not civilians).

38 Anne Speckhard and Ahmet Yayla, *ISIS Defectors: Inside Stories of the Terrorist Caliphate* (McLean, VA, 2016), p. 62.

39 *Per capita*, the top three Arab countries were Libya (50 *per capita*); Jordan (30.1 *per capita*), and Tunisia (27.4 *per capita*).

40 Two interpretations of *Wahhabism* are (1) 'a puritanical form of Islam virtually synonymous with Salafism' (see Assaf Moghadam, *The Globalization of Martyrdom: Al Qaeda, Salafi Jihad, and the Diffusion of Suicide Attacks* (Baltimore, 2011), p. 122); and (2) 'a particularly puritanical, bland, ultra-orthodox and forbidding interpretation of Islam concerned with . . . notions of moral corruption and the need for purity'. See Guilain Denoeux, 'The Forgotten Swamp: Navigating Political Islam', in F. Volpi (ed.), *Political Islam: A Critical Reader* (London, 2011), p. 59.

41 Isabelle Duyvesteyn and Bram Peters, 'Fickle foreign fighters? A cross-case analysis of seven Muslim foreign fighter mobilisations (1980–2015)', *International Centre for Counter-Terrorism (ICCT) Research Paper* (October 2015), p. 4.

42 Stephane Lacroix, 'Saudi Islamists and the Arab Spring', *The London School of Economics and Political Science*, 36 (May 2014), p. 5.

43 Aaron Y. Zelin, 'The Saudi foreign fighter presence in Syria', *CTC Sentinel* 7/1 (April 2014a), pp. 10–14.

44 Nawaf Obaid, 'Saudi Arabia's master plan against ISIS, Assad and Iran in Syria', *The National Interest*, 16 February 2016.

45 Al-Jazeera, Saudi Arabia arrests hundreds of suspected ISIL members. *Al-Jazeera*, 18 July 2015.

46 Toby Matthiesen, 'The domestic sources of Saudi foreign policy: Islamists and the state in the wake of the Arab Uprisings', *Rethinking Political Islam Series*, *Brookings Institute* (August 2015), p. 1.

47 See Al-Moslim.net, *'ulama' wa-du'a fi-l-mamlaka yasduroon bayanaan li-ta'yeed al-jabhat al-islamiyya fi-Sham wa yad'una ila da'miha* (Scholars in the Kingdom issue a statement in support of the Islamic Front in Syria and call for support), 5 December 2013. Available at http://almoslim.net/node/195146 (link no longer working). The Islamic Front was formed on 22 November 2013, consisting of Ahrar al-Sham, Suqour al-Sham, the Tawhid Brigade, the Haq Brigade, Ansar al-Sham, the Islam Army, and the Kurdish Islamic Front. See also Aron Lund, 'The politics of the Islamic Front, Part 1: Structure and Support', *Carnegie Endowment for International Peace*, 14 January 2014.

48 Abdullah Al-Muhaysani, *kalama Abdullah al-muhaysani amaam majmoo' isra' ba'd tahhreer mataar abu al-dhuhoor al-askararee* (speech by Abdullah al-Muhaysani in front of a group of prisoners after the capture of Abu Dhuhoor Military airport). September 2015. Available at www.youtube.com/watch?v=aSFE-nD0gmA (accessed 7 June 2016).

49 Other clerics that have great influence in Saudi Arabia include Egyptian Yusuf al-Qaradawi (based in Qatar) who decreed that 'anyone who has the ability, who is trained to fight . . . has to go; I call on Muslims to support their brothers in Syria' (see Zelin, 'The Saudi foreign fighter presence in Syria').

50 Matthiesen, 'The domestic sources of Saudi foreign policy', p. 6.

51 Thomas Hegghammer, *Jihad in Saudi Arabia: Violence and Pan Islamism since 1979* (Cambridge, 2010b), p. 121.

52 Roger P. Warren, *Why Radical Islamist Ideology is a Threat: A Study of Gulf Arab Detainees Recommended for 'Continued Detention' in Guantanamo Bay.* M.Litt Thesis. University of St Andrews. May 2012. Unpublished.

53 Speckhard and Yayla, *ISIS Defectors: Inside Stories of the Terrorist Caliphate*, p. 62.

54 Ibid., p. 103.

55 Muhammad Al-Khatib, 'Why we joined ISIS', *Al Jumhuriya*, 5 July 2018. Available at www.aljumhuriya.net/en/content/why-we-joined-isis (accessed 6 July 2018).

56 An excellent empirical study of such discrimination was authored by Claire L. Adida, David D. Laitin, and Marie-Anne Valfort, *Why Muslim Integration Fails in Christian-Heritage Societies* (Cambridge, 2016).

57 See Maxwell Taylor and John Horgan, 'A conceptual framework for addressing psychological process in the development of the terrorist', *Terrorism and Political Violence* 18/4 (2006), p. 592.

58 Mubaraz Ahmed, Milo Comerford and Emman El-Badawy, 'Milestones to Militancy: What the Lives of 100 Jihadis Tell us about a Global Movement', *Centre on Religion and Politics*, Tony Blair Faith Foundation, April 2016, p. 5.

59 Many of these individuals had participated in multiple defensive jihads. The seventy-four identified had participated in eighty-nine defensive jihads.

60 Involvement in the Libyan jihad (which was supported by NATO) was not exclusive to Libyan fighters. The book dataset also reveals the presence of two Egyptian (Ahmad al-Barra and Walid Badr) and one Palestinian foreign fighter (Osama Kishta).

61 See Michael Weiss and Hassan Hassan, *ISIS: Inside the Army of Terror* (New York, 2015); Gerges, *ISIS: A History*, p. 50; and Ahmed et al., 'Milestones to Militancy', p. 19.

62 Tony Blair, 'Tony Blair says he's sorry for Iraq War "mistakes," but not for ousting Saddam', *CNN Interview with Fareed Zakaria GPS*, 26 October 2015. Available at http://edition.cnn.com/2015/10/25/europe/tony-blair-iraq-war/ (accessed 10 March 2016).

63 The book dataset reveals Muhammad al-Qab (www.facebook.com/Strangers.sy4 posted 29 October 2013, link no longer working); Husaam al-Shataywi (Convoy of Martyrs); Abdul Qadir al-Misrati (http://documents.sy/image. php?id=2443&lang=en posted 28 July 2013, link no longer working); Abu Ibrahim al-Libi, Abu Dharr, and Mu'aweeya al-Libi (Zaman al-Wasl, March 8, 2016) were involved in the Libyan jihad to overthrow the Gaddafi regime in 2011.

64 They were Ibrahim Shakaran, Muhammad Ahmad Mazouz, and Muhammad Sulayman al-Alami, who incidentally, were also former detainees at Guantanamo Bay prison. Other Arab and non-Arab groups with national identities include *Jund ash-Shaam* and *Fatah al-Islam* (Lebanese); *Jaysh al-Muhajjireen wa-Ansar* (Chechens); *Kateebat Tawhid wa Jihad* (Uzbeks); and *Crimean Jamaat* (Russian and Crimean Tartars).

65 The remaining nine belonged to either Egyptian Islamic Jihad (EIJ), the Egyptian Islamic Group (EIG), Fatah al-Islam, the Libyan Islamic Fighting Group (LIFG), and/or the Moroccan Islamic Fighting Group (MIFG).

66 Ahmed et al., 'Milestones to Militancy', p. 5.

67 Ibid., p. 9 and p. 29.

68 See Marco Nilsson, 'Foreign fighters and the radicalization of local jihad: Interview evidence from Swedish jihadists', *Studies in Conflict and Terrorism*, 38/1 (2015), pp. 343–358; Dodwell et al., 'The Caliphate's Global Workforce', p. 10; and Randy Borum and Robert Fein, 'The psychology of foreign fighters', pp. 1–19. It is

important to recognise that many Arab foreign fighters went to Syria and joined a group, often based on their geographic origin, only to later join groups such as *Jabhat al-Nusrah* or ISIS.

69 J.M. Berger and Jessica Stern, 'Why are foreign fighters joining ISIS?', *The Atlantic*, 8 March 2015.

70 See United Nations Security Council Counter-Terrorism Committee, 'Background Note: Stemming the flow of foreign terrorist fighters', Madrid, 27–28 July 2015a. Available at www.un.org/en/sc/ctc/docs/2015/0721Special%20Meeting%20 Madrid%20-%20General%20background%20Note.pdf (link no longer working).

71 See Hegghammer, 'Syria's foreign fighters', and Jennifer Cafarella, 'Jabhat al-Nusra in Syria: An Islamic Emirate for al-Qaeda', *Institute for the Study of War*, *Middle East Security Report* 25 (2014), p. 9. The EU's Director of Justice and Home Affairs, Gilles de Kerchove, told the BBC on 24 April 2013, that 'not all of them are radical when they leave, but most likely many of them will be radicalised there'. See Gilles de Kerchove, 'Hundreds of Europeans fighting in Syria, says EU expert', *BBC*, 24 April 2013.

72 Nathan Patin, 'The other foreign fighters: An open-source investigation into American volunteers fighting the Islamic State in Iraq and Syria', *A Bellingcat Investigation*, August 2015, pp. 21, 23, 26, 29, and 30.

73 Ibid., p. 1.

74 Ahmed et al., 'Milestones to Militancy', p. 5.

75 Nathan Patin, 'The other foreign fighters', p. 32.

76 See also Henry Tuck, Tanya Silverman and Candace Smalley, '*Shooting in the right direction': Anti-ISIS Foreign Fighters in Syria and Iraq*, Institute for Strategic Dialogue, Horizons Series No. 1 (2016).

77 Mohammad Ballout, 'In Syria, US sides with local jihadists to defeat global ones', *Al Monitor*, 7 January 2014.

78 Barak H. Obama, 'Readout of the President's Call with President Vladimir Putin of Russia', *The White House. Office of the Press Secretary*, 14 February 2016.

79 John F. Kerry, 'Press Availability at the International Syria Support Group', *Embassy of the United States, Damascus, Syria*, 12 February 2016a. Available at http:// damascus.usembassy.gov/statedept021216en2.html (accessed 18 February 2016).

80 Mowaffaq Safadi, 'Don't rely on Syria's "moderate" fighting force. It doesn't exist', *The Guardian*, 16 December 2015.

81 L. Rosen, US Authorizes Financial Support for the Free Syrian Army. *Al Monitor*. 27 July 2012. See also Tyler Durden, 'Ben Rhodes Admits Obama Armed Jihadists in Syria in Bombshell Interview', *Zero Hedge*, 24 June 2018. Available at www. zerohedge.com/news/2018-06-24/ben-rhodes-admits-obama-armed-jihadists-syria-bombshell-interview.

82 The martyrdom operations included attacks against Syrian Army checkpoints 'Panorama', 'Wadi Elbow', Barrier 68, and 'Tumeah'; Nabq military intelligence building, and Mingh airbase.

83 For example, on 23 December 2011, an Iraqi Arab foreign fighter conducted a martyrdom operation against the Military Intelligence building in Damascus. The UN Security Council (SC/10506 dated 23 December 2011) denounced the attacks as 'terrorist attacks'. Additionally, *Agence France Presse* (23 December 2011); *The Daily Beast* (4 January 2012); and *Jerusalem Post* (25 December 2011) also labelled the attack a 'suicide attack' (all cited under CPOST Attack ID 377522234).

84 Hegghammer, 'Syria's foreign fighters'.

85 Miguel Carreras and Ajay Verghese, 'Violence, Insecurity, and Religiosity: A Multilevel Analysis of 71 Countries', *Terrorism and Political Violence* (2018).

86 Saudi fighter Abdul Kareem al-Thabeeti arrived 12 July 2014 and departed 15 July 2014.

87 Libyan fighter Alaa' Muhammad al-Libi, arrived 1 July 2014 and departed 23 July 2014.

88 Libyan fighter Nazaar Fathi al-Badri arrived 20 July 2014 and departed 15 August 2014.

89 Speckhard and Yayla, *ISIS Defectors: Inside Stories of the Terrorist Caliphate*, p. 261.

90 Ibid, p. 181.

91 Saif Allah al-Muhajjir, *Sharia 4 Sham*, Facebook, 11 July 2013.

92 Lorne Dawson, *In Their Own Words: Religiosity and the Islamic State Foreign Fighters*, Oxford Research Group, 27 April 2018. Available at https://sustainablesecurity.org/2018/04/27/in-their-own-words-religiosity-and-the-islamic-state-foreign-fighters/ (accessed 5 May 2018).

93 Chicago Project on Security and Threats (CPOST) Suicide Attack Database and the Global Terrorism Database (GTD).

94 Martyrdom of Hamza al-'Awani (Abu Hajjir al-Tunisi). *Al-Ghuraabaa'* [Strangers]. Facebook. 16 July 2013. Available at www.facebook.com/Strangers.sy2 (link no longer working).

95 Obituary of Hamza al-'Awani (Abu Hajjir al-Tunisi). *Shaghor*. Facebook. 8 September 2013. Available at www.shaghor.com/index.php?s=27&id=33#.UiyhmvpYEpI.facebook (link no longer working).

96 Alastair Reed, Jeanine de Roy van Zuijdewin, and Edwin Bakker, 'Pathways of foreign fighters: Policy options and their (un)intended consequences', *International Centre for Counter-Terrorism Policy Brief*, April 2015, p. 1.

97 Ibid., p. 2.

98 Gerges, *ISIS: A History*, p. 223.

99 Assaf Moghadam, *The Globalization of Martyrdom: Al Qaeda, Salafi Jihad, and the Diffusion of Suicide Attacks* (Baltimore, 2011), pp. 102–110.

100 Fawaz A. Gerges, 'ISIS and the Third Wave of Jihadism', *Current History*, December 2014, p. 343.

101 Charles J. M. Drake, 'The role of ideology in terrorists' target selection', *Terrorism and Political Violence* 10/2 (1998), p. 54.

102 ISIS was designated a terrorist organisation on 13 December 2011, 30 May 2013, 14 May 2014, and 2 June 2014 under the UN 1267 Sanctions List (20 June 2016), p. 53. *Jabhat al-Nusrah* was designated a terrorist organisation on 14 May 2014 under the UN 1267 Sanctions List (20 June 2016), p. 50.

103 The Paris terrorist attacks on 13 November 2015 killed 130 civilians; the Brussels terrorist attacks on 22 March 2016, killed thirty-five civilians; and the Nice terrorist attack on 14 July 2016, killed eighty-four civilians.

104 United Nations Human Rights Council, 'Independent International Commission of Inquiry on the Syrian Arab Republic established pursuant to United Nations Human Rights Council Resolutions S-17/1, 19/22 and 21/26', 20 December 2012. Available at www.ohchr.org/Documents/Countries/SY/ColSyriaDecember2012.pdf (accessed 21 December 2012).

105 United Nations Human Rights Council 'They came to destroy': ISIS Crimes against the Yazidis. Human Rights Council', Thirty-second session. Agenda Item 4. 15 June 2016. Available at www.ohchr.org/Documents/HRBodies/HRCouncil/ColSyria/
A_HRC_32_CRP.2_en.pdf (accessed 6 July 2016).

106 Quran: Ash-Shuraa 42: 40 'And the retribution for an evil act is an evil one like it'.

107 See Louise Richardson, *What Terrorists Want: Understanding the Enemy, Containing the Threat* (New York, 2007); Mohammed M. Hafez, *Suicide Bombers in Iraq: The Strategy and Ideology of Martyrdom* (Washington, 2007b), p. 44; Moghadam, *The Globalization of Martyrdom*, p. 230; Andrew Silke, 'Holy Warriors: Exploring the Psychological Processes of Jihadi Radicalization', *European Journal of Criminology* 5/1 (2008), p. 113.

108 Joas Wagemakers, 'What Should an Islamic State Look Like? Jihadi-Salafi Debates on the War in Syria', *The Muslim World* 106/3 (2016), p. 501.

109 Shiraz Maher, *Salafi-Jihadism: The History of an Idea* (London, 2016a), p. 12.

110 Quintan Wiktorowicz, *Radical Islam Rising: Muslim Extremism in the West* (Maryland, 2005b), p. 25.

111 David C. Hofmann and Lorne L. Dawson, 'The neglected role of charismatic authority in the study of terrorist groups and radicalization', *Studies in Conflict and Terrorism* 37/4 (2014), p. 358.

112 See Hassan Hassan, 'The sectarianism of the Islamic State: Ideological roots and political context', *Carnegie Endowment for International Peace*, June 2016, p. 9.

113 Mironova et al. 'The motivations of Syrian Islamist fighters', p. 16.

114 Gerges, *ISIS: A History*, p. 292.

115 See Shadi Hamid, 'The roots of the Islamic State's appeal', *The Atlantic*, 31 October 2014; Graeme Wood, 'What ISIS really wants', *The Atlantic*, March 2015; and Dodwell et al., 'The Caliphate's Global Workforce', p. 32.

116 See Jurgen Todenhöfer, 'Islamic State – Seven Impressions of a Difficult Journey', 2014. Available at http://juergentodenhoefer.de/seven-impressions-of-a-difficult-journey/?lang=en (accessed 8 December 2015).

117 Thomas Hegghammer, 'Jihadi-Salafis or revolutionaries? On religion and politics in the study of militant Islamism', in R. Meijer (ed.) *Global Salafism: Islam's New Religious Movement* (London, 2009a), p. 255.

118 Hassan, 'The sectarianism of the Islamic State', p. 7.

119 *Dabiq* 10 (p. 58).

120 Cole Bunzel, 'From Paper State to Caliphate: The Ideology of the Islamic State', *The Brookings Project on US Relations in the Islamic World* (March 2015), p. 11.

121 Abu Muhammad Al-Maqdisi, *A Call to the Ummah and Mujahideen*, May 2014. Available at www.justpaste.it/Maqdisi-ISIS (accessed 30 May 2014).

122 Abu Muhammad Al-Maqdisi, *Why did I not name them Khawarij even until now?* June 2015. Available at https://pietervanostaeyen.com/2015/06/25/shaykh-abu-muhammad-al-maqdisi-why-did-i-not-name-them-khawarij-even-until-now/ (accessed 30 June 2015).

123 See A.S. Ali, 'IS disciplines some Emirs to avoid losing base', *Al Monitor*, 2 September 2014. The arrested Arab foreign fighters included Abu Musab al-Tunisi, Abu Asid al-Maghrabi, Abu al-Hawra al-Jazari, and Abu Abdullah al-Maghrabi, who were charged with excessive *takfir* accusations.

124 Hassan, 'The sectarianism of the Islamic State', p. 1.

125 Kenneth M. Pollack, *Arabs at War: Military Effectiveness, 1948–1991* (Lincoln, 2004), p. 573.

126 Salah Al-Ansari and Usama Hasan, *Tackling Terror: A Response to Takfiri Terrorist Theology*. Quilliam Foundation, 2018, pp. 41–42.

127 See Christopher Reuter, 'I'm Not a Butcher': An Interview with Islamic State's Architect of Death, *Spiegel Online International*, 16 July 2015; Weiss and Hassan, *ISIS: Inside the Army of Terror*, p. 168; Dodwell et al., 'The Caliphate's Global Workforce', p. 31; Gerges, *ISIS: A History*, p. 67.

128 For example, see Al-Baqarah (2:154): '*And do not say about those who are killed in the way of Allah, "They are dead." Rather they are alive, but you perceive it not.*' Also, see Muhammad (47: 7), Al-Imaran (3: 169) and Al-Imran (3: 157).

129 As cited in Lorne L. Dawson, 'Challenging the curious erasure of religion from the study of religious terrorism', *Numen* 65 (2018), p. 158. Dawson was referring to works by William I. Thomas and Dorothy Swaine Thomas. 1928. The Child in America: Behavior Problems and Programs. New York: Knopf, 1928, pp. 571–572.

130 The August 2013 spike may have been influenced by a *Jabhat al-Nusrah*/FSA offensive in Latakia. Certainly the November 2013 spike reflects a *Jabhat al-Nusrah* and FSA defence of Base 80 near Aleppo airport.

131 See Jomana Karadsheh, 'US: Iraq suicide attacks rising during *Ramadan*', *CNN*, 27 September 2006.

132 See Jason Warner and Hilary Matfess, *Exploding Stereotypes: The Unexpected Operational and Demographic Characteristics of Boko Haram's Suicide Bombers*. Combating Terrorism Center at West Point, August 2017, p. 21.

133 Amarnath Amarasingam and Charlie Winter, *ISIS's Perverse, Bloody Interpretation of Ramadan*. The Atlantic, 26 May 2017. Available at www.theatlantic.com/international/archive/2017/05/ramadan-isis-attack-muslim/528336/ (accessed 7 June 2018).

134 See Michael J. Reese, Keven G. Ruby and Robert A. Pape, *Days of Action or Restraint? How the Islamic State Calendar Impacts Violence*, American Political Science Review 111/3 (2017), pp. 439–459.

135 As noted in Chapter 3, CPOST defines a suicide attack 'as an attack in which an attacker kills himself or herself in a deliberate attempt to kill others'.

136 CPOST Attack ID 147281505 (20 December 2013).

137 Out of an original total of forty-six attacks, three were duplicate entries and removed. That left twenty-eight attacks targeting civilians and non-combatants, twelve attacks against combatants, and three attacks with no clearly identifiable intended target.

138 C. Winter 'War by suicide'; p. 17.

139 Tracy Shelton, 'Syria: From IT to rebel commander', *Global Post*, 3 March 2013.

140 Reuter, 'I'm Not a Butcher'.

141 Martin Chulov, 'No regrets, no remorse: ISIS mastermind who sent out 15 suicide bombers', *The Guardian*, 31 August 2015.

142 Moghadam, *The Globalization of Martyrdom*, p. 5.

143 Thomas Hegghammer, 'Should I stay or should I go? Explaining variation in Western jihadists' choice between domestic and foreign fighting', *American Political Science Review*, February 2013b.

144 David Cook, 'Suicide Attacks or "Martyrdom Operations" in Contemporary *Jihad* Literature', *Nova Religio: The Journal of Alternative and Emergent Religions* 6/1 (2002), p. 9.

145 The Arabic verb *ghamasa* means 'to plunge, immerse, submerse' (Wehr, *A Dictionary of Modern Written Arabic*, p. 684.

146 The first mention of an *inghimasi* operation (in Syria) was a Jabhat al-Nusrah attack on 100 Syrian Arab Army soldiers occupying the Al-Kindi Hospital in Aleppo on 20 December 2013 (CPOST Attack ID 47281505).

147 Zelin, 'The Saudi foreign fighter presence in Syria', p. 13.

148 Emma El-Badawy, Milo Comerford and Peter Welby, 'Inside the Jihadi Mind:
     Understanding Ideology and Propaganda', *Centre on Religion and Politics* (October
     2015), p. 20.

149 Aymenn J. Al-Tamimi, 'Stories of the mujahideen: Unseen Islamic State
     biographies of outstanding members', *Jihadology*, 24 August 2016. Available at
     http://jihadology.net/2016/08/24/the-archivist-stories-of-the-mujahideen-unseen-
     islamic-state-biographies-of-outstanding-members/ (accessed 12 October 2016).

150 Mustafa Al-Kadhimi, 'Iraq struggles to combat evolving terrorist threat', *Al
     Monitor*, 31 January 2016; Dodwell et al., 'The Caliphate's Global Workforce', p. 28.

151 Hafez, *Suicide Bombers in Iraq*, p. 117; David Cook, *Martyrdom in Islam*
     (Cambridge, 2007), p. 153; Assaf Moghadam, *The Globalization of Martyrdom:
     Al Qaeda, Salafi Jihad, and the Diffusion of Suicide Attacks* (Baltimore, 2011),
     p. 104; Mia Bloom, John Horgan and Charlie Winter, 'Depictions of Children and
     Youth in the Islamic State's Martyrdom Propaganda, 2015–2016', *CTC Sentinel*
     9/2 (February 2016), pp. 30–31.

152 C. Winter 'War by suicide'; p. 5.

153 David J. Slavicek, 'Deconstructing the Shariatic justification of suicide bombings',
     Studies in Conflict and Terrorism 31/6 (2008), p. 560; Charlie Winter, 'Suicide
     tactics and the Islamic State', *International Centre for Counter-Terrorism – The
     Hague*. 10 January 2017a.

154 Alex P. Schmid, *The Routledge Handbook of Terrorism Research* (Oxon: (2013a),
     p. 86.

155 Rebecca Molloy, 'Deconstructing Ibn Taymiyya's views on suicidal missions', *CTC
     Sentinel* 2/3 (March 2009), p. 17.

156 Abu Basir Al-Tartusi, 'Suspicions of sin in martyrdom or suicide attacks', *Al-Tartosi
     Website*, 11 November 2005. Available at www.en.altartosi.com/suicide.htm#A
     (link no longer working).

157 Dabiq, Issue 2, p. 13.

158 Dabiq, Issue 11, p. 29.

159 Dabiq, Issue 13, p. 17.

160 The Islamic State (2015). *The Inghimasis – The Pride of the Nation*.

161 Dabiq, Issue 14, p. 20.

162 Dabiq, Issue 2, p. 13.

163 Dabiq, Issue 14, p. 23.

164 Inspire, Issue 14, p. 43.

165 Inspire, Issue 14, p. 44.

166 Karin M. Fierke, *Political Self-Sacrifice: Agency, Body and Emotion in International
     Relations* (Cambridge, 2014), p. 207.

167 The US Commission on International Religious Freedom, 'Annual Report
     2016 – Syria', p. 121, 'concluded that ISIL was committing genocide against the

Christian, Yazidi, Shi'a, Turkmen'; while the UN Human Rights Council confirmed that 'ISIS has committed the crime of genocide as well as multiple crimes against humanity and war crimes against the Yazidis'. See United Nations Human Rights Council 'They came to destroy': ISIS Crimes against the Yazidis. Human Rights Council', Thirty-second session, Agenda Item 4, 15 June 2016, p. 1. Available at www.ohchr.org/Documents/HRBodies/HRCouncil/CoISyria/A_HRC_32_CRP.2_en.pdf (accessed 6 July 2016).

168   According to the Office of the UN Special Advisor on the Prevention of Genocide (n.d.), 'ethnic cleansing' is one of 'the elements of the crime of genocide as defined in Article 6 of the Rome Statute' (p. 3).

169   Article II of the United Nations (1948) *Convention on the Prevention and Punishment of the Crime of Genocide* (p. 280).

170   John F. Kerry, 'Remarks on Daesh and Genocide', Secretary of State Press Briefing Room, *US Department of State*, Washington, DC, 17 March 2016b. Available at www.state.gov/secretary/remarks/2016/03/254782.htm (accessed 10 July 2016). Academically genocide may be considered an ideology. See Alison Des Forges, *The Ideology of Genocide*, Issue: A Journal of Opinion 23/2 (1995), pp. 44–47.

171   Ervin Staub, *The Roots of Evil: The Origins of Genocide and Other Group Violence* (Cambridge, 1989), p. 13.

172   According to former Canadian General Dallaire, 800,000 Rwandans were killed by 30 June 1993 in a genocide. See Romeo A. Dallaire, *Shake Hands with the Devil: The Failure of Humanity in Rwanda* (Toronto, 2003), p. 375.

173   Twitter @meisny 6 May 2015.

174   Wehr, *A Dictionary of Modern Written Arabic*, p. 85.

175   See Hassan, 'The sectarianism of the Islamic State', p. 17. According to Fawwaz Gerges, Abu Bakr al-Naji (possibly also known as Muhammad Hassan Khalil al-Hakim) authored a 'blue print' for the establishment of an Islamic State, which ISIS draws upon selectively. See Gerges, *ISIS: A History*, p. 34.

176   William McCants, 'The Management of Savagery: The Most Critical Stage Through Which the Umma Will Pass. Translation of Al-Naji, Abu Bakr (2004)', *John M. Olin Institute for Strategic Studies* (23 May 2006).

177   Gerges, *ISIS: A History*, p. 36.

178   Dabiq, Issue 12 (p. 39).

179   See *Dabiq*, Issue 1 (p. 38) and *Dabiq*, Issue 5 (p. 31). Hans Wehr translates *at-tawahhush* as 'wildness, savageness, barbarity, brutality', see Wehr, *A Dictionary of Modern Written Arabic*, p. 1056.

180   See *Dabiq* 8 (p. 60) and McCants, 'The Management of Savagery', p. 26.

181   McCants, 'The Management of Savagery', p. 36.

182   Shiraz Maher, 'Shiraz Maher on ISIS: The Management of Savagery', *The New Statesman*, 12 July 2016b.

183 Abu Bakr Al-Naji, 'The Management of Savagery: The Most Critical Stage Through
     Which the Umma Will Pass' (2004). Translated by W. McCants. *John M. Olin
     Institute for Strategic Studies*, 23 May 2006, p. 76. This call for moderation by
     al-Naji contradicted his earlier guidance that 'the ingredient of softness is one of
     the ingredients of failure for any jihadi action' (p. 72).
184 Al-Naji, 'The Management of Savagery', p. 47.
185 Human Rights Watch, 'World Report 2014: Syria (Events for 2013)', *Human Rights
     Watch*, 2014.
186 Al-Naji, 'The Management of Savagery', p. 235.
187 Ibid., p. 73.
188 Dabiq, Issue 12 (p. 39).
189 Drake, 'The role of ideology in terrorists' target selection', p. 54.
190 Philip G. Zimbardo, *The Lucifer Effect: How Good People Turn Evil* (London, 2007),
     p. 8.
191 Staub, *The Roots of Evil*, p. 13.
192 Guy Sajer, *The Forgotten Soldier* (London, 1971), p. 234.
193 British Security Service (MI5), 'Terrorist training and indoctrination' (2016b).
     Available at www.mi5.gov.uk/terrorist-training-and-indoctrination (accessed
     7 June 2016).
194 According to Brynjar Lia, this emphasis on obedience to a leader and the leader's
     power over the group was a cornerstone of the training doctrine of veteran
     Afghan Arab, Abdul Aziz al-Sharif (aka Dr Fadl) who authored '*The Compendium
     of the Pursuit of Divine Knowledge*' – later a core Islamist reference. See Brynjar
     Lia, 'Doctrines for jihadi terrorist training', *Terrorism and Political Violence*
     20/1 (2008a), p. 520.
195 See Dabiq, Issue 1, p. 35).
196 See Dabiq, Issue 12, p. 9.
197 See Dabiq 12, p. 10. As an addendum, a later ISIS document dated 17 May 2017,
     entitled *That Those Who Perish Would Perish Upon Proof and Those Who Live
     Would Live Upon Proof*, demanded that even if authority figures 'command
     something that the soul dislikes, obeying them is obligatory'. See Bryan Price and
     Muhammad Al-'Ubaydi, 'CTC perspectives: The Islamic State's internal rifts and
     social media ban', *Combating Terrorism Center at West Point*, 21 June 2017.
198 Speckhard and Yayla, *ISIS Defectors: Inside Stories of the Terrorist Caliphate*, p. 234.
199 Stanley Milgram, 'Behavioral study of obedience', *Journal of Abnormal and Social
     Psychology* 67 (1963), pp. 371–378.
200 Staub, *The Roots of Evil*.
201 Milgram, 'Behavioral study of obedience', p. 252.
202 Staub, *The Roots of Evil*, p. 19.
203 Ibid., p. 28.
204 Perliger and Milton, 'From cradle to grave', p. 37.

205 Ibid., p. iv.

206 The Islamic State. *Terrify the Enemy of God and Your Enemy*, 3 January 2016. Available at http://heavy.com/news/2016/01/new-isis-islamic-state-news-pictures-videos-terrorist-terrorism-special-forces-military-training-wilayat-hims-syria-full-uncensored-youtube/ (accessed 16 July 2016).

207 An example of a Syrian training camp regime included a 'timetable ... which detailed when [recruits] had to train, eat, pray and stressed that they had to be in bed by 10pm unless they were on guard duty'. See Tom Whitehead, 'Life in a terror training camp: lights out 10pm, cleaning, military training', *The Telegraph*, 26 November 2014.

208 It is acknowledged that videos for 'martyrdom/suicide' operations have considerable overlaps, as both are used to revere the 'martyr' and to recruit new members.

209 Hassan Hassan, 'The secret world of ISIS training camps', *The Guardian*, 25 January 2015.

210 Ibid.

211 Al-Tamimi, 'Islamic State training camp textbook: Course in monotheism – complete text'.

212 Quintan Wiktorowicz, 'A genealogy of radical Islam, *Studies in Conflict and Terrorism* 28/2 (2005a), p. 81.

213 Al-Tamimi, 'Islamic State training camp textbook: Course in monotheism – complete text'.

214 Natana J. Delong-Bas, *Wahhabi Islam: From Revival and Reform to Global Jihad* (Oxford, 2004), p. 59.

215 Recent examples of the preparation of SVBIEDs in Aleppo are found at @AABoroma 19 October 2016 (1:50PM), and 21 October 2016 (2:40PM).

216 Lord Moran, *The Anatomy of Courage* (London, 1945), p. 170.

217 Lia, 'Doctrines for jihadi terrorist training', p. 519.

218 There is a training camp named after Abdullah Azzam near Tabqa in Syria (Jenan Moussa, @jenanmoussa, Twitter, 13 May 2018).

219 Dr Fadl was an Egyptian plastic surgeon, veteran Afghan Arab and member of Egyptian Islamic Jihad. He became an Islamist ideologue and authored 'The Compendium of the Pursuit of Divine Knowledge' – later a core Islamist reference. After the 9/11 attacks, he was arrested and imprisoned for three years. In 2004, he was returned to Egypt where he denounced Al Qaeda and terrorism.

220 See Brynjar Lia, *Architect of Global Jihad: The Life of Al-Qaida Strategist Abu Mus'ab al-Suri* (New York, 2008b). According to Lia, Abu Musab al-Suri, author of *Call to Global Islamic Resistance,* 'advocated mass casualty terrorism in the West' (p. 3) and that 'confrontation with America is fundamental' (p. 412).

221 Lia, 'Doctrines for jihadi terrorist training', p. 518.

222 Hassan 'The secret world of ISIS training camps'.

223 Lia, 'Doctrines for jihadi terrorist training', p. 527.

224   Ibid., p. 518.

225   According to the Oxford Concise Dictionary (1995), p. 693, indoctrination includes 'the teaching of a person ... to accept ideas uncritically'.

226   See Martha Crenshaw, 'Political violence in Algeria', *Terrorism and Political Violence* 6/1 (1994), pp. 261–280; Fathali M. Moghaddam, 'The Staircase to Terrorism: A Psychological Exploration', *American Psychologist* 60/2 (2005), pp. 161–169; Quintan Wiktorowicz, *Radical Islam Rising: Muslim Extremism in the West* (Maryland, 2005b); and Clark McCauley and Sophie Moskalenko, 'Mechanisms of Political Radicalization: Pathways Toward Terrorism', *Terrorism and Political Violence* 20/3 (2008), pp. 415–433.

227   Lia, 'Doctrines for jihadi terrorist training', p. 518.

228   Meg Aubrey, Rosie Aubrey, Frances Brodrick, and Caroline Brooks, 'Why young Syrians choose to fight: Vulnerability and resilience to recruitment by violent extremist groups in Syria', *International Alert*, May 2016, p. 10.

229   John Horgan, *The Psychology of Terrorism* (London, 2005), p. 103.

230   See Annika Waldeck, *The ideology of ISIS – a motivation for Europeans to become foreign fighters?* Master Thesis in Global Studies. Roskilde Universitet, 29 June 2015, p. 66. This arrival procedure is also corroborated by Byman and Shipiro who noted that 'foreign fighters often have their passports taken away when they join ... and become highly dependent on the group'. See Daniel Byman and Jeremy Shapiro, 'Be Afraid. Be a Little Afraid: The Threat of Terrorism from Western Foreign Fighters in Syria and Iraq', *Foreign Policy at Brookings*, Policy Paper 34 (2014), p. 6.

231   Noted in Chapter 3, indoctrination and brainwashing are different. Brainwashing involves 'the surrender of strongly held beliefs and the adoption of new beliefs often diametrically opposed to them'. See William Sargant, *Battle for the Mind: A Physiology of Conversion and Brain-washing* (London, 1959), p. xvii.

232   Jacob Olidort, 'Inside the Caliphate's Classroom: Textbooks, Guidance Literature, and Indoctrination Methods of the Islamic State', *The Washington Institute for Near East Policy*, *Policy Focus* 147 (August 2016).

233   Ibid., p. 8.

234   Ibid., p. 6.

235   Jurgen Todenhöfer, 'Blindsided: How ISIS shook the world', *CNN (Fareed Zakaria GPS)*, 29 November 2015. Available at http://transcripts.cnn.com/TRANSCRIPTS/1511/29/fzgps.01.html (accessed 18 December 2015).

236   Mironova et al. 'The motivations of Syrian Islamist fighters', p. 16.

237   Gerges, *ISIS: A History*, p. 266.

238   Hassan, 'The sectarianism of the Islamic State', p. 18.

239   Nagieb Khaja, 'On the frontline in Syria: the Danish gangster who turned Jihadi', *The Guardian*, 7 July 2014.

240 CPOST Attack ID 1457441285, includes Syrian Documentary on Al-Nusrah Front. Damascus Television Service. 9 June 2012.

241 The attack 'killed 55 people and injured 372' (CPOST Attack ID 1457441285), but they were not designated military or civilian personnel.

242 See CPOST Attack ID 1457441285.

243 Mohammad Azzam, 'Islamic State's "suicide squad": Zealots, footballers and French chefs', *The New Arab*, 28 March 2016.

244 Ibid.

245 Jafar Al-Tayyar Crying before Suicide bombing in Syria Terrorists. YouTube. 27 September 2015. www.youtube.com/watch?v=fHaxkHtWBZE (last accessed 15 July 2016).

246 John Hall, 'The Unwilling Suicide Bomber', *The Daily Mail*, 23 September 2015.

Chapter 5

1 Philip G. Zimbardo, *The Lucifer Effect: How Good People Turn Evil* (London, 2007), pp. 5–8.

2 United Nations Security Council, 'Resolution 2178 (2014), 24 September 2014, p. 2. Available at www.un.org/en/sc/ctc/docs/2015/SCR%202178_2014_EN.pdf (accessed 6 July 2016).

3 Alex P. Schmid, 'Foreign (terrorist) fighter estimates: Conceptual and data issues', *International Centre for Counter-Terrorism Policy Brief*, October 2015, p. 5.

4 Andrew Silke, *Terrorists, Victims and Society* (Chichester, 2009), p. 34.

5 Thomas Hegghammer, 'Jihadi-Salafis or revolutionaries? On religion and politics in the study of militant Islamism', in R. Meijer (ed.) *Global Salafism: Islam's New Religious Movement* (London, 2009a), p. 252.

6 It is important to note that those who participate in terrorism do not label themselves *irhaabiyeen*, but as *mujahhideen*, within the rubric of political Islam.

7 The book dataset (noted in Chapter 4) identified three Arab foreign fighters who fought against the Gaddafi regime in Libya: two Egyptians (Ahmad al-Barra and Walid Badr) and a Palestinian (Osama Kishta).

8 The book dataset identified 126 Arab foreign fighters within the US-backed Free Syrian Army (FSA), of which ten conducted self-sacrificial ('martyrdom/suicide') attacks against Syrian Arab Army (SAA) units.

9 Examples of pre-eminent scholars include Natana J. Delong-Bas, *Wahhabi Islam: From Revival and Reform to Global Jihad* (Oxford, 2004); Fawaz A. Gerges, *The Far Enemy: Why Jihad went Global* (Cambridge, 2005); and Brynjar Lia, '"Destructive doctrinarians": Abu Musa'b al-Suri's critique of the Salafis in the jihadi current', in R. Meijer (ed.), *Global Salafism: Islam's New Religious Movement* (London, 2009).

10 Philip Gibbs, *Realities of War* (London, 1929), p. 52.

11 Abdullah Y. Azzam, *Defense of Muslim Lands: The First Obligation After Imam*, 1983. Available at www.kalamullah.com/Books/defence.pdf (accessed 25 January 2012).

12 Abu Musab al-Zarqawi, Dialogue with Shaykh Abu Musab al-Zarqawi, Part One, *Al-Furqan Media Productions*, 2006.

13 Saif Allah al-Muhajjir, *Sharia 4 Sham*, Facebook, 11 July 2013.

14 Charles J.M. Drake, 'The role of ideology in terrorists' target selection', *Terrorism and Political Violence* 10/2 (1998), p. 53.

15 Stephen E. Ambrose, 'Atrocities in historical perspective', in D.L. Anderson (ed.), *Facing My Lai: Moving Beyond the Massacre* (Kansas, 1998), p. 116.

16 As noted in Chapter 3, UN Secretary General Kofi Annan believed that the invasion of Iraq 'was not in conformity with the UN Charter ... it was illegal'. Later UK former Lord Chief Justice Lord Bingham described the war as 'a serious violation of international law'.

17 The United Nations Security Council Resolution 2254 (2015) called on the Syrian government and all parties to 'engage in formal negotiations on a political transition process on an urgent basis' (p. 2). Implicit in the resolution was a transition without President Bashar al-Assad. The governments of the United States, United Kingdom, Turkey, and Saudi Arabia have publicly denounced the legitimacy of the al-Assad regime.

18 From Chapter 3, an insurgency was understood to mean 'a hybrid form of conflict that combines subversion, guerrilla warfare and terrorism ... [in] an internal struggle in which a disaffected group seeks to gain control of a nation'. See Thomas R. Mockaitis, *British Counterinsurgency 1919–1960* (London, 1990), p. 3.

19 Alex Schmid's 'revised academic consensus definition of terrorism' includes 'targeting mainly civilians and non-combatants' – which Iraqi military units are not. See Alex P. Schmid, *The Routledge Handbook of Terrorism Research* (Oxon: (2013a), p. 86.

20 As noted in Chapter 1, according to Boaz Ganor 'the targets of terrorism are civilians', thus excluding Iraqi military and police units. Attacks on these units appear more akin to defensive jihad as part of an insurgency. The US Department of State label 'military personnel (whether or not armed or on duty) who are not deployed in a war zone or a war-like setting' as civilians. As Iraq was reasonably considered a war zone or a war-like setting', Iraqi military personnel would not qualify as civilians. See US Department of State, 'Country Reports on Terrorism 2014', June 2015, p. 388. Available at www.state.gov/documents/organization/239631.pdf (accessed 15 December 2015).

21 The adjective 'trained' is used to differentiate between untrained recruits (who are more akin to civilians) and fully trained soldiers or policemen who are operationally active, in a 'war zone'.

22 As noted in Chapter 4, genocide is defined in Article 2 of the Convention on the Prevention and Punishment of the Crime of Genocide (1948) and includes acts that are 'committed with intent to destroy, in whole or in part, a national, ethnical, racial or religious group'.

23 Quintan Wiktorowicz and John Kaltner, 'Killing in the Name of Islam: Al-Qaeda's Justification for September 11', *Middle East Policy* X/2 (2003), p. 90.

24 According to the 2007 US Joint Fires and Targeting Handbook collateral damage is an 'the unintentional or incidental injury or damage to persons or objects that would not be lawful military targets in the circumstances ruling at the time' (pp. 1–22), and thus a Collateral Damage Estimate (CDE) is conducted as part of the planning process.

25 Chairman of the Joint Chiefs of Staff Instruction. *No-Strike and the Collateral Damage Estimation Methodology*. 12 October 2012, p. D-1.

26 In Chapter 3, the Arabic word *daroorah* was defined as 'necessity' and chimes with the 'doctrine of necessity'. See H.H.A. Cooper, 'What is a terrorist?: A psychological perspective', *Legal Medical Quarterly* 1/1 (1977), pp. 16–32.

27 See Abu Musab Al-Zarqawi, 'The Return of Ibn Al-'Alqami's Grandchildren. 90-minute audio heard on the Internet on 18 May 2005', *The Middle East Media Research Institute*, Special Dispatch 917, 7 June 2005.

28 Abu Muhammad Al-Adnani, *Indeed Your Lord is Ever Watchful*, 21 September 2014.

29 Martin Chulov, 'No regrets, no remorse: ISIS mastermind who sent out 15 suicide bombers', *The Guardian*, 31 August 2015.

30 Tracy Shelton, 'Syria: From IT to rebel commander', *Global Post*, 03 March 2013.

31 Eleanor Beevor, 'Coercive radicalization: Charismatic authority and the internal strategies of ISIS and the Lord's Resistance Army', *Studies in Conflict and Terrorism*, 0/0, 2016, p. 3.

32 Rik Coolsaet, *Jihadi Terrorism and the Radicalisation Challenge: European and American Experiences* (London, 2011), p. 260. Chapter 1 noted the existence of TRAP-18, but this is more applicable to lone actor terrorists.

33 See INTERPOL, Foreign Terrorist Fighters. Available at www.interpol.int/ Crime-areas/Terrorism/Foreign-terrorist-fighters (accessed 14 June 2018).

34 Peter R. Neumann, 'The trouble with radicalization', *International Affairs*, 89/4 (2013), p. 873.

35 See Jamie Bartlett and Carl Miller, 'The edge of violence: Towards telling the difference between violent and non-violent radicalization', *Terrorism and Political Violence*, 24/1, 2012, p. 2.

36 Jonathan Githens-Mazer and Robert Lambert, 'Why Conventional Wisdom on Radicalization Fails: The Persistence of a Failed Discourse', *International Affairs*, 86/1 (2010), p. 901.

37 Neumann, 'The trouble with radicalization', p. 878.

38 David Cook, 'Suicide Attacks or "Martyrdom Operations" in Contemporary *Jihad* Literature', *Nova Religio: The Journal of Alternative and Emergent Religions* 6/1 (2002), p. 35.

39 Karin M. Fierke, *Political Self-Sacrifice: Agency, Body and Emotion in International Relations* (Cambridge, 2014), p. 207.

40 Maxwell Taylor, *The Fanatics: A Behavioural Approach to Political Violence* (Oxford, 1991), p. 191.

41 As noted in Chapter 4, while ISIS employed *inghimasi* attacks as a military tactic (Dabiq Magazine Issue 2, p. 13); Jabhat al-Nusrah employed them against civilians and non-combatants (Inspire Magazine Issue 14, p. 42).

42 The research conducted for this study identified 187 self-sacrificial attacks (both martyrdom operations and suicide attacks) – 110 in Iraq (post-2003) and 77 in Syria (post-2011). The actual identity of the individuals (Arab foreign fighter/ Islamist terrorist) and their intended targets amounted to 33 in Iraq, and 77 in Syria.

43 According to the US Department of Navy, '14.7 percent of kamikaze sorties ... were effective in hitting ships'. See US Department of the Navy, 'Defense against Kamikaze Attacks in World War 2 and its relevance to anti-ship missile defense. Volume 1, an analytical history of kamikaze attacks against ships of the United States Navy during World War 2. *Center for Naval Analyses Alexandria VA*, November 1970, p. 80.

44 Examples include Saudi Ahmad Abdullah al-Shaya in December 2004 in Iraq; Muhammad Jarrallah in February 2014 in Syria (The Meir Amit Intelligence and Information Centre, 2014, p. 19); and Abu Alaa' al-Muhajir in August 2014 in Syria (@JihadNews2, 03 August 2014).

45 See Global Terrorism Database (GTD) ID:200412240004, and Chicago Project on Security and Threats (CPOST) Attack ID: 1006327513.

46 Ariel Merari, *Driven to Death: Psychological and Social Aspects of Suicide Terrorism* (Oxford, 2010), p. 9.

47 The Concise Oxford Dictionary (Oxford, 1995), p. 1393. The other definition is 'the intentional killing of oneself', which within the context of a 'suicide attack' does not accurately reflect the action.

48 Hannsjoachim W. Koch, *The Hitler Youth: Origins and Developments 1922–1945* (New York, 2000), p. 228.

49 Ibid., p. 249.

50 Assaf Moghadam makes the argument that a suicide attack should 'not be labelled a terrorist attack if it is targeted against members of an army, because attacks are ordinarily labelled terrorist attacks when they are aimed at non-combatants'. See Assaf Moghadam, *The Globalization of Martyrdom: Al Qaeda, Salafi Jihad, and the Diffusion of Suicide Attacks* (Baltimore, 2011), p. 5.

51 Charles J.M. Drake, 'The role of ideology in terrorists' target selection', *Terrorism and Political Violence* 10/2 (1998), pp. 53–85.

52 Bruce Hoffman, *Inside Terrorism* (New York, 2006), p. 155; and Fierke, *Political Self-Sacrifice*, p. 199.

53 Al-Zarqawi made no distinction between Iraqi military targets and Iraqi civilians/ non-combatants. This was based on the view that the Shi'a had taken 'control of the institutions of the state and their security, military, and economic branches' making them 'the real enemy'. See Abu Musab Al-Zarqawi, 'February 2004 Coalition Provisional Authority English translation of terrorist Musab al Zarqawi letter obtained by United States Government in Iraq' (2004a). Available at http://2001-2009.state.gov/p/nea/rls/31694.htm http://2001-2009.state.gov/p/nea/rls/31694.htm (accessed 12 February 2012).

54 US Commission on International Religious Freedom, 'Annual Report 2011 – Saudi Arabia', p. 141; an International Centre for Religion and Diplomacy, *The State of Tolerance in the Curriculum of the Kingdom of Saudi Arabia*, 2013, p.v. Available at https://assets.documentcloud.org/documents/3022108/State-Dept-Study-on-Saudi-Textbooks.pdf (accessed 31 January 2015).

55 Michael Weiss and Hassan Hassan, *ISIS: Inside the Army of Terror* (New York, 2015), p. 168; Brian Dodwell, Daniel Milton and Don Rassler, 'The Caliphate's Global Workforce: An Inside Look at the Islamic State's Foreign Fighter Payroll', *Combating Training Centre at West Point, United States Military Academy* (April 2016a), p. 31; and Fawaz A. Gerges, *ISIS: A History* (Oxford, 2016), p. 67.

56 This finding was also corroborated by Charlie Winter. See Charlie Winter, 'War by suicide: A statistical analysis of the Islamic State's martyrdom industry', *International Centre for Counter-Terrorism – The Hague*. February 2017b. Available at https://icct.nl/wp-content/uploads/2017/02/ICCT-Winter-War-by-Suicide-Feb2017.pdf (accessed 10 March 2017), p. 17.

57 Mohammed M. Hafez, 'Rationality, culture, and structure in the making of suicide bombers: A preliminary theoretical synthesis and illustrative case study', *Studies in Conflict and Terrorism* 29/2 (2006a), pp. 165–185.

58 Andrea Beccaro, 'Modern Irregular Warfare: The ISIS Case Study', *Small Wars & Insurgencies* 29/2 (2018), p. 210.

59 Al-Adnani, *Indeed Your Lord is Ever Watchful*.

60 Merari, *Driven to Death*, p. 24.

61 See Ehud Sprinzak, 'Rational Fanatics', *Foreign Policy*, September/October 2000, pp. 66–73; Raphael Israeli, *Islamikaze: Manifestations of Islamic Martyrology* (London, 2003); Jon Elster, 'Motivations and beliefs in suicide missions', in D. Gambetta (ed.), *Making Sense of Suicide Missions* (Oxford, 2005); and Robert A. Pape, *Dying to Win: The Strategic Logic of Suicide Terrorism* (New York, 2005).

62 Moghadam, *The Globalization of Martyrdom*, p. 5.

63 Cole Bunzel, 'The Caliphate's Scholar-in-Arms', *Jihadica*, 9 July 2014. Available at www.jihadica.com/the-caliphate%e2%80%99s-scholar-in-arms/ (accessed 24 October 2014).

64 Shiv Malik, 'The ISIS papers: leaked documents show how ISIS is building its state', *The Guardian*, 7 December 2015.

65 Jurgen Todenhöfer, *My Journey into the Heart of Terror: Ten Days in the Islamic State* (Vancouver, 2016), p. 218.

66 Gerges, *ISIS: A History*, p. 224.

67 Weiss and Hassan, *ISIS: Inside the Army of Terror*, p. xv.

68 Moghadam, *The Globalization of Martyrdom*, p. 14.

69 Shelton, 'Syria: From IT to rebel commander'.

70 Eline Gordts, '15,000 foreign fighters have joined extremist groups in Iraq and Syria. Here's why they went', *Huffington Post*, 8 November 2014.

71 Thomas Hegghammer, 'Syria's foreign fighters', *The Middle East Channel*, 9 December 2013a.

72 Bernhard B. Fall, *Hell in a Very Small Place: The Siege of Dien Bien Phu* (New York, 1985), p. 368.

73 Martin Windrow, *The Last Valley: Dien Bien Phu and the French Defeat in Vietnam* (London, 2004), p. 398.

74 Ted Morgan, *Valley of Death: The Tragedy at Dien Bien Phu that Led America into the Vietnam War* (London, 2010), pp. 536–537.

75 Shmuel Bar, 'Jihad ideology in light of contemporary fatwas', *Hudson Institute*, Center on Islam, Democracy, and the Future of the Muslim World, 1/1 (August 2006), p. 14.

76 Hoffman, *Inside Terrorism*, p. 155.

77 Ami Pedahzur, *Root Causes of Suicide Terrorism: The Globalization of Martyrdom* (Oxon, 2006).

78 As Karin Fierke noted, '"suicide bombing" and "suicide attack" are examples of Western terminology'. See Fierke, *Political Self-Sacrifice*, p. 205.

79 See Sophia Akram, 'Suicide bombings: Martyrdom or military tactic?', *The New Arab*, 8 March 2016. An excellent example of a potential self-sacrificial attack involving an Arab fighter (of unknown nationality) may be found on YouTube (www.youtube.com/watch?v=1nBc0ksZLHg). He successfully destroyed a Syrian army tank with just a hand grenade. He survived, although had he died, it could reasonably be conceptualised as a self-sacrificial attack.

80 E. Beevor, 'Coercive radicalization: Charismatic authority', p. 3.

81 Merari, *Driven to Death*, p. 213.

82 Githens-Mazer and Lambert, 'Why Conventional Wisdom on Radicalization Fails'.

83 This 'conventional wisdom' would include the conflation of defensive jihad and Islamist terrorism, and the labelling of all self-sacrificial attacks as 'suicide attacks'.

84 Philip G. Zimbardo, *The Lucifer Effect: How Good People Turn Evil* (London, 2007), p. 5.

85 Ibid., p. 8.

86 Ibid., p. 7.

87 See Martha Crenshaw, 'The causes of terrorism', *Comparative Politics* 13/4 (1981), p. 381; Ervin Staub, *The Roots of Evil: The Origins of Genocide and Other Group Violence* (Cambridge, 1989), p. 22; Maxwell Taylor, *The Fanatics: A Behavioural Approach to Political Violence* (Oxford, 1991), p. 257; and Christopher R. Browning, *Ordinary Men: Reserve Police Battalion 101 and the Final Solution in Poland* (New York, 1998), p. 209. Additionally, Max Taylor argued that the 'origins of fanatical violence ... seem to lie in situational ... factors' (p. 257); whilst Browning posited that 'situational factors were very strong indeed' (p. 209) turning 'ordinary men into willing executioners' (p. 216).

88 See Stanley Milgram, *Obedience to Authority: An Experimental View* (London, 1974).

89 Oxford Concise Dictionary, p. 960.

90 Floris Vermeulen and Frank Bovenkerk, *Engaging with Violent Extremism: Local Policies in Western European Cities* (Amsterdam, 2012), p. 48.

91 Mitchell D. Silber and Arvin Bhatt, 'Radicalization in the West: The Homegrown Threat', *The New York City Police Department*, 2007, p. 6.

92 Asef Bayat, *Life as Politics: How Ordinary People Change the Middle East* (Amsterdam, 2010), p. ix.

93 See Fred E. Katz, *Ordinary People and Extraordinary Evil: A Report on the Beguilings of Evil* (Albany, 1993); and Browning, *Ordinary Men: Reserve Police Battalion 101*.

94 Hannah Arendt, *Eichmann in Jerusalem: A Report on the Banality of Evil* (London, 1994), p. 276.

95 Ibid., p. 287.

96 Milgram, *Obedience to Authority*, p. 6.

97 Introduced in Chapter 2, Abu Zubaydah was a Palestinian expatriate living in Saudi Arabia, who became an Afghan Arab and maintained a diary of his experiences. He was later 'wrongly' considered (Sageman, 2013) to be 'the third or fourth man in Al-Qaeda'. See US Central Intelligence Agency, 'Psychological Assessment of Zain al-'Abedin al-Abideen Muhammad Hassan, a.k.a. Abu Zubaydah', 31 January 2003. Available at www.thetorturedatabase.org/files/foia_subsite/pdfs/CIA000544.pdf (accessed 6 July 2014).

98 Ibid., p. 546.

99 Marc Sageman, 'A Frighteningly Normal Man', *Al-Jazeera*, 26 November 2013.

100 Alex Strick van Linschoten and Felix Kuehn, *An Enemy We Created: The Myth of the Taliban-Al-Qaeda Merger in Afghanistan* (London, 2012), p. 69.

101 See Zimbardo, *The Lucifer Effect*, p. 8. Chapter 2 found these factors and situational variables included, but were not limited to, terrorist training and ideological indoctrination (often by those with known previous terrorist links); obedience to authority (in this case Osama bin Laden); the inability of many Afghan Arabs to reintegrate back into their societies; and 'comradeship' ties.

102 Abu Musab Al-Zarqawi, 'February 2004 Coalition Provisional Authority English translation of terrorist Musab al Zarqawi letter obtained by United States Government in Iraq' (2004a). Available at http://2001-2009.state.gov/p/nea/rls/31694.htmhttp://2001-2009.state.gov/p/nea/rls/31694.htm (accessed 12 February 2012).

103 Zimbardo, *The Lucifer Effect*, p. 17.

104 Browning, *Ordinary Men: Reserve Police Battalion 101*, p. 216.

105 Zimbardo, *The Lucifer Effect*, p.8.

106 Ibid., p. 11.

107 Gerges, *ISIS: A History*, p. 50.

108 Zimbardo, *The Lucifer Effect*, p. 11.

109 Richard Holmes, *Acts of War: The Behaviour of Men in Battle* (Reading, 2004), p. x.

110 The book dataset identifies twenty-two cases of internecine deaths, most generally as a result of kidnapping, torture and eventual execution.

111 Holmes, *Acts of War: The Behaviour of Men in Battle*, p. 28.

112 Pieter van Ostaeyen, 'My first battlefield experience. Text by Abu Salman al-Britani published by Fursan Al Sham Media', 12 November 2016. Available at https://pietervanostaeyen.com/2016/11/13/fursan-al-sham-media-my-first-battlefield-experience/ (accessed 14 November 2016).

113 Arie Perliger and Daniel Milton, 'From cradle to grave: The life cycle of foreign fighters in Iraq and Syria', *Combating Terrorism Center* (November 2016), p. 39.

114 Michael Bilton and Kim Sim, *Four Hours in My Lai: A War Crime and its Aftermath* (London, 1993), p. 370.

115 Browning, *Ordinary Men: Reserve Police Battalion 101*, p: 160.

116 Stephen E. Ambrose, 'Atrocities in historical perspective', p. 108.

117 Kendrick Oliver, *The My Lai Massacre in American History and Memory* (Manchester, 2006), p. 111.

118 Hugh Thompson, 'Moral courage in combat: The My Lai Story', Presentation to the US Naval Academy (n.d.). Available at www.usna.edu/Ethics/Publications/ThompsonPg1-28_Final.pdf (accessed 14 March 2012).

119 Arguably it may have been a common occurrence. According to Claude Cookman, on the same day as the My Lai massacre, 'another company massacred ninety women and children a mile away in My Khe'. See Claude Cookman, 'An American atrocity: The My Lai massacre concretized in a victim's face', *The Journal of American History* (June 2007), p. 154.

120 Whilst ISIS label their enemy *kufr, rafidah, nusairi, taghoot, and murtadd*, the US Marines in Vietnam used 'gooks', 'dinks', and 'slopes'. See Cookman, 'An American atrocity: The My Lai massacre', p. 156.

121 Taylor, *The Fanatics: A Behavioural Approach to Political Violence*, p. 265.

122 Oliver, *The My Lai Massacre in American History and Memory*, pp. 109–110.

123 Holmes, *Acts of War: The Behaviour of Men in Battle*, p. 391.

124 Bilton and Sim, *Four Hours in My Lai*, p. 368.

125 Crenshaw, 'The causes of terrorism', p. 385.

126 Andrew Mumford, 'Minimum Force Meets Brutality: Detention, Interrogation and Torture in British Counter-Insurgency Campaigns', *Journal of Military Ethics* 11/1 (2012), p. 11.

127 Ibid., p. 12.

128 For example, Anthony Beevor, John Keegan, Cornelius Ryan and Richard Holmes.

129 Anthony Beevor, *Ardennes 1944: Hitler's Last Gamble* (London, 2015), p. 364.

130 Weiss and Hassan, *ISIS: Inside the Army of Terror*, p. 129.

131 It was noted in Chapter 4, that Guy Sajer, an Alsatian Wehrmacht soldier on the Russian front in World War II, recalled that the brutality both on and off the battlefield often induced 'the most innocent of youths on whatever side to commit inconceivable atrocities'. See Guy Sajer, *The Forgotten Soldier* (London, 1971), p. 234.

132 Oxford Concise Dictionary, p. 693.

133 Andrew Silke, *Terrorists, Victims and Society*, p. 96.

134 William Sargant, *Battle for the Mind: A Physiology of Conversion and Brainwashing* (London, 1959), p. xxii.

135 Ibid., p. 234.

136 As Chapter 4 discovered, this was in large part due to their respective regimes' refusal to reintegrate them back into society.

137 Mohammed M. Hafez, 'Jihad after Iraq: Lessons from the Arab Afghans', *Studies in Conflict and Terrorism* 32/2 (2009), p. 78.

138 Mustafa Hamid and Leah Farrall, *The Arabs at War in Afghanistan* (London, 2015), p. 165.

139 As Chapter 2 found, only 14 per cent of the Afghan Arab cohort had documented pre-existing terrorist links.

140 The Algerians attended the *Abdul Majid al-Jazairi* Camp. See Hamid and Farrall, *The Arabs at War in Afghanistan*, p. 167. The Jordanians attended the *Tawhid wal-Jihad* camp in Herat. See Jean-Charles Brisard and Damien Martinez, *Zarqawi: The New Face of al-Qaeda* (Cambridge, 2005), p. 72.

141 United Nations Security Council Counter-Terrorism Committee, 'Background Note: Group I: Technical sessions on detection, intervention against, and prevention of incitement, recruitment and facilitation of FTF travel', Madrid,

27–28 July 2015b. Available at www.un.org/en/sc/ctc/docs/2015/0721Tehnical%20
Session%20Group%20I%20-%20background%20note.pdf (link no longer
working).

142	US Homeland Security Institute, 'Recruitment and radicalization of school-aged
youth by international terrorist groups', 23 April 2009, p. 2.

143	John Horgan, *The Psychology of Terrorism* (London, 2005), p. 102.

144	According to Christopher Browning, during the occupation of Poland in World
War II, 'the age of men affected their susceptibility to indoctrination'. See
Browning, *Ordinary Men: Reserve Police Battalion 101*, p. 182.

145	Vera Mironova, Loubna Mrie and Sam Whitt, 'The motivations of Syrian Islamist
fighters, *CTC Sentinel Terrorism Monitor* 7/10 (2014), p. 16; and Annika Waldeck,
The ideology of ISIS – a motivation for Europeans to become foreign fighters?
Master Thesis in Global Studies. Roskilde Universitet, 29 June 2015, p. 66.

146	George Joffe, 'Global jihad and foreign fighters', *Small Wars and Insurgencies*,
27/5 (2016), p. 800.

147	Hamid as cited in Hamid and Farrall, *The Arabs at War in Afghanistan*, p. 61.

148	Maximillian K. Weber, [1919] 'Politics as a Vocation', in H.H. Gerth and C. Wright
Mills (eds), *From Max Weber: Essays in Sociology* (London, 2009), p. 78.

149	David C. Hofmann and Lorne L. Dawson, 'The neglected role of charismatic
authority in the study of terrorist groups and radicalization, *Studies in Conflict
and Terrorism* 37/4 (2014), p. 340.

150	Ibid., p. 351.

151	See Martha Crenshaw, 'Political violence in Algeria', *Terrorism and Political
Violence* 6/1 (1994), p. 264; R. Hrair Dekmejian, *Islam in Revolution:
Fundamentalism in the Arab World* (New York, 1995), p. 63; Quintan Wiktorowicz,
Radical Islam Rising: Muslim Extremism in the West (Maryland, 2005b), p. 135;
Tore Bjorgo, *Roots Causes of Terrorism* (London, 2005), p. 260; and Gerges, *The Far
Enemy*, p. 36; and Haroro J. Ingram, *The Charismatic Leaders of Modern Islamist
Radicalism and Militancy* (New York, 2016), p. 4.

152	Wiktorowicz, *Radical Islam Rising: Muslim Extremism in the West*, pp. 24–26.

153	Bjorgo, *Roots Causes of Terrorism*, p. 260.

154	The label 'bunch of guys' is attributed to Marc Sageman. See Marc Sageman,
Understanding Terror Networks (Philadelphia, 2004).

155	Hofmann and Dawson, 'The neglected role of charismatic authority', p. 358.

156	Bartlett and Miller, 'The edge of violence', p. 15.

157	See Steven Emerson, 'Inside the Osama Bin Laden Investigation', *Journal of
Counterterrorism & International Security* (Fall 1998), pp. 16–26; Andrew
McGregor, 'Jihad and the Rifle Alone: Abdullah Azzam and the Islamist
Revolution', *The Journal of Conflict Studies* XXIII/2 (2003); Trevor Stanley,
'Abdullah Azzam: The Godfather of Jihad', *Perspectives on World History and*

Current Events, 2003–2005 (2005); and Thomas Hegghammer, 'Abdullah Azzam: The Imam of Jihad', in G. Kepel and J-P. Milelli (eds), *Al Qaeda in its Own Words* (London, 2008b).

158 See Simon Reeve, *The New Jackals: Ramzi Yousef, Osama bin Laden and the Future of Terrorism* (London, 1999); Jossef Bodansky, *Bin Laden: The Man who Declared war on America* (New York, 2001); Elaine Landau, *Osama Bin Laden: A War Against the West* (New York, 2002); Peter L. Bergen, *Holy War Inc. Inside the Secret World of Osama Bin Laden* (London, 2002); and Omar Saghi, 'Osama Bin Laden, the iconic orator', in G. Kepel and J-P. Milelli (eds), *Al Qaeda in its Own Words* (London, 2008).

159 Lawrence Wright, *The Looming Tower: Al-Qaeda and the Road to 9/11* (New York, 2006); and Roxanne L. Euben and Muhammad Q. Zaman, *Princeton Readings in Islamist Thought: Texts and Contexts from al-Banna to Bin Laden* (Princeton, 2009).

160 See Brisard and Martinez, *Zarqawi: The New Face of al-Qaeda*; Loretta Napoleoni, *Insurgent Iraq: Al Zarqawi and the New Generation* (New York, 2005); Murad B. Al-Shishani, 'Al-Zarqawi's rise to power: Analyzing tactics and targets', *Terrorism Monitor*, 3/22 (2005a), pp. 5–7; and Jean-Pierre Milelli, 'Abu Musab al-Zarqawi, Jihad in Mesopotamia', in G. Kepel and J-P. Milelli (eds), *Al Qaeda in its Own Words* (London, 2008).

161 Beevor, 'Coercive radicalization: Charismatic authority'; David C. Hofmann, 'The influence of charismatic authority on operational strategies and attack outcomes of terrorist groups', *Journal of Strategic Security* 9/2 (2016), pp. 14–44.

162 Beevor 'Coercive radicalization: Charismatic authority', p. 1.

163 Peter R. Neumann, 'Victims, perpetrators, assets: The Narratives of Islamic State defectors', *The International Centre for the Study of Radicalisation and Political Violence* (2015).

164 Milgram, *Obedience to Authority*, p. xii.

165 ISIS magazine Dabiq 12, p. 10.

166 Milgram, *Obedience to Authority*, p. 3.

167 Ibid., p. 6.

168 All forty subjects obeyed the experimental commands to administer Shock Level 20 (a fake 300 volts) to their victims. Subsequently twenty-six (65 per cent) continued to obey the experimenter's orders to the end, administering a fake 450 volts (Milgram, *Obedience to Authority*).

169 Jerry M. Burger, 'Replicating Milgram: Would people still obey today?' *American Psychologist*, 64/1 (2009), pp. 1–11.

170 Milgram, *Obedience to Authority*, p. 189.

171 Staub, *The Roots of Evil*, p. 19.

172 Bilton and Sim, *Four Hours in My Lai*, p. 362.

173 Milgram, *Obedience to Authority*, p. 7.

Chapter 6

1. Daniel Byman, 'The homecomings: What happens when Arab foreign fighters in Iraq and Syria return?', *Studies in Conflict and Terrorism*, 38/1 (2015), p. 582.

2. Countering extremism/countering violent extremism/preventing violent extremism.

3. Mosques in Saudi Arabia were bombed on 22 May 2015 (Qatif); 29 May 2015 (Dammam); 6 August 2015 (Abha); 4 July 2016 (Medina and Qatif).

4. ISIS-inspired attacks in Tunisia include the 18 March 2015 Bardo Museum attack; the 6 June 2015 Port El Kantaoui beach resort attack; and the 24 November 2015 bombing in Tunis (against the Presidential Guard).

5. ISIS-inspired attacks in Egypt include the 11 July 2015 attack on the Italian Consulate in Cairo; the 8 January 2016 attack on the Red Sea city of Hurghada; and the 22 October 2016 assassination of an Egyptian general (Adil Rageea).

6. In addition to ISIS expansion in Benghazi, Sirte, and Tripoli (A. Engel, 2015), ISIS-inspired attacks within the country include the 27 January 2015 Corinthia Hotel (Tripoli) attack, and the 7 January 2016 Zliten truck bombing (killing sixty policemen and wounding 200).

7. ISIS-inspired attacks in Kuwait include the 26 June 2015 bombing of a Shi'a mosque in Kuwait City (killing twenty-seven and wounding 227).

8. ISIS-inspired attacks in Yemen include the 20 March 2015 Sanaa mosque quadruple suicide bombing (killing 142 and wounding 351); the 25 March 2016 triple suicide bombing in Aden; the 26 May 2016 bombing of army recruits in Aden.

9. For example, the United Arab Emirates 'sentenced four Emiratis (whose ages ranged from eighteen to twenty-nine) to death in absentia for joining the militant ISIS group and fighting alongside the militant group's members in Syria' (Al-Arabiya, 2016). Interestingly in the early 1990s, the United Arab Emirates 'instigated a particularly generous package of rewards' for Emirati Afghan Arabs. See Alex Strick van Linschoten and Felix Kuehn, *An Enemy We Created: The Myth of the Taliban-Al Qaeda Merger in Afghanistan* (London, 2012), p. 109).

10. See Abdullah F. Al-Ansary, 'Combating Extremism: A brief overview of Saudi Arabia's approach', Middle East Policy Council, *Middle East Policy Journal*, 15/2 (2008); Naif A. Al-Saud, 'Saudi Arabia's strategy to combat terrorism: An insider's perspective', *RUSI Journal*, 154/6 (2009), pp. 74–80; and Caryle Murphy, 'Saudi Arabia tried to keep the Islamic State from recruiting its youth', *Global Post*, 2 March 2015.

11. Fatma Al-Sayegh, 'Post 9/11 changes in the Gulf: The case of the UAE', *Middle East Policy*, 11/2 (2004), pp. 107–124, and Al-Arabiya, 'UAE court gives four death sentences for supporting ISIS', *Al-Arabiya*, 14 February 2016.

12. Vish Sakthivel, 'Weathering Morocco's Syria returnees', *The Washington Institute*, 25 September 2013.

13. Murtaza Hussain, 'ISIS recruitment thrives in brutal prisons run by US-backed Egypt', *The Intercept*, 24 November 2015.

14. Michael Pizzi, 'Foreign fighters come home to roost', *Al Jazeera America*, 5 June 2015.

15. Byman, 'The homecomings', p. 587.

16. Muhammad Al-Khatib, 'Why we joined ISIS', *Al-Jumhuriya*, 5 July 2018. Available at www.aljumhuriya.net/en/content/why-we-joined-isis (accessed 6 July 2018).

17. Byman, 'The homecomings', p. 591.

18. Joe Odell, 'How the UAE's pro-democracy movement fell into a spiral death', *Middle East Eye*, 2 April 2018. Available at www.middleeasteye.net/columns/how-uae-s-pro-democracy-movement-fell-death-spiral-477436739 (accessed 7 June 2018).

19. More widely, see the seminal book by Mohammed Hafez, *Why Muslims Rebel: Repression and Resistance in the Islamic World* (London, 2003).

20. Legitimacy is used here to mean 'logically admissible or defendable'. See the Concise Oxford Dictionary (Oxford, 1995), p. 777.

21. David Cook, *Martyrdom in Islam* (Cambridge, 2007), p. 151.

22. Rachel Briggs and Tanya Silverman, 'Western foreign fighters: Innovations in responding to the threat', *Institute for Strategic Dialogue* (2014), p. 37.

23. Simon Hooper, 'Denmark introduces rehab for Syrian fighters', *Al Jazeera*. 7 September 2014.

24. Frank Gardiner, 'Inside Saudi Arabia's rehab centre for jihadists', *BBC World*, 26 May 2017.

25. Erin Martz, *Trauma Rehabilitation After War and Conflict* (London, 2010), p. 4.

26. David C. Hofmann and Lorne L. Dawson, 'The neglected role of charismatic authority in the study of terrorist groups and radicalization', *Studies in Conflict and Terrorism* 37/4 (2014), p. 362.

27. Stanley Milgram, *Obedience to Authority: An Experimental View* (London, 1974).

28. Ibid., p. 6.

29. John Horgan, *Walking Away from Terrorism: Accounts of Disengagement from Radical and Extremist Movements* (London, 2009), p. 13.

30. Amber Atteridge, 'Foreign fighters post conflict: Assessing the impact of Arab Afghans and Syrian Iraqi foreign fighters on global security', *International Institute for Counter-Terrorism*, IDC Herzliya, Spring 2016, p. 23; and Peter R. Neumann, *Radicalized: New Jihadists and the Threat to the West* (London, 2016), p. 104.

Bibliography

Abdul-Ahad, Ghaith, 'From here to eternity', *The Guardian*, 8 June 2005.

Abdul-Rahman, Omar, 'Sentencing Statement of Blind Sheikh Omar Abdel Rahman and the New York Terrorists', *Intelwire*, 1996. Available at http://intelfiles.egoplex.com/61HKRAHS-sentencing.htm (Link no longer working).

Abedin, Mahan, 'From mujahid to activist: An interview with a Libyan veteran of the Afghan jihad', *The Jamestown Foundation*, Terrorism Monitor, 3/2 (2005).

Aboul-Enein, Youssef H., *Militant Islamist Ideology: Understanding the Global Threat* (Annapolis, 2010).

Adida, Claire L., David D. Laitin, and Marie-Anne Valfort, *Why Muslim Integration Fails in Christian-Heritage Societies* (Cambridge, 2016).

Ahmed, Mubaraz, Milo Comerford and Emman El-Badawy, 'Milestones to Militancy: What the Lives of 100 Jihadis Tell us about a Global Movement', *Centre on Religion and Politics*, Tony Blair Faith Foundation, April 2016.

Akram, Sophia, 'Suicide bombings: Martyrdom or military tactic?', *The New Arab*, 8 March 2016.

Al-Adaam, Abdullah, 'Do not consult anyone in killing the Alawites', *Ansar al-Mujahideen English Forum*, 22 Shaban 1433 A.H. (12 July 2012).

Al-Adnani, Abu Muhammad, *Indeed Your Lord is Ever Watchful*, 21 September 2014.

Al-Adnani, Tamim, 'Lawrence Islamic video presents an interview with Tamim Adnani, Director of the Afghan Mujahideen Service Office in Afghanistan', *Why Islam*, 1989.

Al-Ansari, Salah and Usama Hasan, *Tackling Terror: A Response to Takfiri Terrorist Theology*, Quilliam Foundation, 2018, pp. 41–42.

Al-Ansary, Abdullah F., 'Combating Extremism: A brief overview of Saudi Arabia's approach', Middle East Policy Council, *Middle East Policy Journal*, 15/2 (2008).

Al-Bahri, Nasser, Interview with Nassir al-Bahri (Abu Jandal). Part 1. *Al-Quds al-Arabi*, 20 March 2005a.

Al-Bahri, Nasser, Interview with Nassir al-Bahri (Abu Jandal). Part 3. *Al-Quds al-Arabi*, 28 March 2005b.

Al-Bahri, Nasser, Interview with Nassir al-Bahri (Abu Jandal). Part 7. *Al-Quds al-Arabi*, 2 April 2005c.

Al-Bahri, Nasser, Interview with Nassir al-Bahri (Abu Jandal). Part 8. *Al-Quds al-Arabi*, 31 March [*sic*] 2005d.

Al-Bahri, Nasser, *Guarding Bin Laden: My Life in al-Qaeda* (UK, 2013).

Al-Jazeera, 'Saudi Arabia arrests hundreds of suspected ISIL members', *Al-Jazeera*, 18 July 2015.

Al-Kadhimi, Mustafa, 'Iraq struggles to combat evolving terrorist threat', *Al Monitor*, 31 January 2016.

Al-Khatib, Muhammad, 'Why we joined ISIS', *Al Jumhuriya*, 5 July 2018. Available at www.aljumhuriya.net/en/content/why-we-joined-isis (accessed 6 July 2018).

Al-Maqdisi, Abu Muhammad, *A Call to the Ummah and Mujahideen*, May 2014. Available at www.justpaste.it/Maqdisi-ISIS (accessed 30 May 2014).

Al-Maqdisi, Abu Muhammad, *Why did I not name them Khawarij even until now?* June 2015. Available at https://pietervanostaeyen.com/2015/06/25/shaykh-abu-muhammad-al-maqdisi-why-did-i-not-name-them-khawarij-even-until-now/ (accessed 30 June 2015).

Al-Moslim.net, *'ulama' wa-du'a fi-l-mamlaka yasduroon bayanaan li-ta'yeed al-jabhat al-islamiyya fi-Sham wa yad'una ila da'miha* [Scholars in the Kingdom issue a statement in support of the Islamic Front in Syria and call for support], 5 December 2013. Available at http://almoslim.net/node/195146 (Link no longer working).

Al-Muhaysani, Abdullah, *kalama Abdullah al-muhaysani amaam majmoo' isra' ba'd tahhreer mataar abu al-dhuhoor al-askararee* [Speech by Abdullah al-Muhaysani in front of a group of prisoners after the capture of Abu Dhuhoor Military airport]. September 2015. Available at www.youtube.com/watch?v=aSFE-nD0gmA (accessed 7 June 2016).

Al-Naji, Abu Bakr, The Management of Savagery: The Most Critical Stage Through Which the Umma Will Pass (2004). Translated by W. McCants. *John M. Olin Institute for Strategic Studies*, 23 May 2006.

Al-Qarni, Musa, 'Saudi Cleric Musa Al-Qarni on Iqra TV', *Middle East Media Research Institute*, 29 October 2004. Available at http://memritv.org/clip/en/339.htm (accessed 7 June 2016).

Al-Qarni, Musa, 'Saudi Cleric Musa Al-Qarni on Iqra TV', *Middle East Media Research Institute*, 3 February 2005a. Available at http://memritv.org/clip/en/523.htm (accessed 7 June 2016).

Al-Qarni, Musa, 'Saudi Preacher Musa Al-Qarni: 'The Jews and Christians are Allah's Enemies . . . We Ask Allah to Strengthen the Jihad Fighters in Iraq', *Middle East Media Research Institute*, Special Dispatch No. 859, 8 February 2005b. Available at www.memri.org/report/en/0/0/0/0/0/0/0/1312.htm (accessed 18 December 2015).

Al-Qarni, Musa, 'Saudi Cleric Musa Al-Qarni on Iqra TV', *Middle East Media Research Institute*, 18 March 2006a. Available at http://memritv.org/clip/en/1082.htm (accessed 7 June 2016).

Al-Qarni, Musa, 'Saudi academic recounts experiences from Afghan war', *Al-Hayat*, 20 March 2006b. Available at www.e-ariana.com/ariana/eariana.nsf/allPrintDocs/60 F915EE3EE3AA61F8725713700594314?OpenDocument (accessed 7 June 2016).

Al-Qudri, Muhammad T., 'Fatwa on terrorism and suicide bombings', *Minhaj-ul-Quran International*, December 2010 (Norfolk, 2010).

Al-Saud, Naif A., 'Saudi Arabia's strategy to combat terrorism: An insider's perspective', *RUSI Journal*, 154/6 (2009), pp. 74–80.

Al-Sayegh, Fatma, 'Post 9/11 changes in the Gulf: The case of the UAE', *Middle East Policy,* 11/2 (2004), pp. 107–124.

Al-Shishani, Murad B., 'Al-Zarqawi's rise to power: Analyzing tactics and targets', *Terrorism Monitor*, 3/22 (2005a), pp. 5–7.

Al-Shishani, Murad B., 'The Salafi-Jihadist movement in Iraq: recruitment methods and Arab volunteers', *Terrorism Monitor*, 3/23 (2005b), pp. 6–8.

Al-Tamimi, Aymenn J., 'Islamic State training camp textbook: Course in monotheism – complete text', *aymennjawad.org*, 26 July 2015. Available at www.aymennjawad. org/17633/islamic-state-training-camp-textbook-course-in (accessed 12 February 2016).

Al-Tamimi, Aymenn J., 'Stories of the mujahideen: Unseen Islamic State biographies of outstanding members', *Jihadology*, 24 August 2016. Available at http://jihadology. net/2016/08/24/the-archivist-stories-of-the-mujahideen-unseen-islamic-state-biographies-of-outstanding-members/ (accessed 12 October 2016).

Al-Tartusi, Abu Basir, 'Suspicions of sin in martyrdom or suicide attacks', *Al-Tartosi Website*, 11 November 2005. Available at www.en.altartosi.com/suicide.htm#A (link no longer working).

Al-Uyayri, Yusuf, *The Future of Iraq and the Arabian Peninsula After the Fall of Baghdad*. 5 September 2003. Available at www.freerepublic.com/focus/f-news/976932/posts (accessed 1 May 2018).

Al-Zarqawi, Abu Musab, 'February 2004 Coalition Provisional Authority English translation of terrorist Musab al Zarqawi letter obtained by United States Government in Iraq' (2004a). Available at http://2001-2009.state.gov/p/nea/ rls/31694.htmhttp://2001-2009.state.gov/p/nea/rls/31694.htm (accessed 12 February 2012).

Al-Zarqawi, Abu Musab, 'Al-Zarqawi's message to the fighters of jihad in Iraq on September 11, 2004', *The Middle East Media Research Institute,* Special Dispatch 785, 15 September 2004b.

Al-Zarqawi, Abu Musab, 'The Return of Ibn Al-'Alqami's Grandchildren. 90-minute audio heard on the Internet on 18 May 2005', *The Middle East Media Research Institute,* Special Dispatch 917, 7 June 2005.

Al-Zarqawi, Abu Musab, 'Dialogue with Shaykh Abu Musab Al-Zarqawi', Parts 1–3. *Al-Furqan Media Production*, 2006.

Al-Zawahiri, Ayman, *Al-Kitaab al-Aswad: Qissaat Ta'dheeb al-Muslimeen fi Ahd Hosni Mubarak* (1992).

Al-Zawahiri, Ayman, 'Personal letter to Abu Musab al-Zarqawi 9 July 2005'. Available at www.ctc.usma.edu/posts/zawahiris-letter-to-zarqawi-english-translation-2 (accessed 12 September 2012).

Al-Zayyat, Montasser, *The Road to Al-Qaeda: The Story of Bin Laden's Right-Hand* Man (London, 2004).

Ali, A.S., 'IS disciplines some Emirs to avoid losing base', *Al Monitor*, 2 September 2014.

Allam Shawqi S., *Open Letter to Abu Bakr al-Baghdadi*, 19 September 2014. Originated by Shaykh Shawqi Allam and 125 Islamic Scholars. Available at www.lettertobaghdadi.com (Link no longer working).

Amarasingam, Amarnath and Charlie Winter, *ISIS's Perverse, Bloody Interpretation of Ramadan*. The Atlantic, 26 May 2017. Available at www.theatlantic.com/international/archive/2017/05/ramadan-isis-attack-muslim/528336/ (accessed 7 June 2018).

Ambrose, Stephen E., 'Atrocities in historical perspective', in D.L. Anderson (ed.), *Facing My Lai: Moving Beyond the Massacre* (Kansas, 1998).

Amjad-Ali, Charles W., 'Jihad and Just War Theory: Dissonance and Truth', *Dialog: A Journal of Theology*, 48/3 (2009), pp. 239–247.

Anas, Abdullah, 'Jihad, then and now: The Majalla speaks to Abdullah Anas', *Al Majalla*, 8 February 2014.

Anas, Abdullah, 'Naheed Mustafa talks to Abdullah Anas, who fought alongside bin Laden', *CBC News*, 16 September 2015.

Ani, Marwan and Caryle Murphy, 'Bombing in Kurdish City in Northern Iraq Kills 60', *Washington Post Foreign Service*, 5 May 2005.

Annan, Kofi, 'Iraq War Illegal, Says Annan', *BBC*, 16 September 2004.

Arendt, Hannah, *Eichmann in Jerusalem: A Report on the Banality of Evil* (London, 1994).

Atteridge, Amber, 'Foreign fighters post conflict: Assessing the impact of Arab Afghans and Syrian-Iraqi foreign fighters on global security', *International Institute for Counter-Terrorism*, IDC Herzliya, Spring 2016.

Atwan, Abdel Bari, *The Secret History of Al Qaeda* (Los Angeles, 2006).

Aubrey, Meg, Rosie Aubrey, Frances Brodrick, and Caroline Brooks, 'Why young Syrians choose to fight: Vulnerability and resilience to recruitment by violent extremist groups in Syria', *International Alert*, May 2016.

Azzam, Abdullah Y., *Defense of Muslim Lands: The First Obligation After Imam*, 1983. Available at www.kalamullah.com/Books/defence.pdf (accessed 25 January 2012).

Azzam, Abdullah Y., *Join the Caravan* (1987). Available at https://islamfuture.wordpress.com/2009/08/20/join-the-caravan/ (accessed 15 May 2015).

Azzam, Abdullah Y., *The Lofty Mountain* (1989). Available at https://ebooks.worldofislam.info/ebooks/Jihad/The%20Lofty%20Mountain.pdf (accessed 15 May 2015).

Azzam, Abdullah Y., *Fi Dhilal Surat at-Tawbah* [In the shade of the at-Tawbah chapter]. (Date, place, and publisher unknown.) *In the Words of Abdullah Azzam*. (Date, place, and publisher unknown.) Available at http://ahlulislam.com/books/words_azzam.pdf (accessed 15 May 2015).

Azzam, Mohammad, 'Islamic State's "suicide squad": Zealots, footballers and French chefs', *The New Arab*, 28 March 2016.

Ballen, Ken, *Terrorists in Love: The Real lives of Islamic Radicals* (London, 2011).

Ballout, Mohammad, 'In Syria, US sides with local jihadists to defeat global ones', *Al Monitor*, 7 January 2014.

Bar, Shmuel, 'Jihad ideology in light of contemporary fatwas', *Hudson Institute*, Center on Islam, Democracy, and the Future of the Muslim World 1/1 (August 2006).

Bartlett, Jamie and Carl Miller, 'The edge of violence: Towards telling the difference between violent and non-violent radicalization', *Terrorism and Political Violence* 24/1 (2012), pp. 1–21.

Bayat, Asef, *Life as Politics: How Ordinary People Change the Middle East* (Amsterdam, 2010).

BBC, 'Islamic State assassin: How I killed more than 100 people', *BBC World News*, 4 May 2018. Available at www.bbc.com/news/world-middle-east-43881659 (accessed 5 May 2018).

Beaumont, Peter, '"Living suicide bomb" rejoins al-Qaida after Saudi deprogramming', *The Guardian*, 18 January 2014.

Beccaro, Andrea, 'Modern Irregular Warfare: The ISIS Case Study', *Small Wars & Insurgencies* 29/2 (2018), pp. 207–228.

Beevor, Anthony, *Ardennes 1944: Hitler's Last Gamble* (London, 2015).

Beevor, Eleanor, 'Coercive radicalization: Charismatic authority and the internal strategies of ISIS and the Lord's Resistance Army', *Studies in Conflict and Terrorism*, 0/0, 2016, pp. 1–26.

Beit-Hallahmi, Benjamin, 'The return of martyrdom: Honour, death and immortality', *Totalitarian Movements and Political Religions* 4/1 (2003), pp. 11–34.

Bergen, Peter L., *Holy War Inc. Inside the Secret World of Osama Bin Laden* (London, 2002).

Bergen, Peter L., *The Osama Bin Laden I Know: An Oral History of al Qaeda's Leader* (London, 2006).

Berger, J.M. and Jessica Stern, 'Why are foreign fighters joining ISIS?', *The Atlantic*, 8 March 2015.

Bilton, Michael and Kim Sim, *Four Hours in My Lai: A War Crime and its Aftermath* (London, 1993).

Bin Laden, Osama, *Declaration of War against the Americans Occupying the Land of the Two Holy Places*. Published in Al Quds Al Arabi, August 1996. Public Broadcasting Service. Available at www.pbs.org/newshour/terrorism/international/fatwa_1996.html (accessed 15 May 2012).

Bin Laden, Osama, *Jihad Against Jews and Crusaders*. World Islamic Front Statement, 23 February 1998. *Federation of American Scientists*. Washington: FAS. Available at www.fas.org/irp/world/para/docs/980223-fatwa.htm (accessed 15 May 2012).

Bingham, Tom, 'Lord Bingham delivers Annual Grotius Lecture on the Rule of Law in the International Order', *British Institute of International and Comparative Law*, 18 November 2008. Available at www.biicl.org/newsitem/109 (accessed 15 May 2012).

Bjorgo, Tore, *Root Causes of Terrorism* (London, 2005).

Blair, Tony, 'Tony Blair says he's sorry for Iraq War "mistakes," but not for ousting Saddam', *CNN Interview with Fareed Zakaria GPS*, 26 October 2015. Available at http://edition.cnn.com/2015/10/25/europe/tony-blair-iraq-war/ (accessed 10 March 2016).

Bloom, Mia, John Horgan and Charlie Winter, 'Depictions of Children and Youth in the Islamic State's Martyrdom Propaganda, 2015–2016', *CTC Sentinel* 9/2 (February 2016), pp. 29–32.

Bodansky, Jossef, *Bin Laden: The Man Who Declared War on America* (New York, 2001).

Bonner, Michael, *Jihad in Islamic History* (New Jersey, 2008).

Borum, Randy and Robert Fein, 'The psychology of foreign fighters', *Studies in Conflict and Terrorism* (2016), pp. 1–19.

Bradley, John R., *After the Arab Spring: How the Islamists Hijacked the Middle East Revolts* (New York, 2012).

Briggs, Rachel and Tanya Silverman, 'Western foreign fighters: Innovations in responding to the threat', *Institute for Strategic Dialogue* (2014).

Brisard, Jean-Charles and Damien Martinez, *Zarqawi: The New Face of al-Qaeda* (Cambridge, 2005).

British Security Service (MI5), 'Foreign Fighters' (2016a). Available at www.mi5.gov.uk/foreign-fighters?adhoc_referrer=011607016011 (accessed 7 June 2016).

British Security Service (MI5), 'Terrorist training and indoctrination' (2016b). Available at www.mi5.gov.uk/terrorist-training-and-indoctrination (accessed 7 June 2016).

Browning, Christopher R., *Ordinary Men: Reserve Police Battalion 101 and the Final Solution in Poland* (New York, 1998).

Bruce, James, 'Arab Veterans of the Afghan War', *Jane's Intelligence Review*, 7/4 (1995), pp. 175–180.

Bunzel, Cole, 'The Caliphate's Scholar-in-Arms', *Jihadica*, 9 July 2014. Available at www.jihadica.com/the-caliphate%e2%80%99s-scholar-in-arms/ (accessed 24 October 2014).

Bunzel, Cole, 'From Paper State to Caliphate: The Ideology of the Islamic State', *The Brookings Project on US Relations in the Islamic World* (March 2015).

Burger, Jerry M., 'Replicating Milgram: Would people still obey today?' *American Psychologist*, 64/1 (2009), pp. 1–11.

Butcher, Tim, 'Troops show true grit in desert storms', *The Telegraph*, 20 March 2003.

Byman, Daniel, 'The homecomings: What happens when Arab foreign fighters in Iraq and Syria return?', *Studies in Conflict and Terrorism*, 38/1 (2015), pp. 581–602.

Byman, Daniel and Jeremy Shapiro, 'Be Afraid. Be a Little Afraid: The Threat of Terrorism from Western Foreign Fighters in Syria and Iraq', *Foreign Policy at Brookings*, Policy Paper 34 (2014).

Cafarella, Jennifer, 'Jabhat al-Nusra in Syria: An Islamic Emirate for al-Qaeda', *Institute for the Study of War, Middle East Security Report* 25 (2014).

Callimachi, Rukmini and Jim Yardley, 'From amateur to ruthless jihadist in France: Cherif and Said Kouachi's path to Paris attack at Charlie Hebdo', *The New York Times*, 17 January 2015.

Canetti, Daphna, Stevan E. Hobfall, Ami Pedahzur and Eran Zaidise, 'Much ado about religion: Religiosity, resource loss, and support for political violence', *Journal of Peace Research* 45/5 (2010), pp. 575–587.

Carreras, Miguel and Ajay Verghese, 'Violence, Insecurity, and Religiosity: A Multilevel Analysis of 71 Countries', *Terrorism and Political Violence* (2018).

Chehab, Zaki, *Inside the Resistance: The Iraqi Insurgency and the Future of the Middle East* (New York, 2005).

Chicago Project on Security and Threats (CPOST). *Suicide Attack Database*. Available at http://cpostdata.uchicago.edu/search_new.php (Accessed 7 June 2016).

Chulov, Martin, 'No regrets, no remorse: ISIS mastermind who sent out 15 suicide bombers', *The Guardian*, 31 August 2015.

Cigar, Norman, *'Abd Al-'Aziz Al-Muqrin's A Practical Course for Guerrilla War* (Dulles, VA, 2009).

Cilluffo, Frank J., Jeffrey B. Cozzens, and Magnus Ranstorp, 'Foreign Fighters: Trends, Trajectories and Conflict Zones', *Homeland Security Policy Institute*, 1 October 2010.

Combating Terrorism Centre (CTC) West Point. *Harmony Program*. Available at www. ctc.usma.edu/programs-resources/harmony-program (accessed 18 December 2012).

Cook, David, 'Suicide Attacks or "Martyrdom Operations" in Contemporary *Jihad* Literature', *Nova Religio: The Journal of Alternative and Emergent Religions* 6/1 (2002), pp. 7–44.

Cook, David, 'The Implications of "Martyrdom Operations" for Contemporary Islam', *Journal of Religious Ethics* 32/1 (2004), pp. 129–151.

Cook, David, *Understanding Jihad* (Berkeley, 2005).

Cook, David, *Martyrdom in Islam* (Cambridge, 2007).

Cookman, Claude, 'An American atrocity: The My Lai massacre concretized in a victim's face', *The Journal of American History* (June 2007), pp. 154–162.

Coolsaet, Rik, *Jihadi Terrorism and the Radicalisation Challenge: European and American Experiences* (London, 2011).

Cooper, H.H.A., 'What is a terrorist?: A psychological perspective', *Legal Medical Quarterly* 1/1 (1977), pp. 16–32.

Cordesman, Anthony, 'Iraq and foreign volunteers', *Center for Strategic and International Studies* (18 November 2005).

Crenshaw, Martha, 'The causes of terrorism', *Comparative Politics* 13/4 (1981), pp. 379–399.

Crenshaw, Martha, 'Political violence in Algeria', *Terrorism and Political Violence* 6/1 (1994), pp. 261–280.

Crenshaw, Martha, The Causes of Terrorism. In C.W. Kegley (ed.) *The New Global Terrorism: Characteristics, Causes, Controls* (New Jersey, 2003).

Crenshaw, Martha, 'Explaining Suicide Terrorism: A Review Essay', *Security Studies* 16/1 (2007a), pp. 133–162.

Crenshaw, Martha, 'Foreword by Martha Crenshaw', in M.M. Hafez (Author), *Suicide Bombers in Iraq: The Strategy and Ideology of Martyrdom* (Washington, 2007b).

Crenshaw, Martha, *Understanding Terrorism: Causes, Processes and Consequences* (Oxon, 2011).

Cunningham, Erin, 'In stark transformation, Egyptian rights activist dies fighting for the Islamic State', *The Washington Post*, 5 November 2014. Available at www.washingtonpost.com/world/in-stark-transformation-egyptian-rights-activist-dies-fighting-for-the-islamic-state/2014/11/05/d03d0339-203e-42f0-9e87-95cff45cd1cb_story.html (accessed 10 November 2014).

Dalacoura, Katerina, 'Islamist terrorism and the Middle East democratic deficit: Political exclusion, repression and the causes of extremism', *Democratization* 13/3 (2006), pp. 508–525.

Dalacoura, Katerina, *Islamist Terrorism and Democracy in the Middle East* (Cambridge, 2011).

Dallaire, Romeo A., *Shake Hands with the Devil: The Failure of Humanity in Rwanda* (Toronto, 2003).

Dawson, Lorne L., *In their own words: Religiosity and the Islamic State Foreign Fighters*, Oxford Research Group, 27 April 2018. Available at https://sustainablesecurity.org/2018/04/27/in-their-own-words-religiosity-and-the-islamic-state-foreign-fighters/ (accessed 5 May 2018).

Dawson, Lorne L., 'Challenging the curious erasure of religion from the study of religious terrorism', *Numen* 65 (2018), pp. 141–164.

de Kerchove, Gilles, 'Hundreds of Europeans fighting in Syria, says EU expert', *BBC*, 24 April 2013.

de La Corte Ibanez, Luis, 'The social psychology of suicide terrorism', *IDC Herzliya/International Institute for Counter-Terrorism* (October 2014).

Dekmejian, R. Hrair, *Islam in Revolution: Fundamentalism in the Arab World* (New York, 1995).

Delong-Bas, Natana J., Wahhabi Islam: From Revival and Reform to Global Jihad (Oxford, 2004).

Denoeux, Guilain, 'The Forgotten Swamp: Navigating Political Islam', in F. Volpi (ed.), *Political Islam: A Critical Reader* (London, 2011).

Des Forges, Alison, *The Ideology of Genocide*, Issue: A Journal of Opinion 23/2 (1995), pp. 44–47.

Dodwell, Brian, Daniel Milton and Don Rassler, 'The Caliphate's Global Workforce: An Inside Look at the Islamic State's Foreign Fighter Payroll', *Combating Training Centre at West Point, United States Military Academy* (April 2016a).

Dodwell, Brian, Daniel Milton and Don Rassler, 'Then and Now: Comparing the Flow of Foreign Fighters in AQI and the Islamic State', *Combating Training Centre at West Point, United States Military Academy* (December 2016b).

Drake, Charles J.M., 'The role of ideology in terrorists' target selection', *Terrorism and Political Violence* 10/2 (1998), pp. 53–85.

Durden, Tyler, 'Ben Rhodes Admits Obama Armed Jihadists in Syria in Bombshell Interview', *Zero Hedge*, 24 June 2018. Available at www.zerohedge.com/news/

2018-06-24/ben-rhodes-admits-obama-armed-jihadists-syria-bombshell-interview.

Duyvesteyn, Isabelle and Bram Peters, 'Fickle foreign fighters? A cross-case analysis of seven Muslim foreign fighter mobilisations (1980–2015)', *International Centre for Counter-Terrorism (ICCT) Research Paper* (October 2015).

Eatwell, Roger, 'The concept and theory of charismatic leadership', *Totalitarian Movements and Political Religions* 7/2 (2006), pp. 141–156.

Edwards, David B., *Before Taliban: Genealogies of the Afghan Jihad* (Berkeley, 2002).

El-Badawy, Emma, Milo Comerford and Peter Welby, 'Inside the Jihadi Mind: Understanding Ideology and Propaganda', *Centre on Religion and Politics* (October 2015).

Elster, Jon, 'Motivations and beliefs in suicide missions', in D. Gambetta (ed.), *Making Sense of Suicide Missions* (Oxford, 2005).

Emerson, Steven, 'Inside the Osama Bin Laden Investigation', *Journal of Counterterrorism & International Security* (Fall 1998), pp. 16–26.

Esposito, John L., *Unholy War: Terror in the Name of Islam* (Oxford, 2003).

Euben, Roxanne L. and Muhammad Q. Zaman, *Princeton Readings in Islamist Thought: Texts and Contexts from al-Banna to Bin Laden* (Princeton, 2009).

Fall, Bernhard B., *Hell in a Very Small Place: The Siege of Dien Bien Phu* (New York, 1985).

Felter, Joseph and Brian Fishman, 'Al Qaeda's Foreign Fighters in Iraq: A First Look at the Sinjar Records', *Harmony Project* (2007).

Fierke, Karin M., *Political Self-Sacrifice: Agency, Body and Emotion in International Relations* (Cambridge, 2014).

Fishman, Brian, Peter Bergen, Joseph Felter, Vahid Brown and Jacob Shapiro, 'Bombers, bank accounts, and bleedout: Al-Aa'ida's road in and out of Iraq', *Harmony Project* (22 July 2008).

Fisk, Robert, 'Freedom, democracy and human rights in Syria', *Independent*, 16 September 2010.

Fitzgerald, Mary, 'The son of the father of jihad', *The Irish Times*, 7 July 2006. Available at www.irishtimes.com/news/the-son-of-the-father-of-jihad-1.1027271 (accessed 15 April 2018).

Gambetta, Diego, *Making Sense of Suicide Missions* (Oxford, 2005).

Ganor, Boaz, 'Defining terrorism: Is one man's terrorist another man's freedom fighter?' *International Institute for Counter-Terrorism* (1 January 2010).

Gardiner, Frank, 'Inside Saudi Arabia's rehab centre for jihadists', *BBC World*, 26 May 2017.

Gerges, Fawaz A., *The Far Enemy: Why Jihad went Global* (Cambridge, 2005).

Gerges, Fawaz A., *The Rise and Fall of Al-Qaeda* (New York, 2011).

Gerges, Fawaz A., 'ISIS and the Third Wave of Jihadism', *Current History*, December 2014.

Gerges, Fawaz A., *ISIS: A History* (Oxford, 2016).

Ghosh, Aparisim, 'Inside the Mind of an Iraqi Suicide Bomber', *Time Magazine*, 28 June 2005.

Gibbs, Philip, *Realities of War* (London, 1929).

Githens-Mazer, Jonathan and Robert Lambert, 'Why Conventional Wisdom on Radicalization Fails: The Persistence of a Failed Discourse', *International Affairs*, 86/1 (2010), pp. 889–901.

Glasse, Charles, *The Concise Encyclopedia of Islam* (London, 2008).

Gonzalez, Nathan, *The Sunni-Shia Conflict: Understanding Sectarian Violence in the Middle East* (Mission Viejo, 2009).

Gordts, Eline, '15,000 foreign fighters have joined extremist groups in Iraq and Syria. Here's why they went', *Huffington Post*, 8 November 2014.

Grossman, David, *On Killing: The Psychological Cost of Learning to Kill in War and Society* (London, 2009).

Hafez, Mohammed M., *Why Muslims Rebel: Repression and Resistance in the Islamic World* (London, 2003).

Hafez, Mohammed M., 'Rationality, culture, and structure in the making of suicide bombers: A preliminary theoretical synthesis and illustrative case study', *Studies in Conflict and Terrorism* 29/2 (2006a), pp. 165–185.

Hafez, Mohammed M., 'Suicide terrorism in Iraq: A preliminary assessment of the quantitative data and documentary evidence', *Studies in Conflict and Terrorism* 29/6 (2006b), pp. 591–619.

Hafez, Mohammed M., 'Martyrdom mythology in Iraq: How jihadists frame suicide terrorism in videos and biographies', *Terrorism and Political Violence* 19/1 (2007a), pp. 95–115.

Hafez, Mohammed M., *Suicide Bombers in Iraq: The Strategy and Ideology of Martyrdom* (Washington, 2007b).

Hafez, Mohammed M., 'Jihad after Iraq: Lessons from the Arab Afghans', *Studies in Conflict and Terrorism* 32/2 (2009), pp. 73–94.

Hafez, Mohammed M., 'Martyrs without borders: The puzzle of transnational suicide bombers' in M. Breen-Smyth (ed.), *The Ashgate Companion to Political Violence* (Surrey, 2012a).

Hafez, Mohammed M., 'Martyrs without borders: Iraq's foreign fighters and the third generation of global jihad', *National Consortium for the Study of Terrorism and Responses to Terrorism* (2012b).

Hall, Edward T., *Beyond Culture* (Garden City NY, 1976).

Hall, John, 'The Unwilling Suicide Bomber', *The Daily Mail*, 23 September 2015.

Hamden, Raymond H., 'Psychology of Terrorists: 4 Types', *The Foundation of International Human Relations*, Washington, DC, 2006,

Hamid, Mustafa and Leah Farrall, *The Arabs at War in Afghanistan* (London, 2015).

Hamid, Shadi, 'The roots of the Islamic State's appeal', *The Atlantic*, 31 October 2014.

Hashim, Ahmed S., *Insurgency and Counter-Insurgency in Iraq* (New York, 2006).

Hassan, Hassan, 'The secret world of ISIS training camps', *The Guardian*, 25 January 2015.

Hassan, Hassan, 'The sectarianism of the Islamic State: Ideological roots and political context', *Carnegie Endowment for International Peace*, June 2016.

Hassan, Riaz, 'What motivates the suicide bombers? Study of a comprehensive database gives a surprising answer', *YaleGlobal*, 3 September 2009.

Hegghammer, Thomas, 'Terrorist recruitment and radicalization in Saudi Arabia', *Middle East Policy*, VIII/4 (2006), pp. 39–60.

Hegghammer, Thomas, 'Saudi militants in Iraq: Backgrounds and recruitment patterns', *Norwegian Defence Research Establishment* (FFI), 5 February 2007.

Hegghammer, Thomas, 'Deconstructing the myth about al-Qa'ida and Khobar', *CTC Sentinel*, 1/3 (2008a), pp. 2–22.

Hegghammer, Thomas, 'Abdullah Azzam: The Imam of Jihad', in G. Kepel and J-P. Milelli (eds), *Al Qaeda in its Own Words* (London, 2008b).

Hegghammer, Thomas, 'Jihadi-Salafis or revolutionaries? On religion and politics in the study of militant Islamism', in R. Meijer (ed.) *Global Salafism: Islam's New Religious Movement* (London, 2009a).

Hegghammer, Thomas, 'The ideological hybridization of jihadi groups', Hudson Institute, *Current Trends in Islamist Ideology*, 9 (2009b), pp. 26–45.

Hegghammer, Thomas, 'The Origins of Global Jihad: Explaining the Arab Mobilization to 1980s Afghanistan', *Belfer Center for Science and International Affairs*, 22 January 2009c.

Hegghammer, Thomas, 'The rise of Muslim foreign fighters: Islam and the globalization of jihad', *International Security*, 35/3 (2010a), pp. 53–94.

Hegghammer, Thomas, — *Jihad in Saudi Arabia: Violence and Pan Islamism since 1979* (Cambridge, 2010b).

Hegghammer, Thomas, 'The foreign fighter phenomenon: Islam and transnational militancy', *Belfer Center for Science and International Affairs*, February 2011a.

Hegghammer, Thomas, 'Global jihadism after the Iraq war', in F. Volpi (ed.) *Political Islam: A Critical Reader* (London, 2011b).

Hegghammer, Thomas, 'Syria's foreign fighters', *The Middle East Channel*, 9 December 2013a.

Hegghammer, Thomas, 'Should I stay or should I go? Explaining variation in Western jihadists' choice between domestic and foreign fighting', *American Political Science Review*, February 2013b.

Hellmich, Christina, 'The physiology of al-Qaeda: From ideology to participation', in M. Ranstorp (ed.), *Understanding Violent Radicalization: Terrorist and Jihadist Recruitment in Europe* (Oxon, 2010).

Hewitt, Christopher and Jessica Kelley-Moore, 'Foreign fighters in Iraq: A cross-national analysis of jihadism', *Terrorism and Political Violence* 21/1 (2009), pp. 211–220.

Hinnebusch, Raymond, *Syria: Revolution from Above* (London, 2001).

Hoffman, Bruce, *Inside Terrorism* (New York, 2006).

Hofmann, David C., 'The influence of charismatic authority on operational strategies and attack outcomes of terrorist groups', *Journal of Strategic Security* 9/2 (2016), pp. 14–44.

Hofmann, David C. and Lorne L. Dawson, 'The neglected role of charismatic authority in the study of terrorist groups and radicalization', *Studies in Conflict and Terrorism* 37/4 (2014), pp. 348–368.

Holmes, Richard, *Acts of War: The Behaviour of Men in Battle* (Reading, 2004).

Holtmann, Philipp, 'Terrorism and jihad: Differences and similarities', *Perspectives on Terrorism* 8/3 (2014), pp. 140–143.

Hooper, Simon, 'Denmark introduces rehab for Syrian fighters', *Al Jazeera*. 7 September 2014.

Horgan, John, *The Psychology of Terrorism* (London, 2005).

Horgan, John, *Walking Away from Terrorism* (London, 2009).

Human Rights Watch, 'World Report 2014: Syria (Events for 2013)', *Human Rights Watch*, 2014.

Hussain, Murtaza, 'ISIS recruitment thrives in brutal prisons run by US-backed Egypt', *The Intercept*, 24 November 2015.

Ingram, Haroro J., *The Charismatic Leaders of Modern Islamist Radicalism and Militancy* (New York, 2016).

International Centre for Religion and Diplomacy, *The State of Tolerance in the Curriculum of the Kingdom of Saudi Arabia*, 2013. Available at https://assets. documentcloud.org/documents/3022108/State-Dept-Study-on-Saudi-Textbooks.pdf (accessed 31 January 2015).

International Committee of the Red Cross, 'International Humanitarian Law. Chapter 1, Rule 5 (Definition of Civilians)', *International Committee of the Red Cross* (2015a).

International Committee of the Red Cross, 'International Humanitarian Law. Chapter 1, Rule 1 (The Principle of Distinction between Civilians and Combatants)', *International Committee of the Red Cross* (2015b).

Iraq Survey Group, 'Comprehensive Report of the Special Advisor to the DCI on Iraq's WMD, with Addendums (Duelfer Report)', *US Government Publishing Office*, 25 April 2005. Accessed at www.gpo.gov/fdsys/pkg/GPO-DUELFERREPORT/ content-detail.html (accessed 31 January 2015).

Israeli, Raphael, *Islamikaze: Manifestations of Islamic Martyrology* (London, 2003).

Jacquard, Roland, *In the Name of Osama bin Laden: Global Terrorism and the Bin Laden Brotherhood* (London, 2002).

Jalali, Ali A. and Lester W. Grau, *The Other Side of the Mountain: Mujahideen Tactics in the Soviet-Afghan War*, The US Marine Corp Studies and Analysis Division (1998).

Jansen, Johannes J.G., *The Neglected Duty: The Creed of Sadat's Assassins and Islamic Resurgence on the Middle East* (New York, 1986).

Joffe, George, 'Global jihad and foreign fighters', *Small Wars and Insurgencies*, 27/5 (2016), pp. 800–816.

Jones, Robert A., *Emile Durkheim: An Introduction to Four Major Works* (Beverly Hills, 1986).

Karadsheh, Jomana, 'US: Iraq suicide attacks rising during *Ramadan*', *CNN*, 27 September 2006.

Katz, Fred E., *Ordinary People and Extraordinary Evil: A Report on the Beguilings of Evil* (Albany, 1993).

Katz, Mark N., 'Civil conflict in South Yemen', *Middle East Review*, Fall 1986.

Keegan, John, *The Face of Battle* (London, 1986).

Kelsay, John, *Arguing the Just War Theory in Islam* (London, 2009).

Kepel, Gilles, *Jihad: The Trail of Political Islam* (London, 2008).

Kepel, Gilles and Jean-Pierre Milelli, *Al Qaeda in its Own Words* (London, 2008).

Kerry, John F., 'Press Availability at the International Syria Support Group', *Embassy of the United States*, Damascus, Syria, 12 February 2016a. Available at http://damascus. usembassy.gov/statedept021216en2.html (accessed 18 February 2016).

Kerry, John F., 'Remarks on Daesh and Genocide', Secretary of State Press Briefing Room, *US Department of State*, Washington, DC, 17 March 2016b. Available at www. state.gov/secretary/remarks/2016/03/254782.htm (accessed 10 July 2016).

Khaja, Nagieb, 'On the frontline in Syria: the Danish gangster who turned Jihadi', *The Guardian*, 7 July 2014.

Koch, Hannsjoachim W., *The Hitler Youth: Origins and Developments 1922–1945* (New York, 2000).

Kohlmann, Evan F., *Al-Qaida's Jihad in Europe: The Afghan-Bosnian Network* (New York, 2004).

Kohlmann, Evan F., 'The Foreign Martyrs of Iraq: 2003–04', *Global Terror Alert*, 2005a.

Kohlmann, Evan F., 'Profiles of Saudi Arabian Islamic Militants Killed in Iraq: 2004–2005. *Global Terror Alert*, 2005b.

Kohlmann, Evan F., 'The Mujahideen of Bosnia: Origins, Training, and Implications', in J.J.F. Forrest (ed.), *The Making of a Terrorist: Recruitment, Training, and Root Causes.* Volume II: Training (London, 2006).

Komarow, Steven and Sabah Al-Anbaki, 'Would-be suicide bomber angry at those who sent him', *USA Today*, 24 January 2005.

Kuehn, Felix, Leah Farrall and Alex Strick Van Linschoten, 'Expert Report in US vs. Talha Ahsan; US vs. Babar Ahmad; Exhibit F', April 2014. Available at from www. sacc.org.uk/sacc/docs/ba_expert_reports.pdf (accessed 10 May 2014).

Lacroix, Stephane, 'Saudi Islamists and the Arab Spring', *The London School of Economics and Political Science*, 36 (May 2014).

Lahoud, Nelly, 'Jihadi recantations and their significance', in A. Moghadam and B. Fishman (eds), *Fault Lines in Global Jihad: Organizational, Strategic, and Ideological Fissures* (London, 2011).

Landau, Elaine, *Osama Bin Laden: A War against the West* (New York, 2002).

Lawrence, Thomas E., 'Seven Pillars of Wisdom' (London, 1935).

Lehr, Peter, '(No) Princes of the Sea: Reflections on Maritime Terrorism', in J. Krause and S. Bruns (eds), *Routledge Handbook of Naval Strategy and Security* (Oxon, 2016).

Li, Darryl, 'Afghan Arabs, real and imagined', *Middle East Report* 260, 41 (Fall 2011).

Lia, Brynjar, *Globalisation and the Future of Terrorism: Patterns and Predictions* (London, 2005).

Lia, Brynjar, 'Doctrines for jihadi terrorist training', *Terrorism and Political Violence* 20/1 (2008a), pp. 518–542.

Lia, Brynjar, *Architect of Global Jihad: The Life of Al-Qaida Strategist Abu Mus'ab al-Suri* (New York, 2008b).

Lia, Brynjar, 'Destructive doctrinarians': Abu Musa'b al-Suri's critique of the Salafis in the jihadi current', in R. Meijer (ed.), *Global Salafism: Islam's New Religious Movement* (London, 2009).

Lister, Charles, 'Profiling Jabhat al-Nusra', *The Brookings Project on US Relations with the Islamic World*, Analysis Paper 24 (July 2016).

Maclean, Fitzroy, *Eastern Approaches* (London, 1950).

Maher, Shiraz, *Salafi-Jihadism: The History of an Idea* (London, 2016a).

Maher, Shiraz, 'Shiraz Maher on ISIS: The Management of Savagery', *The New Statesman*, 12 July 2016b.

Malet, David, 'Why Foreign Fighters? Historical Perspectives and Solutions', *Foreign Policy Research Institute, Orbis* 54/1 (2010), pp. 97–114.

Malet, David, *Foreign Fighters: Transnational Identity in Civic Conflicts* (Oxford, 2013).

Malet, David, 'Foreign fighter mobilization and persistence in a global context', *Terrorism and Political Violence* 0 (2015), pp. 1–20.

Malik, Shahid, 'Not all fighters going to Syria are extremists, says former UK minister Shahid Malik', *The Sydney Morning Herald*, 18 May 2014.

Malik, Shiv, 'The ISIS papers: leaked documents show how ISIS is building its state', *The Guardian*, 7 December 2015.

Martz, Erin, *Trauma Rehabilitation After War and Conflict* (London, 2010).

Matthiesen, Toby, *Sectarian Gulf: Bahrain, Saudi Arabia, and the Arab Spring that Wasn't* (Stanford, 2013).

Matthiesen, Toby, 'The domestic sources of Saudi foreign policy: Islamists and the state in the wake of the Arab Uprisings', *Rethinking Political Islam Series, Brookings Institute* (August 2015).

McAdam, Doug, 'Recruitment to high-risk activism: The case of Freedom Summer', *American Journal of Sociology* 92/1 (1986), pp. 64–90.

McCants, William, 'The Management of Savagery: The Most Critical Stage Through Which the Umma Will Pass. Translation of Al-Naji, Abu Bakr (2004).' *John M. Olin Institute for Strategic Studies* (23 May 2006).

McCants, William and Jarret Brachman, 'Militant Ideology Atlas – Executive Report', *Combating Terrorism Center West Point* (2006a).

McCants, William and Jarret Brachman, 'Militant Ideology Atlas – Research Compendium', *Combating Terrorism Center West Point* (2006b).

McCauley, Clark and Sophie Moskalenko, 'Mechanisms of Political Radicalization: Pathways Toward Terrorism', *Terrorism and Political Violence* 20/3 (2008), pp. 415–433.

McDermott, Terry, 'Abu Zubaydah and the banality of "jihadism"', *Al Jazeera America*. 19 December 2013.

McGregor, Andrew, 'Jihad and the Rifle Alone: Abdullah Azzam and the Islamist Revolution', *The Journal of Conflict Studies* XXIII/2 (2003).

McHugo, John, 'The roots of Syria's tragedy', *Al-Jazeera*, 5 October 2015.

McMillan, M.E., *From the First World War to the Arab Spring: What's really going on in the Middle East?* (New York, 2016).

Meloy, J. Reid, 'The Operational Development and Empirical Testing of the Terrorism Radicalization Assessment Protocol (TRAP-18)', *Journal of Personality Assessment*, 21 June 2018.

Merari, Ariel, 'Terrorism as a strategy of insurgency', *Terrorism and Political Violence* 5/4 (1993), pp. 213–251.

Merari, Ariel, *Driven to Death: Psychological and Social Aspects of Suicide Terrorism* (Oxford, 2010).

Milelli, Jean-Pierre, 'Abu Musab al-Zarqawi, Jihad in Mesopotamia', in G. Kepel and J-P. Milelli (eds), *Al Qaeda in its Own Words* (London, 2008).

Milgram, Stanley, 'Behavioral study of obedience', *Journal of Abnormal and Social Psychology* 67 (1963), pp. 371–378.

Milgram, Stanley, *Obedience to Authority: An Experimental View* (London, 1974).

Mironova, Vera, Loubna Mrie and Sam Whitt, 'The motivations of Syrian Islamist fighters, *CTC Sentinel Terrorism Monitor* 7/10 (2014).

Mockaitis, Thomas R., *British Counterinsurgency 1919–1960* (London, 1990).

Mockaitis, Thomas R., *Osama Bin Laden: A Biography* (Santa Barbara, 2010).

Moghadam, Assaf, 'Motives for martyrdom: Al Qaeda, Salafi Jihad, and the spread of suicide attacks', *International Security* 3/3 (2008), pp. 46–78.

Moghadam, Assaf, *The Globalization of Martyrdom: Al Qaeda, Salafi Jihad, and the diffusion of suicide attacks* (Baltimore, 2011).

Moghadam, Assaf, 'The connectivity between terrorism, insurgency, and civil war', *The Site Intel Group*, 20 June 2014.

Moloney, Ed, *A Secret History of the IRA* (London, 2002).

Moore, Cerwyn, and Paul Tumelty, 'Foreign Fighters and the Case of Chechnya: A Critical Assessment', *Studies in Conflict and Terrorism* 31/5 (2008), pp. 412–433.

Moran, Lord, *The Anatomy of Courage* (London, 1945).

Morgan, Ted, *Valley of Death: The Tragedy at Dien Bien Phu that Led America into the Vietnam War* (London, 2010).

Mumford, Andrew, 'Minimum Force Meets Brutality: Detention, Interrogation and Torture in British Counter-Insurgency Campaigns', *Journal of Military Ethics* 11/1 (2012), pp. 10–25.

Murphy, Caryle, 'Saudi Arabia tried to keep the Islamic State from recruiting its youth', *Global Post*, 2 March 2015.

Napoleoni, Loretta, *Insurgent Iraq: Al Zarqawi and the New Generation* (New York, 2005).

Neumann, Peter R., 'The trouble with radicalization', *International Affairs*, 89/4 (2013), pp. 873–893.

Neumann, Peter R., 'Suspects into collaborators: Assad and the Jihadists', *London Review of Books* 36/7 (2014), pp. 19–21.

Neumann, Peter R., 'Victims, perpetrators, assets: The Narratives of Islamic State defectors', *The International Centre for the Study of Radicalisation and Political Violence* (2015).

Neumann, Peter R., *Radicalized: New Jihadists and the Threat to the West* (London, 2016).

Neumann, Peter R. and Scott Kleinmann, 'How rigorous is radicalization research?', *Democracy and Security* 9/4 (2013), pp. 360–382.

Nilsson, Marco, 'Foreign fighters and the radicalization of local jihad: Interview evidence from Swedish jihadists', *Studies in Conflict and Terrorism*, 38/1 (2015), pp. 343–358.

Norwegian Defence Research Establishment (FFI). Retrieved December 18, 2012, from http://english.nupi.no/

Noueihed, Lin and Alex Warren, *The Battle for the Arab Spring: Revolution, Counter-Revolution and the Making of a New Era* (New Haven, 2012).

Obaid, Nawaf, 'Saudi Arabia's master plan against ISIS, Assad and Iran in Syria', *The National Interest*, 16 February 2016.

Obama, Barak H., 'Readout of the President's Call with President Vladimir Putin of Russia', *The White House. Office of the Press Secretary*, 14 February 2016.

Odell, Joe, 'How the UAE's pro-democracy movement fell into a death spiral', *Middle East Eye*, 2 April 2018. Available at www.middleeasteye.net/columns/how-uae-s-pro-democracy-movement-fell-death-spiral-477436739 (accessed 7 June 2018).

Office of the UN Special Advisor on the Prevention of Genocide. *OSAPG Analysis Framework* (n.d.). Available at www.un.org/en/preventgenocide/adviser/pdf/osapg_analysis_framework.pdf (accessed 16 February 2016).

Olidort, Jacob, 'Inside the Caliphate's Classroom: Textbooks, Guidance Literature, and Indoctrination Methods of the Islamic State', *The Washington Institute for Near East Policy, Policy Focus* 147 (August 2016).

Oliver, Kendrick, *The My Lai Massacre in American History and Memory* (Manchester, 2006).

Orton, Kyle W., 'Al-Qaeda in Syria and American Policy', *The Syrian Intafada*, 4 October 2016.

Pape, Robert A., *Dying to Win: The Strategic Logic of Suicide Terrorism* (New York, 2005).

Partlow, Joshua, 'An uphill battle to stop fighters at border', *Washington Post*, 5 May 2007.

Patin, Nathan, 'The other foreign fighters: An open-source investigation into American volunteers fighting the Islamic State in Iraq and Syria', *A Bellingcat Investigation*, August 2015.

Paz, Reuven, 'Arab volunteers killed in Iraq: An analysis', *The Project for the Research of Islamist Movements* 3/1 (March 2005).

Pedahzur, Ami, *Suicide Terrorism* (Cambridge, 2005).

Pedahzur, Ami, *Root Causes of Suicide Terrorism: The Globalization of Martyrdom* (Oxon, 2006).

Pedahzur, Ami and Arie Perlinger, 'The making of suicide bombers: A comparative perspective', in J.J.F. Forest (ed.) *The Making of a Terrorist: Recruitment, Training, and Root Causes.* Volume 1: Recruitment (London, 2000).

Perliger, Arie and Daniel Milton, 'From cradle to grave: The life cycle of foreign fighters in Iraq and Syria', *Combating Terrorism Center* (November 2016).

Piazza, James A., 'Is Islamist terrorism more dangerous?: An empirical study of group ideology, organisation, and goal structure', *Terrorism and Political Violence* 21/1 (2009), pp. 62–88.

Pipes, Daniel, *Greater Syria: The History of an Ambition* (Oxford, 1990).

Pizzi, Michael, 'Foreign fighters come home to roost', *Al Jazeera America.* 5 June 2015.

Pokalova, Elena, 'Driving factors behind foreign fighters in Syria and Iraq', *Studies in Conflict and Terrorism* 0/0 (2018), pp. 1–34.

Pollack, Kenneth M., *Arabs at War: Military Effectiveness, 1948–1991* (Lincoln, 2004).

Post, Jerrold M., *The Mind of the Terrorist* (Basingstoke, 2007).

Price, Bryan and Muhammad Al-'Ubaydi, 'CTC perspectives: The Islamic State's internal rifts and social media ban', *Combating Terrorism Center at West Point*, 21 June 2017.

Public Broadcasting Service (PBS), 'The fatwa of the 26 Clerics: Open sermon to the militant Iraqi people' [given on 5 November 2004], *Frontline*, 8 February 2005. Available at www.pbs.org/wgbh/pages/frontline/shows/saud/etc/fatwa.html (accessed 7 June 2016).

Public Broadcasting Service (PBS), The Secret History of ISIS, *Frontline*, Season 34 (2018), Episode 10. Available at www.pbs.org/video/frontline-secret-history-isis/ (accessed 29 April 2018).

Quilliam. Available at www.quilliaminternational.com/about/ (accessed 14 August 2017).

Rana, Muhammad A. and Mubasher Bukhari, *Arabs in Afghan Jihad* (Lahore, 2007).

Ranstorp, Magnus, 'Interpreting the broader context and meaning of Bin-Laden's Fatwa', *Studies in Conflict & Terrorism* 21/4 (1998), pp. 321–330.

Reagan, Ronald W., Proclamation 4908. Afghanistan Day. By the President of the United States of America, 10 March 1982. Available at, www.reagan.utexas.edu/archives/ speeches/1982/31082c.htm (accessed 20 January 2014).

Reed, Alastair, Jeanine de Roy van Zuijdewin, and Edwin Bakker, 'Pathways of foreign fighters: Policy options and their (un)intended consequences', *International Centre for Counter-Terrorism Policy Brief*, April 2015.

Reese, Michael J., Keven G. Ruby and Robert A. Pape, *Days of Action or Restraint? How the Islamic State Calendar Impacts Violence*, American Political Science Review 111/3 (2017), pp. 439–459.

Reeve, Simon, *The New Jackals: Ramzi Yousef, Osama bin Laden and the Future of Terrorism* (London, 1999).

Ressam, Ahmad, 'United States of America v. Mokhtar Haouari', *United States District Court Southern District of New York*, 3 July 2001.

Reuter, Christoph, 'I'm Not a Butcher': An Interview with Islamic State's Architect of Death, *Spiegel Online International*, 16 July 2015.

Richardson, Louise, *What Terrorists Want: Understanding the Enemy, Containing the Threat* (New York, 2007).

Rosen, L., 'US Authorizes Financial Support for the Free Syrian Army', *Al Monitor*. 27 July 2012. Retrieved August 26, 2013, from www.al-monitor.com/pulse/originals/2012/al-monitor/us-authorizes-financial-support.html.

Rosenblatt, Nate, 'All jihad is local: What ISIS's files tell us about its fighters', *New America*, July 2016.

Rosenthal, Franz, 'On suicide in Islam', *Journal of the American Oriental Society* 66/3 (July–September 1946), pp. 239–259.

Roy, Jules, *The Battle of Dienbienphu* (London, 1965).

Roy, Olivier, *Islam and Resistance in Afghanistan* (Cambridge, 1990).

Rubin, Barnett R., 'Arab Islamists in Afghanistan', in John L. Espositi (ed.), *Political Islam: Revolution, Radicalism, and Reform?* (Colorado, 1997).

Rubin, Barnett R., *The Tragedy of the Middle East* (Cambridge, 2002).

Safadi, Mowaffaq, 'Don't rely on Syria's "moderate" fighting force. It doesn't exist', *The Guardian*, 16 December 2015.

Sageman, Marc, *Understanding Terror Networks* (Philadelphia, 2004).

Sageman, Marc, 'The normality of global jihadi terrorism', *The Journal of International Security Affairs* 8 (2005).

Sageman, Marc, *Leaderless Jihad: Terror Networks in the Twenty-First Century* (Philadelphia, 2008).

Sageman, Marc, 'A Frighteningly Normal Man', *Al-Jazeera*, 26 November 2013.

Saghi, Omar, 'Osama Bin Laden, the iconic orator', in G. Kepel and J-P. Milelli (eds), *Al Qaeda in its Own Words* (London, 2008).

Sajer, Guy, *The Forgotten Soldier* (London, 1971).

Sakthivel, Vish, 'Weathering Morocco's Syria returnees', *The Washington Institute*, 25 September 2013.

Sambanis, Nicholas, 'What is civil war?: Conceptual and empirical complexities of an operational definition', *Journal of Conflict Resolution* 48/6 (2004), pp. 814–858.

Sanders, Edmond, *War Blazed Imam's Path to Extremism*, *LA Times*, 27 September 2004.

Sargant, William, *Battle for the Mind: A Physiology of Conversion and Brain-washing* (London, 1959).

Schmid, Alex P., *The Routledge Handbook of Terrorism Research* (Oxon: (2013a).

Schmid, Alex P., 'Radicalisation, de-radicalisation, counter-radicalisation: a conceptual discussion and literature review', *International Centre for Counter-Terrorism Research Paper*, March 2013b.

Schmid, Alex P., 'Foreign (terrorist) fighter estimates: Conceptual and data issues', *International Centre for Counter-Terrorism Policy Brief*, October 2015.

Schmid, Alex P. and Albert J. Jongman, *Political Terrorism: A New Guide to Actors, Authors, Concepts, Databases, Theories, and Literature* (New Brunswick, 1988).

Seifert, Katherine R. and Clark McCauley, 'Suicide Bombers in Iraq, 2003–2010: Disaggregating Targets Can Reveal Insurgent Motives and Priorities', *Terrorism and Political Violence* 26/5 (2014), pp. 803–820.

Shaghor, 'After Surviving a Suicide Attack in Iraq, Mujahid Ahmad Abdullah al-Shaya Goes to Jihad in the Levant & Pays Allegiance to ISIS', *Facebook*, 18 November 2013. Available at www.shaghor.com/index.php?s=23&cat=7&id=368#.Uon4ely4s_A. facebook (link no longer working).

Shelton, Tracy, 'Syria: From IT to rebel commander', *Global Post*, 03 March 2013.

Silber, Mitchell D. and Arvin Bhatt, 'Radicalization in the West: The Homegrown Threat', *The New York City Police Department*, 2007, p. 6.

Silke, Andrew, 'Holy Warriors: Exploring the Psychological Processes of Jihadi Radicalization', *European Journal of Criminology* 5/1 (2008), pp. 99–123.

Silke, Andrew, *Terrorists, Victims and Society* (Chichester, 2009).

Slavicek, David J., 'Deconstructing the Shariatic justification of suicide bombings', *Studies in Conflict and Terrorism* 31/6 (2008), pp. 553–571.

Speckhard, Anne and Mubin Shaikh, *Undercover Jihadi: Inside the Toronto 18 Al Qaeda Inspired, Homegrown Terrorism in the* West (McLean, 2014).

Speckhard, Anne and Ahmet Yayla, *ISIS Defectors: Inside Stories of the Terrorist Caliphate* (McLean, VA, 2016).

Springer, Devin R., James L. Regens and David N. Edger, *Islamic Radicalism and Global Jihad* (Washington, 2009).

Sprinzak, Ehud, 'Rational Fanatics', *Foreign Policy*, September/October 2000, pp. 66–73.

Stahl, Lesley (Producer) 'Interview with Madeleine Albright', *60 Minutes*, 12 May 1996). Available at www.youtube.com/watch?v=FbIX1CP9qr4 (accessed 21 December 2012).

Stanley, Trevor, 'Abdullah Azzam: The Godfather of Jihad', *Perspectives on World History and Current Events, 2003–2005* (2005).

Staub, Ervin, *The Roots of Evil: The Origins of Genocide and Other Group Violence* (Cambridge, 1989).

Stenerson, Anne, 'Al Qaeda's foot soldiers: A study of the biographies of foreign fighters killed in Afghanistan and Pakistan between 2002 and 2006', *Studies in Conflict and Terrorism* 34/1 (2011), pp. 171–198.

Stepanova, Ekaterina, 'Terrorism in asymmetrical conflict: Ideological and structural aspects', *SIPRI Research Report* 23 (Oxford, 2008).

Stern, Jessica, 'How Terrorists Hijacked Islam', *USA Today*, 1 October 2001.

Strick van Linschoten, Alex and Felix Kuehn, *An Enemy We Created: The Myth of the Taliban-Al-Qaeda Merger in Afghanistan* (London, 2012).

Syrian Network for Human Rights, 'Statistics Since March 2011', *Syrian Network for Human Rights*, November 2016. Available at http://sn4hr.org (accessed 24 January 2017).

Syrian Observatory for Human Rights, 'More than 400,000 were killed in 63 months of the Syrian Revolution', *Syrian Observatory for Human Rights*, 28 May 2016. Available at www.syriahr.com/en/?p=46478 (accessed 7 June 2016).

Tankel, Stephen, 'Universal soldiers or parochial actors: Understanding jihadists as products of their environments', *Terrorism and Political Violence* 0/0 (2016), pp. 1–24.

Tawil, Camille, *Brothers in Arms: The Story of Al-Qa'ida and Arab Jihadists* (London, 2010).

Taylor, Maxwell, *The Fanatics: A Behavioural Approach to Political Violence* (Oxford, 1991).

Taylor, Maxwell and John Horgan, 'A conceptual framework for addressing psychological process in the development of the terrorist', *Terrorism and Political Violence* 18/4 (2006), pp. 585–601.

Testas, Abdelaziz, 'The roots of Algeria's religious and ethnic violence', *Studies in Conflict and Terrorism* 25/3 (2002), pp. 161–183.

The 9/11 Commission Report, *The 9/11 Commission Report* (London, 2005).

The Concise Oxford Dictionary (Oxford, 1995).

The Guardian, 'Doomed to failure in the Middle East: A Letter from 52 former senior British diplomats to Tony Blair', *The Guardian*, 27 April 2004. Available at www.theguardian.com/politics/2004/apr/27/foreignpolicy.world (accessed 5 January 2015).

The Islamic State. 'The Inghimasis – The Pride of the Nation – Wiliyat al-Barakah. *Jihadology*, August 2015. Available at http://jihadology.net/2015/08/03/new-video-message-from-the-islamic-state-the-inghimasis-the-pride-of-the-nation-wilayat-al-barakah/ (accessed 12 February 2016).

The Islamic State. *Terrify the Enemy of God and Your Enemy*, 3 January 2016. Available at http://heavy.com/news/2016/01/new-isis-islamic-state-news-pictures-videos-terrorist-terrorism-special-forces-military-training-wilayat-hims-syria-full-uncensored-youtube/ (accessed 16 July 2016).

The North Atlantic Treaty, *The North Atlantic Treaty* 4 April 1949. Available at www.nato.int/cps/ic/natohq/official_texts_17120.htm (accessed 15 April 2018).

Thomas, William I., and Dorothy Swaine Thomas. 1928. The Child in America: Behavior Problems and Programs. New York: Knopf, 1928, pp. 571–572.

Thompson, Hugh, 'Moral courage in combat: The My Lai Story', Presentation to the US Naval Academy (n.d.). Available at www.usna.edu/Ethics/Publications/ThompsonPg1-28_Final.pdf (accessed 14 March 2012).

Todenhöfer, Jurgen, 'Islamic State – Seven Impressions of a Difficult Journey', 2014. Available at http://juergentodenhoefer.de/seven-impressions-of-a-difficult-journey/?lang=en (accessed 8 December 2015).

Todenhöfer, Jurgen, 'Blindsided: How ISIS shook the world', *CNN (Fareed Zakaria GPS)*, 29 November 2015. Available at http://transcripts.cnn.com/TRANSCRIPTS/1511/29/fzgps.01.html (accessed 18 December 2015).

Todenhöfer, Jurgen, *My Journey into the Heart of Terror: Ten Days in the Islamic State* (Vancouver, 2016).

Tripp, Charles, *A History of Iraq* (Cambridge, 2002).

Trofimov, Yaroslav, *The Siege of Mecca: The Forgotten Uprising in Islam's Holiest Shrine and the Birth of Al Qaeda* (New York, 2007).

Tuck, Henry, Tanya Silverman and Candace Smalley, '*Shooting in the right direction*': *Anti-ISIS Foreign Fighters in Syria and Iraq*. Institute for Strategic Dialogue, Horizons Series No. 1 (2016).

UK Government, 'Roots of violent radicalisation', *House of Commons Home Affairs Committee*. Nineteenth Report of Session 2010–2012. Volume 1 (6 February 2012). Available at www.publications.parliament.uk/pa/cm201012/cmselect/cmhaff/1446/1446.pdf (accessed 7 June 2014).

UK Government, 'Channel Duty Guidance: Protecting vulnerable people from being drawn into terrorism', 2015. Available at www.gov.uk/government/uploads/system/uploads/attachment_data/file/425189/Channel_Duty_Guidance_April_2015.pdf (accessed 7 June 2016).

UK Ministry of Defence, *The Joint Service Manual of the Law of Armed Conflict*, JSP 383 (2004 Edition).

United Nations Children's Fund, *The Situation of Children in Iraq: An Assessment Based on the UN Convention on the Rights of a Child*, February 2002. Available at www.casi.org.uk/info/unicef0202.pdf (accessed 21 December 2012).

United Nations Department of Economic and Social Affairs, Population Division (2013). World Population Prospects: The 2012 Revision: Estimates, 1950–2010. June 2013.

United Nations Human Rights Council, 'Independent International Commission of Inquiry on the Syrian Arab Republic established pursuant to United Nations Human Rights Council Resolutions S-17/1, 19/22 and 21/26', 20 December 2012. Available at www.ohchr.org/Documents/Countries/SY/ColSyriaDecember2012.pdf (accessed 21 December 2012).

United Nations Human Rights Council 'They came to destroy': ISIS Crimes against the Yazidis. Human Rights Council', Thirty-second session. Agenda Item 4. 15 June 2016. Available at www.ohchr.org/Documents/HRBodies/HRCouncil/CoISyria/A_HRC_32_CRP.2_en.pdf (accessed 6 July 2016).

United Nations Security Council, 'Resolution 2178 (2014), 24 September 2014. Available at www.un.org/en/sc/ctc/docs/2015/SCR%202178_2014_EN.pdf (accessed 6 July 2016).

United Nations Security Council, 'Resolution 2254 (2015), 18 December 2015. Available at www.securitycouncilreport.org/atf/cf/%7B65BFCF9B-6D27-4E9C-8CD3-CF6E4FF96FF9%7D/s_res_2254.pdf (accessed 6 July 2016).

United Nations Security Council Counter-Terrorism Committee, 'Background Note: Stemming the flow of foreign terrorist fighters', Madrid, 27–28 July 2015a. Available at www.un.org/en/sc/ctc/docs/2015/0721Special%20Meeting%20Madrid%20-%20General%20background%20Note.pdf (link no longer working).

United Nations Security Council Counter-Terrorism Committee, 'Background Note: Group I: Technical sessions on detection, intervention against, and prevention of incitement, recruitment and facilitation of FTF travel', Madrid, 27–28 July 2015b. Available at www.un.org/en/sc/ctc/docs/2015/0721Tehnical%20Session%20Group%20I%20-%20background%20note.pdf (link no longer working).

United Nations, 'Convention on the Prevention and Punishment of the Crime of Genocide', 9 December 1948. Available at https://treaties.un.org/doc/publication/unts/volume%2078/volume-78-i-1021-english.pdf (accessed 21 December 2012).

United Nations, 'ISIL (Da'esh) & Al-Qaida Sanctions List (1267/1989/2253). Last updated on 14 March 2017. Available at https://scsanctions.un.org/fop/fop?xml=htdocs/resources/xml/en/consolidated.xml&xslt=htdocs/resources/xsl/en/al-qaida.xsl (accessed 15 March 2017).

US Central Intelligence Agency, 'Psychological Assessment of Zain al-'Abedin al-Abideen Muhammad Hassan, a.k.a. Abu Zubaydah', 31 January 2003. Available at www.thetorturedatabase.org/files/foia_subsite/pdfs/CIA000544.pdf (accessed 6 July 2014).

US Central Intelligence Agency, *The World Fact Book 2014 – Iraq*. Available at www.cia.gov/library/publications/download/download-2014 (accessed 8 April 2015).

US Commission on International Religious Freedom, 'Annual Report 2011 – Saudi Arabia', pp. 141–156.

US Commission on International Religious Freedom, 'Annual Report 2016 – Syria' (pp. 119–125).

US Defence Intelligence Agency, '*Declassified Report: Syria and Muslim Brotherhood*, 1982. Released 2016. Available at https://syria360.files.wordpress.com/2013/11/dia-syria-muslimbrotherhoodpressureintensifies-2.pdf (accessed 21 December 2016).

US Department of State, 'Country Reports on Terrorism 2014', June 2015. Available at www.state.gov/documents/organization/239631.pdf (accessed 15 December 2015).

US Department of State, 'International Religious Freedom Report 2004', Bureau of Democracy, Human Rights, and Labor. Available at www.state.gov/j/drl/rls/irf/2004/35507.htm (accessed 18 December 2014).

US Department of State, 'The wandering mujahidin: Armed and dangerous', Bureau of Intelligence and Research, *The Washington Institute*. Weekend Edition. 21–22 August 1993. Available at www.washingtoninstitute.org/uploads/Documents/other/StateDept199308WanderingMujahidin.pdf (accessed 21 December 2014).

US Department of the Navy, 'Defense against Kamikaze Attacks in World War 2 and its relevance to anti-ship missile defense. Volume 1. an analytical history of kamikaze attacks against ships of the United States Navy during World War 2. *Center for Naval Analyses Alexandria VA*, November 1970.

Van Ostaeyen Pieter, 'My first battlefield experience. Text by Abu Salman al-Britani published by Fursan Al Sham Media', 12 November 2016. Available at https://pietervanostaeyen.com/2016/11/13/fursan-al-sham-media-my-first-battlefield-experience/ (accessed 14 November 2016).

Vermeulen, Floris and Frank Bovenkerk, *Engaging with Violent Extremism: Local Policies in Western European Cities* (Amsterdam, 2012).

Violations Documentation Centre in Syria. Available at www.vdc-sy.info/index.php/en/martyrs (accessed 17 June 2017).

Wagemakers, Joas, *A Quietist Jihadi: The Ideology and Influence of Abu Muhammad al-Maqdisi* (Cambridge, 2012).

Wagemakers, Joas, 'What Should an Islamic State Look Like? Jihadi-Salafi Debates on the War in Syria', *The Muslim World* 106/3 (2016), pp. 501–522.

Waldeck, Annika, *The ideology of ISIS – a motivation for Europeans to become foreign fighters?* Master Thesis in Global Studies. Roskilde Universitet, 29 June 2015.

Warner, Jason and Hilary Matfess, *Exploding Stereotypes: The Unexpected Operational and Demographic Characteristics of Boko Haram's Suicide Bombers.* Combating Terrorism Center at West Point, August 2017.

Warren, Roger P., *Why Radical Islamist Ideology is a Threat: A Study of Gulf Arab Detainees Recommended for 'Continued Detention' in Guantanamo Bay.* M.Litt Thesis. University of St Andrews. May 2012. Unpublished.

Warren, Roger P., 'Ideological motivations of Arab foreign fighters as insurgents and terrorists: From 1980s Afghanistan to the Syrian insurgency'. in S.N. Romaniuk and S.T. Webb (eds), *Insurgency and Counterinsurgency in Modern War* (London, 2015).

Warren, Roger P., 'The journey from jihad to Islamist terrorism', *The Conversation*, 23 March 2016.

Watson, Peter, *War on the Mind: The Military Uses and Abuses of Psychology* (New York, 1978).

Weber, Maximillian K., [1919] 'Politics as a Vocation', in H. H. Gerth and C. Wright Mills (eds), *From Max Weber: Essays in Sociology* (London, 2009).

Wehr, Hans, *A Dictionary of Modern Written Arabic* (London, 1980).

Weiss, Michael and Hassan Hassan, *ISIS: Inside the Army of Terror* (New York, 2015).

Whitaker, Brian, 'Bereaved father to sue over jihad call', *The Guardian*, 22 November 2004.

Whitehead, Tom, 'Life in a terror training camp: lights out 10pm, cleaning, military training', *The Telegraph*, 26 November 2014.

Wieland, Carsten, *Syria – a decade of lost chances: Repression and revolution from Damascus spring to Arab Spring* (Seattle, 2012).

Wiktorowicz, Quintan, *Islamic Activism: A Social Movement Approach* (Indianapolis, 2004).

Wiktorowicz, Quintan, 'A genealogy of radical Islam', *Studies in Conflict and Terrorism* 28/2 (2005a), pp. 75–97.

Wiktorowicz, Quintan, *Radical Islam Rising: Muslim Extremism in the West* (Maryland, 2005b).

Wiktorowicz, Quintan, 'Anatomy of the salafi movement', *Studies in Conflict and Terrorism* 29/3 (2006), pp. 207–239.

Wiktorowicz, Quintan and John Kaltner, 'Killing in the Name of Islam: Al-Qaeda's Justification for September 11', *Middle East Policy* X/2 (2003), pp. 76–92.

Williams, Brian G., 'On the Trail of the "Lions of Islam": Foreign Fighters in Afghanistan and Pakistan 1980–2010', *Orbis* 55/2 (2011).

Windrow, Martin, *The Last Valley: Dien Bien Phu and the French Defeat in Vietnam* (London, 2004).

Winter, Charlie, 'Suicide tactics and the Islamic State', *International Centre for Counter-Terrorism – The Hague*, 10 January 2017a. Available at https://icct.nl/publication/suicide-tactics-and-the-islamic-state/ (accessed 11 January 2017).

Winter, Charlie, 'War by suicide: A statistical analysis of the Islamic State's martyrdom industry', *International Centre for Counter-Terrorism – The Hague*. February 2017b. Available at https://icct.nl/wp-content/uploads/2017/02/ICCT-Winter-War-by-Suicide-Feb2017.pdf (accessed 10 March 2017).

Wood, Graeme, 'What ISIS really wants', *The Atlantic*, March 2015.

World Public Opinion, 'Public Opinion in the Islamic world on terrorism, al Qaeda, and US Policies', *The Program on International Policy Attitudes*, 25 February 2009.

Wright, Lawrence, *The Looming Tower: Al-Qaeda and the Road to 9/11* (New York, 2006).

Yusuf, Ramzi, 'Statement by Ramzi Yousef at Sentencing', *The New York Times* 9 January 1998.

Zaidi, Manzar, 'A taxonomy of jihad', *Arab Studies Quarterly* 41/3 (2009), pp. 21–34.

Zaman Al Wasl, 'Exclusive: 1736 documents reveal ISIS jihadists personal data', *Zaman Al Wasl*, 8 March 2016. Available at https://en.zamanalwsl.net/news/14541.html (accessed 9 March 2016).

Zelin, Aaron Y., 'The Ghosts of Sinjar in Tripoli and Benghazi', *Al-Wasat*, 10 January 2013a.

Zelin, Aaron Y., 'Foreign Jihadists in Syria: Tracking Recruitment Networks', *The Washington Institute for Near East Policy*, Policy Watch 2186 (19 December 2013b).

Zelin, Aaron Y., 'The Saudi foreign fighter presence in Syria', *CTC Sentinel* 7/1 (April 2014a), pp. 10–14.

Zill, Oriana, 'A portrait of Wadih El Hage', *Frontline – Public Broadcasting Service*, 12 September 2001. Available at www.pbs.org/wgbh/pages/frontline/shows/binladen/upclose/elhage.html (accessed 12 November 2014).

Zimbardo, Philip G., *The Lucifer Effect: How Good People Turn Evil* (London, 2007).

Zimmerman, John C., 'Sayyid Qutb's Influence on the 11 September Attacks', *Terrorism and Political Violence* 16/2 (2004), pp. 222–252.

Zubaydah, Abu, 'Original document: Abu Zubaydah diaries volume one', *United States Department of Justice. Federal Bureau of Investigation.* Unclassified. *Al-Jazeera America*, 5 November 2013. Available at http://america.aljazeera.com/multimedia/2013/11/original-documentabuzubaydahdiariesvolumeone.html (accessed 12 February 2014).

Zubaydah, Abu, 'Original document: Abu Zubaydah diaries volume two', *United States Department of Justice. Federal Bureau of Investigation.* Unclassified. *Al-Jazeera America*, 26 November 2013. Available at http://america.aljazeera.com/multimedia/2013/11/original-documentabuzubaydahdiariesvolumetwo.html (accessed 12 February 2014).

Zubaydah, Abu, 'Original document: Abu Zubaydah diaries volume three', *United States Department of Justice. Federal Bureau of Investigation.* Unclassified. *Al-Jazeera America*, 26 November 2013. Available at http://america.aljazeera.com/ multimedia/2013/11/original-documentabuzubaydahdiariesvolumethree.html (accessed 12 February 2014).

Index

The letter *f* following an entry indicates a page that includes a figure